Commodity Prices and Markets

NBER—East Asia Seminar on Economics
Volume 20

Following is a list of the conference volumes in the East Asia Seminar on Economics series. Since the first EASE conference, in June 1990 in Seoul, Korea, coorganizing research organizations in the Asia-Pacific countries have taken turns hosting a conference every year. The longevity of the seminar series testifies to the success of collaborations among the coorganizing research institutions, which are listed in each volume. The printed editions of the conference volumes will cease at volume 20, but annual conferences will continue to take place, and the papers presented will be available on the NBER website.

Takatoshi Ito and Anne O. Krueger, Editors and Seminar Chairs

Takatoshi Ito and Andrew K. Rose, Editors and Seminar Chairs

Commodity Prices and Markets

Edited by **Takatoshi Ito and Andrew K. Rose**

The University of Chicago Press

Chicago and London

TAKATOSHI ITO is a professor in the Graduate School of Economics at the University of Tokyo, and a research associate of the National Bureau of Economic Research. ANDREW K. ROSE is the B. T. Rocca Professor of Economic Analysis and Policy at the Haas School of Business, University of California, Berkeley, and a research associate of the National Bureau of Economic Research.

The University of Chicago Press, Chicago 60637
The University of Chicago Press, Ltd., London
© 2011 by the National Bureau of Economic Research
All rights reserved. Published 2011.
Printed in the United States of America

20 19 18 17 16 15 14 13 12 11   1 2 3 4 5
ISBN-13: 978-0-226-38689-8 (cloth)
ISBN-10: 0-226-38689-9 (cloth)

Library of Congress Cataloging-in-Publication Data

Commodity prices and markets / edited by Takatoshi Ito and
    Andrew K. Rose
        p. cm. — (NBER East Asia seminar on economics ; v. 20)
    ISBN-13: 978-0-226-38689-8 (hardcover : alk. paper)
    ISBN-10: 0-226-38689-9 (hardcover : alk. paper) 1. Prices—East
    Asia—Congresses. 2. Petroleum industry and trade—East Asia—
    Congresses. 3. Futures market—East Asia—Congresses. I. Ito,
    Takatoshi, 1950– II. Rose, Andrew, 1959– III. Series: NBER–East
    Asia Seminar on Economics (Series) ; v. 20.
    HB235.E18C66 2011
    332.63′28095—dc22
                                                                    2010028438

Relation of the Directors to the
Work and Publications of the
National Bureau of Economic Research

1. The object of the NBER is to ascertain and present to the economics profession, and to the public more generally, important economic facts and their interpretation in a scientific manner without policy recommendations. The Board of Directors is charged with the responsibility of ensuring that the work of the NBER is carried on in strict conformity with this object.

2. The President shall establish an internal review process to ensure that book manuscripts proposed for publication DO NOT contain policy recommendations. This shall apply both to the proceedings of conferences and to manuscripts by a single author or by one or more co-authors but shall not apply to authors of comments at NBER conferences who are not NBER affiliates.

3. No book manuscript reporting research shall be published by the NBER until the President has sent to each member of the Board a notice that a manuscript is recommended for publication and that in the President's opinion it is suitable for publication in accordance with the above principles of the NBER. Such notification will include a table of contents and an abstract or summary of the manuscript's content, a list of contributors if applicable, and a response form for use by Directors who desire a copy of the manuscript for review. Each manuscript shall contain a summary drawing attention to the nature and treatment of the problem studied and the main conclusions reached.

4. No volume shall be published until forty-five days have elapsed from the above notification of intention to publish it. During this period a copy shall be sent to any Director requesting it, and if any Director objects to publication on the grounds that the manuscript contains policy recommendations, the objection will be presented to the author(s) or editor(s). In case of dispute, all members of the Board shall be notified, and the President shall appoint an ad hoc committee of the Board to decide the matter; thirty days additional shall be granted for this purpose.

5. The President shall present annually to the Board a report describing the internal manuscript review process, any objections made by Directors before publication or by anyone after publication, any disputes about such matters, and how they were handled.

6. Publications of the NBER issued for informational purposes concerning the work of the Bureau, or issued to inform the public of the activities at the Bureau, including but not limited to the NBER Digest and Reporter, shall be consistent with the object stated in paragraph 1. They shall contain a specific disclaimer noting that they have not passed through the review procedures required in this resolution. The Executive Committee of the Board is charged with the review of all such publications from time to time.

7. NBER working papers and manuscripts distributed on the Bureau's web site are not deemed to be publications for the purpose of this resolution, but they shall be consistent with the object stated in paragraph 1. Working papers shall contain a specific disclaimer noting that they have not passed through the review procedures required in this resolution. The NBER's web site shall contain a similar disclaimer. The President shall establish an internal review process to ensure that the working papers and the web site do not contain policy recommendations, and shall report annually to the Board on this process and any concerns raised in connection with it.

8. Unless otherwise determined by the Board or exempted by the terms of paragraphs 6 and 7, a copy of this resolution shall be printed in each NBER publication as described in paragraph 2 above.

Contents

Acknowledgments

This volume is a collection of papers that were presented at the twentieth annual East Asia Seminar on Economics (EASE). EASE is coorganized by the National Bureau of Economic Research (NBER) in Cambridge, MA; the Australian National University; the Hong Kong University of Science and Technology; the Korea Development Institute in Seoul; Singapore Management University; the Chung-Hua Institution for Economic Research in Taipei; the Tokyo Center for Economic Research; and the Chinese Center for Economic Research at Beijing University. EASE-20 was held in Hong Kong, June 26–27, 2008; the Hong Kong University of Science and Technology (HKUST) was the local organizer, and the Hong Kong Institute for Monetary Research (HKIMR) was a gracious host.

We thank all our sponsors: the NBER, All Nippon Airways, HKUST, and the HKIMR, for making EASE-20 possible. The conference department of the NBER led by Carl Beck with support by Brett Maranjian for this conference, and the publication department led by Helena Fitz-Patrick, as usual, made the organization and publication process run smoothly. The local team led by Francis Lui at HKUST deserves special mention for ensuring that the conference and all local arrangements ran as smoothly as they did.

Introduction

Takatoshi Ito and Andrew K. Rose

The chapters of this volume were first presented at the twentieth annual East Asian Seminar on Economics, and are all focused on the theme of commodity prices and markets.

Commodity price fluctuations represent tremendous challenges and opportunities for economists and policymakers. For economists, they often represent large, plausibly exogenous shocks of tremendous importance, especially for small open economies. For societies dependent upon commodity sales, price changes are either disasters or windfalls. The statistical linkages between commodity prices—especially the price of oil—have been well-known for a long period of time, though the exact interpretation is not universally agreed upon. For policymakers of oil-importing countries, oil price increases represent an adverse supply shock, posing difficult policy options. Due to an increase in imported energy price, domestic prices tend to increase and output tends to be depressed. Monetary easing (intended to help stimulate aggregate demand) may result in further increases in prices, which may prompt workers' demand wage increases to maintain real wages. Moreover, lower interest rates may depreciate the exchange rate, further aggravating inflation. An inflationary spiral of price and wage increases may thus be ignited. Knowing this risk, an inflation targeting central bank might be reluctant to relax monetary policy to support output. On the other hand, if the central bank tightens monetary policy in fear of inflation, output activities will contract further, deepening the recession. Although a contrac-

Takatoshi Ito is professor in the Graduate School of Economics at the University of Tokyo, and a research associate of the National Bureau of Economic Research. Andrew K. Rose is the B.T. Rocca Professor of Economic Analysis and Policy at the Haas School of Business, University of California, Berkeley, and a research associate of the National Bureau of Economic Research.

1

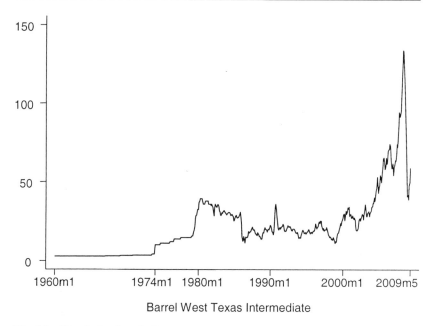

Barrel West Texas Intermediate

Fig. I.1   Nominal price of oil

tion in output is inevitable in the face of the adverse supply shock, and the standard of living of the oil-importing economy has to fall, it may be difficult for policymakers to convince the public of this consequence.

Before we introduce the chapters, we first provide a brief background to the material. We begin with oil prices. Oil represents one of the most important sources of energy used in both advanced and developing economies. Other fossil fuels (e.g., coal and natural gas) are also used widely around the world, especially to produce electricity. Other important sources of energy exist, including hydro, nuclear, and renewable power such as wind and solar. Still, oil has played, and will continue to play, a vital role in a number of key transportation types (e.g., cars, trucks, ships, and airplanes) in the foreseeable future. Fluctuations in oil prices are imperfectly but substantially associated with business cycle fluctuations, especially in the United States. Thus, it is eminently reasonable to begin with a brief overview of the oil market.

Figure I.1 provides a time-series plot of a standard measure of the price of oil (in this case, the nominal dollar price of a barrel of West Texas Intermediate Crude). Several features of the data jump out, upon even casual observation. First, the price of oil was exceptionally smooth until 1973. In fact, the price of oil fluctuated between only $2.57/bbl (oil barrel) and $3.56/bbl from January 1948 until July 1973. In the 1950s, oil "majors" controlled the oil price, and in the 1960s the OPEC (Organization of Petroleum Exporting Countries) became influential in fixing oil prices. This period of exceptional tranquility ended with the first oil price shock. Oil prices jumped from around $3/bbl to $12/bbl in a matter of a few months, in the aftermath of a war in the Middle East. After another period of low volatility, the price of oil again rose steeply between the summers of 1979 and 1980, a period known widely as the second oil price shock. The oil market has been relatively volatile since the second oil crisis, and has exhibited some dramatic price fluctuations. Of special note are the collapse of oil prices in the mid-1980s (possibly due to increases in new supply from the North Sea and other oil field discovery and delivery), the spike in oil prices associated with the Gulf War of 1990, and the very dramatic run-up in oil prices, which began around 2004. The price movement in the latest episode is said to be amplified by speculative money. Finally, the global recession of 2008 to 2009 coincides with an equally dramatic collapse in oil prices.

What caused these oil price changes? Hamilton has argued in a long series of papers (e.g., Hamilton 2009) that supply disruptions and discovery of the North Sea oil have characterized most of the post-war oil price shocks. However, he argues that the most recent increases in the price of oil seem to have been caused by strong demand confronting stagnant production. This characterization has been widely but not universally accepted; Kilian (2008) argues that most oil price shocks have been driven by global demand for industrial commodities (including crude oil), along with shocks to the precautionary demand for crude oil. In any case, it is unclear that the nature of the shock has important consequences for the macroeconomy of a typical oil importer.

As is well-known, the timing of the price changes seems to coincide remarkably well with macroeconomic fluctuations. The big oil price increases associated with OPEC-I, OPEC-II, the 1990 Gulf War, and 2007 to 2008 all closely lead business cycle downturns that hit a number of industrial countries at about the same time. Accordingly, much conventional macroeconomic theory takes oil price shocks as exogenous supply shocks. Significant increases in the price of oil might be expected to create both inflation and recession; this "stagflation" has been famously modeled by Bruno and Sachs (1985) in an important analysis of the first two OPEC shocks. However, it is not completely obvious that oil price shocks need cause enduring inflation. Any recessionary effects of oil prices are necessarily transient, and oil price shocks are simply a large and important relative price change (rather than an intrinsic source of persistent changes in the absolute price level). Thus some authors, notably Bernanke, Gertler, and Watson (1997), have argued that the endogenous monetary response to oil price shocks (rather than the shocks themselves) are what has caused many of the adverse consequences of oil prices. In any case, the macroeconomy seems to respond differently to oil price shocks of late than it did during the period of the large OPEC shocks of the 1970s. Blanchard and Galí (2007) argue that this is the result of a combination of better monetary policy, more flexible labor markets, a

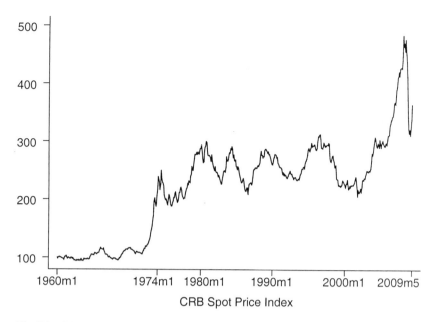

Fig. I.2   Nominal commodity prices

reduced importance of oil, and simple good luck (in that adverse oil price shocks did not coincide with other shocks).

Where figure I.1 portrays the price of oil, figure I.2 is an analogous time-series plot of a commonly used index of commodity prices (in this case, the spot market index provided by the Commodity Research Bureau including twenty-two basic commodities). One of the striking features of the broader index of commodity price index is its close similarity to the oil price series of figure I.1 (even though the index does not include petroleum products).[1] The two series share a long period of low volatility at the beginning of the sample, which ends at around the same time. After thirty years of continuing volatility, they share the same enormous run-up, collapse, and small rebound during the dramatic events of 2007 to 2009. The common and dramatic nature of the recent price movements suggests that while oil and general commodity prices may help cause business cycle fluctuations, they may also be responsive to global economic fluctuations, as argued by Kilian (2008).

With these features of the data in mind, we now turn to the chapters of *Commodity Prices and Markets*. Rather than begin with the macroeconomy, we begin with more narrow examinations of commodity prices, then gradually begin to broaden our scope.

1. See http://www.crbtrader.com/crbindex/spot_background.asp.

Forecasting Currencies with Commodity Prices

In a well-known recent working paper, Chen, Rogoff, and Rossi (2008) (hereafter CRR) argue that the exchange rates of countries that produce disproportionate amounts of commodities can be used to forecast future commodity prices themselves. Forecasting commodity prices is not only important for a large number of businesses and official agencies, but has also proven to be remarkably difficult to forecast (even via prices of commodity futures). Thus, this positive result has the potential to be quite significant, if it stands up to scrutiny. In "Commodity Prices, Commodity Currencies, and Global Economic Developments," Groen and Pesenti (chapter 1, this volume) provide exactly the sort of independent robustness analysis that is standard in other sciences, but deplorably rare in economics.

Groen and Pesenti do a very thorough job of scrutinizing the results of CRR. Where CRR focus on one commodity price index at the quarterly frequency, Groen and Pesenti exhaustively analyze ten commodity price indices using monthly data to forecast ahead at four different horizons. More importantly, CRR are interested in asking whether commodity prices can be forecast with *either* exchange rates or arbitrary combinations of other macroeconomic and commodity-relevant variables. The latter is the most intriguing part of their study, since they cast their net widely to examine a host of economic "fundamentals" that might be of relevance in forecasting commodity prices. In fact, their potential set of fundamentals are so large as to require factor-analytic procedures to reduce the "curse of dimensionality," which might otherwise eliminate all available degrees of freedom. They compare statistical models that are augmented with extra information from either exchange rates or economic fundamentals to laughably simple time-series benchmark models such as the simple random walk popularized by Meese and Rogoff. Unfortunately, despite all the judicious use of econometric technology, Groen and Pesenti consistently find only weak results. Any improvement in forecasting commodity prices over simple benchmarks tend to be ephemeral, sensitive to the exact measure of commodity prices used in the forecasting index, the precise horizon, and so forth. This cannot be considered definitive until it completely encompasses the much more positive results first found by CRR. However, it represents serious pushback for those who believe in the forecasting ability of commodity currencies, and is likely to trigger a lively debate in the reviving field of exchange rate economics.

Why do Groen and Pesenti fail to find that commodity currencies do not provide significant forecasting ability for commodity prices? One possible explanation is that commodity markets are fully efficient, quickly and completely reflecting all possible sources of information. If commodity prices were fully efficient, then it might be impossible for currencies—or any other information—to help forecast their movements. Considerable skepticism is warranted here, since futures markets for commodities have a long and ignoble history of providing awful forecasts for future spot prices of commodities. Still, the hypothesis seems worth investigating; in the (unlikely) event that it is a reasonable characterization, an efficient commodity market would lead to a number of radical conclusions concerning commodity prices. And surprisingly—at least to us—Chan, Tse, and Williams (chapter 2, this volume) examine futures markets for commodities and find considerable evidence consistent with the hypothesis of market efficiency in "The Relationship between Commodity Prices and Currency Exchange Rates."

Chan, Tse, and Williams are, like Groen and Pesenti, particularly interested in the relationship between commodity prices and currencies; they are similarly motivated by the findings of CRR. But, they depart from other investigators in looking at the price/currency relationships with higher-frequency data. Their daily data set has more observations (though a shorter span) than those of others working in the area, so that they can tease out even relatively short-lived forecasting relationships. They also depart from other researchers in using the futures data for commodities actually employed by speculators and hedgers, rather than the more illiquid spot prices. Their results are consistent with Fama's notion of "semistrong" market efficiency in that they find that a week's worth of lags in currencies returns do not, in fact, help improve forecasts of commodity returns. In this, they are consistent with the results of Groen and Pesenti (and inconsistent with those of CRR) in that they find no advantage to using currencies when forecasting commodity prices. Indeed, an (unjustified) extrapolation of their findings implies that *nothing* can be used to forecast future commodity returns.

We find this result to be narrow, but intriguing. The findings are narrow because they rely on linear Granger-causality tests for a limited number of currencies and commodities forecast at short horizons. Still, they are unusually positive in a literature often plagued by unexplained rejections of market efficiency. We look forward to future work in the area, as additional forecasting variables (such as the "order flow" used in foreign exchange markets) are applied with more general statistical techniques. If the results stand up—an outcome that is far from certain—they could represent the beginnings of a shift in one of the field's deeply held priors.

Commodity Prices, the Terms of Trade, and Exchange Rates

Commodity prices are of interest to economists for a great many reasons. One of these is that the characteristics of commodity prices are quite different from those of other prices in the economy. For instance, where many nominal prices of goods and services exhibit "stickiness" of one sort or another, it is well-known that commodity prices are volatile—indeed, scarily so. The effect of commodity price fluctuations on more traditional prices can then be examined, and, indeed, this is done by a number of the following chapterq that estimate "pass-through" equations. We return to these issues later in the book.

Another difference between commodity and more traditional prices for goods and services is that commodity prices are often denominated in one currency—almost always the U.S. dollar—and thus show essentially full and instantaneous pass-through of exchange rate changes. For instance, if the dollar price of gold stays constant, but the euro/dollar exchange rate fluctuates, the price of oil in euros will change 1:1 with the exchange rate. This difference between commodities and a more conventional price series is exploited by Broda and Romalis (chapter 3, this volume) in a novel and interesting way. In "Identifying the Relationship between Trade and Exchange Rate Volatility," they use the difference between the negligible effects of exchange rate volatility on commodity trade with the fact that exchange rate volatility might have a large effect on trade in noncommodity sectors. This is a plausible identifying restriction that allows them to incorporate the possibility that trade—whether from commodities or other goods— might, in turn, have a feedback effect on exchange rate volatility. This clever identification strategy allows them to model the simultaneous determination of exchange rate volatility and trade in a way that is more satisfying and plausible than other approaches. Allowing for simultaneity turns out to have a big effect in practice; it dramatically lowers the much-disputed effect of currency unions on trade first identified by one of the editors.

It has long been known that shocks to commodity prices are responsible for much of the variation in a country's terms of trade, especially for developing countries that export disproportionate amounts of commodities. The terms of trade is conventionally defined as the ratio of a country's export to import prices. To measure the numerator of the terms of trade, one simply adds up the prices faced by the country's exporters, weighting by the importance of a particular good in a country's aggregate exports; the denominator is constructed analogously. Commodity-exporting countries tend to produce specialized export bundles, so that the volatility of their terms of trade tends to derive from shocks to their exports rather than their more widely diversified imports. All this is well-known and has been much studied.

Do the consumers of a country face the same terms of trade as producers? If not, then the marginal rate of substitution across goods faced by consumers differs from the marginal rate of transformation faced by producers. This inefficiency can potentially have serious consequences for welfare. It would also be interesting to understand the proximate causes for the wedges between consumer and producer prices, which are often caused by tariffs, taxes, and other aspects of government policy. These, in turn, may have political-economy origins that are also worthy of study. First, though, it is necessary to see if there are, in fact, nontrivial differences between the traditional (producer) terms of trade and the consumers' terms of trade (hereafter CTT). This initial measurement task is the one set for themselves by Berka and Crucini (chapter 4, this volume) in "The Consumption Terms of Trade and Commodity Prices."

Berka and Crucini create consumer terms of trade using underlying price data from the Economist Intelligence Unit, which is a panel of disaggregated prices for a number of individual goods collected in a number of important global cities across time. Rather than using city-specific prices, however, the authors average prices across cities to create average consumer prices. This procedure might be problematic, given the existence of dramatic and persistent deviations from the law of one price studied by many authors (including Crucini). However, it does deliver a single set of worldwide consumer prices that can then be aggregated up to create the CTT when weighted by net export shares. (The aggregation scheme necessarily means that any good in which a country's trade is approximately balanced will contribute little to the CTT.) Since the study depends on a dubious assumption as well as a narrow panel of goods, cities, and time, we view this study as a preliminary one, necessary to determine whether a larger effort is warranted.

After creating the consumer terms of trade, Berka and Crucini then perform some intriguing empirical analysis. While their results are preliminary, at least two results are compelling. First, they find that just a few goods—oil, automobiles, and pharmaceuticals—contribute disproportionately to volatility in the CTT. Second, they find considerable differences between the traditional (producers') terms of trade and CTT. We view this work as far from definitive; the set of caveats necessary for a broad interpretation is long. However, the subject material has now passed this initial "smell test" and warrants a more comprehensive and grounded study; we look forward to more analysis from the authors in the future.

"Pass-through" of Commodity Prices to the General Price Level

Periods immediately after large increases in commodity prices—especially the price of oil—have sometimes been associated with inflation; these inflations have often been large and persistent. However, the great inflations associated with the first two OPEC price shocks of the 1970s seem now to be a thing of the past. During the last few years, oil prices have risen very dramatically without any clear and strong inflationary consequences. That is, the "pass-through" of oil prices (which are determined on global markets) to domestic prices seems to be changing. Given the extreme volatility of oil prices that the world has experienced of late, it is important to understand *why* pass-through patterns seem to be changing. Accordingly, three of the chapters in this volume examine the changing nature of pass-through.

In "Pass-Through of Oil Prices to Japanese Domestic Prices," Shioji and Uchino (chapter 5, this volume) study pass-through issues for Japan. They begin by quantifying the size and nature of pass-through of oil prices to domestic in inflation for Japan. However, their real interest lies in understanding why the effects of oil price shocks seems to have declined so much over the last few decades. They use time-series techniques (vector autoregressions, or VARs), which allow for variation over time in their coefficients, and examine disaggregated price data. They compare a number of different and plausible explanations for declining pass-through. It might be the case that the Bank of Japan is slowly asserting its recent monetary independence and establishing greater credibility for monetary policy. If so, a more credible nominal anchor for the Japanese economy means that a given oil price shock is viewed increasingly as a shift in relative prices that need not result in greater inflation. Alternatively, more flexible Japanese labor markets might also result in lower pass-through. Another possible explanation is simply that energy is less important to the Japanese economy, in part because of the sharp increases in energy prices of the 1970s. Based upon a close examination of input-output tables for Japan, this turns out to be the most plausible explanation. It states, essentially, that Japanese firms reacted to the first two OPEC oil price shocks by changing their cost structures. For instance, switching to less oil-intensive production structures over time lessens the effects of subsequent oil price shocks (such as the one currently being experienced). The contrast between Japanese and American automotive firms is not only implicit, but striking. Still, Shioji and Uchino leave much room for future work. It is unclear which mechanism led to the changing responses of Japanese firms to energy price signals. Did the exchange rate play a role? Were public policies—especially energy taxes—important? How were consumers affected by all this? We enjoyed reading this step along the path toward a complete understanding of the effects of oil price shocks, and look forward to more.

Fukunaga, Hirakata, and Sudo (chapter 6, this volume) broaden the range of inquiry in "Effects of Oil Price Changes on the Industry-Level Production and Prices in the United States and Japan" in two key ways. They are interested in the effects of oil price shocks on prices (the focus of Shioji and Uchino) and also output. This allows them to characterize the consequences for the real economy both at a macroeconomic level, and at a more disaggregated industry level. They also do comparable work for both the United States and Japan. The choice of this pair of countries is natural: they constitute the two largest economies in the world, and have reacted quite differently to large changes in energy prices. Like Shioji and Uchino, Fukunaga and colleagues also use time-series data in their VAR-based empirical analysis. However, they diverge in exploiting a set of identification assumptions recently popularized by Kilian (2008).

Kilian's identification scheme relies on splitting the economy into three separate blocks, which are identified recursively. A global oil market depends only on itself, but also affects the aggregate macroeconomy. Both of these markets spill out to affect individual industries. Oil price shocks can then be identified to be either demand or supply in nature, and one can analyze their effects on different sorts of industries in both countries. We find this identification scheme eminently plausible, though the authors' modeling of the domestic macroeconomies is narrower than we would prefer (omitting, for instance, the exchange rate and all measures of monetary policy). In any case, the empirics deliver plausible results concerning the effects of different oil shocks, particularly for the United States, on oil and nonoil industries. As one would expect, the effects of oil price changes depend on the exact nature of the shock and of the industry being affected. More interestingly, the transmission of different shocks is very different for the United States and Japan. The United States, for example, is oil-intense and less export-dependent compared with Japan. Perhaps most intriguing is the fact that there seem to be weaker, or even positive effects of unexpected oil (supply) price increases on Japan, a result that stands in contrast with strong negative effect on the United States. The authors provide a plausible explanation for their findings, since the effect of oil price increases can potentially be positive because Japan produces energy-efficient goods (e.g., fuel-efficient Japanese cars). While we do not believe that the authors have presented enough evidence to be completely persuasive, we consider this finding fascinating, and well worth further study.

Kuo and Peng (chapter 7, this volume) are also interested in pass-through issues and study them using Taiwanese data in "Price Pass-Through, Household Expenditure, and Industrial Structure: The Case of Taiwan." Theirs is a primarily descriptive analysis that characterizes Taiwan, reasonably enough, as an emerging economy that is not yet rich enough to have the low pass-through effects that characterize a typical advanced economy. They find that when global commodity prices rise, only around a fifth of these increases eventually show up in domestic consumer prices of energy and food; these are two of the most volatile parts of consumer prices, which are substantially driven by commodity prices. These components are also worthy of study since their volatility means that they are often omitted from inflationary measures that focus on core underlying inflation. Kuo and Peng analyze the effects of these price changes on household expenditures using coarsely disaggregated Taiwanese data and the "Almost Ideal Demand System" developed by Deaton and Muellbauer. The causes, however, of these relatively small responses are left unmodeled, so it is difficult to know how to interpret these effects or forecast them in the future.

Macroeconomic Effects of Oil Prices

As we noted earlier, the periods of time after oil price increases have historically been associated with recessions in richer economies, which tend to be oil importers (with a few exceptions, such as Norway and the United

Kingdom, after the discovery of the North Sea oil field). This might be because of the direct consequences of higher oil prices for production and consumption. Alternatively and plausibly, it may well be the indirect result of endogenous monetary policy actions that are induced by oil prices. However, both monetary policy and the apparent effects of oil prices seem to have changed of late. Monetary authorities around the world have slowly gained inflation credibility, often by adopting inflation-targeting regimes; simultaneously, the effects of higher oil prices on the economy seem to have shrunk. Is this a coincidence? In "Oil and the Macroeconomy," Lee and Song (chapter 8, this volume) investigate these possibly interrelated issues and find that in the case of Korea, monetary policy is indeed managed close to optimally, at least when it comes to the responsiveness of monetary policy to oil price shocks.

Lee and Song first establish that oil price rises seem to have a different effect on the Korean economy recently than they did in the 1970s, which were days of the large shocks. They do this through means of a conventionally identified VAR model of the Korean economy estimated on two separate periods of time (before the Asian crisis of 1997, and after 2000). They find that the adverse effects of oil prices on Korean real gross domestic product (GDP) have indeed shrunk during the later period. This result is consistent with intuition, as well as the well-known results of Blanchard and Galí (2007). Still, the real question is why exactly has the adverse effect of these supply shocks diminished over time? Since one of the most obvious answers is the response of monetary policy, Lee and Song construct a conventional dynamic stochastic general equilibrium (DSGE) model with both oil and monetary policy built in. After estimating the model, they are able to compare the actual response of monetary policy to oil shocks, with the optimal response delivered by their model. Since the two are relatively close, they conclude that the Bank of Korea seems to have used its monetary independence well (though some caution is necessary since some of the estimates are quite imprecise).

A completely different take on the role of oil in the Korean economy is provided by An and Kang (chapter 9, this volume) in "Oil Shocks in a DSGE Model for the Korean Economy." Like Lee and Song, the authors provide a state-of-the-art modern macroeconomic model of the Korean economy. The model is a relatively conventional one of a small open economy, but it has been augmented to allow for oil imports to be used either for consumption or production purposes. The authors fit the model to fifteen years of recent Korean data, and then use their model to make a set of somewhat unusual comparisons. Specifically, they are interested in understanding how much worse the model performs if oil is excluded entirely from (a) Korean production or (b) Korean consumption. Precisely what one is to make of this comparison is not completely clear to us, though we find it interesting that removing the oil inputs to production has a much more substantive effect than removing the consumption channel. Whether this results from the absence of capital in the model (which limits the amount of factor substitutability in production) is also unclear. We think of this as a very hypothetical set of thought experiments estimated in a sophisticated manner (though with relatively little data); an answer, in other words, awaiting a suitable question.

References

Bernanke, B. S., M. Gertler, and M. Watson. 1997. Systematic monetary policy and the effects of oil price shocks. *Brookings Papers on Economic Activity* 1: 91–142.

Blanchard, O. J., and J. Galí. 2007. The macroeconomic effects of oil shocks: Why are the 2000s so different from the 1970s? NBER Working Paper no. 13368. Cambridge, MA: National Bureau of Economic Research, September.

Bruno, M., and J. Sachs. 1985. *Economics of worldwide stagnation.* Oxford: Basil Blackwell.

Chen, Y.-C., K. Rogoff, and B. Rossi. 2008. Can exchange rates forecast commodity prices? NBER Working Paper no. 13901. Cambridge, MA: National Bureau of Economic Research, March.

Hamilton, J. 2009. Causes and consequences of the oil shock of 2007–08. NBER Working Paper no. 15002. Cambridge, MA: National Bureau of Economic Research, May.

Kilian, L. 2008. The economic effects of energy price shocks. *Journal of Economic Literature* 46 (4): 871–909.

I

Forecasting Currencies
with Commodity Prices

Commodity Prices, Commodity Currencies, and Global Economic Developments

Jan J. J. Groen and Paolo A. Pesenti

1.1 Introduction

In a June 2008 speech, significantly titled "Outstanding Issues in the Analysis of Inflation," Federal Reserve Chairman Bernanke (Bernanke 2008) singled out the role of commodity prices among the main drivers of price dynamics, "underscoring the importance for policy of both forecasting commodity price changes and understanding the factors that drive those changes." (Speech is posted online at http://www.federalreserve.gov/news events/speech/bernanke20080609a.htm.) While inflationary pressures were very much in the minds of monetary policymakers across the globe at that time, the macroeconomic outlook changed rapidly and dramatically in the months following the speech, as the global economy experienced the near collapse of trade volumes, and the associated plunge in commodity prices was the harbinger of pervasive disinflation risks. During the second half of 2009, the signs of an approaching recovery did reemerge worldwide. At the time of this writing (end of 2009), a rally in commodity prices, once again, is resurrecting inflationary threats.

Are they justified? Are they premature? The answers to these questions depend on a long list of variables, and are subject to many caveats. First,

Jan J. J. Groen is a senior economist at the Federal Reserve Bank of New York. Paolo A. Pesenti is Vice President and Head of the International Research Function at the Federal Reserve Bank of New York. He is affiliated with the Centre for Economic Policy Research (CEPR) and the National Bureau. We thank Kalok Chan, Takatoshi Ito, Warwick McKibbin, Roberto Mariano, John Romalis, Andrew Rose, two reviewers, and conference participants at the EASE-20 conference in Hong Kong for many helpful suggestions, as well as Spencer Amdur for excellent research assistance. The views expressed here are those of the authors, and do not necessarily reflect the position of the Federal Reserve Bank of New York, the Federal Reserve System, or any other institution with which the authors are affiliated.

pass-through of commodity price swings to final retail prices takes time; IMF (International Monetary Fund 2008) reports estimates of an average propagation lag of about nine to twelve months for the transmission of oil price shocks, and up to thirty months for the transmission of food price shocks. Second, intensity of use affects a country's Consumer Price Index (CPI) vulnerability to commodity price swings. For instance, energy intensity is typically lower in advanced economies than in emerging and developing countries, and food expenditure represents over one-third of consumption in emerging economies, but only one-tenth of consumption in advanced economies. Third, monetary policy credibility matters. Under regimes of high credibility, changes in the prices of oil, industrial metals, and agricultural commodities can have a significant impact on headline inflation without unmooring medium-term inflation expectations. But, expectations under weak policy credibility depend on current and past inflation, enhancing the impact of commodity price shifts on core inflation. Fourth, exchange rates can amplify or mitigate the transmission mechanism, as commodities are typically priced in dollars, while retail prices are denominated in local currencies (according to International Monetary Fund [2008], a 1 percent effective dollar depreciation raises oil prices in dollars by more than 1 percent).[1]

More than anything, the link between commodity price cycles and inflation is bound to be affected by the size and persistence of commodity price movements, and in this respect, recent swings in commodity prices have been nothing short of spectacular. Following large increases between 2003 and 2006, oil prices accelerated and more than doubled between the end of 2006 and the time of the aforementioned Bernanke speech. Food prices rose by about 50 percent over the same time horizon, with particularly rapid trajectories for corn, wheat, rice, and soybeans. To find traces of a comparable boom one has to go back to the early 1970s, as no major commodity cycle materialized during the 1980s or the 1990s. The subsequent price bust in late 2008 was just as dramatic as this most recent pick-up. Between July 2008 and February 2009, energy prices collapsed by 70 percent, and agricultural prices by 37 percent.[2]

Long-term trends in fundamentals, slower population growth, and weaker global income and output growth suggest that the recent peaks are unlikely to be the new norm (see World Bank [2009]). But what will come next is by no means an easy prediction—which is precisely the key message of the current contribution.

The "easy way out" of relying on commodity futures as signals of future spot price movements is, in practice, highly inadequate.[3] A long literature

1. See also Keyfitz (2004) and Verleger (2008).
2. On the links between commodity prices and inflation, see also Cecchetti and Moessner (2008) and Hobijn (2008).
3. See the chapter by Chan, Tse, and Williams in this volume for a recent assessment.

emphasizes that commodity price dynamics are influenced in theory and in practice by a large variety of factors, including, but not limited to, growth in large emerging economies, inventory and supply constraints, monetary and exchange rate policies, and possibly financial speculation. Section 1.2 of this chapter provides a succinct summary of the different arguments. In light of these considerations, the search for a comprehensive approach to forecasting is bound to be quixotic. Nevertheless, a recent paper by Chen, Rogoff, and Rossi (2008) (hereafter, CRR) appears to provide a pragmatic Ariadne's thread to approach the maze.

According to CRR, exchange rate fluctuations of relatively small commodity-exporting countries such as Canada, Australia, New Zealand, Chile, and South Africa with market-based floating exchange rates have "remarkably robust power in predicting future global commodity prices." While the basic notion that changes in commodity currencies are correlated with commodity prices is not new in the literature, CRR provides a systematic attempt to document and test the forecasting properties of a small set of commodity currencies as explanatory variables, with surprisingly promising results both in-sample (using Granger-causality tests robust to parameter instabilities) and out-of-sample.

The results from CRR (2008) are the direct motivation for our contribution. The basic idea is to take a broad index of different spot commodity prices as the forecast variable (we consider ten alternative indices and sub-indices for three different commodity classes), and compare the forecasting properties of three approaches against a baseline autoregressive or random walk process. The three approaches include a model in which forecasts are based only on the information embedded in observed past movements of commodity currencies, as in CRR, and two variants of a factor-augmented regression model that makes use of information from a relatively large data set, as described later. The purpose of our exercise is ultimately to provide an agnostic but reasonably systematic look at the global roots of commodity price dynamics. Rather than attempting to answer questions such as "why are commodity prices so high or so low" and "how long are they going to stay where they are," our contribution has the more modest purpose of providing an empirical assessment of the extent to which information embedded in indicators of global economic developments may help in predicting movements of commodity prices, by improving upon the naive statistical benchmarks, or the CRR approach.

The main conclusions of the chapter can be summarized as follows. We are able to provide some corroboration, albeit rather mild, for the CRR results. For one specific commodity index, at the shortest forecasting horizons (up to one-quarter ahead), the predictions of an exchange rate-based model are significantly better than those based on a random walk, although they do not outperform an autoregressive specification; at the one-year ahead horizon, the performance is reverted, as the CRR model significantly outperforms the autoregressive benchmark but not the random walk. When other indices are considered, the results are nuanced. We also find that a model encompassing principal components extracted from a panel of global economic explanatory variables generally performs poorly. We obtain more promising results when we replace the principal components approach with a different methodology (a partial least squares factor-augmented model), suggesting that information from a larger set of macrovariables can have some predictive power. However, across commodity indices we cannot generate forecasts that are, on average, structurally more accurate and robust than those based on a random walk or autoregressive specifications.

The chapter is organized as follows. Section 1.2 provides a synthetic survey of the different arguments used to rationalize and predict shifts in commodity prices. Section 1.3 describes the methodology used in constructing our exchange rate-based and factor-augmented regression models and assessing their forecasting properties against the naive statistical benchmarks. Section 1.4 reports and discusses our results. Section 1.5 concludes.

1.2   Interpreting Commodity Price Cycles

In retrospect, and with the advantage of hindsight, one can always attempt to rationalize movements of commodity prices in terms of supply and demand fundamentals.[4] Taking for instance the case of oil prices, Hamilton (2009) emphasizes that, while historical oil price shocks were primarily caused by physical disruptions of supply, the price run-up of 2007 to 2008 was caused by strong demand confronting stagnating world production and little spare capacity.[5] A mismatch between fast demand growth and increasing intensity of the gross domestic product (GDP) in countries such as China on the one hand,[6] and slow-growing supply capacity due to sluggish investment until the early 2000s on the other hand, similarly explains the path of industrial metals (see World Bank 2009). As far as food prices were concerned, weather shocks and supply bottlenecks certainly played a role in the recent cycle. But the decline in global inventory in the mid-2000s was mainly the result of strong growth of consumption in emerging and developing economies. Also, attempts to avoid the consequences of rising fuel prices by exploring alternative sources of energy led governments to revise their biofuel mandates and subsidize production. The outcome was

4. Structural macroeconomic fundamentals were emphasized in early papers on the determination and forecasting of commodity prices such as Reinhart (1988) and Borensztein and Reinhart (1994).
5. Kilian (2009) downplays the contribution of current supply disruptions to price movements, attributing fluctuations in the price of oil to "precautionary demand associated with market conditions about the availability of future oil supplies."
6. Currently GDP metal intensity in China is four times higher than in developed countries. Going forward, China's metal intensity is expected to peak and move closer to the world's average (see World Bank 2009).

soaring demand for corn and some vegetable oils. Because of corn-based ethanol production in the United States, about 30 percent of the entire corn crop was diverted toward production of biofuels (see International Monetary Fund 2008).[7]

Understanding long-run trend movements in fundamentals, however, does little to enhance our ability to predict the extent, persistence, or volatility of changes in short-term supply and demand, nor their effects on commodity prices. Take once again the case of oil. The argument can be made that increasing extraction costs in marginal fields imply that future capacity will be built at higher costs. At the same time, short-term demand price elasticity is likely to remain rather low (below 0.1 according to most estimates), even though income elasticities are somewhat higher.[8] As a result, small revisions in the expected path of future supply expansion can have large and highly volatile effects on expected future prices. Heuristically, one can understand the difficulties related to predicting oil price changes by visualizing the market for oil as the overimposition of a virtually vertical line (inelastic demand) with another vertical line (inelastic supply). While the quantity traded is not in doubt, the equilibrium price in such market is very much in the eye of the beholder. Minor movements of either curves, related to small adjustments in inventories or marginal changes in extraction decisions, can have sizable (and unpredictable) effects on prices.[9] Similar considerations may apply, ceteris paribus, to other commodity classes.

The extent and volatility of recent swings have prompted some observers to dismiss attempts to rationalize and predict commodity price movements in terms of fundamentals, and focus instead on the role of other factors such as speculative behaviors in the futures markets. The basic idea is that speculative strategies that drive futures prices up must be reflected in higher spot prices today regardless of long-term fundamentals, or agents would have an incentive to accumulate inventories that could be sold later at higher prices. More generally, commodity prices are forward-looking variables that reflect and process expectations about future price changes. The effects of speculative and forward-looking behaviors are likely to be stronger in an environ-

7. Going forward, even assuming that food demand will slow with lower population growth and strong productivity growth will ensure adequate food supply, biofuels could expand demand rapidly, with associated upside risks for corn prices (see World Bank 2009).

8. The price elasticity may be time varying. For instance, in the early part of the past decade the initial response of U.S. consumers to oil price increases was relatively muted due, among other factors, to the low share of gasoline in consumption spending. By 2007 to 2008, energy had returned to an importance for a typical budget not seen since the 1970s, enhancing the sensitivity of consumers' behaviors to bad news about energy prices (see Hamilton 2009).

9. The observed large volatility in the rate of change of nonrenewable minerals and fossil fuels, as well as the absence of long-term positive trends, makes it difficult to reconcile the empirical evidence with the prescriptions of the Hotelling's rule (Hotelling 1931). According to this rule, the price of nonrenewable resources should be growing continuously at a rate that tends toward the rate of interest as the share of cost in price gets smaller and smaller over time. For a recent assessment see Gaudet (2007).

ment of rapid declines in short-term interest rates, lowering the opportunity cost of physical commodity holding as emphasized by Frankel (2008), and prompting investors in money market instruments to seek higher yields in alternative asset classes such as commodity futures. In this light, very rapid declines of short-term rates in early 2008 may have "fanned the flames of commodity speculation," as Hamilton (2009) puts it.[10]

The jury is still out on whether speculation can effectively drive spot prices. A 2008 report of the Interagency Task Force on Commodity Markets (Interagency Task Force on Commodity Markets 2008) did not find speculation behind higher oil prices. If anything, speculators tended to react *after,* rather than in anticipation of, price changes. Skeptic rebuffs of the speculation theory point out that speculation in the futures market can raise spot prices to the extent that it is accompanied by increasing physical hoarding. But there is no systematic inventory hoarding evidence in recent episodes of high volatility in spot commodity prices. If anything, oil inventories were moving downward, not upward at the time of sharpest price movements, suggesting that inventory changes served to mitigate rather than aggravate the magnitude of oil price shocks (see Interagency Task Force on Commodity Markets 2008). A related mechanism linking futures and spot prices requires current production to be foregone (including the deliberate choice to keep oil in the ground) in response to anticipated higher future prices. The fact is that, to rationalize a speculation-based interpretation of the oil shocks of 2007 to 2008, one needs a combination of two elements: low price elasticity of demand, and failure of physical production to increase. But these are precisely the two key ingredients of a fundamentals-only explanation as pointed out by Hamilton (2009), so that, ultimately, the two approaches are observationally equivalent.[11]

One could argue that, regardless of speculation, futures prices should help to predict the direction of future price movements, as they efficiently incorporate information available to market participants. But futures prices provide, at best, highly noisy signals about future spot prices.[12] The difference between the futures price and the current spot price (or futures basis) is not in itself an indicator of the expected direction of change of spot commodity prices, as it reflects both the expected decline in the spot price and a risk premium. Gorton and Rouwenhorst (2005) suggest that the basis "seems to carry important information about the risk premium of individual commodities," somewhat downplaying the role of market expectations about the expected spot return. Also, it is unclear whether prices in relatively illiquid segments of the futures market such as longer-dated contracts can be considered unbiased and effective aggregators of information.

10. See also Akram (2008).
11. See also Slade and Thille (2004).
12. For a survey of the evidence, see Bowman and Husain (2004).

A different—and more promising—approach exploits the forward-looking nature of a different category of asset prices, namely, exchange rates. As shown forcefully by Engel and West (2005), bilateral exchange rates between any pair countries reflect expectations about future changes in the underlying relative economic fundamentals. Therefore, exchange rates of predominantly commodity-exporting economies vis-à-vis, say, the United States, should reflect expectations about demand and supply conditions in world commodity markets. This is the rationale for the finding by CRR (2008) that commodity exchange rates can be remarkably effective predictors of future commodity prices. CRR observe that primary commodity products represent a key component of output in the five commodity-exporting countries under consideration, affecting a large fraction (between 25 and more than 50 percent) of their export earnings. At the same time, these countries are too small to have monopoly power on international relative prices through the manipulation of the supply of their exports, so that global commodity price changes end up representing sizable terms-of-trade shocks for these countries. Market expectations of these changes are priced into current exchange rates, through standard forward-looking mechanisms. Ultimately, observable movements in a small number of exchange rates embed valuable information on the direction of change of future commodity prices, making commodity currencies significantly better predictors than standard approaches based on traditional statistical models (such as a random walk or a mean-reverting autoregressive process).

In light of the aforementioned considerations, a pragmatic approach to commodity prices forecasting is to use information from a large variety of indicators of supply and demand conditions across major developed and developing countries, complementing the forecasting power of commodity currencies with the one embedded in current global economic developments. The set of macroeconomic time series we consider includes industrial production, business and consumer confidence data, retail sales volumes, unemployment rates, core consumer prices (excluding food and energy), money aggregates and interest rates, as well as data on inventories and production of industrial metals, oil, natural gas, and coal, and more unusual variables such as the Baltic Dry Index (BDI)—an index that captures the average price of ocean shipping, aggregating prices of many different routes and types of shipping vessels. The complete list of variables we consider can be found in appendix table 1A.1.

1.3   Methodological Issues

1.3.1   Three Specifications of the Forecasting Equation

Turning now to the formal aspects of our exercise, in what follows we focus on the performance of direct forecasts from fundamentals-based regressions for a number of commodity price indices.[13] Following standard practice in the forecasting literature, we use an autoregressive (AR) model as the forecasting benchmark for such regressions. The *AR benchmark model* in the context of direct forecasting can be written as:

$$(1) \qquad \Delta p_{t+h,t} = \alpha^h + \sum_{i=1}^{k} \rho_i \Delta p_{t-i+1,t-i} + \epsilon_{t+h,t}, \qquad t = 1, \ldots, T,$$

where $p_t = \ln(P_t)$ and P_t is a spot commodity price index, $\Delta p_{t+h,t} = p_{t+h} - p_t$ for the forecasting horizon $h > 0$, and $\Delta p_{t-i+1,t-i} = p_{t-i+1} - p_{t-i}$ for $i = 1, \ldots,$ k. The number of lagged first differences k in equation (1) is determined by sequentially applying the standard Schwarz (1978) Bayesian information criterion (BIC) starting with a maximum lag order of $k = k_{max}$ down to $p = 1$. The unconditional mean benchmark is simply:

$$(2) \qquad \qquad \Delta p_{t+h,t} = \alpha^h + \epsilon_{t+h,t},$$

which implies a *random walk (RW) forecast* for the level of the forecast variable p_t.

The benchmark models in equations (1) and (2) use solely the information embedded in the commodity price time series itself. However, when forecasting commodity price changes, it might be useful to incorporate information from additional, theoretically relevant variables. For instance, CRR (2008) explore the usefulness of exchange rates to predict commodity prices. Consistently, we follow CRR (2008) and modify equation (1) by adopting the following specification for the *exchange rate-based model:*

$$(3) \qquad \Delta p_{t+h,t} = \alpha^h + \sum_{m=1}^{M} \gamma_m \Delta e_t^m + \sum_{i=1}^{k} \rho_i \Delta p_{t-i+1,t-i} + \epsilon_{t+h,t}.$$

In equation (3), $\Delta e_t^1, \ldots, \Delta e_t^M$ are the first differences of the log U.S. dollar exchange rates of M commodity-exporting economies.

More generally, from a forecasting vantage point, it might be useful to exploit information from a set of economically relevant variables not limited to commodity exchange rates. For this purpose, *factor-augmented regressions* provide a convenient approach. One seminal application of the use of factor-augmented regressions is Stock and Watson (2002b), where a limited number of principal components extracted from a large data set are added to a standard linear regression model that is then used to forecast key macroeconomic variables. Stock and Watson (2002a) and Bai (2003) formalized the underlying asymptotic theory, which allows the use of principal com-

---

13. While the time-series reduced-form approach of the chapter provides a simple and flexible framework for our forecasting exercise, it sacrifices the information embedded in a medium- or large-scale econometric model. As an example of a stochastic dynamic general equilibrium model dealing with the transmission of commodity prices in the global economy, see Elekdag et al. (2008).

ponents to identify the common factors in very large data sets. Our factor-augmented regressions adhere to the following specification:

$$(4) \qquad \Delta p_{t+h,t} = \alpha^h + \sum_{i=1}^{r} \beta_i^h f_{i,t}^{PC} + \sum_{j=1}^{k} \rho_j \Delta p_{t-j+1,t-j} + \epsilon_{t+h,t}.$$

Following Stock and Watson (2002b) we take a $T \times N$ matrix of N indicator variables, say $X = (x_1' \ldots x_T')'$, and normalize X such that the variables are in zero-mean and unity variance space, which results in the $T \times N$ matrix $\tilde{X}$. We then compute the r eigenvectors of the $N \times N$ matrix $\tilde{X}'\tilde{X}$ that correspond to the first $\hat{r}$ largest eigenvalues of that matrix. By postmultiplying $\tilde{X}$ with these eigenvectors, we obtain the estimated factors $f_{i,t}^{PC}$ used in equation (4).

The drawback of the aforementioned factor-augmented regression approach is that the use of principal components does not always guarantee that the information extracted from a large number of predictors is particularly useful in the context of the specific forecasting exercise. Boivin and Ng (2006) make it clear that if the forecasting power comes from a certain factor, this factor can be dominated by other factors in a large data set, as the principal components solely provide the best fit for the large data set and not for the target variable of interest. We, therefore, consider an alternative to principal components in which only the factors relevant for modeling the target variable, commodity price changes in our case, are extracted from the predictor variable set. One possible approach is partial least squares (PLS) regression. As Groen and Kapetanios (2008) show, PLS regression outperforms the usual principal components-based approach both in simulations and empirically, and especially when the underlying factor structure is weak.[14]

We implement PLS regression by constructing the factors as linear, orthogonal combinations of the (normalized) predictor variables assembled in the $T \times N$ matrix $\tilde{X} = (\tilde{x}_1' \ldots \tilde{x}_T')'$, such that the linear combinations maximize the covariance between the h-period ahead commodity price changes and each of the common components constructed from the predictor variables. In practice, we specify the corresponding *factor-augmented regression model* as:

$$(5) \qquad \Delta p_{t+h,t} = \alpha^h + \sum_{i=1}^{r} \beta_i^h f_{i,t}^{PLS} + \sum_{j=1}^{k} \rho_j \Delta p_{t-j+1,t-j} + \epsilon_{t+h,t},$$

where the PLS factors are extracted according to a similar scheme as in Groen and Kapetanios (2008), namely:

14. One condition under which principal components provide consistent estimates of the unobserved factor structure in a large data set is when these factors strongly dominate the dynamics of the series in such a data set relative to the nonfactor components of the data (see Bai 2003). However, in practice, the factors might not dominate the nonstructural dynamics as strongly as assumed in the underlying asymptotic theory. This affects the accuracy of the factors estimated through principal components. The PLS regression, on the other hand, yields consistent factor estimates even in the latter case—see Groen and Kapetanios (2008).

1. Demean $\Delta p_{t+h,t}$, resulting in $\Delta \tilde{p}_{t+h,t}$, and set $u_t = \Delta \tilde{p}_{t+h,t}$ and $v_{i,t} = \tilde{x}_{l,t}$, $l = 1, \ldots, N$. If lagged price changes are included in equation (5), regress both $\Delta \tilde{p}_{t+h,t}$ as well as the $\tilde{x}_{l,t}$'s on $\Delta p_{t-j+1,t-j}$ for $l = 1, \ldots, N$ and $j = 1, \ldots, k$.[15] Denote the resulting residuals as $\Delta \check{p}_{t+h,t}$ and $\check{x}_{l,t}$'s $l = 1, \ldots, N$. Set $u_t = \Delta \check{p}_{t+h,t}$ and $v_{i,t} = \check{x}_{l,t}$, $l = 1, \ldots, N$. Finally, set $i = 1$.

2. Determine the $N \times 1$ vector of loadings $w_i = (w_{1i} \ldots w_{Ni})'$ by computing individual covariances: $w_{li} = Cov(u_t, v_{it})$, $l = 1, \ldots, N$, and $t = 1, \ldots, T - h$. Construct the i-th PLS factor by taking the linear combination given by $w_i' v_t$ and denote this factor by $f_{i,t}^{PLS}$.

3. Regress u_t and $v_{l,t}$, $l = 1, \ldots, N$, $t = 1, \ldots, T - h$ on $f_{i,t}^{PLS}$. Denote the residuals of these regressions by $\tilde{u}_t$ and $\tilde{v}_{l,t}$, respectively.

4. If $i = r$ stop, then set $u_t = \tilde{u}_t$, $v_{l,t} = \tilde{v}_{l,t}$, $l = 1, \ldots, N$ and $i = i + 1$ and go to step 2.

Selecting the optimal number of factors in the aforementioned factor-augmented regression approaches is a crucial issue, as is the optimal lag order. Moreover, this selection process is complicated by the fact the factors in equations (4) and (5) are generated regressors. In finite samples, the estimation error from a generated regressor adds to the overall estimation error variance in a regression. So, in determining whether to include a regressor, one should balance in the standard case the increase in goodness of fit with adding the noise of an extra free parameter, whereas in the case of a generated regressor, the trade-off is between improvement of fit and adding noise of *both* an extra parameter and an extra, estimated, variable. The latter model selection problem rules out the usage of standard measures such as BIC. Instead, in the cases of equations (4) and (5), we adopt the factor- and lag-order selection criterion as proposed in Groen and Kapetanios (2009). The following information criterion is valid for both regressions (4) and (5) under the framework spelled out in theorem 2 of Groen and Kapetanios (2009):

$$(6) \qquad BICM = \frac{T}{2} \ln\{\hat{\sigma}_\epsilon^2\} + (1 + k)\ln(T) + r\ln(T)\left(1 + \frac{T}{N}\right),$$

where $\hat{\sigma}_\epsilon$ is the standard ordinary least squares (OLS) variance estimator. The third right-hand side term in the *BICM* measure is a penalty term for adding the estimated factors to regressions (4) and (5). This term is motivated by the result that, when in the underlying panel of predictor variables the dimensions T and N go to infinity, the factors become observed. Therefore, the dimensions of this underlying panel determine the penalization for the number of factors in finite samples. Hence, searching for the optimal values of the modified IC in equation (6) provides the econometrician with a consistent, simultaneous estimate of the optimal values of r and k in regressions (4) and (5).

---

15. As the weights (also known as loadings) of the predictor variables in each of the constructed PLS factors depend on the covariance of these with commodity price changes, the inclusion of lagged commodity price changes will affect these loading estimates.

1.3.2   Assessing the Forecasting Properties

Before we proceed, we need to deal with the realistic possibility that the dynamics of the forecasting variable (commodity prices in our case) have not been stable over time. Our approach is to update the forecasting models based on a fixed rolling window of historical data encompassing ω periods. In detail, the steps are as follows:

1. For any given forecast horizon h, the first forecast is generated on $t_0 = \omega$.
2. Extract r^{max} principal components and PLS factors from the N predictor variables over the sample $t = t_0 - \omega + 1, \ldots, t_0 - h$.
3. Determine over the sample $t = t_0 - \omega + 1, \ldots, t_0 - h$ the optimal lag order and optimal number of factors in both (4) and (5) for our criterion BICM (see [6]) across the range $j = 0, \ldots, k^{max}$ and $i = 1, \ldots, r^{max}$. This results in $(\hat{k}^{PC}_{BICM}, \hat{r}^{PC}_{BICM})$ and $(\hat{k}^{PLS}_{BICM}, \hat{r}^{PLS}_{BICM})$. In a similar vein, determine also the optimal lag order for the AR benchmark (1) and the exchange rate-based model (3) based on BIC.
4. Given the outcome of step 3, estimate (1)–(5) over the sample $t = t_0 - \omega + 1, \ldots, t_0 - h$ for each h.
5. Extract r^{max} principal components and PLS factors from the N predictor variables over the sample $t = t_0 - \omega + 1, \ldots, t_0$.
6. Generate the forecast $\Delta\hat{p}_{t+h,t}$ using the estimated dimensions from step 3 and the parameter estimates from step 4 as well as, in the case of (4) and (5), the factors from step 5.
7. Repeat for $t_0 + 1, \ldots, T - h$ and for any forecast horizon h.

To assess the forecasting performance of the respective models we consider the mean of the squared forecast errors (MSE):

$$(7) \qquad \mathrm{MSE} = \frac{1}{T - t_0 - h} \sum_{s=t_0}^{T-h} \varepsilon^2_{s,s+h},$$

where $\varepsilon_{s,t+h}$ is the forecast error of the model-generated prediction of the commodity price change, based on the previously described recursive updating scheme, relative to the *observed* commodity price change over h periods. It is, however, questionable whether one should compare the "raw" MSE (7) of the fundamentals-based predictions; that is, those based on (3), (4), or (5) (denoted as $\mathrm{MSE_F}$), with the MSE of our more parsimonious benchmark models (labeled as $\mathrm{MSE_B}$). Clark and West (2006, 2007) show both theoretically, as well as in Monte Carlo simulations, that $\mathrm{MSE_{RW}} - \mathrm{MSE_F}$ or $\mathrm{MSE_{AR}} - \mathrm{MSE_F}$ is biased downwards as $\mathrm{MSE_F}$, is inflated by spurious noise as the result of inappropriately fitting a larger model on the data. Asymptotically, this spurious noise in $\mathrm{MSE_F}$ disappears, but it can be quite pervasive in finite samples, especially in the case of (4) and (5) where the factors have to be estimated first before a forecast can be constructed. Thus, for sample sizes comparable to those used in practice, tests based on raw MSE differentials relative to (1) or (2) are severely undersized, which makes it harder to find any evidence against the benchmark forecast.

Following Clark and West (2006, 2007), we compare the MSE (7) based on either (1) or (2) with corrected MSE measures for (3), (4), and (5); that is,

$$(8) \qquad \text{MSE}_F^{adj} = \text{MSE}_F - \left(\frac{1}{T - t_0 - h} \sum_{s=t_0}^{T-h} (\Delta\hat{p}_{s,s+h}^B - \Delta\hat{p}_{s,s+h}^F)^2 \right);$$

$$B = AR \text{ or } RW$$

where $\Delta\hat{p}_{s,s+h}^B$ and $\Delta\hat{p}_{s,s+h}^F$ are the h-period ahead commodity price change forecasts from, respectively, the benchmark models and the fundamentals models (3), (4), and (5). We then report the relative MSE differentials as:

$$(9) \qquad RMSE = \frac{\text{MSE}_B - \text{MSE}_F^{adj}}{\text{MSE}_B},$$

with $B = AR$ or RW. So, a positive (negative) value of equation (9) equal to x ($-x$) suggests that the fundamentals-based h-quarter ahead forecast is on average $100\,x$ percent more (less) accurate than the corresponding benchmark forecast.

Given equation (8), we can formulate a test statistic for H_0: $\text{MSE}_B - \text{MSE}_F = 0$

$$(10) \quad z_{\text{MSE}}^{adj} = \sqrt{T - t_0 - h} \left(\frac{\text{MSE}_B - \text{MSE}_F^{adj}}{\sqrt{Var(\tilde{u}_{t+h}^{adj})}} \right); \qquad B = AR \text{ or } RW$$

with

$$\tilde{u}_{t+h}^{adj} = u_{t+h}^{adj} - (\text{MSE}_B - \text{MSE}_F^{adj}),$$

and

$$u_{t+h}^{adj} = \varepsilon_{B,s,s+h}^2 - (\varepsilon_{Fs,s+h}^2 - (\Delta\hat{p}_{s,s+h}^B - \Delta\hat{p}_{s,s+h}^F)^2); \qquad s = t_0, \ldots, T - h.$$

We compute the variance of the $\tilde{u}_{t+h}^{adj}$ terms based on a heteroskedasticity and autocorrelation consistent (HAC) variance estimator, as time-varying variance is a feature of commodity price changes, and the overlap in observations at forecast horizons $h > 1$ induces serial correlation in the disturbances of our forecasting models.

More specifically, we employ the parametric HAC variance estimator proposed by Den Haan and Levin (1997), which has been shown to have good finite sample properties.[16] Clark and West (2006, 2007) show that in case of

---

16. In our case, the Den Haan and Levin (1997) approach entails fitting an AR model to the $\tilde{u}_{t+h}^{adj}$ terms, with the lag order determined by minimizing BIC, and using this estimated AR model to compute the unconditional variance of the $\tilde{u}_{t+h}^{adj}$ terms.

rolling window-based parameter updating, as is the case in our specification, equation (10) will be asymptotically distributed according to a standard normal distribution; that is, $z_{MSE}^{adj} \sim N(0, 1)$ in (10). In the forecast evaluation, we use (10) to conduct a *one-sided* test for the null hypothesis that fundamentals-based commodity price predictions do not significantly outperform those based on our naive, parsimonious benchmark specifications vis-à-vis the alternative hypothesis that (3), (4), or (5) outperform either (1) or (2).

1.4 Empirical Results

1.4.1 Data Description

There are ten spot indices in total, taken from four distinct sources. Details about the composition and calculation of the different indices appear in appendix table 1A.2.

From the Commodity Research Bureau, we use the Reuters/Jefferies CRB Index (CRB), which dates back the farthest of any cross-commodity index. Both the overall index and the industrial metals subindex start in 1947. However, we only go as far back as 1973, based on the availability of the economic fundamental variables. The next longest series, the S&P/Goldman Sachs Index (SPG), starts in 1970, although once again we use data from 1973 onward. The SPG subindices for industrial metals and energy start in 1977 and 1983, respectively. We also evaluate the series used in CRR (2008), the IMF Nonfuel Commodity Prices Index (IMF), which starts in 1980, along with the IMF industrial metals subindex. Finally, the Dow Jones-AIG Commodity Index (DJ-AIG) is the shortest series we use, beginning in 1991, along with its subindices for energy and metals. All commodity price data come directly from the companies who publish them, except for the SPG subindices, which come from Bloomberg. As discussed in section 1.3.1, we take log first differences of all commodity price indices, a transformation chosen to guarantee covariance stationarity.

The exchange rate data for the CRR model come from Bloomberg. We use monthly averages of daily bilateral dollar exchange rates for the Canadian dollar, the Australian dollar, the New Zealand dollar, the South African rand, and the Chilean peso. Chilean exchange rate data are only used when evaluating our models for the DJ-AIG indices, since these data only extend back as far as 1991.

For the factor-augmented models (4) and (5), we combine the exchange rate data with additional fundamental predictor variables in a panel. These additional variables comprise a set of standard macroeconomic time series across major developed and developing countries, such as industrial production, business and consumer confidence data, retail sales volumes, unemployment rates, core consumer prices (excluding food and energy), money

aggregates, and interest rates (OECD; stat databases available at http://www
.oecd.org/statsportal). They also include data on inventories and production of industrial metals, oil, natural gas, and coal (Energy Information
Administration; data have been obtained via Haver Analytics DLX databases [http://www.haver.com/]), as well as the Baltic Dry Index (BDI). The
BDI is an index that captures the costs of ocean shipping, aggregating the
prices of many different routes and types of shipping vessels. It is maintained by the Baltic Exchange, a commodity exchange. Our BDI data come
from Bloomberg as far back as 1985, and they are averaged over the month
from daily data. Before that, going back to 1973, we use monthly data on
aggregated ocean shipping rates that we splice onto our BDI data for the
pre-1985 period.[17]

The predictor variables are also transformed to guarantee covariance stationarity. In general, this means that the real variables are expressed in log
first differences, and the rate variables, such as unemployment and interest
rate, are simply expressed in first differences; see appendix table 1A.2 for
more details. With respect to prices and monetary aggregates, we transform
these series into first differences of annual growth rates to guarantee that
the dynamic properties of the transformed series are comparable to those
of the rest of the predictor variable panel.[18] Except for the BDI, exchange
rate data, and interest rates, the remaining series in our predictor variable
panels for models (4) and (5) are assumed to be observable with a one-month
lag. So, for example, in February 2009 agents only observe industrial production or the consumer price index up to January 2009. Hence, for these
(typically macroeconomic) time series we lag the series by one month before
including them in our panels, thus reducing the potential bias in favor of our
factor-augmented models in the forecast evaluations.

The cross-sectional sizes of the panels used in the factor-augmented models vary across the different commodity price indices we evaluate, as different
indices have different time spans that determine the availability of the variables used in the panel. For the CRB aggregate and industrial metals indices,
the full sample for both the commodities prices and the predictor variables
panel is 1973.03 to 2009.2, with a total of $N = 96$ series in the panel. For
the aggregate SPG commodities price index, the full sample also equals
1973.03 to 2009.2 with $N = 96$. For the SPG industrial metals subindex, the
full sample equals 1977.02 to 2009.2 with cross-sectional size of $N = 112$ for
the predictor variable panel, whereas for the SPG energy subindex they are
1983.02 to 2009.02 and $N = 127$, respectively. For the two IMF commodi-

17. We thank Lutz Kilian for providing us with this data, which he uses in Kilian (2009).
For our purposes, we use the nominal raw version of his series, instead of the real detrended
version used in his paper.
18. This particular transformation acknowledges that series like log price levels and log
money aggregate levels behave as if they were $I(2)$, possibly because of mean growth shifts due
to policy regime changes, financial liberalizations, and other phenomena.

ties price series, the full sample spans the period 1980.02 to 2009.02, and we use $N = 122$ series in the panels used for our factor-augmented models. Finally, for the three DJ-AIG series, the data span the period 1991.02 to 2009.02, and there are $N = 143$ series in the corresponding panels of predictor variables.

1.4.2   Results

As discussed in section 1.3.1, for all ten commodity price indices listed earlier we assess the forecasting performance of our three fundamentals-based forecast methods (the CRR exchange rate-based model [3] and our two factor-augmented models [4] and [5]) relative to two simple benchmark forecasts: those based on an autoregressive (AR) specification, and those based on the unconditional mean or random walk (RW) model (respectively, [1] and [2]). In tables 1.1 to 1.10, the last columns (denoted FX) report comparisons of the factor-augmented models against the CRR model used as a benchmark, as will be explained later. All forecasting models, including the benchmark models, are updated for each forecast based on a fixed rolling window of data (see section 1.3.2), which we set equal to a ten-year period resulting in 120 monthly observations.[19]

The forecasts for our ten commodity price indices apply to five time horizons (in months): $h = 1$, $h = 3$, $h = 6$, $h = 12$, and $h = 24$, as commonly analyzed in the literature. In each reestimation of our forecasting models, we determine a version of each of our two factor-augmented regressions, (4) and (5), based on our modified information criterion in (6). Using this criterion in (6), we simultaneously select the optimal lag order from $j = 0, \ldots, 12$ (where $p = 0$ means no lagged commodity price changes included in the model) as well as the optimal number of factors across $i = 1, \ldots, 6$ such that the value of the criterion is minimized. In case of the AR benchmark (1), as well as the CRR exchange rates-based model (3), we select that lag order from $p = 0, \ldots, 12$ that minimizes the BIC criterion for these two models.

The forecasting results for the CRB commodity price indices are reported in tables 1.1 and 1.2. When we first focus on the performance of the CRR specification (3), it becomes clear that in an out-of-sample context it is not structurally outperforming random walk and autoregressive forecasts: at the shortest horizons its predictions are only significantly better than those based on a random walk, whereas one and two years ahead the CRR model can only significantly outperform the AR benchmark.

Factor-augmented models that utilize principal components extracted from the corresponding panel of global economic data perform quite poorly, and never really significantly outperform the naive benchmark predictions. However, when PLS regression is used to generate factor-augmented com-

---

19. Thus, $\omega = 120$ in the forecast scheme outlined in section 1.3.2.

Table 1.1   Forecast evaluation for the aggregate CRB commodity price index; 1973.03–2009.02

	CRR		PC regression		PLS regression		
h	RW	AR	RW	AR	RW	AR	FX
1	0.07	–0.01	0.00	–0.01	0.20	0.14	0.18
	(1.34)**	(–0.56)	(0.03)	(–0.63)	(1.86)**	(0.99)*	(1.44)**
3	0.02	0.02	–0.02	0.00	0.14	0.14	0.25
	(0.34)	(0.59)	(–0.88)	(–0.16)	(1.26)**	(0.82)*	(1.95)***
6	0.02	0.05	–0.06	–0.02	–0.10	–0.09	–0.05
	(0.25)	(1.14)*	(–0.71)	(–0.55)	(–0.56)	(–0.73)	(–0.41)
12	0.02	0.06	–0.09	–0.02	0.00	0.02	0.14
	(0.25)	(0.93)*	(–0.85)	(–0.24)	(0.00)	(0.16)	(1.43)**
24	–0.01	0.07	–0.19	–0.05	–0.59	–0.48	–0.09
	(–0.08)	(1.56)**	(–1.97)	(–0.57)	(–2.84)	(–2.40)	(–0.37)

Notes: The table reports the relative improvement in the MSE for either the CRR exchange rate-based model (3), versions of the principal components-based factor-augmented model (4), or versions of the PLS regression-based factor-augmented model (5) relative to either the AR model (1) or the random walk-based model (2). This relative MSE improvement is defined in (9). In parentheses we report the test statistic (10) for the null hypothesis that the corresponding MSE differential is zero, whereas a * (**) [***] denotes a rejection of this null hypothesis in favor of the alternative hypothesis that the MSE differential is positive at a 10 percent (5 percent) [1 percent] significance level. Under the heading CRR we report the results for model (3) relative to the AR benchmark (column *AR*) and the random walk-based benchmark (column *RW*), under the heading PC we report these for the principal components-based model (4) with factor- and lag order selection based on the BICM criterion as in (6), and under the heading PLS we report the results for the PLS regression-based model (5) with factor- and lag order selection also based on the BICM criterion as in (6). Finally, in case of PLS regression, the column dented by *FX* reports forecast results of (11), using PLS factors extracted from a predictor variable panel without exchange rates, relative to (3) as a benchmark.

modity price forecasts, the results are more encouraging. For the overall CRB index (see table 1.1), PLS regression-based specifications provide significantly better predictions than both benchmark models at the one-month and one-quarter horizons. In table 1.2, we have a similar outcome for the industrial medals CRB subindex, although PLS-based factor models are also outperforming both benchmarks one year ahead.

In case of the DJ-AIG commodity price indices in tables 1.3 to 1.5, there is arguably some value added in using exchange rate-based models when predicting the overall index (table 1.3), but a lot less so for the energy and metals subindices (tables 1.4 and 1.5). Compared to the CRB indices, factor-augmented models appear to be less useful: only the overall DJ-AIG index PLS-based models are able to significantly outperform both benchmarks at the three-month and six-month horizons.

Tables 1.6, 1.7, and 1.8 report on the out-of-sample performance for our next group of commodity price indices: the S&P/Goldman-Sachs (SPG) indices. The CRR exchange rates-based model (3) is able to significantly outperform naive benchmark projections only at the two-year horizon. Also,

Table 1.2   **Forecast evaluation for the CRB industrial metals subindex; 1973.03–2009.02**

	CRR		PC regression		PLS regression		
h	RW	AR	RW	AR	RW	AR	FX
1	0.12	0.01	0.11	0.03	0.20	0.09	0.10
	(2.30)***	(0.43)	(2.71)***	(1.37)**	(3.88)***	(1.10)*	(1.26)**
3	0.06	0.00	0.00	0.00	0.14	0.10	0.18
	(1.23)**	(0.04)	(0.11)	(−0.11)	(0.90)*	(0.72)	(1.33)**
6	0.03	0.02	−0.01	0.02	−0.01	0.01	0.03
	(0.70)	(0.70)	(−0.19)	(0.26)	(−0.04)	(0.10)	(0.27)
12	0.02	0.04	−0.09	0.00	0.13	0.17	0.23
	(0.22)	(0.73)	(−1.01)	(0.04)	(0.92)*	(1.26)**	(2.12)***
24	0.00	0.08	−0.13	0.01	−0.37	−0.30	0.08
	(−0.04)	(1.80)**	(−1.42)	(0.07)	(−1.92)	(−1.64)	(0.23)

Note: See the notes for table 1.1.

Table 1.3   **Forecast evaluation for the aggregate DJ-AIG commodities price index; 1991.02–2009.02**

	CRR		PC regression		PLS regression		
h	RW	AR	RW	AR	RW	AR	FX
1	0.24	0.09	0.19	0.03	0.40	0.18	0.19
	(2.96)***	(1.59)**	(0.58)	(0.95)*	(0.60)	(1.03)*	(1.48)**
3	0.05	0.05	0.00	0.03	0.48	0.48	0.43
	(1.16)*	(0.98)*	(0.05)	(1.06)*	(0.94)*	(0.93)*	(0.98)*
6	0.00	0.01	−0.08	0.03	0.06	0.17	0.18
	(0.00)	(0.50)	(−0.22)	(0.55)	(1.31)**	(0.80)	(3.85)***
12	0.18	0.09	0.25	0.34	0.20	0.33	0.39
	(0.83)*	(1.93)***	(0.84)*	(1.33)**	(0.62)	(0.86)*	(1.26)**
24	0.17	0.13	0.62	0.82	0.04	0.08	0.17
	(0.71)	(1.62)**	(2.14)***	(1.80)**	(0.07)	(0.19)	(0.57)

Note: See the notes for table 1.1.

forecasts based on both (4) and (5) cannot be deemed to be structurally more accurate than those based on a random walk or autoregressive specifications, although PC-based regressions are successful at $h = 24$ in case of the SPG-Energy index.

Finally, we discuss the results for the IMF indices, as reported in tables 1.9 and 1.10. The CRR specification is doing well in outperforming both benchmark models at the one-month horizon in case of the aggregate index (table 1.10), but not for the industrial metals subindex. Turning to the factor-augmented approaches we find a rather counterintuitive result: PLS-based factor model forecasts significantly outperform the benchmark projections one month and three months ahead for aggregate IMF index, but this result disappears in the case of the metals subindex.

Table 1.4   Forecast evaluation for the DJ-AIG energy subindex; 1991.02–2009.02

	CRR		PC regression		PLS regression		
_h_	_RW_	_AR_	_RW_	_AR_	_RW_	_AR_	_FX_
1	0.17	–0.05	0.24	0.01	0.29	0.06	0.16
	(1.44)**	(–1.23)	(0.13)	(0.32)	(0.51)	(0.30)	(0.33)
3	–0.03	–0.05	–0.03	–0.04	0.35	0.37	0.40
	(–0.52)	(–1.24)	(–0.62)	(–0.88)	(0.72)	(0.83)*	(0.96)*
6	–0.08	–0.04	–0.09	–0.03	0.10	0.22	0.28
	(–0.69)	(–2.89)	(–0.62)	(–1.43)	(0.28)	(0.48)	(0.55)
12	0.07	0.00	–0.12	0.02	–0.03	0.22	0.32
	(0.32)	(0.11)	(–0.49)	(0.10)	(–0.07)	(0.49)	(0.79)
24	0.12	0.12	0.37	0.51	0.02	0.48	0.52
	(0.05)	(2.05)***	(1.01)*	(1.11)*	(0.04)	(0.56)	(0.93)*

Note: See the notes for table 1.1.

Table 1.5   Forecast evaluation for the DJAIG Industrial Metals subindex; 1991.02–2009.02

	CRR		PC regression		PLS regression		
_h_	_RW_	_AR_	_RW_	_AR_	_RW_	_AR_	_FX_
1	0.30	0.04	0.23	–0.02	0.21	–0.12	–0.05
	(1.43)**	(1.16)*	(0.32)	(–0.54)	(1.15)*	(–0.68)	(–0.31)
3	0.10	–0.03	0.04	0.00	0.18	0.08	0.13
	(1.09)*	(–0.50)	(0.64)	(0.02)	(0.77)	(0.36)	(0.87)*
6	0.01	0.00	0.02	0.07	0.03	0.10	0.13
	(0.10)	(–0.39)	(0.04)	(0.69)	(0.07)	(0.71)	(1.16)*
12	–0.08	–0.04	0.22	0.32	0.20	0.26	0.33
	(–0.36)	(–0.73)	(1.36)**	(1.53)**	(0.12)	(1.92)***	(2.42)***
24	–0.24	0.00	–0.19	0.02	–0.13	0.06	0.11
	(–1.35)	(–0.13)	(–1.26)	(0.27)	(–0.34)	(0.66)	(0.64)

Note: See the notes for table 1.1.

The earlier results suggest that neither the exchange rate approach (as in the CRR model) nor a broader approach that uses information from larger data sets, including both exchange rates and other macrovariables (as in our factor-augmented models), are overwhelmingly successful in predicting commodity price dynamics. Nonetheless, the results in tables 1.1 to 1.10 show that the CRR and the PLS-based factor models are occasionally able to outperform simple benchmark models in an out-of-sample context. In light of this outcome, one wonders whether the extra information of the PLS-based factor model vis-à-vis the CRR model is significant enough to warrant its use. To investigate this we compare the out-of-sample commodity price changes from the CRR framework with the following model:

$$(11) \quad \Delta p_{t+h,t} = \alpha^h + \sum_{m=1}^{M} \gamma_m \Delta e_t^m + \sum_{i=1}^{r} \beta_{i,}^{h} f_{i,t}^{PLS} + \sum_{j=1}^{k} \rho_i \Delta p_{t-j+1,t-j} + \epsilon_{t+h,t},$$

Table 1.6   **Forecast evaluation for the aggregate SPG commodities price index; 1973.03–2009.02**

	CRR		PC regression		PLS regression		
h	RW	AR	RW	AR	RW	AR	FX
1	0.15	–0.02	0.16	–0.02	0.10	–0.06	–0.02
	(1.80)**	(–1.02)	(0.89)*	(–1.16)	(0.69)	(–0.71)	(–0.20)
3	–0.06	–0.01	0.00	0.04	–0.03	0.04	0.11
	(–1.65)	(–0.54)	(–0.13)	(1.86)**	(–0.27)	(0.30)	(0.71)
6	–0.03	–0.01	–0.04	0.01	–0.04	0.02	0.08
	(–0.23)	(–0.30)	(–0.01)	(0.87)*	(–0.49)	(0.23)	(1.15)*
12	0.10	0.04	0.03	0.01	–0.07	–0.07	0.06
	(0.69)	(1.13)*	(0.14)	(0.22)	(–0.59)	(–0.45)	(0.35)
24	0.13	0.14	–0.07	–0.02	–0.49	–0.39	–0.07
	(1.16)*	(1.55)**	(–0.73)	(–0.23)	(–0.89)	(–2.04)	(–0.31)

Note: See the notes for table 1.1.

Table 1.7   **Forecast evaluation for the SPG energy subindex; 1983.02–2009.02**

	CPR		PC regression		PLS regression		
h	RW	AR	RW	AR	RW	AR	FX
1	0.14	–0.04	0.15	–0.01	0.35	0.18	0.23
	(1.46)**	(–1.56)	(1.51)**	(–0.63)	(1.59)**	(1.15)*	(1.54)**
3	–0.06	–0.02	–0.02	0.01	0.13	0.21	0.25
	(–0.67)	(–0.90)	(–0.19)	(0.52)	(0.71)	(0.92)*	(1.08)*
6	–0.05	0.00	–0.10	–0.03	–0.01	0.02	0.06
	(–0.46)	(0.10)	(–0.35)	(–0.84)	(–0.09)	(0.18)	(0.54)
12	0.10	0.02	–0.08	–0.09	–0.05	–0.09	–0.03
	(0.32)	(0.71)	(–0.94)	(–1.92)	(–0.19)	(–0.27)	(–0.11)
24	0.18	0.04	0.27	0.16	0.40	0.23	0.31
	(1.59)**	(0.77)	(2.09)***	(1.21)*	(0.65)	(0.45)	(0.43)

Note: See the notes for table 1.1.

where the r PLS factors are now extracted from a panel of predictor variables that *excludes* the M commodity dollar exchange rates, and we again use the BICM criterion (6) to determine r and k. An out-of-sample comparison between model (11) and model (3), therefore, provides insight about how valuable for forecasting purposes is the extra information (on top of the exchange rates) embedded in the large data set. The out-of-sample analysis for (11) is carried out as outlined in section 1.3.2, but now with the CRR model (3) as the benchmark.

In the *last* columns of tables 1.1 to 1.10, denoted *FX*, we report the results of the out-of-sample comparison between (11) and (3). Of these fifty out-of-sample exercises (five horizons for ten commodity price indices), the extra information embedded in the predictor variable panels turns out to

Table 1.8   Forecast evaluation for the SPG industrial metals subindex; 1977.02–2009.02

	CRR		PC regression		PLS regression		
h	RW	AR	RW	AR	RW	AR	FX
1	0.13	–0.02	0.17	0.02	0.16	0.01	0.02
	(1.61)**	(–1.16)	(0.28)	(0.97)*	(1.22)*	(0.08)	(0.15)
3	–0.03	–0.07	0.07	0.06	0.11	0.06	0.13
	(–0.59)	(–1.97)	(1.65)**	(1.95)***	(0.74)	(0.47)	(1.13)*
6	–0.03	–0.04	0.01	0.02	–0.08	–0.12	–0.05
	(–0.25)	(–1.36)	(0.11)	(0.62)	(–0.24)	(–0.45)	(–0.26)
12	–0.02	0.01	–0.03	0.02	–0.05	–0.10	–0.04
	(–0.16)	(0.16)	(–0.28)	(0.22)	(–0.19)	(–0.67)	(–0.25)
24	–0.12	–0.01	–0.38	–0.25	–0.19	–0.12	–0.09
	(–0.49)	(–0.63)	(–2.01)	(–1.58)	(–1.29)	(–0.88)	(–0.51)

Note: See the notes for table 1.1.

Table 1.9   Forecast evaluation for the aggregate, nonfuel IMF commodities price index; 1980.02–2009.02

	CRR		PC regression		PLS regression		
h	RW	AR	RW	AR	RW	AR	FX
1	0.34	0.03	0.32	–0.01	0.44	0.18	0.17
	(1.49)**	(1.49)**	(1.20)*	(–0.69)	(2.33)***	(1.37)**	(1.48)**
3	0.15	–0.01	0.13	–0.01	0.25	0.10	0.14
	(3.31)***	(–0.29)	(1.86)**	(–0.37)	(2.15)***	(1.00)*	(1.31)**
6	0.01	0.01	0.00	0.03	–0.10	–0.10	–0.06
	(0.36)	(0.37)	(–0.01)	(0.98)*	(–0.37)	(–0.46)	(–0.24)
12	0.03	0.04	–0.07	–0.02	0.15	0.14	0.23
	(0.40)	(0.93)*	(–0.75)	(–0.06)	(0.18)	(0.41)	(0.83)*
24	–0.08	0.00	–0.39	–0.29	–0.14	–0.07	–0.03
	(–1.03)	(–0.03)	(–2.31)	(–2.20)	(–0.91)	(–0.49)	(–0.26)

Note: See the notes for table 1.1.

improve significantly their forecasting performance against the exchange-rate approach in twenty-four cases, in particular for the CRB and DJ-AIG indices. In the majority of those twenty-four cases, both the CRR model and the *original* PLS-based factor model significantly outperform at least one of the two simple, naive, benchmark models. Hence, the case can be made that the PLS-based factor model has a slight edge over the CRR model in modeling commodity price dynamics.

A potential reason why both the CRR and the factor-augmented models cannot structurally outperform naive benchmark forecast might well be due to the fact that market-specific information is the dominant driver of commodity price dynamics. This market-specific information, such as speculative strategies, should, however, be present in futures and forwards contracts that price in expectations for commodity prices in the near future.

Table 1.10   Forecast evaluation for the IMF Industrial Metals subindex; 1980.02–2009.02

	CRR		PC regression		PLS regression		
h	RW	AR	RW	AR	RW	AR	FX
1	0.15	0.01	0.14	0.02	0.10	–0.04	0.01
	(1.80)**	(0.25)	(1.35)**	(0.46)	(0.85)*	(–0.32)	(0.04)
3	0.02	–0.05	0.05	0.02	0.14	0.06	0.12
	(0.34)	(–0.80)	(0.71)	(0.39)	(0.90)*	(0.50)	(1.38)**
6	0.01	–0.02	0.05	0.07	0.10	0.08	0.12
	(0.05)	(–0.50)	(0.18)	(0.84)*	(0.24)	(0.31)	(0.59)
12	0.05	0.03	–0.01	0.02	0.23	0.19	0.25
	(0.41)	(0.92)*	(–0.06)	(0.14)	(0.30)	(0.63)	(0.90)*
24	–0.08	0.01	–0.38	–0.30	–0.09	–0.08	–0.05
	(–0.52)	(0.47)	(–1.78)	(–1.83)	(–0.32)	(–0.37)	(–0.24)

Note: See the notes for table 1.1.

We therefore collected a number of time series on one, three, six, and twelve months ahead futures and forward rates for prices of food commodities, oil, precious metals, and industrial metals; see the appendix tables for more details. Next, we took appropriate transformations of these futures and forward rates (to make them covariance stationary), added them to our panels of predictor variables, and evaluated whether the addition of such market-specific information enables the factor-augmented models to structurally outperform the naive benchmark predictions. Regrettably, however, consistent time series on a broad set of commodity futures and forward rates are only available from the mid-1980s onwards. Thus, a proper comparison with the factor-augmented results in tables 1.1 to 1.10 is not feasible for all ten commodity price indices. We therefore limit the previously mentioned experiment to the DJ-AIG price indices, and the corresponding results can be found in tables 1.11, 1.12, and 1.13.

If one compares the results in tables 1.11 to 1.13 with the results of the factor-augmented model in tables 1.3 to 1.5, which exclude information embedded in commodities futures/forwards rates, it becomes quite clear that the forecasting performances are substantially unchanged across data sets. Thus, qualitatively, the factor-augmented model results in tables 1.11 to 11.13 relative to the naive benchmark models remain as weak as was originally the case in tables 1.3 to 1.5.

1.5   Conclusion

Can we obtain forecasts of commodity price movements that systematically improve upon naive statistical benchmarks? The basic message of the chapter is one of inconclusiveness. While our results corroborate the notion that commodity currencies are somewhat privileged variables in terms of their predictive power, we are unable to obtain robust validation of this

Table 1.11   **Forecast evaluation for the aggregate DJ-AIG commodities price index with futures included in the underlying panel; 1991.02–2009.02**

	PC regression		PLS regression	
h	RW	AR	RW	AR
1	0.26	0.09	0.58	0.32
	(0.33)	(0.87)*	(1.23)*	(0.46)
3	0.10	0.11	0.45	0.45
	(0.68)	(1.15)*	(0.95)*	(0.98)*
6	0.03	0.05	0.07	0.17
	(0.27)	(2.17)***	(1.04)*	(0.75)
12	0.10	−0.02	0.22	0.32
	(0.25)	(−0.18)	(0.58)	(0.36)
24	0.00	−0.04	0.09	0.12
	(−0.02)	(−0.19)	(0.15)	(0.35)

Note: See the notes for table 1.1.

Table 1.12   **Forecast evaluation for the aggregate DJ-AIG energy subindex with futures included in the underlying panel; 1991.02–2009.02**

	PC regression		PLS regression	
h	RW	AR	RW	AR
1	0.25	0.03	0.32	0.07
	(0.73)	(0.58)	(0.37)	(0.27)
3	0.04	0.02	0.39	0.40
	(0.37)	(0.59)	(0.66)	(0.78)
6	−0.07	−0.03	0.13	0.24
	(−0.25)	(−0.56)	(0.27)	(0.76)
12	−0.30	−0.40	0.02	0.19
	(−0.47)	(−0.97)	(0.04)	(0.26)
24	−0.03	0.10	0.02	0.41
	(−0.09)	(0.34)	(0.03)	(0.83)*

Note: See the notes for table 1.1.

notion across commodity indices and across forecasting horizons. Information from larger sets of macrovariables can help improve our predictions, but their forecasting properties are nuanced, and by no means overwhelming.

To make a point of some potential relevance for the current (late 2009) policy debate in light of our results, stronger exchange rates in commodity-exporter countries, improved confidence and business conditions in China and other Asian newly industrialized countries (NICS), as well as the positive drift of the BDI, all point to buoyant conditions in commodity markets going forward. The risks of a recrudescence in global headline inflation are skewed on the upside. But acknowledging these risks is not tantamount to fostering concerns about policymakers' ability to guarantee price stability,

Table 1.13   **Forecast evaluation for the aggregate DJ-AIG industrial metals subindex with futures included in the underlying panel; 1991.02–2009.02**

	PC regression		PLS regression	
h	RW	AR	RW	AR
1	0.35	0.08	0.41	0.07
	(0.30)	(1.08)*	(1.29)**	(0.54)
3	0.16	0.09	0.17	0.08
	(0.70)	(1.59)**	(0.73)	(0.42)
6	0.07	0.08	–0.03	0.03
	(0.28)	(1.06)*	(–0.04)	(0.12)
12	0.06	0.10	0.15	0.24
	(0.23)	(0.30)	(0.13)	(1.78)**
24	–0.20	0.04	–0.09	0.11
	(–0.90)	(0.37)	(–0.25)	(1.54)**

Note: See the notes for table 1.1.

thus advocating a fast withdrawal of accommodation worldwide. Analyses like ours suggest that forecasts of commodity prices provide at their very best only highly noisy information about their actual future trajectories and persistence. All the more so, estimates of the inflationary pressures associated with expected commodity price swings remain tentative at best. Excessive confidence in the forecast of a forthcoming commodity price surge, or even increased dispersion in global policymakers' views and beliefs about future inflation risks, can become the catalyzer of (or the pretext for) a premature tightening of the global policy mix even though the international outlook remains vulnerable to negative shocks, with potentially devastating consequences for the real economy worldwide.

Concluding as we started with a quote by Bernanke (2008), there is a key open question for a research agenda focused on understanding and predicting swings in commodity prices: "What are the implications for the conduct of monetary policy of the high degree of uncertainty that attends forecasts of commodity prices? Although theoretical analyses often focus on the case in which policymakers care only about expected economic outcomes and not the uncertainty surrounding those outcomes, in practice policymakers are concerned about the risks to their projections as well as the projections themselves. How should those concerns affect the setting of policy in this context?" It is our (strong) prediction that future research will very much take these questions to heart.

Appendix

Table 1A.1 **Data codes**

Code	Country
a	Canada
b	France
c	Germany
d	Italy
e	Japan
f	United Kingdom
g	United States
h	Brazil
i	India
j	Indonesia
k	South Africa
l	OECD
m	G7

Transformation X_t of raw series Y_t

1	$X_t = \ln(Y_t) - \ln(Y_{t-1})$
2	$X_t = Y_t - Y_{t-1}$
3	$X_t = \ln(Y_t/Y_{t-12}) - \ln(Y_{t-1}/Y_{t-13})$
4	$X_t = \ln(\Sigma_{k=0}^{11} Y_{t-k}/12) - \ln(\Sigma_{k=1}^{12} Y_{t-k}/12)$
5	$X_t = Y_t$

Commodity price series

v	CRB, CRB ind. metal, SPG
w	DJAIG, DJAIG energy, DJAIG ind. metal
x	IMF, IMD ind. metal
y	SPG energy
z	SPG ind. metal

Table 1A.2 **Data description**

Variable	Countries	Source	Transform	Indices
Australian Dollar Exchange Rate	—	Bloomberg	1	vwxyz
Canadian Dollar Exchange Rate	—	Bloomberg	1	vwxyz
New Zealand Dollar Exchange Rate	—	Bloomberg	1	vwxyz
South African Rand Exchange Rate	—	Bloomberg	1	vwxyz
Chilean Peso Exchange Rate	—	Bloomberg	1	w
Baltic Dry Index (BDI)	—	Bloomberg	1	vwxyz
Industrial Production	abcdefg	OECD	1	vwxyz
Industrial Production	j	OECD	1	w
Nominal short-term interest rates (3 month)	abceg	OECD	2	vwxyz
Nominal short-term interest rates (3 month)	df	OECD	2	wxyz
Real short-term interest rates (3 month)	abceg	OECD	2	vwxyz

Table 1A.2 (continued)

Variable	Countries	Source	Transform	Indices
Real short-term interest rates (3 month)	df	OECD	2	wxyz
Long-term interest rates (10 year)	abcfgk	OECD	2	vwxyz
Long-term interest rates (10 year)	e	OECD	2	w
Business Confidence Indicator	g	OECD	5	vwxyz
Business Confidence Indicator	e	OECD	5	wxyz
Business Confidence Indicator	bcdeflm	OECD	5	w
Consumer Confidence Indicator	bcdf	OECD	5	wxyz
Consumer Confidence Indicator	fl	OECD	5	wxy
Consumer Confidence Indicator	a	OECD	5	w
Unemployment	aefg	OECD	2	vwxyz
Unemployment	b	OECD	2	wxy
Unemployment	h	OECD	2	wy
Retail Trade Volume	acefg	OECD	1	vwxyz
Retail Trade Volume	b	OECD	1	wxyz
Retail Trade Volume	k	OECD	1	wxy
Retail Trade Volume	d	OECD	1	w
Hourly Earnings in Manufacturing	dfg	OECD	1	vwxyz
Hourly Earnings in Manufacturing	e	OECD	4	vwxyz
Hourly Earnings in Manufacturing	a	OECD	1	vxyz
Goods Exports	abcgefghk	OECD	1	vwxyz
Goods Exports	ij	OECD	1	w
Goods Imports	abcgefghk	OECD	1	vwxyz
Goods Imports	ij	OECD	1	w
Term Slope Structure (Long-term—short-term rates)	abcg	OECD	5	vwxyz
Term Slope Structure (Long-term—short-term rates)	f	OECD	5	wxy
Term Slope Structure (Long-term—short-term rates)	e	OECD	5	w
Core CPI	abcdefgl	OECD	3	vwxyz
Core CPI	m	OECD	3	vz
Broad money (M3)	agk	OECD	3	vwxyz
Broad money (M3)	i	OECD	3	wxyz
Broad money (M3)	el	OECD	3	wy
Broad money (M3)	f	OECD	3	w
Narrow money (M1)	aegl	OECD	3	vwxyz
Narrow money (M1)	ik	OECD	3	wxyz
Narrow money (M1)	f	OECD	3	w
LME Copper Warehouse Stocks	—	EIA	1	vwxyz
LME Lead Warehouse Stocks	—	EIA	1	vwxyz
LME Zinc Warehouse Stocks	—	EIA	1	vwxyz
LME Aluminum Warehouse Stocks	—	EIA	1	wxy
LME Nickel Warehouse Stocks	—	EIA	1	wxy
LME Tin Warehouse Stocks	—	EIA	1	w
Crude Oil Stocks, Non-SPR (Strategic Petrol Reserve)	—	EIA	1	vwxyz
Crude Oil Stocks, total	—	EIA	1	vwxyz
Crude Oil Stocks, SPR	—	EIA	1	wxy

(continued)

Table 1A.2 (continued)

Variable	Countries	Source	Transform	Indices
Jet Fuel Stocks	—	EIA	1	vwxyz
Motor Gasoline Stocks	—	EIA	1	vwxyz
Residual Fuel Oil Stocks	—	EIA	1	vwxyz
Other Petroleum Products Stocks	—	EIA	1	vwxyz
Total Petroleum Stocks	—	EIA	1	vwxyz
United States Crude Oil Production	—	EIA	1	vwxyz
Non-OPEC Crude Oil Production	—	EIA	1	vwxyz
World Crude Oil Production	—	EIA	1	vwxyz
OPEC Crude Oil Production	—	EIA	1	vwxyz
Total World Coal Stocks	—	EIA	1	vwxyz
Distillate Fuel Oil Stocks	—	EIA	1	wxyz
Propane/Propylene Stocks	—	EIA	1	wxyz
Liquefied Petroleum Gases Stocks	—	EIA	1	wxyz
Natural Gas in Underground Storage— working gas	—	EIA	1	wyz
Natural Gas in Underground Storage— total	—	EIA	1	wyz
Currency: Banknotes and Coin	f	Bank of England	1	vwxyz
Wheat Futures Price (1, 3, and 6 month)	—	Bloomberg	1	w^a
Corn Futures Price (1 and 3 month)	—	Bloomberg	1	w^a
Hogs Futures Price (1, 3, and 6 month)	—	Bloomberg	1	w^a
WTI Futures Price (1, 3, 6, and 12 month)	—	Bloomberg	1	w^a
Heating Oil Futures Price (1, 3, 6, and 12 month)	—	Bloomberg	1	w^a
Brent Crude Futures Price (3 and 6 month)	—	Bloomberg	1	w^a
Copper Futures Price (3 and 6 month)	—	Bloomberg	1	w^a
Gold Futures Price (3, 6, and 12 month)	—	Bloomberg	1	w^a
Silver Futures Price (3, 6, and 12 month)	—	Bloomberg	1	w^a
Lead Forward Price (3 and 15 month)	—	Bloomberg	1	w^a
Copper Forward Price (3 month)	—	Bloomberg	1	w^a
Nickel Forward Price (3 month)	—	Bloomberg	1	w^a
Tin Forward Price (3 month)	—	Bloomberg	1	w^a
Zinc Forward Price (3 month)	—	Bloomberg	1	w^a
Aluminum Forward Price (3 month)	—	Bloomberg	1	w^a
Dependent variables				
Reuters/Jefferies Commodity Price Index	—	CRB	1	v
CRB Industrial Metals Price Index	—	CRB	1	v
S&P/Goldman Sachs Commodity Price Index	—	Goldman Sachs	1	v
Dow Jones/AIG Commodity Price Index	—	Dow Jones	1	w
DJAIG Energy Commodity Price Index	—	Dow Jones	1	w
DJAIG Industrial Metals Price Index	—	Dow Jones	1	w
IMF Global Commodity Price Index	—	IMF	1	x
IMF Industrial Metals Price Index	—	IMF	1	x

Table 1A.2   (continued)

Variable	Countries	Source	Transform	Indices
S&P/Goldman Sachs Energy Commodities Price Index	—	Goldman Sachs	1	y
S&P/Goldman Sachs Industrial Metals Price Index	—	Goldman Sachs	1	z

Note: Dashed cells indicate these variables are not country-specific (such as a global price index), or—in the case of currencies—the country code differs from the abc. . .m conventions.
[a]These are only used in the DJAIG models for tables 1.11 and 1.12.

References

Akram, Q. F. 2008. Commodity prices, interest rates and the dollar. Norges Bank Research Department, Working Paper no. 2008/12, August.

Bai, J. 2003. Inferential theory for factor models of large dimensions. *Econometrica* 71 (1): 135–72.

Bernanke, B. S. 2008. Outstanding issues in the analysis of inflation. Speech at the Federal Reserve Bank of Boston's 53rd Annual Economic Conference. June 9, Chatham, MA.

Boivin, J., and S. Ng. 2006. Are more data always better for factor analysis? *Journal of Econometrics* 132 (1): 169–94.

Borensztein, E., and C. M. Reinhart. 1994. The macroeconomic determinants of commodity Prices. IMF Working Paper no. WP/94/9. Washington, DC: International Monetary Fund, January.

Bowman, C., and A. M. Husain. 2004. Forecasting commodity prices: Futures versus judgment. IMF Working Paper no. WP/04/41. Washington, DC: International Monetary Fund, March.

Cecchetti, S. G., and R. Moessner. 2008. Commodity prices and inflation dynamics. *Bank for International Settlements Quarterly Review* 2008 (December): 55–66.

Chen, Y., K. Rogoff, and B. Rossi. 2008. Can exchange rates forecast commodity prices? NBER Working Paper no. 13901. Cambridge, MA: National Bureau of Economic Research, March.

Clark, T. E., and K. D. West. 2006. Using out-of-sample mean squared prediction errors to test the Martingale difference hypothesis *Journal of Econometrics* 135 (1-2) 155–86.

———. 2007. Approximately normal tests for equal predictive accuracy in nested models. *Journal of Econometrics* 138 (1): 291–311.

Den Haan, W. J., and A. Levin. 1997. A practitioner's guide to robust covariance matrix estimation. *Handbook of Statistics* 24:291–341.

Elekdag, S., R. Lalonde, D. Laxton, D. Muir, and P. Pesenti. 2008. Oil price movements and the global economy: A model-based assessment. *IMF Staff Papers* 55 (June): 297–311. Washington, DC: International Monetary Fund.

Engel, C., and K. D. West. 2005. Exchange rates and fundamentals. *Journal of Political Economy* 113 (3): 485–517.

Frankel, J. 2008. The effects of monetary policy on real commodity prices. In *Asset prices and monetary policy,* ed. J. Y. Campbell, 291–334. Chicago: University of Chicago Press.

Gaudet, G. 2007. Natural resource economics under the rule of Hotelling. *Canadian Journal of Economics / Revue Canadienne d'Économique* 40 (4): 1033–59.

Gorton, G., and K. G. Rouwenhorst. 2005. Facts and fantasies about commodity futures. Yale University, Yale International Center for Finance. Working Paper.

Groen, J. J. J., and G. Kapetanios. 2008. *Revisiting useful approaches to data-rich macroeconomic forecasting.* Federal Reserve Bank of New York Staff Reports no. 327. New York.

———. 2009. *Model selection criteria for factor-augmented regressions.* Federal Reserve Bank of New York Staff Reports no. 363. New York.

Hamilton, J. 2009. Causes and consequences of the oil shock of 2007–08. In *Brookings papers on economic activity,* ed. D. Romer and J. Wolfers, 1–68. Washington, DC: Brookings Institution Press.

Hobijn, B. 2008. Commodity price movements and PCE inflation. *Federal Reserve Bank of New York Current Issues in Economics and Finance* 14 (8): 1–7.

Hotelling, H. 1931. The economics of exhaustible resources. *Journal of Political Economy* 39:137–75.

Interagency Task Force on Commodity Markets. 2008. *Interim report on crude oil.* Washington, DC. July.

International Monetary Fund. 2008. Is inflation back? Commodity prices and inflation. In *World economic outlook: Financial stress, downturns, and recoveries,* 83–128. Washington, DC: International Monetary Fund.

Keyfitz, R. 2004. Currencies and commodities: Modeling the Impact of exchange rates on commodity prices in the world market. Washington, DC: The World Bank, Development Prospects Group.

Kilian, L. 2009. Not all oil price shocks are alike: Disentangling demand and supply shocks in the crude oil Market. *American Economic Review* 99:1053–69.

Reinhart, C. M. 1988. Real exchange rates and commodity prices in a neoclassical model. IMF Working Paper no. WP/88/55. Washington, DC: International Monetary Fund, June.

Schwarz, G. 1978. Estimating the dimension of a model. *Annals of Statistics* 6: 461–64.

Slade, M. E., and H. Thille. 2004. Commodity spot prices: An explanatory assessment of market-structure and forward-trading effects. University of Warwick and University of Guelph. Working Paper, September.

Stock, J. H., and M. W. Watson. 2002a. Forecasting using principal components from a large number of predictors. *Journal of the American Statistical Association* 97:1167–79.

———. 2002b. Macroeconomic forecasting using diffusion indexes. *Journal of Business and Economic Statistics* 20:147–62.

Verleger, P. K. 2008. The oil-dollar link. *The International Economy* 2008 (Spring): 46–50.

World Bank. 2009. *Global economic prospects. Commodities at the crossroads.* Washington, DC: The International Bank for Reconstruction and Development / The World Bank.

Comment   Kalok Chan

There have been surges in commodity prices in the last decade, at least before the financial tsunami. There are many explanations being provided, such as political uncertainty, a significant growth in world outputs, and monetary expansion, as well as low real interest rates.

A few academic studies seek to investigate whether we can forecast global commodity prices. A notable study is Chen, Rogoff, and Rossi (2008), who find that a small number of commodity currencies can forecast global commodity prices. The explanations being given are that exchange rate reflects expectations of future changes of the economic fundamentals, which can affect demand/supply in commodity markets. A natural question being raised is: Can we use macroeconomic variables to forecast commodity prices?

In this chapter, Professors Groen and Pesenti examine whether we can forecast commodity prices using three models: benchmark models, based on random walk or autoregressive process, exchange rate-based model following Chen, Rogoff, and Rossi (2008, hereafter CRR), and factor-augmented models.

The strength of the chapter lies on it asking a very important question, based on a large data set and rigorous econometric analysis. Results indicate some evidence on forecastability of commodity prices using commodity currencies and macroeconomic variables.

However, the overall evidence is weak, as CRR finds that exchange-rate movement can predict all commodity price indices. On the other hand, this chapter finds that the predictive ability of macroeconomic variables is much weaker. But, given that exchange rates should incorporate information about the demand and supply for commodities, while macroeconomic variables represent business activities that lag behind financial transactions, the weak evidence on using macroeconomic variables might not be surprising. Even though the chapter attempts to use factor-augmented models, their performance is still poor, as the aggregation of macroeconomic variables might not be as effective as the currency market incorporating the relevant information.

Rather than looking at individual commodities, this chapter examines the commodity price indices instead. There are at least a few problems associated with using commodity price indices. First, there is heterogeneity across commodity price indices, so that different commodity price indices might vary in terms of number of commodities, commodity exchanges, and the weightings. Second, commodity price indices reflect both spot and futures

Kalok Chan is the Synergis-Geoffrey Yeh Professor of Finance and Director of the Centre for Fund Management at the Hong Kong University of Science and Technology, Hong Kong, China.

contracts, so that they reflect information expected for different time periods. Third, commodity indices comprise a basket of commodities, and it could well be that any autoregressive process for the commodity indices come from cross-predictability across different commodities within the indices.

In addition, I have some other comments. One is that the chapter is not clear on the methodologies and variables being used. For example, it is not clear how many macroeconomic variables are being used for forecasting commodity prices. It is also not clear how the authors select the variables to predict commodity prices. There is also no mention about the number of principal components or number of factors being extracted in factor-augmented regression models.

Overall, I do not think the chapter has fully achieved the objective of answering what really affects commodity prices. While there are a few key factors, such as macroeconomic activities, commodity supply, and monetary policy, the chapter is unable to distinguish them.

Reference

Chen, Y., K. Rogoff, and B. Rossi. 2008. Can exchange rates forecast commodity prices? NBER Working Paper no. 13901. Cambridge, MA: National Bureau of Economic Research, March.

Comment   Roberto S. Mariano

In dealing with commodity price movements, this chapter compares the forecasting performance of fundamentals-based methods with baseline autoregressive or random walk models. Though still preliminary, this chapter shows thoroughness and care in dealing with the motivation, the substance, and the technical details of the study.

The authors begin the chapter with the result of Chen, Rogoff, and Rossi (2008, hereafter CRR), that exchange rate fluctuations of relatively small commodity-exporting countries (Canada, Australia, New Zealand, Chile, and South Africa) with market-based floating exchange rates have "remarkably robust power in predicting future global commodity prices."

The forecast variable in the chapter is a broad index of different spot commodity prices (ten alternative indices and subindices for three different commodity classes). The three forecasting models analyzed in the chapter are:

Roberto S. Mariano is professor of economics and statistics and dean of the School of Economics at Singapore Management University, and professor emeritus of economics and statistics at the University of Pennsylvania.

1. A baseline autoregressive or random walk process (equations [1] and [2] in the chapter).

2. An "exchange-rate model" that adds to the baseline model only commodity currencies, as in CRR (equation [3] in the chapter).

3. A factor-augmented regression model that makes use of information from a relatively large data set of economically relevant "indicator" or "predictor" variables, including commodity exchange rates, again, in conjunction with the baseline model (equations [4] and [5] in the chapter).

In the third group of models, the authors consider two ways of obtaining proxies for the latent (unobservable) factors in the model, based on a large number of observable predictors including commodity currencies:

1. Use a fixed number of principal components of the predictor variables. As the authors point out, one of the problems with this approach is that while the first few principal components generate, by definition, the linear combinations with maximum variation, they need not be the best predictors for commodity price fluctuations.

2. The authors use partial least squares to determine observable factors that are "relevant for modeling the target variable." These are orthogonal linear combinations of the predictor variables (just like the principal components), but this time they are so chosen to maximize the correlation with the h-period-ahead commodity price changes. The procedure is based on an earlier paper of Groen. The authors also point out correctly the additional complication in this procedure due to the fact that the factor proxies are generated regressors that require further modification in the selection procedure (again, based on another earlier paper of Groen).

In this third group of models, I wonder if it would be useful for the authors to consider a third alternative that nests the exchange-rate model. That is, why not separate the commodity currencies as separate regressors as in model 2, and then get the PCs or PLS proxy factors from the rest of the predictor variables?

The authors provide a detailed analysis of their assessment of forecasting properties. I endorse their approach of updating their forecasting models based on a fixed rolling window of historical data, since commodity price dynamics have not been stable over time. They also provide enough technical details for their testing procedure for the null hypothesis that the fundamentals-based predictor (model 2 or 3) does not significantly outperform the benchmark predictor. The argument they present is compelling for the bias correction in the mean square error (MSE) calculations for the fundamentals-based forecasts, but I wonder if even the HAC variance estimator still may need a further finite-sample correction.

One other technical question I have pertains to the fact that in model 2 and model 3, the predictor variables themselves have to be predicted. Are forecast errors on their prediction also taken into account in the forecast assessment in the chapter?

The main conclusions of the chapter, as the authors put it, are:

- The chapter shows mild corroboration of the CRR results that . . . commodity currencies are "somewhat priveleged variables" in terms of their predictive power for forecasting commodity price movements.
- The results in the chapter are unable to provide robust validation of this notion across commodity indices and across forecasting horizons.
- Empirical results also show that information from larger sets of macrovariables can help, but their forecasting properties are "nuanced and by no means overwhelming."
- From a policy perspective, the tentative results in the chapter indicate that forecasts of commodity prices provide highly noisy information— hence, "estimates of the inflationary pressures associated with expected commodity price swings remain tentative at best."

I would add that the results in the chapter are encouraging, and point to further research directions in getting more signals and less noise from the forecasts of commodity prices.

Reference

Chen, Y., K. Rogoff, and B. Rossi. 2008. Can exchange rates forecast commodity prices? NBER Working Paper no. 13901. Cambridge, MA: National Bureau of Economic Research, March.

2

The Relationship between Commodity Prices and Currency Exchange Rates
Evidence from the Futures Markets

Kalok Chan, Yiuman Tse, and Michael Williams

2.1 Introduction

We examine relationships among currency and commodity futures markets based on four commodity-exporting countries' currency futures returns and a range of index-based commodity futures returns. These four commodity-linked currencies are the Australian dollar, Canadian dollar, New Zealand dollar, and South African rand. We find that commodity/currency relationships exist contemporaneously, but fail to exhibit Granger-causality in either direction. We attribute our results to the informational efficiency of futures markets. That is, information is incorporated into the commodity and currency futures prices rapidly and simultaneously on a daily basis.

There are a few studies on the relationship between currency and commodity prices. A recent study by Chen, Rogoff, and Rossi (2008) using quarterly data finds that currency exchange rates of commodity-exporting countries have strong forecasting ability for the spot prices of the commodities they export. The authors argue that the currency market is price efficient and can incorporate useful information about future commodity price movements. In contrast, the commodities spot market is far less developed than

Kalok Chan is the Synergis-Geoffrey Yeh Professor of Finance and Director of the Centre for Fund Management at the Hong Kong University of Science and Technology, Hong Kong, China. Yiuman Tse is professor of Finance at the University of Texas at San Antonio and a U.S. Global Investors, Inc., research fellow. Michael Williams is a doctoral student at the University of Texas at San Antonio.

We appreciate the comments of Taka Ito, Tokuo Iwaisako, Andy Rose, Doo Yong Yang, and the participants of the 2009 NBER-EASE Conference in Hong Kong. Tse acknowledges the financial support from a summer research grant of U.S. Global Investors, Inc., and the College of Business at the University of Texas at San Antonio.

the exchange rate market. Therefore, exchange rates contain forward-looking information beyond what is already reflected in commodity prices.

However, Chen, Rogoff, and Rossi (2008) use commodity prices from either the spot market or the forward market, both of which are less price efficient than the currency spot market. As a result, their evidence cannot be interpreted as absolute superior information processing ability in the currency exchange market over the commodity market. In this chapter, we extend Chen and colleagues by employing futures market data. Relative to the commodity spot market, the futures market offers more convenient, lower cost trading due to its high liquidity, transparent pricing system, high leverage, and allowance of short positions. We, therefore, expect a higher level of informational efficiency for the futures market.

Another advantage of studying the futures market is that we can use higher-frequency data. Most previous literature examines commodity/currency relationships using lower-frequency data (e.g., Chen, Rogoff, and Rossi [2008] use quarterly data). This allows the previous literature to examine commodity/currency relationships based on business transactions. Using daily data allows us to examine the fast dynamics between commodity prices and currency rates in terms of the information transmission brought about by informed and speculative transactions.

Literature studying commodity/currency relationships began with the Meese-Rogoff Exchange Rate Puzzle, which states that fundamentals-based currency forecasting models cannot outperform random walk benchmarks (Meese and Rogoff 1983). The puzzle thus suggests that no economic fundamental-to-exchange rate relationship exists. An extensive literature following Meese and Rogoff, however, finds contradictions to the Exchange Rate Puzzle (e.g., MacDonald and Taylor 1994; Chinn and Meese 1995; MacDonald and Marsh 1997; Mark and Sul 2001; Groen 2005; and others).

Previous studies often cite three explanations for fundamentals-to-currency relationships in general, and commodity-to-currency relationships in particular. The sticky price model states that commodity price increases lead to inflationary pressures on a commodity-exporting country's real wages, nontraded goods prices, and exchange rate. However, wages and nontraded goods prices are upwards sticky, leading only commodity price increases to impact the country's exchange rate. The efficient relative price between traded and nontraded goods is then restored by the currency appreciation.

The portfolio balance model states that a commodity-exporting country's exchange rate is heavily dependent on foreign-determined asset supply and demand fluctuations. Thus, commodity price increases lead to a balance of payments surplus and an increase in foreign holdings of the country's currency. Both of these factors, in turn, lead to an increase in the relative demand for the country's currency, leading to positive currency returns (see

Chen and Rogoff [2003]; Chen [2004]; and Chen, Rogoff, and Rossi [2008] for further detailed discussions).

The third explanation for commodity-to-currency relationships states that commodity price changes proxy exogenous shocks in a commodity-exporting country's terms-of-trade (Cashin, Cespedes, and Sahay 2003; Chen and Rogoff 2003). Terms-of-trade shocks then lead to a shift in the relative demand for an exporter's currency, which, in turn, leads to changes in that exporter's exchange rate (Chen 2004; Chen, Rogoff, and Rossi 2008).

Currency-to-commodity relationships are explained by changes in macro-economic expectations embedded within currency prices being incorporated into commodity price changes (Mark 1995; Sephton 1992; Gardeazabal, Regulez, and Vasquez 1997; Engel and West 2005; Klaassen 2005). This is made possible given that exchange rates are forward-looking while commodity prices are based on short-term supply and demand imbalances (Chen, Rogoff, and Rossi 2008). Under this framework, economic expectations embedded within currency prices contain information regarding a commodity exporter's capacity to meet supply expectations. Thus, expectations regarding future commodity conditions can lead to hedging or hoarding behavior, which, in turn, leads to commodity price changes.

Each of the previous models assumes that economic agents adjust their commodity (or currency) holdings based on business activities (i.e., hedging). Additionally, economic agents are capable of capturing incoming commodity/currency information, accurately interpreting that information in light of their business-specific conditions, and then acting according to their needs. While these assumptions likely hold over longer periods of time, it is questionable whether they hold for frequencies as low as one day.

Our study examines short-horizon commodity/currency relationships using two types of restriction-based causality tests as well as a rolling, out-of-sample forecasting methodology. We find no evidence of cross-asset causality or predictive ability in either direction. These results suggest that commodity returns information is rapidly incorporated into currency returns (and vice versa) on a daily level. In light of previous literature, our results also suggest that economic expectations embedded in currency returns are rapidly incorporated into a country's terms-of-trade, which are embedded in commodity returns (and vice versa).

We suggest that daily commodity/currency relationships within futures markets are facilitated by relatively informed speculators and these markets' ability to rapidly incorporate information shocks into prices. As a result, commodity/currency lead-lag relationships are not found over daily horizons given that asymmetric information profits have already been captured by informed speculators.

Many studies provide evidence that the previous explanation is aided by futures markets having an important role in the price discovery process. Specifically, futures prices represent unbiased estimates of future spot prices when markets are efficient. While we do not suggest that markets are perfectly efficient, we do recognize that futures markets provide a large proportion of forward-looking price discovery. As such, market participants look to futures prices for information regarding future spot prices. Note that our analysis is not predicated on futures prices being unbiased estimates of future spot prices. Rather, our analysis is based on a much less restrictive assumption that futures markets provide forward-looking price discovery for spot markets.

Chan (1992) and many others show that futures lead stock index movements. In commodity futures markets, Schwarz and Szakmary (1994) report that futures prices lead spot prices in petroleum markets such as crude oil, heating oil, and unleaded gasoline. Bessler and Covey (1991) find that cattle futures prices provide more price discovery than cattle cash prices. Thus, futures markets provide higher levels of price discovery than spot markets.

Futures markets offer individual and institutional investors the opportunity to trade (for hedging and speculation) in assets that they may not easily access in commodity spot and forward markets. Investors can also readily trade simultaneously in the commodity and currency futures markets on a real time basis. Accordingly, commodities and currencies are more closely linked and more responsive to one another in the futures market than in the spot market.

We continue in section 2.2 with a description of the study's data set and empirical methodology. Section 2.3 reports the study's results while section 2.4 summarizes the study's findings and provides concluding remarks.

2.2   Data and Methodology

We collect daily commodity and currency futures data from Commodity Systems Inc.'s (CSI) database spanning a maximum range from July 28, 1992 to January 28, 2009. We use the active nearby futures contracts where prices are denominated in U.S. dollars. A separate analysis is performed on data denominated in euros. Our results remain qualitatively unchanged, indicating that dollar denomination and dollar effects do not impact our study's results. We avoid using forward contracts because commodity forward contracts are notoriously illiquid. Prior research has reported that currency and commodity futures contracts traded on the Chicago Mercantile Exchange (CME) are liquid and efficient. Moreover, we do not face nonsynchronous trading problems in our analysis given that all CME futures contracts used in this study trade within one hour of each other.

We calculate returns throughout our analysis using the difference in log prices for both commodities and currencies. Given that our data originate from the futures markets, these returns actually represent the excess returns made possible by securing a futures position. Futures contracts do not generally necessitate an initial monetary outlay in order to secure a position (beyond, of course, exchange-specific margin requirements). As such, any gains or losses incurred by a trader are free and clear of additional transactions costs associated with funding requirements and opportunity loss. Any individual or index return mentioned throughout the chapter should be considered as an excess return.

Note that multiple contracts may trade simultaneously in futures markets depending on contract maturity. To determine a contract's price, we select the price of the most active nearby contract before that contract's last trading day. This is done in a "rolling" fashion throughout each contract's data span. We calculate returns for each contract prior to rolling over to the next contract. See, for example, Bessembinder and Chan (1992) and Tse and Booth (1996).

Most previous studies examine commodity/currency relationships using lower-frequency data. Using lower-frequency data allows the previous literature to examine these relationships in the context of business transactions. We use daily data to capture fast dynamics occurring within the futures markets and to focus on the impact of informed and other speculative activity on commodity/currency relationships.

We employ two broad commodity index futures, the S&P GSCI (formerly Goldman Sachs Commodity Index) and the Reuters/Jefferies Commodity Research Bureau (CRB) commodity indices that began trading on July 28, 1992 and March 6, 1996, respectively. While the GSCI contract is more popular than the CRB contract, we include both due to differing index coverage. Among the currency futures, the Japanese yen is the most active contract, followed by the Canadian dollar, Australian dollar, New Zealand dollar, and South African rand.

Investors may not have easy access to many commodity spot markets and, as discussed in Chen, Rogoff, and Rossi (2008), many commodities lack liquid forward markets. However, most of the commodity and currency futures contracts used in this study are actively traded by individual and institutional investors. Thus, our study avoids infrequent trading and liquidity biases that may exist in forward and spot commodity markets.

Rosenberg and Traub (2008) and many others point out that futures markets' wide range of participants (from hedge funds to corporate hedgers and retail traders), centralized location, anonymous trading, and highly transparent trading systems suggest that futures prices can aggregate rich sources of private information. As a result, price discovery is much faster in futures markets. More importantly, daily futures settlement prices are readily available from various futures exchanges and news media. Daily settlement prices are determined by the futures exchange near the close of trading in order to calculate daily profits and losses on investors' positions. These profits and losses are both realized (resulting from actual purchases and sales) and unrealized (resulting from daily marking-to-market revaluations).

Table 2.1   Sample beginning dates

	AD	CD	RA	NZ	JY
S&P GSCI Commodity Index	7/29/1992	7/29/1992	5/08/1997	5/08/1997	7/29/1992
CRB Commodity Index	3/07/1996	3/07/1996	5/08/1997	5/08/1997	3/07/1996
Country specific indices	7/29/1992	7/29/1992	5/08/1997	5/08/1997	

Notes: The table reports the beginning dates for each currency/commodity pair. Abbreviations AD, CD, NZ, RA, and JY refer to the Australian dollar, Canadian dollar, New Zealand dollar, South African rand, and Japanese yen, respectively.

All but three futures contracts are traded on the CME Group (Chicago Mercantile Exchange/Chicago Board of Trade/New York Mercantile Exchange Company) based in the United States. The CRB commodity index futures are traded on ICE Futures U.S. (formerly named the New York Board of Trade). Using data predominantly from one exchange has the benefit of avoiding different trading platform and exchange bias.

Lead and zinc futures used to construct country-specific commodity return indices are traded on the London Metals Exchange (LME). We include the two non-U.S. traded commodity futures into these indices given that each contribute a small percentage to the indices' composition. For robustness purposes, we test our results after omitting lead and zinc futures. We find that our results (available on request) are virtually the same, indicating that our results are not affected by multiple exchange bias.

As previously discussed, unlike other studies that employ data of lower frequencies, we use daily data as in Sephton (1992) to account for commodity/currency relationships being sensitive to time aggregation (Klaassen 2005). As shown in table 2.1, there is a variation of the data period for different commodity/currency combinations due to data reporting limitations. In addition to the full sample, we also base our analyses on two subsamples. The first subsample ranges from July 28, 1992 to June 29, 2007, and represents the prefinancial crisis period. The second subsample ranges from July 1, 2007 to January 28, 2009, which covers conditions during the financial crisis. We find that the two subsamples' results are qualitatively similar to the full sample results (see appendix table 2A.1). Examining the subsamples relative to the full sample ensures that our results are not biased by the recent financial crisis that began with the Bear Stearns hedge fund collapse in July 2007.

Australian, Canadian, New Zealand, and South African currencies are often referred to as "commodity currencies," reflecting that the underlying countries are large commodity exporters. According to the World Bank's World Development Indicators database in 2007, commodities contributed a 68 percent share of Australia's total exports, 43 percent for Canada, 71 percent for New Zealand, and 49 percent for South Africa. Raw commodities comprise a significant percentage of these countries' exports such that an increase in commodity prices may directly increase their currency prices. It is worth noting that these countries are still price takers in world markets for most of their commodity exports (Chen and Rogoff 2003).

Given their strong dependence on commodity exports and data availability, we include the aforementioned countries in our analysis. Note that we do not include Chile in our analysis as in Chen, Rogoff, and Rossi (2008), even though Chile is a raw commodity exporter. We omit Chile from the analysis given that peso futures are not available on the CME, and that including non-CME peso futures could introduce exchange bias into the results.

Both the S&P GSCI and Reuters/Jefferies CRB commodity index futures track various commodity sectors including energy, agricultural, livestock, precious metal, and industrial metal products. The GSCI is relatively concentrated in energy commodity futures (approximately 68 percent in May 2009), whereas the CRB is more commodity diverse (39 percent invested in energy futures). Consistent results between the two indices indicate that our results are not sensitive to index basket diversity or focus.

In addition to the two broad commodity indices, we construct daily "country commodity" return indices that proxy changes in a commodity-exporting country's terms-of-trade (Cashin, Cespedes, and Sahay 2003; Chen and Rogoff 2003; Chen 2004). This process begins by identifying commodity series from the CSI database whose export shares are known (IMF Global Financial Database from appendix 1, table-A1 of Chen, Rogoff, and Rossi [2008]). From there, country-specific returns are calculated as the export share-weighted average of individual commodity returns.

In some cases, early sample data are not fully available for a given country returns index. We use export share reweighting in these cases to compensate for the missing series and to prevent return attenuation. Using the post-weights found in table 2.2, the country commodity futures return series for country i at time t consisting of j commodities during unavailable data dates is calculated as follows:

$$\text{Country Commodity Return}_{it} = \sum_{j} \text{Individual Commodity Return}_{jt} * \left(\frac{w_{ij}}{\sum_{j} w_{ij}} \right)$$

where the commodity-specific weights (w_{ij}) are reweighted according to data availability.

It is important to note that several futures contracts do not have long data histories. In particular, coal contracts are important components in the Australian and South African country indices, but whose futures data are unavailable until July 12, 2001. Thus, these country indices can only replicate 46.3 percent and 78.0 percent of the true Australian and South African indices, respectively. Moreover, aluminum futures contracts are important components in both the Australian and Canadian indices, yet

Table 2.2   **Export shares**

Australia	Pre	Post
Coal	24.4	34.5
Gold	9.4	13.3
Wheat	8.3	11.7
Aluminum	8.1	11.5
Beef	7.9	11.2
Natural Gas	4.8	6.8
Cotton	2.8	4.0
Copper	2.8	4.0
Zinc	1.5	2.1
Lead	0.7	1.0
Total	70.7	

New Zealand	Pre	Post
Beef	9.4	36.4
Aluminum	8.3	32.2
Lumber	8.1	31.4
Total	25.8	

Canada	Pre	Post
Crude Oil	21.4	29.4
Lumber	13.6	18.7
Natural Gas	10.7	14.7
Beef	7.8	10.7
Aluminum	5.0	6.9
Wheat	3.4	4.7
Gold	2.3	3.2
Zinc	2.3	3.2
Copper	2.0	2.7
Coal	1.8	2.5
Hogs	1.8	2.5
Corn	0.5	0.7
Silver	0.3	0.4
Total	72.9	

South Africa	Pre	Post
Gold	48.0	48.0
Platinum	30.0	30.0
Coal	22.0	22.0
Total	100	

Notes: The table reports pre- and post-weighting export shares for four commodity exporting countries. The pre-weighting column refers to International Monetary Fund (IMF) export shares reported in Chen, Rogoff, and Rossi (2008). The post weighting column refers to IMF export shares that are reweighted based on data availability in the CSI data set. Note that the CSI data set does not include a futures contract on beef. As such, beef returns are proxied by an average of live cattle and feeder cattle returns.

only begin to have consistent data coverage on May 14, 1999. Therefore, our country commodity indices may underrepresent the true indices under full information.

All commodity futures contracts in table 2.2 have consistent trade data after July 12, 2001 for the Australian, Canadian, and South African commodity return indices and after May 14, 1999 for the New Zealand commodity returns index. After these corresponding trading dates, country commodity indices contain an average 70.7 percent, 72.9 percent, and 100 percent of the available commodities for Australia, Canada, and South Africa, respectively. For robustness purposes, we conduct our analyses on a data set that begins on July 29, 1992, as well as a second data set that begins on July 12, 2001 for the Australian, Canadian, and South African return indices, and May 14, 1999 for the New Zealand returns index. We find that the results (i.e., no significant causality and forecasting improvement in all countries) are similar across samples. We summarize these results in appendix tables 2A.2 and 2A.3.

Due to data availability, the New Zealand commodity returns index comprises only 25.8 percent of New Zealand commodity exports. While some New Zealand futures data are available from the Australian Securities Exchange, the twelve-hour lag between U.S. and Australian futures trading may introduce nonsynchronous trading problems. These omitted futures comprise a large percentage of New Zealand's total exports, implying that nonsynchronous bias could be large if these components are included. As such, we trade off likely exchange bias in favor of possible index construction bias.

Unlike previous literature, we use currency futures data to mitigate the impacts of overnight currency transaction interest payments. Specifically, spot rate changes are only one component of currency trading profit. Interest earned (paid) on long (short) currency transactions must be included to accurately estimate profits in currency spot markets. Levich and Thomas (1993), Kho (1996), and many others use currency futures to eliminate the need for overnight interest rate accounting.

Pukthuanthong-Le, Levich, and Thomas (2007) point out the computational advantages of using futures over spot data in forecasting currency returns. Specifically, price trends and returns can be measured simply by the log difference of futures prices given that futures prices reflect contemporaneous interest differentials between a foreign currency and the U.S. dollar. Thus, using futures data allows us to conveniently measure currency returns.

We use two separate analyses to assess causality between commodity and currency returns, which is equivalent to testing semistrong form (cross-asset) efficiency for a given futures contract. The first analysis uses coefficient restriction tests on the following two models to examine currency-to-commodity and commodity-to-currency causal relationships, respectively:

(1) $$\text{Comm}_{j,t} = \alpha_{j,0} + \sum_{k=1}^{5} \beta_{j,k}\text{Comm}_{j,t-k} + \sum_{l=1}^{5} \gamma_{j,l}\text{Curr}_{i,t-l} + \varepsilon_{j,t}$$

(2) $$\text{Curr}_{i,t} = \alpha_{i,0} + \sum_{k=1}^{5} \beta_{i,k}\text{Curr}_{i,t-k} + \sum_{l=1}^{5} \gamma_{i,l}\text{Comm}_{j,t-l} + \varepsilon_{i,t},$$

where $\text{Curr}_{i,t}$ are daily log returns for the ith currency at time t and $\text{Comm}_{j,t}$ are daily log returns for the jth commodity at time t.

While our study's aim is cross-asset predictability, we include own-autoregressive lags in both models. This is done for the sake of consistency, as well as the fact that exchange rates can exhibit nontrivial, own serial dependence (Klaassen 2005). Further, including five lags for each variable allows the tests to account for semistrong form (cross-asset) efficiency violations spanning more than one trading day and up to one trading week.

The models shown earlier are estimated using ordinary least squares (OLS) with the Newey-West heteroskedasticity and autocorrelation consistent covariance matrix. For coefficient testing, two restriction tests are employed on the cross-market coefficients, γ, as follows:

$$H_{O,1} : \gamma_1 = \ldots = \gamma_5 = 0$$
$$H_{O,2} : \gamma_1 + \ldots + \gamma_5 = 0.$$

The first test assumes that all cross-market coefficients are jointly equal to zero. The second test assumes that the sum of all cross-market coefficients is equal to zero. In addition, the magnitude (sign) of summed coefficients indicates economic significance (relationship directionality).

Note that our commodity/currency samples span an average of 2,000 to 4,000 trading days. Given such large sample sizes, we use the 1 percent statistical significance level as the significance benchmark, while we also discuss results significant at the 5 percent level. Doing so frees our inferences from concluding that significant commodity/currency relationships exist when, in fact, they do not.

Our second analysis involves comparing rolling out-of-sample forecasts between models 1 and 2 against their respective own-autoregressive benchmark forecasts. Specifically, models 1 and 2 and the following benchmark models are estimated using the first half of each available sample:

(3) $$\text{Comm}_{j,t} = \alpha_{j,0} + \sum_{k=1}^{5} \beta_{j,k}\text{Comm}_{j,t-k} + \varepsilon_{j,t}$$

(4) $$\text{Curr}_{i,t} = \alpha_{i,0} + \sum_{k=1}^{5} \beta_{i,k}\text{Curr}_{i,t-k} + \varepsilon_{i,t}.$$

A one-step ahead, out-of-sample forecast is then computed using the initial estimation. From there, both the beginning and the end of the estimation sample are advanced by one time period while a second one-step ahead, out-of-sample forecast is made. This process continues until the holdout sample is exhausted.

After computing the out-of-sample returns forecasts, Root Mean Square Error (RMSE) percentage differences are calculated as follows:

$$\frac{RMSE_{Model} - RMSE_{Benchmark}}{RMSE_{Benchmark}},$$

where negative (positive) values indicate that a given augmented (benchmark) model provides superior forecasting power relative to a given benchmark (augmented) model. Significant negative values also indicate that a given commodity (currency) return series has predictive power for a given currency (commodity) return series.

Note that other fundamental information exists that may help in explaining exchange rate and commodity price movements, as well as the interlinkages between them. Examples could include economy size (real gross domestic product), export basket diversity, country commodity supply elasticities, and commodity production efficiency measures. However, like Chen, Rogoff, and Rossi (2008), our focus is solely on cross-asset returns predictability at daily intervals. Thus, including other macroeconomic fundamental information would be beyond the scope of our work and would make estimation difficult given that most macroeconomic information is of lower-than-daily frequency.

2.3   Results

2.3.1   Contemporaneous Correlations

Figure 2.1 illustrates monthly futures price movements of the two broad commodity indices and five currencies from July 1992 through January 2009. There is evidence of comovement between the commodity indices and the currencies, although these relationships are less obvious for the South African rand and Japanese yen. We also notice that the commodity and currency futures prices have become more volatile since the second half of 2007.

Panel A of table 2.3 reports cross-asset contemporaneous correlations for the full sample. We find that all commodity-exporting countries' currency returns are contemporaneously correlated with both broad commodity index as well as each respective country-commodity index returns. All correlation coefficients are significantly positive, indicating that commodity price increases are associated with positive currency returns. Australian dollar futures returns are generally more correlated with the broad commodity indices (0.250 with S&P GSCI and 0.412 with CRB) than are other currency futures returns. All other full-sample futures returns also have coefficients

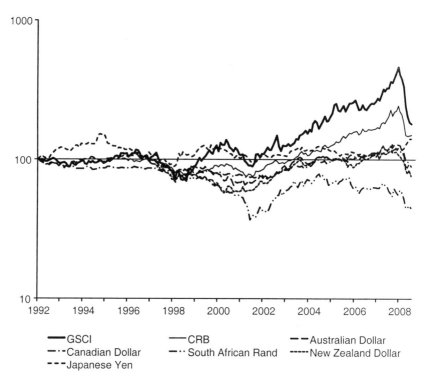

Fig. 2.1   Monthly futures prices, July 1992–January 2009

Notes: This figure reports end-of-the-month futures prices (log scale), each with a scaled starting value of 100 in July 1992. The price series are the S&P GSCI commodity index, CRB commodity index, AD (Australian dollar), CD (Canadian dollar), AR (South African rand), NZ (New Zealand dollar), and JY (Japanese yen).

larger than 0.20 with both indices, except for the relationship between the rand and GSCI (0.162).

We also find that yen returns are not correlated with the two broad commodity index returns (0.001 and 0.055). One may wonder why little correlation exists for the yen given that Japan is heavily dependent on commodity imports. One explanation for this is that the yen was used in the carry trade over the past decade and is a "safe harbor" currency during times of crisis. Thus, the yen being linked to significant nonimport price pressures may reduce its comovement with commodity prices. A second explanation may be that contemporaneous commodity/currency relationships only exist for heavy commodity exporters as opposed to importers.

Of particular note is the fact that while statistically significant, the correlation magnitude for the New Zealand dollar and its country-commodity returns index (0.163) is lower than for the other pairs (0.319 for Australia, 0.225 for Canada, and 0.225 for South Africa). The low correlation for New

Table 2.3   **Contemporaneous correlations**

	AD	CD	RA	NZ	JY
A. Full sample (7/29/1992 or later to 1/28/2009)					
S&P GSCI Commodity Index	0.250	0.261	0.162	0.214	0.001
CRB Commodity Index	0.412	0.375	0.266	0.349	0.055
Country specific indices	0.319	0.225	0.225	0.163	
B. Sub-sample (7/29/1992 or later to 6/29/2007)					
S&P GSCI Commodity Index	0.133	0.136	0.073	0.102	0.056
CRB Commodity Index	0.290	0.239	0.178	0.237	0.157
Country specific indices	0.213	0.122	0.185	0.074	

Notes: The tables report contemporaneous correlations between various commodity and currency returns. Abbreviations AD, CD, RA, NZ, and JY refer to the Australian dollar, Canadian dollar, South African rand, New Zealand dollar, and Japanese yen currency return series, respectively. All correlations are statistically different from zero at the 1 percent significance level except for the full sample GSCI/JY pair.

Zealand may be a result of index construction. As seen in table 2.2, our New Zealand commodity returns index comprises only 25.8 percent of the IMF export shares.

The GSCI and CRB commodity indices are highly cross-correlated (0.710). The significance of this relationship can be explained by both indices tracking the same major commodity categories. The lack of perfect correlation suggests that different index allocations lead each index to reflect different commodity return aspects. This latter fact affirms that our use of the two indices is not an exercise in redundancy.

Panel B shows that the correlation coefficients between commodity and currency returns decrease substantially during the subsample, although the results are still significant at the 1 percent level. For instance, the correlation coefficient between the Australian dollar and the GSCI index is 0.133, 0.290 for the CRB, and 0.213 for the Australian commodity index returns. These results suggest that the financial crisis had some marginal, but not statistically significant, impact on commodity/currency relationships.

It is also worth noting that correlations between the currency futures and the country-specific commodity return indices are generally higher if the sample starts from the day when all of the component commodities have started trading (i.e., July 12, 2001 for Australia, Canada, and South Africa and May 14, 1999 for New Zealand; see panel A of table 2A.2 in the appendix). Given that correlations are still significant, these results indicate that data availability only impacts country index construction in a marginal, nonsignificant manner.

2.3.2 Currency-to-Commodity Lead-Lag Relationships

Table 2.4 reports the results of cross-market coefficient restriction tests on currency-to-commodity return relationships. Panels A and B report zero-

Table 2.4   **Currency-to-commodity Granger causality tests**

	AD	CD	RA	NZ
A. P-values of cross-market zero-coefficient tests, full sample				
S&P GSCI Commodity Index	0.721	0.654	0.477	0.780
CRB Commodity Index	0.419	0.551	0.378	0.957
Country specific indices	0.847	0.407	0.979	0.258
B. P-values of cross-market zero-coefficient tests, subsample				
S&P GSCI Commodity Index	0.381	0.784	0.661	0.900
CRB Commodity Index	0.065	0.309	0.434	0.731
Country specific indices	0.362	0.645	0.393	0.874
C. Sum of cross-market coefficients, full sample				
S&P GSCI Commodity Index	0.152	0.009	0.138	0.009
CRB Commodity Index	0.104	0.069	0.087	0.019
Country specific indices	0.056	0.044	0.030	0.073
D. Sum of cross-market coefficients, subsample				
S&P GSCI Commodity Index	0.153	0.004	0.066	0.102
CRB Commodity Index	0.121**	0.096	0.056	0.030
Country specific indices	0.079	0.094	−0.034	0.040

Notes: The tables report coefficient restriction tests on the following OLS estimated model:

$$\text{Comm}_{j,t} = \alpha_{j,0} + \sum_{k=1}^{5} \beta_{j,k}\text{Comm}_{j,t-k} + \sum_{l=1}^{5} \gamma_{j,l}\text{Curr}_{i,t-l} + \varepsilon_{j,t}$$

In each panel, AD, CD, RA, and NZ refer to the Australian dollar, Canadian dollar, South African rand, and New Zealand dollar return series, respectively. The sample period starts on July 29, 1992 (or later depending on data availability; see Table 2.1, Panel A) and ends on January 28, 2009 for the full sample (June 29, 2007 for the subsample). *P*-values are reported for the cross-market zero-coefficient results while the sum of cross-market coefficients are reported for the coefficient-sum results.
***Significant at the 1 percent level.
**Significant at the 5 percent level.

coefficient restriction test *p*-values for the full and subsamples, respectively. We find that no significant currency-to-commodity relationships exist. The lowest *p*-value is 0.065 for the subsample Australian dollar-CRB index relationship.

Panels C and D report the sum of cross-market coefficients for the full and subsamples, respectively. Again, we find little evidence of currency-to-commodity relationships for commodity-exporting countries. The only exception to this finding is the Australian dollar-to-CRB index relationship. This sum is 0.121 and is significant at the 5 percent, but not 1 percent level.

Note that the previous relationships are reexamined using ten lags for both commodities and currencies. We find that results throughout the chapter remain qualitatively unchanged between the two model specifications (results available on request). This finding indicates that the results in table 2.4 are robust to lag specification.

Table 2.5   **Currency-to-commodity forecasting results**

	AD (%)	CD (%)	RA (%)	NZ (%)
A. RMSE percentage differences, full sample				
S&P GSCI Commodity Index	−0.06	−0.20	0.85	1.06
CRB Commodity Index	0.88	1.35	0.80	1.05
Country specific indices	0.27	0.04	0.29	−0.09
B. RMSE percentage differences, subsample				
S&P GSCI Commodity Index	−1.33	−1.25	0.06	0.97
CRB Commodity Index	−0.66	0.16	−1.10	−0.24
Country specific indices	0.14	−0.02	0.26	0.29

Notes: The tables report RMSE percentage differences between a currency-augmented commodity forecasting model

$$\text{Comm}_{j,t} = \alpha_{j,0} + \sum_{k=1}^{5} \beta_{j,k}\text{Comm}_{j,t-k} + \sum_{l=1}^{5} \gamma_{j,l}\text{Curr}_{i,t-l} + \varepsilon_{j,t},$$

and an own-autoregressive forecasting model

$$\text{Comm}_{j,t} = \alpha_{j,0} + \sum_{k=1}^{5} \beta_{j,k}\text{Comm}_{j,t-k} + \varepsilon_{j,t}.$$

Each model is estimated using OLS with the first half of available data while rolling, out-of-sample forecasts are computed for the remaining half. Negative (positive) values indicate that the currency-augmented commodity (benchmark) forecasting model is superior to the benchmark (currency-augmented commodity) forecasting model. In each panel, AD, CD, RA, and NZ refer to the Australian dollar, Canadian dollar, South African rand, and New Zealand dollar return series, respectively. The sample period starts on July 29, 1992 (or later, depending on data availability) and ends on January 28, 2009 for the full sample and June 29, 2007 for the subsample.

Table 2.5 compares out-of-sample forecasting accuracy between currency-augmented commodity forecasting models and their own-autoregressive commodity forecasting benchmarks. Panels A and B report RMSE percentage differences for the full and subsamples, respectively. We find that RMSE percentage differences are mixed with respect to sign, but are all economically insignificant. The greatest forecasting improvement is still less than 5 percent. Insignificant differences suggest that currency returns are not capable of forecasting future commodity returns. In other words, daily currency returns do not possess causal relationships with commodity returns.

Chen, Rogoff, and Rossi (2008) find that currency returns are able to predict future broad commodity index returns at quarterly frequencies. Based on the present-value model of exchange rate determination (Campbell and Shiller 1987; Engel and West 2005), they argue that the currency exchange rate can predict economic fundamentals because the currency rate reflects expectations of future changes in its fundamentals. Specifically, currency rates are forward-looking while commodity prices are focused on short-run supply and demand conditions. As a result, forward-looking currency exchange rates can predict commodity prices.

A refinement of their explanation for currency-to-commodity relationships may be in macroeconomic expectations leading to changes in a country's terms-of-trade. Currency returns' forward-looking nature suggest that they contain economic expectations information (Mark 1995; Sephton 1992; Gardeazabal, Regulez, and Vazquez 1997; Engel and West 2005; Klaassen 2005). Commodity returns, on the other hand, contain information regarding a commodity exporter's terms-of-trade, given that commodity price shocks originate from exogenous, international markets and that these exporters are world-price takers (Cashin, Cespedes, and Sahay 2003; Chen and Rogoff 2003; Chen 2004).

Under the aforementioned framework, economic expectations embedded within currency returns contain information regarding a commodity exporter's capacity to meet exporting expectations. While this exporter is likely a price taker, commodity market elasticity conditions imply that small supply imbalances induce high price responses (Chen, Rogoff, and Rossi 2008). Thus, expectations regarding future commodity conditions could lead to commodity transactions and, therefore, commodity price changes.

We suggest that the incorporation of economic expectations into trade terms takes place over intervals shorter than what economic agents need to alter their commodity positions after an exchange rate shock. These short-run intervals are, however, of sufficient length for commodity speculators to profit from economic expectations information embedded in currency prices. These speculators have greater information interpretation abilities relative to the average economic agent and, therefore, are able to capture asymmetric information profits. Given commodity futures markets' ability to rapidly incorporate information, speculative activity brings about rapid currency (economic expectations) to commodity (terms-of-trade) comovement.

Note that our explanation does not contradict previous findings of long-horizon commodity/currency relationships. Rather, we make a distinction between speculative versus business commodity transactions. The former transaction takes place over daily frequencies in liquid futures markets and involves informed traders profiting from superior information collection and processing skills. The latter transaction takes place over much longer time frames, and involves relatively uninformed agents adjusting commodity positions according to their economic outlooks.

2.3.3   Commodity-to-Currency Lead-Lag Relationships

Table 2.6 reports cross-market coefficient restriction causality tests for commodity-to-currency return relationships. Panels A and B report zero-coefficient restriction test p-values for the full and subsamples, respectively. We find little evidence that commodities cause currency returns. Two pos-

Table 2.6   **Commodity-to-currency granger causality tests**

	AD	CD	RA	NZ
A. P-values of cross-market zero-coefficient tests, full sample				
S&P GSCI Commodity Index	0.196	0.029	0.817	0.258
CRB Commodity Index	0.264	0.098	0.671	0.260
Country specific indices	0.011	0.043	0.828	0.995
B. P-values of cross-market zero-coefficient tests, subsample				
S&P GSCI Commodity Index	0.167	0.738	0.396	0.088
CRB Commodity Index	0.433	0.288	0.188	0.052
Country specific indices	0.070	0.590	0.704	0.823
C. Sum of cross-markets coefficients, full sample				
S&P GSCI Commodity Index	0.033	0.045***	−0.016	0.019
CRB Commodity Index	0.077	0.057	−0.070	0.066
Country specific indices	0.130***	0.052***	−0.031	0.019
D. Sum of cross-markets coefficients, subsample				
S&P GSCI Commodity Index	0.011	0.019	−0.008	−0.021
CRB Commodity Index	0.011	−0.007	−0.083	0.000
Country specific indices	0.095**	0.020	−0.050	−0.018

Notes: The tables report coefficient restriction tests on the following OLS estimated model:

$$\text{Curr}_{i,t} = \alpha_{i,0} + \sum_{k=1}^{5} \beta_{i,k}\text{Curr}_{i,t-k} + \sum_{l=1}^{5} \gamma_{i,l}\text{Comm}_{j,t-l} + \varepsilon_{i,t}.$$

In each panel, AD, CD, RA, and NZ refer to the Australian dollar, Canadian dollar, South African rand, and New Zealand dollar return series, respectively. The sample period starts on July 29, 1992 (or later, depending on data availability) and ends on January 28, 2009 for the full sample and June 29, 2007 for the subsample. *P*-values are reported for the cross-market zero-coefficient results while the sum of cross-market coefficients are reported for the coefficient-sum results.

***Significant at the 1 percent level.

**Significant at the 5 percent level.

sible exceptions to this finding are the Australian returns index-to-Australian dollar and the Canadian returns index-to-Canadian dollar relationships. While these relationships are significant at the 5 percent level in the full sample (*p*-values of 0.011 and 0.043 for the Australian-index and Canadian-index, respectively), they are not significant in the subsample (*p*-values of 0.070 and 0.590, respectively).

Panels C and D report the sum of cross-market coefficients. There is no evidence of significant daily lead-lag, commodity-to-currency relationships. Neither broad nor country-specific commodity returns can consistently explain future currency returns. The sums of coefficients are generally economically insignificant. Two exceptions are, again, the Australian returns index-to-Australian dollar and the Canadian returns index-to-Canadian dollar causal relationships. Both of these relationships are significant at the 1 percent level in the full sample, but only the former relationship is significant

Table 2.7   Commodity-to-currency forecasting results

	AD (%)	CD (%)	RA (%)	NZ (%)
A. RMSE percentage differences, full sample				
S&P GSCI Commodity Index	0.32	−0.02	0.22	0.21
CRB Commodity Index	0.54	0.05	0.34	0.50
Country specific indices	−0.29	−0.07	0.14	0.14
B. RMSE percentage differences, sub-sample				
S&P GSCI Commodity Index	0.59	0.00	−0.23	−0.55
CRB Commodity Index	−0.17	−0.49	−1.10	−0.72
Country specific indices	−0.04	0.00	0.15	0.17

Notes: The tables report RMSE percentage differences between a commodity-augmented currency forecasting model

$$\text{Curr}_{i,t} = \alpha_{i,0} + \sum_{k=1}^{5} \beta_{i,k}\text{Curr}_{i,t-k} + \sum_{l=1}^{5} \gamma_{i,l}\text{Comm}_{j,t-l} + \varepsilon_{i,t},$$

and an own-autoregressive forecasting model

$$\text{Curr}_{i,t} = \alpha_{i,0} + \sum_{k=1}^{5} \beta_{i,k}\text{Curr}_{i,t-k} + \varepsilon_{i,t}.$$

Each model is estimated using OLS with the first half of available data while rolling, out-of-sample forecasts are computed for the latter half. Negative (positive) values indicate that the commodity-augmented currency (benchmark) forecasting model is superior to the benchmark (commodity-augmented currency) forecasting model. In each panel, AD, CD, RA, and NZ refer to the Australian dollar, Canadian dollar, South African rand, and New Zealand dollar return series, respectively. The sample period starts on July 29, 1992 (or later, depending on data availability) and ends on January 28, 2009 for the full sample and June 29, 2007 for subsample.

at the 5 percent level in the subsample. Moreover, only the Australian returns index-to-Australian dollar results are moderately economically significant given that the sum of cross-asset coefficients is 0.130 and 0.095 for the full and subsamples, respectively.

Table 2.7 reports forecasting accuracy results between commodity-augmented currency return models and own-autoregressive currency benchmarks. We find that commodity returns are rarely capable of increasing out-of-sample forecasting accuracy for currency returns, relative to own-autoregressive models. Like the currency-to-commodity forecasting results in table 2.5, no improvement for the commodity-to-currency forecasting is larger than 5 percent. In other words, we find evidence that commodity returns do not lead currency returns at relatively short time intervals. Our results are consistent across sample selection, indicating that these results are robust to both index construction and the effects of the financial crisis.

For comparison purposes, we repeat the causality and forecasting analyses on Japanese yen-to-broad commodity index returns to assess if currency-to-commodity relationships exist for a noncommodity exporting country. As in the correlation analysis, we find no significant links between the yen and broad commodity index returns. Again, these results are not surprising given that Japan is not a major raw commodity exporter, and that the yen is used for both carry trade and risk mitigation purposes.

The commodity-to-currency causality and forecasting results in tables 2.6 and 2.7 indicate the efficient information transmission between the commodity and currency markets. This market efficiency also suggests that the terms-of-trade information embedded within commodity returns is rapidly incorporated into the economic expectations embedded in a commodity-exporting country's currency returns.

Theoretical models discussed in the introduction suggest the causal relationship between commodity prices and currency exchange rates. While these models (particularly the sticky price model and portfolio balance model) provide adequate commodity-to-currency explanations over longer time frames, they likely do not hold over shorter intervals in liquid futures markets. The reason for this is that each model requires economic agents to make currency transactions in response to exogenous stimuli. However, the average economic agent will not likely recognize and incorporate economic expectations into their business decisions over very short time intervals.

The lack of commodity-to-currency causal relationships at daily intervals does not, however, preclude rapid information transfers between asset classes as we suggest. In this case, speculators in futures markets rapidly incorporate terms-of-trade information into economic expectations over intraday time frames, while other economic agents cause long-horizon commodity-to-currency relationships through their business-necessitated activity.

Overall, we do not find significant causality and forecasting power between the currency and commodity futures markets in both directions and in both the full and subperiods. If anything, the Australian commodity returns index Granger-causes the Australian dollar in the full period analysis, while we find no forecasting improvement. All pairs of commodity and currency futures are significantly and contemporaneously correlated.

In the context of a broader literature, our findings have implications on the present-value model of exchange rate determination. The present-value model states that a given exchange rate can be represented as the discounted sum of its expected (exogenous) fundamentals. Chen, Rogoff, and Rossi (2008) find Granger-causal relationships from exchange rates to commodity prices over quarterly intervals using spot market data. We, however, find no Granger-causality between the commodity and currency markets using daily futures data. Thus, we provide preliminary evidence that the present-value model of exchange rate determination may not hold for daily durations in the highly efficient exchange rate futures markets.

2.4   Conclusions

We examine short-run commodity/currency relationships in four commodity-exporting countries (Australia, Canada, New Zealand, and South Africa) using restriction-based causality tests and a rolling out-of-sample forecasting analysis. We use daily futures prices from July 1992 through January 2009. While investors do not have easy access to many commodity spot and forward markets, they can readily trade in futures markets. They can even speculate on the commodity and currency futures prices simultaneously on a real time basis.

We find that commodity exporting countries' currency returns are contemporaneously correlated with both broad and country-specific commodity return indices. In contrast, commodity returns do not share causal relationships with currency returns, nor are commodity returns capable of predicting future daily currency returns (and vice versa). These results show that commodity prices and currency exchange rates are closely related, but the lead-lag relationship disappears within a day. In light of previous literature, we conclude that commodity-exporting countries' terms-of-trade information embedded in commodity returns is rapidly incorporated into these countries' economic expectations, which are embedded in their exchange rates (and vice versa).

Our results are different from Chen, Rogoff, and Rossi (2008) who use quarterly spot data. They find that currency exchange rates can remarkably forecast commodity prices, suggesting that currency rates contain information beyond what has been reflected in commodity prices. However, their findings may be a result of the less informationally efficient commodity spot markets.

In our chapter, the rapid information transmission between the commodity and currency markets is a result of informed traders using futures markets to profit from expectations/trade-term information. Previous literature notes that futures markets in general, and commodity futures markets in particular, take price leadership roles with respect to spot markets. This is because futures markets are active, transparent, of low transaction costs, have no short-selling constraints, and allow traders the ability to speculate simultaneously in both commodity and currency futures contracts. Thus, the very nature of futures markets allows informed traders the ability to rapidly incorporate economic expectations (currency return information) into commodity-exporting countries' trade-terms (commodity returns, and vice versa).

For future research, we suggest examining individual commodity futures to individual currency futures relationships. Of particular interest among practitioners is the relationship between the Australian dollar and gold, and the relationship between the Canadian dollar and crude oil (see Lien 2008). Another avenue for further study is how monetary policy and real interest rates impact commodity/currency relationships. Frankel (2005, 2006) and Blanch (2008) note that U.S. monetary policy has significant impacts on commodity prices. It would also be interesting to examine whether investor psychology motivates commodity/currency relationships. An example would be whether increased investor opportunism or risk appetite entices investors into both the commodity and high-yielding currency futures markets. All this warrants future research.

Appendix

Table 2A.1   **Contemporaneous correlations, restriction and forecasting accuracy tests for the crisis only sample**

		Currency-to-Commodity			Commodity-to-Currency		
	Rho	Zero-Coef.	Sum-Coef.	RMSE % Diff	Zero-Coef.	Sum-Coef.	RMSE % Diff
AD							
S&P GSCI	0.509***	0.907	0.186	3.16	0.666	0.096	2.49
CRB	0.590***	0.939	0.045	4.04	0.696	0.235	2.42
Country index	0.518***	0.820	−0.027	4.42	0.304	0.235	−0.56
CD							
GI	0.537***	0.244	−0.122	−0.82	0.070	0.142**	0.01
CRB	0.586***	0.240	−0.130	2.88	0.312	0.188	2.34
Country index	0.508***	0.450	−0.099	−0.39	0.073	0.178	−0.14
RA							
GI	0.390***	0.426	0.338	0.54	0.868	−0.086	6.04
CRB	0.451***	0.544	0.155	2.26	0.854	−0.117	5.85
Country index	0.338***	0.537	0.198	−2.85	0.938	−0.008	4.36
NZ							
GI	0.459***	0.958	−0.060	2.22	0.100	0.144	−1.15
CRB	0.548***	0.948	−0.129	4.26	0.557	0.212	1.52
Country index	0.429***	0.141	0.052	−0.59	0.541	0.132	0.46

Notes: The table reports contemporaneous correlations (rho), zero-sum coefficient restriction test p-values, summed cross-asset coefficients, and RMSE percentage differences for currency-to-commodity and commodity-to-currency relationships for the crisis only period. This sample spans July 1, 2007 to January 28, 2009. Abbreviations AD, CD, RA, and NZ refer to the Australian dollar, Canadian dollar, South African rand, and New Zealand dollar return series, respectively.

***Significant at the 1 percent level.

**Significant at the 5 percent level.

Table 2A.2   **Contemporaneous correlations and currency-to-commodity sample robustness**

	AD	CD	NZ	RA
A. Sample ranges and contemporaneous correlations between currency and country Index				
Sample A				
Beginning	7/12/2001	7/12/2001	5/14/1999	7/12/2001
Ending	1/28/2009	1/28/2009	1/28/2009	1/28/2009
Corr. coeff.	0.393	0.332	0.265	0.161
Sample B				
Beginning	7/12/2001	7/12/2001	5/14/1999	7/12/2001
Ending	6/29/2007	6/29/2007	6/29/2007	6/29/2007
Corr. coeff.	0.239	0.193	0.230	0.063
B. P-values of cross-market zero-Coefficient tests				
Country indices (sample A)	0.746	0.433	0.976	0.287
Country indices (sample B)	0.331	0.408	0.641	0.405
C. Sum of cross-markets coefficients				
Country indices (sample A)	0.015	0.025	0.046	0.019
Country indices (sample B)	0.031	0.132	−0.008	0.027
D. RMSE percentage differences				
Country indices (sample A)	−1.31%	−0.32%	0.25%	−1.71%
Country indices (sample B)	−5.60%	−2.36%	0.20%	−1.48%

Notes: The tables report robustness results for currency-to-commodity relationships across two samples not included in the previous discussions. Panel A reports sample date ranges. Panel B reports cross-market zero-coefficient Granger Causality test *p*-values, while Panel C reports the summed coefficients of cross-market variables as well as indicators of statistical significance. Panel D reports RMSE percentage differences of currency-augmented commodity forecasting models relative to own-autoregressive commodity benchmarks. In each panel, AD, CD, RA, and NZ refer to the Australian dollar, Canadian dollar, South African rand, and New Zealand dollar return series, respectively. The beginning date of each sample corresponds to when a given country-commodity return index's individual commodity components were all trading. The end of Sample B corresponds to the (approximate) beginning of the world financial crisis.

Table 2A.3   **Commodity-to-currency sample robustness**

	AD	CD	NZ	RA
A. Sample Date Ranges				
Sample A				
Beginning	7/12/2001	7/12/2001	5/14/1999	7/12/2001
Ending	1/28/2009	1/28/2009	1/28/2009	1/28/2009
Sample B				
Beginning	7/12/2001	7/12/2001	5/14/1999	7/12/2001
Ending	6/29/2007	6/29/2007	6/29/2007	6/29/2007
B. P-values of Cross-market Zero-Coefficient Tests				
Country index (sample A)	0.038	0.019	0.891	0.956
Country index (sample B)	0.118	0.603	0.841	0.932
C. Sum of cross-markets coefficients				
Country index (sample A)	0.148**	0.083	−0.051	0.029
Country index (sample B)	0.083	0.020	−0.092	−0.011
D. RMSE percentage differences				
Country index (sample A)	−0.33%	0.17%	0.68%	0.44%
Country index (sample B)	1.66%	0.86%	0.80%	0.40%

Notes: The tables report robustness results for commodity-to-currency relationships across two samples not included in the previous discussions. Panel A reports sample date ranges. Panel B reports cross-market zero-coefficient Granger Causality test *p*-values, while Panel C reports the summed coefficients of cross-market variables as well as indicators of statistical significance. Panel D reports RMSE percentage differences of commodity-augmented currency forecasting models relative to own-autoregressive currency benchmarks. In each panel, AD, CD, RA, and NZ refer to the Australian dollar, Canadian dollar, South African rand, and New Zealand dollar return series, respectively. The beginning date of each sample corresponds to when a given country-commodity return index's individual commodity components were all trading. The end of Sample B corresponds to the (approximate) beginning of the world financial crisis.

***Significant at the 1 percent level.
**Significant at the 5 percent level.

References

Bessembinder, H., and K. Chan. 1992. Time-varying risk premia and forecastable returns in futures markets. *Journal of Financial Economics* 32 (2): 169–94.

Bessler, D. A., and T. Covey. 1991. Cointegration: Some results on U.S. cattle prices. *Journal of Futures Markets* 11 (4): 461–74.

Blanch, F. 2008. Insight: Commodities rally driven by fundamentals, not speculators. *Financial Times,* June 24. Available at: http://www.ft.com.

Campbell, J. Y., and R. J. Shiller. 1987. Cointegration and tests of present value models. *Journal of Political Economy* 95 (5): 1062–88.

Cashin, P., L. Cespedes, and R. Sahay. 2003. Commodity currencies: Developing countries reliant on commodity exports see the fate of their exchange rates tied to fickle commodity markets. *Finance and Development* 40 (1): 45–8.

Chan, K. 1992. A further analysis of the lead-lag relationship between the cash market and stock index futures market. *Review of Financial Studies* 5:123–52.

Chen, Y. 2004. Exchange rates and fundamentals: Evidence from commodity economies. Unpublished Working Paper. University of Washington, Department of Economics. Unpublished Working Paper.

Chen, Y., and K. Rogoff. 2003. Commodity currencies. *Journal of International Economics* 60:133–60.

Chen, Y., K. Rogoff, and B. Rossi. 2008. Can exchange rates forecast commodity prices? NBER Working Paper no. 13901. Cambridge, MA: National Bureau of Economic Research, March.

Chinn, M. D., and R. A. Meese. 1995. Banking on currency forecasts: How predictable is change in money? *Journal of International Economics* 38:161–78.

Engel, C., and K. D. West. 2005. Exchange rates and fundamentals. *Journal of Political Economy* 113:485–517.

Frankel, J. 2005. How interest rates cast a shadow over oil. *Financial Times,* April 14. Available at: http://www.ft.com.

———. 2006. The effect of monetary policy on real commodity prices. In *Asset prices and monetary policy,* ed. John Campbell, 291–334. Chicago: University of Chicago Press.

Gardeazabal, J., M. Regulez, and J. Vazquez. 1997. Testing the canonical model of exchange rates with unobservable fundamentals. *International Economic Review* 38:389–404.

Groen, J. J. J. 2005. Exchange rate predictability and monetary fundamentals in a small multi-country panel. *Journal of Money, Credit, and Banking* 37:495–516.

Kho, B.-C. 1996. Time-varying risk premia, volatility, and technical trading rule profits: Evidence from foreign currency futures markets. *Journal of Financial Economics* 41:249–90.

Klaassen, F. 2005. Long swings in exchange rates: Are they really in the data? *Journal of Business and Economic Statistics* 23:87–95.

Levich, R. M., and L. R. Thomas III. 1993. The significance of technical trading rules in the FX market: A bootstrap approach. *Journal of International Money and Finance* 12:451–74.

Lien, K. 2008. *Day trading and swing trading the currency market: Technical and fundamental strategies to profit from market moves* (2nd ed.). Hoboken, NJ: Wiley Trading.

MacDonald, R., and I. W. Marsh. 1997. On fundamentals and exchange rates: A Casselian perspective. *Review of Economics and Statistics* 79:655–64.

MacDonald, R., and M. P. Taylor. 1994. The monetary model of exchange rate: Long-run relationships, short-run dynamics and how to beat a random walk. *Journal of International Money and Finance* 13:276–90.

Mark, N. C. 1995. Exchange rates and fundamentals: Evidence on long-horizon predictability. *American Economic Review* 85:201–18.

Mark, N. C., and D. Sul. 2001. Nominal exchange rates and monetary-fundamentals: Evidence from a small post-Bretton Woods sample. *Journal of International Economics* 53:29–52.

Meese, R. A., and K. Rogoff. 1983. Empirical exchange rate models of the seventies: Do they fit out-of-sample? *Journal of International Economics* 14:3–24.

Pukthuanthong-Le, K., R. M. Levich, and L. R. Thomas III. 2007. Do foreign exchange markets still trend? *Journal of Portfolio Management* 34:114–18.

Rosenberg, J. V., and L. G. Traub. 2008. *Price discovery in the foreign currency futures and spot market.* Federal Reserve Bank of New York Staff Reports no. 262. New York.

Schwarz, T. V., and A. C. Szakmary. 1994. Price discovery in petroleum markets: Arbitrage, cointegration, and time interval of analysis. *Journal of Futures Markets* 14:147–67.

Sephton, P. S. 1992. Modeling the link between commodity prices and exchange rates: The tale of daily data. *Canadian Journal of Economics* 25:156–71.
Tse, Y., and G. G. Booth. 1996. Risk premia in foreign currency futures: A reexamination. *Financial Review* 31:521–34.

Comment   Tokuo Iwaisako

Present value formulation of exchange rates is impeccable as a theory. However, its practical importance has always been questioned, because it seems to be nearly impossible to address the issue of simultaneity between the exchange rate and fundamentals in a persuasive manner. The recent paper by Chen, Rogoff, and Rossi (2008, hereafter CRR) tackles this issue using world commodity prices as an exogenous variable with which to cut through macroeconomics where endogeneity is normally considered to be a problem. Chen, Rogoff, and Rossi present surprisingly strong evidence that foreign exchange values of commodity exporting countries ("commodity currencies") help to predict the prices of the commodities they export in spot/forward markets.

Two chapters in this volume, the chapter by Chan, Tse, and Williams, and the chapter by Groen and Pesanti, ask if the finding in CRR (2008) is really robust. In particular, Chan, Tse, and Williams argue that the predictability that CRR (2008) reports disappears if data on commodity futures are used. However, they also find that contemporaneous correlations between commodity prices and commodity currencies are generally very strong.

At first glance, the contrast between the empirical results in CRR (2008) and Chan, Tse, and Williams seems stark. However, once we realize the different natures of spot, forward, and futures markets of commodities, the difference between the two empirical results is not so surprising. While spot and forward commodity markets are dominated by transactions directly related to the transaction of real goods, commodity futures markets are essentially financial markets, dominated by investors/speculators. Hence, the arbitrage mechanism is expected to work more effectively in futures markets than in the other two types of commodity markets.

While I believe that the main findings by Chan, Tse, and Williams are persuasive and robust, we have to be careful in accepting their empirical results. First, there are some important differences between this chapter's data and those of other studies. While this chapter uses daily data, CRR and Groen and Pesanti use lower-frequency data. Also, the authors use a sample period

Tokuo Iwaisako is the principal economist of the Policy Research Institute, Ministry of Finance, Government of Japan, and a visiting researcher at the Institute of Economic Research, Hitotsubashi University.

that is much shorter than the others, and utilizes only the subset of commodity exporting countries, because of the availability of futures market data. Second, the authors employ a simple linear forecasting framework with very limited forecasting variables and the notion of Granger causality. Naturally, the question arises about the validity of their empirical results if, for example, some nonlinear forecasting techniques are used or additional forecasting variables are introduced. I am not really expecting that these issues would significantly change their main findings. However, it is desirable if the authors could provide further robustness checks of their main findings.

I am convinced that their finding in this chapter and the previous results in CRR are not inconsistent. Together with the Groen and Pesanti chapter in this volume, these chapters provide us with a better and more accurate understanding of the relationship between commodity prices and commodity currencies. Yet it is still interesting to know how different the results might be for the spot, forward, and futures markets. Though the authors repeatedly emphasize uninformed trading as a source of predictability in spot and forward commodity returns found in CRR, they do not provide any concrete evidence about this point. I understand that it is beyond the scope of their current chapter, but the roles of uninformed trading and/or other institutional obstacles in generating observed predictability in spot/forward commodity markets is important information for a comprehensive understanding of the empirical results in the literature.

Finally, Chan, Tse, and Williams emphasize that their empirical results are consistent with the efficient market hypothesis. However, the absence of an arbitrage opportunity does not warrant overall efficiency of financial markets, as Professor Summers noted with his ketchup economics analogy many years ago (Summers 1985). This chapter does not really address the issue of whether large swings in commodity prices in the last ten years can be explained by market fundamentals alone, or if they actually contain speculative bubbles that have motivated the large number of recent empirical researches in macroeconomics and finance, including chapters in this volume. Also, the research in CRR (2008) on commodity currencies is motivated by the present value formulation of exchange rates. It would have been helpful if the authors had provided some discussion about the implications of their findings for broader issues.

References

Chen, Y.-C., K. Rogoff, and B. Rossi. 2008. Can exchange rates forecast commodity prices? NBER Working Paper no. 13901. Cambridge, MA: National Bureau of Economic Research, March.
Summers, L. H. 1985. On economics and finance. *Journal of Finance* 40 (3): 633–35.

Comment   Doo Yong Yang

The relationship between economic fundamentals and exchange rates has been one of the long and unsolved issues in international finance. Asset price approach provides a variety of structural models of the exchange rates and concludes that exchange rates is a function of the discounted sum of its expected future fundamentals as follows:

$$S_t = \alpha \sum_{j=0}^{\infty} \beta^j E_t \left(f_{t+j} | I_t \right),$$

where S_t is exchange rates, and f_t is economic fundamentals. Greek letters α and β are parameters in the structural model specification. According to the model, exchange rates should Granger-cause its fundamental, or exchange rates have abilities to forecast the future fundamentals. This present value representation is well-accepted from a theoretical view, but the empirical findings are not supportive. Meese and Rogoff (1983) show that the structural models of the exchange rates do not outperform random walk benchmarks, implying that there is no relationship between exchange rate and fundamentals.

However, there are several problems in empirical investigation of the relationship between the fundamentals and exchange rates. First, it is not easy to find exogenous fundamentals to exchange rate movements. If fundamentals are endogenous to exchange rates, the positive relationship between fundamentals and exchange rates is related with the other variables' responses. In this case, it is difficult to conclude that the present value representation is valid, even if exchange rates Granger-cause the fundamentals or exchange rates have higher power to predict future fundamental movements. In other words, we face the endogenous problem or reverse causality problem. This is why several studies focus on commodity currencies to investigate the relationship between the currency and commodity prices, since commodity prices are a unique exchange rate fundamental that seems to be exogenous to exchange rate movements.

Second, there is a nonlinearity problem in estimated parameters. If the relationship between the currency and commodity prices is time-varying, then the standard Granger causality test might provide the wrong interpretation. Rossi (2006) shows that exchange rates might not be a random walk after controlling the instability of the parameters. Chen, Rogoff, and Rossi (2008) also find that the commodity currencies Granger-cause commodity prices, and conclude that exchange rates have remarkable robust power in predicting commodity prices.

In line with the previous literature, Chan, Tse, and Williams's chapter

Doo Yong Yang is a research fellow at the Asian Development Bank Institute.

examines relationships between commodity currency returns and commodity index returns in four commodity-exporting countries using both causality tests and an out-of-sample forecasting analysis. They conclude that commodity currency returns are contemporaneously correlated with commodity prices, and currency returns are not capable of predicting commodity returns in both directions. The conclusion is different from the previous literature (Chen, Rogoff, and Rossi [2008]; Chen and Rogoff [2003]), which suggests that exchange rates have a power to predict future commodity prices. The difference between this chapter and previous literature is using high-frequency data and future prices for empirical analysis. The authors conclude that the different empirical finding comes from the information transmission between the commodity and currency markets as a consequence of informed traders using futures markets to profit from expectation/trade information. This implies that relationships between commodity price and exchange rates are related with information efficiency rather than the structural model.

This is interesting, and provides important implications on exchange rate behaviors as well as other financial assets. The authors interpret their controversial empirical findings by depending on the heterogeneity of traders in both currency and commodity markets. They suggest that the incorporation of economic expectations into trade terms takes place over intervals shorter than what business-motivated economic agents need to alter their commodity positions after an exchange rate shock. The short-interval traders are generally speculators who have greater information processing abilities relative to the average economic agent and, therefore, are able to capture asymmetric information profits. As a consequence, speculative activity brings about rapid currency-to-commodity comovement in a short period of time. However, the average uninformed traders do not likely recognize and incorporate economic expectations into their business decisions over very short time intervals, and adjust their commodity positions according to their business-specific economic outlooks.

The question is why there exists a contemporaneous relationship between currency futures and commodity futures in short time intervals, and not in long horizon intervals. Does this come from different characteristics of traders such as informed versus uninformed traders, as the authors suggest? I have a little doubt on this argument. Why are the average traders uninformed or unable to adjust their position over very short time intervals? It is not clear to me why only informed speculators come to currency futures and commodity futures to take advantage of their information.

This may be caused by the nature of future trading itself. For example, some traders who purchase commodity futures also want to hedge their positions to exchange rate risks. Therefore, they purchase currency futures in short time intervals. However, long-term commodity holders do not hedge their exchange rate risks since exchange rates have a robust power to predict future commodity prices.

The chapter also suggests that futures markets have more information efficiency than spot markets. This is the justification to explain why the authors use futures market data to test relationships between commodity prices and exchange rates. I am wondering why the authors do not test some robustness for this issue. In other words, the same empirical analysis can be done using high-frequency spot market data. With this analysis, it becomes more clear that the contemporaneous relationship between commodity prices and exchange rates exists in futures markets, which is more efficient in information processing.

In addition, the information set in commodity traders in the chapter is just commodity prices and currencies. One could argue that the comovement of currencies and commodity prices in the high-frequency world results from the dollar effect. Global commodity demands and prices would go up when the dollar is weak. Therefore, it is worthy to include the U.S. dollar value (effective exchange rates of the U.S. dollar) in the regression to confirm the authors' conclusion.

Related to traders' information, monetary variables also affect global commodity demands. It is possible that higher interest rates reduce commodity prices since the interest rates are related to current and future demand and supply for commodities, and lower interest rates reduce inventory costs (Frankel 2006). This is also related to the global liquidity condition. Higher liquidity possibly contributes to an increase in global commodity demand. Thus, it is also interesting to include monetary variables in the regression.

References

Chen, Y., and K. Rogoff. 2003. Commodity currencies. *Journal of International Economics* 60:130–69.

Chen, Y., K. Rogoff, and B. Rossi. 2008. Can exchange rates forecast commodity prices? NBER Working Paper no. 13901. Cambridge, MA: National Bureau of Economic Research, March.

Frankel, J. A. 2006. The effect of monetary policy on real commodity prices NBER Working Paper no. 12713. Cambridge, MA: National Bureau of Economic Research, December.

Meese, R., and K. S. Rogoff. 1983. Exchange rate models of the seventies: Do they fit out of sample? *Journal of International Economics* 14:3–24.

Rossi, B. 2006. Are exchange rates really random walks? Some evidence robust to parameter instability *Macroeconomic Dynamics* 10:20–38.

II

**Commodity Prices, the Terms
of Trade, and Exchange Rates**

Identifying the Relationship between Trade and Exchange Rate Volatility

Christian Broda and John Romalis

3.1 Introduction

A traditional criticism of flexible exchange rate regimes is that flexible rates increase the level of exchange rate uncertainty, and thus reduce incentives to trade.[1] This criticism has generated a large literature that focuses on the impact of exchange rate volatility on trade. However, Mundell's (1961) optimal currency area hypothesis suggests an opposite direction of causality, where trade flows stabilize real exchange rate fluctuations, thus reducing real exchange rate volatility.[2] These two seminal ideas of international trade imply the existence of a standard identification problem: is the correlation between trade and exchange rate volatility indicative of the effect of volatility on trade, or vice versa?

Few theoretical and empirical papers have attempted to answer this question. Most of the existing studies have focused on the effects of exchange rate regimes or volatility on trade by effectively assuming that the exchange rate process is driven by exogenous shocks, and is unaffected by other endogenous variables.[3] Well-known examples of this approach for currency unions commence with Rose (2000) and include Frankel and Rose (2002). By definition,

Christian Broda is professor of economics at the University of Chicago Booth School of Business, and a faculty research fellow of the National Bureau of Economic Research. John Romalis is associate professor of economics at the University of Chicago Booth School of Business, and a faculty research fellow of the National Bureau of Economic Research.

1. Taussig (1924) was an early advocate of this idea.
2. Central banks in many developing countries have targeted real effective exchange rates in the past. This implies that even if trade does not act as an automatic stabilizer, policy interventions will reduce bilateral volatility with major trading partners.
3. Even in the full general equilibrium models of Baccheta and van Wincoop (2000) and Obstfeld and Rogoff (2001), exchange rate volatility is purely determined by exogenous shocks.

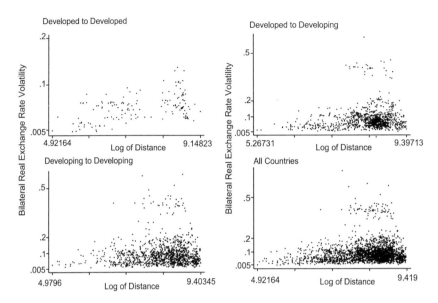

Fig. 3.1   Exchange rate volatility and distance between countries in 1997

this implies that the effect of trade on volatility is assumed inexistent rather than jointly estimated with the effect of volatility on trade.[4] Figure 3.1 illustrates that this is not a benign assumption. This figure shows a strong positive relationship between real exchange rate volatility and distance between trading partners. Since distance cannot be affected by volatility, this strong relationship suggests that greater distance between countries significantly increases bilateral exchange rate volatility through the effect of distance on the intensity of commercial relationships such as trade.[5] Ignoring the causal effect of trade on volatility results in overestimates of the true impact of exchange rate volatility on trade.

We use a model of bilateral trade to structurally estimate the effect on trade of exchange rate volatility and exchange rate regimes such as fixed exchange rates and currency boards. The model highlights the role of trade in determining bilateral real exchange rate volatilities (the source of reverse causality), and the differences in the impact of real exchange rate volatility on trade in different types of goods. These features of the model constitute the main building blocks of our identification strategy. First, real

4. The only exceptions are the empirical papers by Frankel and Wei (1993), Persson (2001), Tenreyro and Barro (2007), and Tenreyro (2007). We discuss the identification strategies of these papers in the main text.
5. This result is related to Engel and Rogers (1996) and Alesina, Barro, and Tenreyro (2003), who examine the importance of distance in the comovement of price shocks across cities and countries, respectively. It also relates to recent work by Hau (2002), discussed on pages 7 and 8, who finds that differences in openness can explain the cross-country variation in the volatility of effective real exchange rates.

exchange rate volatility affects trade in differentiated products, but does not affect where a commodity gets sold. Second, trade in all products affects real exchange rate volatility. These two results will enable us to identify how exchange rate volatility affects trade in differentiated products. The reason for this is that commodity trade can be used to pinpoint how trade affects exchange rate volatility. This enables identification of how volatility affects trade in differentiated products. Since the model predicts that commodity trade is only affected by relative price levels and not by volatility, we identify the effect of volatility on total trade.

The intuition behind the main predictions of the model is fairly simple. First, in our model all trade acts as an automatic stabilizer of real exchange rates. To be consistent with our data, we take the real exchange rate between two countries to be the ratio of consumer price levels expressed in a common currency. In equilibrium, proximate countries have more similar consumption baskets than more distant countries. This implies that more proximate countries have lower real exchange rate volatility than more distant countries, consistent with the data presented in figure 3.1. This is because a shock that changes the price of a country's goods will affect the price of the consumption basket of a neighboring country more than that of a more distant country. In the limit, if baskets are identical, real exchange rates are constant.

Second, in our model exchange rate volatility only affects trade in differentiated products. In a model with more general preferences, the production mix between manufactures and commodities could be affected by exchange rate volatility, but conditional on production, where commodities get sold would remain unaffected. Commodity products are sold in organized exchanges. Subject to transport costs, buyers and sellers do not care who they buy from or sell to; what they end up paying or receiving is identical regardless of the counterparty. With differentiated products the same is not true. Rauch (1999) argues that the heterogeneity of most manufactured products in both characteristics and quality prevents traders from using organized exchanges for these products. Instead, connections between sellers and buyers are made through a costly search process. This cost can be associated with establishing networks, advertising, and marketing in general. Real exchange rate volatility that occurs after these costs are sunk will affect the profitability of these connections. Therefore, in contrast to commodity products, trade in differentiated products is affected by exchange rate volatility.[6]

We use disaggregated data to exploit our identification structure and test the predictions of the model. Rauch (1999) provides a categorization of Standard International Trade Classification (SITC) Revision 2 industries

---

6. The sign of the effect of volatility on trade in differentiated products depends on the degree of risk aversion of the firms that are exporting them. When firms are sufficiently risk averse (loving), relatively more differentiated products will be exported to countries that have low (high) exchange rate volatilities with the exporting country.

according to three possible product types: differentiated, reference priced, and commodity. The Rauch classification is widely used in empirical international trade literature. Bilateral trade data for each SITC industry is available for a large number of developed and developing countries during the period 1970 to 1997. This data is now a little dated, and it would be ideal if we extended it to recent years to identify the early effects of European Monetary Integration (EMU). We calculate several measures of bilateral real exchange rate volatility from monthly real exchange rate series for the same period. We source data on exchange rate regimes from Rose (2000) and Frankel and Rose (2002), the International Monetary Fund (IMF), Rogoff and Reinhart (2003), and Levy-Yeyati and Sturzenegger (2000) (hereafter LYS).

The empirical findings of this chapter provide support for the view that trade depresses real exchange rate volatility. A trading relationship that is 1 percent of the gross domestic product (GDP) greater than the median trade relationship implies that the volatility of the bilateral real exchange rate associated with the intense trading partner is 12 percent smaller than with the less intense partner. The empirical findings also support the view that real exchange rate volatility only moderately depresses exports. We find that doubling real exchange rate volatility decreases exports of differentiated products by 2 percent. The reduction from the ordinary least squares (OLS) estimates is because the model attributes most of the correlation between trade and volatility to the effect that trade has in depressing volatility.

The empirical methodology is suitable for testing the effect of exchange rate regimes on countries' trade performances. While several studies have found large positive effects of fixed regimes on trade (see, for example, Ghosh et al. [1997] and Frankel and Rose [2002]) they do not control for the reverse-causality problem. However, we observe many fixed regimes pegging their currency to that of countries that are their main trading partners, suggesting that reverse causality can be an important problem.[7] Indeed, we find that the effect of fixed regimes on trade is much smaller when the reverse causation is modeled. In particular, the effect of currency unions is substantially reduced from 300 percent to between 10 and 25 percent when we apply our methodology to Frankel and Rose's data, with very little loss of precision.

This chapter departs from the existing literature in several dimensions. First, this chapter represents the first attempt to structurally estimate the relationship between trade and exchange rate volatility. We provide a model that incorporates both directions of causality and suggests an identification structure. Previous attempts to correct for the problem of reverse causality relied on assumptions about appropriate instruments. Frankel and Wei (1993) use the standard deviation of relative money supplies as an instrument for the volatility of exchange rates. Barro and Tenreyro (2007) and

---

7. The European Monetary System and the Central Franc Zone are just two examples of this behavior.

Tenreyro (2007) model the formation of exchange rate regimes to derive an instrument for volatility. They develop an instrument for membership in a currency union (or pegged regime) based on the probability that the countries independently adopt (or peg to) the same common currency. The probability that a single country adopts the currency of another country is a linear combination of the same gravity variables that affect trade directly. They get identification by assuming that "bilateral trade between countries *i* and *j* depends on gravity variables for countries *i* and *j*, but not on gravity variables involving third countries, notably the potential anchors" (Barro and Tenreyo 2007, 5). Their instrumental variable (IV) estimates of the effect of currency unions on trade are substantially larger than OLS estimates, opposite to our results. By contrast, in the case of fixed exchange rates, Tenreyro (2007) finds no effects of fixed exchange rates on trade, whereas we find modest but statistically significant effects. But their identification assumption is unusual. In most models of trade, the trade between countries *i* and *j* will greatly depend on the trading opportunities with third countries. That is an important feature of our relatively standard trade model. Persson (2001) also models selection into currency unions to construct control groups for countries "treated" with a currency union. He finds that a common currency boosts trade by between 13 and 65 percent, which is much closer to our estimates of 10 to 25 percent. His method also identifies exogenous differences in currency union status. Recent papers that examine the trade effects of the euro are also relevant. The introduction of the euro provides an exogenous shift (a "before" and an "after") that can be used to identify the effect of currency unions on trade. Early results using gravity regressions suggest very modest trade increases (see, for example, Micco, Stein, and Ordoñez [2003]). But the experiment may not be as clean as it appears. The introduction of the euro was long anticipated. These papers will need to work hard to separate the trade effects of the common currency from the trade effects of other market integration measures adopted by the European Union in recent years.

Second, we know of no paper that models and estimates the effect of exchange rate volatility on the composition of trade. In previous empirical studies, Bini-Smaghi (1991) and Klein (1990) have attempted to use disaggregate data to test whether uncertainty has different effects for different products. They find that different products are affected differently by volatility, but the characteristics of those products that have larger effects are not identified.

Third, we model how trade costs affect real exchange rate volatility. Hau (2002) shows theoretically and empirically that openness can affect real exchange rate volatility through the share of tradable goods in consumption. In his model, however, this share is exogenously given while in our model differences in consumption baskets are endogenously determined by trading and searching costs. In our model the bilateral pattern of real exchange rate volatility can differ across countries, even though the underlying shocks to each country are identical. This different approach has very real identification implications. Hau (2002) recognizes that openness is an endogenous variable and may be affected by exchange rate volatility. He follows Romer (1993) and uses land area as a suitable instrument for openness in his regressions. In our model we can see why land area is related to openness—it affects individual product prices through trade costs and aggregate price indexes through market size. Trade costs and aggregate price indexes belong in our equation system, suggesting that land area may not be suitable as an instrument.

Last, the focus of most of the theoretical literature is on the role that the invoicing currency plays because prices are set before the exchange rate is observed. Therefore, the invoicing currency determines who bears the exchange rate risk. Note that in this setup uncertainty arises between the time in which prices are set and the time final payment is made, which is usually a short period.[8] We depart from this tradition and focus on the market entry decision of exporting firms. There are no price rigidities in this model.

The chapter proceeds as follows. Section 3.2 contains our trade model. Section 3.3 discusses the implications of that model for exchange rate volatility. Section 3.4 develops our empirical model and identification strategy. Section 3.5 describes our data. Section 3.6 presents the main results of the chapter and the comparisons with the exchange rate regime literature. Section 3.7 presents robustness checks. Section 3.8 concludes.

3.2 A Four-Country, Two-Sector Trade Model

3.2.1 Model Description

The model has four countries and two sectors, manufacturing and commodities. The manufacturing sector is an adaptation of the Krugman (1980) model of intraindustry trade driven by scale economies and product differentiation. The adaptation is that to serve an export market, manufacturers must incur an additional fixed cost in each period before observing that period's exchange rates. After making the entry decision and observing the exchange rate, the manufacturer can set prices optimally for that period. Manufacturers' assumptions about the distribution of exchange rates will affect the entry decision. Exchange rates are affected by productivity shocks that are external to this model. Commodity producers do not face a fixed cost of entry; they are always ready to sell in a market. The realized price levels affect where commodities are sent; exchange rate volatility has no independent effect on commodity trade. Finally, we add "iceberg" trans-

---

8. Informal evidence suggests that this can take between one and six months.

port costs. The transport costs affect the distribution of exchange rates and affect manufacturers' decisions to export. Detailed assumptions are set out as follows:

1. There are four countries $i = 1, \ldots, 4$ on two continents; countries one and two on one continent and three and four on the other.

2. Each country has its own currency that can be freely exchanged for that of another. The price of country i's currency in terms of the currency of country one, which we call the dollar, is s_i.

3. There is one factor of production, labor, supplied inelastically. Labor earns a factor reward of $w_i = 1$ unit of local currency. The total labor supply in each country is one.

4. Trade is always balanced. It is essential to have some long-run trade balance condition, though it need not take this simple and extreme form. Since the model is used to motivate an empirical specification, we do not see this as an important limitation. We will not be estimating deep parameters of our model.

5. Exchange rate movements are driven by shocks to labor productivity $\theta_i^{-1} \in (0,1)$. Any exogenous cause of real exchange rate movements would suffice for our purposes.

6. All consumers in all countries are assumed to maximize identical constant-relative-risk-aversion preferences in each period over a composite manufactured good M and a composite commodity C, with the fraction of income spent on M being b (equation [1]).

(1) $$U = \frac{1}{a}(M^b C^{1-b})^a.$$

7. Commodity sector. The commodity C is a composite good. Perfectly competitive firms in country i produce an identical commodity under constant returns to scale, requiring θ_i units of labor to produce one unit of the commodity. Each country produces a different commodity. For instance, country one might produce wheat while country two produces copper. What is essential for our model is that some commodities are internationally traded between some countries. Commodity C can be interpreted as a subutility function that depends on the quantity of each commodity consumed. We choose the constant elasticity of substitution (CES) function with elasticity of substitution between two different commodities being σ_c. Let q_i^D denote the quantity consumed of the commodity produced in country i. Commodity C is defined by equation (2):

(2) $$C = \left(\sum_{i=1}^{4} (q_i^D)^{(\sigma_c-1)/\sigma_c} \right)^{\sigma_c/(\sigma_c-1)}.$$

8. Monopolistic competition in manufacturing. In manufacturing, there are economies of scale in production, and firms can costlessly differentiate

their products. The output of manufacturing consists of a number of varieties that are imperfect substitutes for one another. The quantity produced of variety v is denoted by q_v^S, the quantity consumed by q_v^D. Variable V is the endogenously determined set of varieties produced, and M can be interpreted as a subutility function that depends on the quantity of each variety of M consumed. We choose the symmetric CES function with elasticity of substitution $\sigma_m > 1$:

$$(3) \qquad M = \left(\int_{v \in V} (q_v^D)^{(\sigma_m - 1)/\sigma_m} dv \right)^{\sigma_m/(\sigma_m - 1)}, \qquad \sigma_m > 1.$$

All manufacturers must serve their domestic market. Manufactures are produced using labor with a marginal cost $w_i \theta_i$, and a per-period fixed cost. The fixed cost must be paid before manufacturers observe the exchange rates for the period. Average costs of production decline at all levels of output, although at a decreasing rate. Production technology for a firm in country e selling q_v units in the domestic market is represented by a total cost function TC that is assumed to be identical for all firms selling in their domestic market:

$$(4) \qquad \mathrm{TC}_e (q_v^S) = w_e (\alpha_1 + q_v^S \theta_e).$$

Manufacturers enter foreign markets through exports only.[9] To export to a foreign market, the manufacturer must incur a per-period fixed cost for market development, which must be paid before observing exchange rates for that period.[10] The manufacturer's cost for market development and producing x_v units for export from country e (exporter) to country i (importer) is represented by the Free On Board (FOB) export cost function XC.

$$(5) \qquad \mathrm{XC}_{ei} (x_v^S) = w_e (\alpha_2 + x_v^S \theta_e).$$

9. Costly international trade. There may be a transport cost for international trade. To avoid the need to model a separate transport sector, transport costs are introduced in the convenient but special iceberg form. The τ_{1m} units of a manufactured good must be shipped for one unit to arrive in the country on the same continent, and τ_{2m} units must be shipped for one unit to arrive in a country on a different continent ($\tau_{2m} \geq \tau_{1m} \geq 1$). The equivalent transport costs for commodities are τ_{1c} and τ_{2c}.

3.2.2   Equilibrium in Commodity Sectors

In general, equilibrium consumers maximize utility, firms maximize profits, all factors are fully employed, and trade is balanced. Productivity determines exchange rates s_e. The equilibrium for commodity sectors

9. If they produce in a foreign country, their cost structure is identical to a domestic firm's.
10. The critical assumption is not the fixed cost α_1 for commencing domestic production, but how large the fixed cost α_2 for entering each export market is relative to α_1.

is straightforward. Firms always price at marginal cost. For their domestic market, marginal cost in local currency is simply equal to the wage rate, one. For export markets, marginal cost is higher due to the transport cost. The price, in dollars, of a commodity produced in country e (exporter) and sold in country i (importer) is given by equation (6).

$$
(6) \qquad p_{ei} = \begin{cases} s_e\theta_e & e=i & \text{domestic sales} \\ s_e\theta_e\tau_{1c} & e\neq i & e,i,\text{on same continent} \\ s_e\theta_e\tau_{2c} & e\neq i & e,i,\text{on different continents.} \end{cases}
$$

Consumers spend a fixed proportion of their income on commodities. They demand some of each commodity. Income in country i in dollars is simply s_i. Maximizing equation (1) yields the following demand functions in country i for commodities produced in e:

$$
(7) \qquad q_{ei}^D = \frac{(s_e\theta_e\tau_{eic})^{-\sigma_c}}{\sum_{e'}(s_{e'}\theta_{e'}\tau_{e'ic})^{1-\sigma_c}}(1-b)s_i,
$$

where $\tau_{eic} = 1$, τ_{ic}, or τ_{2c}, according to model assumption 9. Note how trade costs involving third countries e' directly affect the trade between e and i. It is convenient to define the ideal price index for commodities in country i, P_{ic}:

$$
(8) \qquad P_{ic} = \left(\sum_e(s_e\theta_e\tau_{eic})^{1-\sigma_c}\right)^{1/(1-\sigma_c)}.
$$

Equations (6) through (8) can be solved for log of the value of commodity exports from country e to country i:

$$
(9) \qquad \ln p_{ei}q_{ei}^D = (1-\sigma_c)\ln s_e\theta_e + (1-\sigma_c)\ln\tau_{eic} + \ln(1-b)s_i \\ - (1-\sigma_c)\ln P_{ic}.
$$

We can eliminate country i specific effects, such as its commodity price index P_{ic} and income spent on commodities $(1-b)s_i$, by differencing. In particular, the log value of country i's imports of commodities from country e, $\ln C_{ei}$ less the log value of country i's imports of commodities from country e' is:

$$
(10) \qquad \ln C_{ei} - \ln C_{e'i} = (1-\sigma_c)(\ln s_e\theta_e - \ln s_{e'}\theta_{e'}) \\ + (1-\sigma_c)(\ln\tau_{eic} - \ln\tau_{e'ic}).
$$

3.2.3 Equilibrium in Manufacturing Sectors

The equilibrium in manufacturing sectors is more involved. The crucial difference is that some manufacturers may not end up exporting to some or all foreign markets, and that this proportion will depend on the perceived volatility of exchange rates. The properties of the model's demand structure for manufactures have been analyzed in Helpman and Krugman (1985).[11] Let $p_{ei,v}$

11. See sections 6.1, 6.2, and 10.4 in particular.

be the price paid by consumers in country i, inclusive of transport costs, for a variety v produced in country e, expressed in dollars. Maximization of equation (1) yields the following demand functions for variety v in country i:

$$(11) \qquad q^D_{ei,v} = \frac{p^{-\sigma_m}_{ei,v}}{\int_{v' \in V} p^{1-\sigma_m}_{ei,v} dv'} bs_i; \qquad \forall v \in V.$$

A firm's share of industry revenues depends on its own price and on the prices set by all other firms in that industry. It is convenient to define the ideal price index for manufactures in country i, P_{im}:

$$(12) \qquad P_{im} = \left(\int_{v \in V} p^{1-\sigma_m}_{ei,v} dv \right)^{1/(1-\sigma_m)}.$$

Each firm produces a different variety of the product. Each country produces different varieties. Consumers demand some of every variety made available to them. Profit maximizing firms perceive a demand curve that has a constant elasticity, and therefore, set price at a constant markup over marginal cost.[12] An individual firm in country e sets a single factory gate dollar price $\hat{p}_{e,v}$:

$$(13) \qquad \hat{p}_{e,v} = \frac{\sigma_m}{\sigma_{m-1}} s_e \theta_e.$$

For export markets, marginal cost is higher due to the transport cost. The consumer price $p_{ei,v}$, in dollars, of a manufactured good v produced in country e and sold in country i, is given by equation (14):

$$(14) \qquad p_{ei,v} = \hat{p}_{ei,v} \tau_{eim}.$$

Country $e's$ products sell in its own domestic market at the factory gate price $\hat{p}_{e,v}$, but in export markets the transport cost raises the price to $\hat{p}_{ei,v} \tau_{eim}$. The ideal manufacturing industry price index for country i, P_{im}, is given in equation (15). We assume a symmetric equilibrium if each country faces the same distribution of shocks to productivity, which affects exchange rates. Prior to the realization of the productivity shock, all countries are alike with n firms manufacturing in each country, and that nf_{ei} manufacturing firms from country e export to country i. Let $f_{ei} = f_1$ if e and i are on the same continent, and $f_{ei} = f_2$ if e and i are on different continents. Note that $f_{ei} = 1$ if $e = i$ (domestic sales). The free entry conditions for f_1 and f_2 are examined below.

$$(15) \qquad P_{im} = \left[\sum_e nf_{ei} \left(\frac{\sigma_m}{\sigma_m - 1} s_e \theta_e \tau_{eim} \right)^{1-\sigma_m} \right]^{1/(1-\sigma_m)}.$$

---

12. The demand curve faced by a firm has a constant elasticity if there are an infinite number of varieties.

Equation (16) gives real profits for sales in country i for a manufacturer based in country e: $1/\sigma_m$ is the profit margin; $\alpha_i s_e$ is the fixed market development cost in dollars, where $\alpha_i = \alpha_1$ if $e = i$ (domestic sales) and $\alpha_i = \alpha_2$ if $e \neq i$ (export sales); the remainder of the term in brackets are sales revenues in dollars; while $P_e = (P_{em})^b (P_{ec})^{1-b}$ is the ideal price index in country e.

$$(16) \qquad \frac{\pi_e}{P_e} = \left[\frac{1}{\sigma_m} \left(\frac{(\sigma_m/\sigma_m - 1)s_e \theta_e \tau_{eim}}{P_{im}} \right)^{1-\sigma_m} bs_i - \alpha_i s_e \right] \frac{1}{P_e}.$$

With free entry, manufacturers establish themselves in each country e and make decisions to export to each other country i until for each manufacturer:

$$(17) \qquad \underset{I_{ei}}{\mathrm{Max}} \left[E \left(\sum_i I_{ei} \left(\frac{\pi_e}{P_e} \right)^a \right) \right] = 0,$$

where I_{ei} is an indicator variable that takes a value of 1 if a manufacturer exports from e to i and is 0 otherwise, and a is the parameter governing risk aversion. Profitability in each market is a declining function of the number of domestic firms n and the number of foreign firms $n(f_1 + 2f_2)$ that export to that market, since the price index P_{im} declines with entry and because $\sigma_m > 1$. In general, the proportion of manufacturers that export to nearby markets, f_1, and the proportion, f_2, that export to distant markets will depend on transport costs, market entry costs, risk aversion, and the distribution of exchange rates. The proportion f_2 will in general differ from f_1, directly due to the higher transport cost (which reduces willingness to enter), and indirectly through the impact of transport costs on the distribution of exchange rates.

Proportions f_1 and f_2 are, therefore, different functions of expected exchange rate volatility. The first two equations of our empirical specification will come directly from equations (10) and (19), recognizing that f_1 and f_2 are a function of exchange rate volatility. Let V_e be the set of all manufacturing varieties produced in country e. Equations (11) through (15) solve for the log of the value of manufacturing imports into country i from country e:

$$(18) \qquad \ln \int_{v \in V_e} p_{eiv} q_{eiv}^D = \ln n f_{ei} + (1 - \sigma_m) \ln s_e \theta_e + (1 - \sigma_m) \ln \tau_{eim}$$
$$+ \ln bs_i - (1 - \sigma_m) \ln P_{im}.$$

We again employ differencing to eliminate country i specific effects. Equation (19) gives the log value of country i's manufacturing imports from country e, $\ln M_{ei}$, less the log value of country i's manufacturing imports from country e':

$$(19) \qquad \ln \frac{M_{ei}}{M_{e'i}} = \ln \frac{f_{ei}}{f_{e'i}} + (1 - \sigma_m) \ln \frac{s_e \theta_e}{s_{e'} \theta_{e'}} + (1 - \sigma_m) \ln \frac{\tau_{eim}}{\tau_{e'im}}.$$

Equation (19) for manufacturing trade depends on the difference in the proportions f_{ei} and $f_{e'i}$ of manufacturers who choose to pay the fixed cost to enter country i's market, which will depend on the distribution of exchange rates and attitudes to risk.

3.3   Endogenous Exchange Rate Volatility

In most of the existing theoretical literature, the exchange rate process is purely driven by exogenous shocks. The earlier literature relied on a partial equilibrium approach in which the exchange rate was assumed to be an exogenous random variable (see Ethier 1973; Viaene and de Vries 1992; Hooper and Kohlhagen 1978). More recently, Obstfeld and Rogoff (1998) and Bacchetta and van Wincoop (2000) have focused on general equilibrium models of exchange rate fluctuations. They highlight the importance of having fundamentals such as monetary, fiscal, and productivity shocks drive exchange rate fluctuations. However, in these models, real exchange rates are unaffected by other endogenous variables, and are purely driven by exogenous shocks.

In our model, trade acts as an automatic stabilizer of real exchange rates. The model implies that, *in equilibrium,* proximate countries have more similar consumption baskets than more distant countries. More similar consumption baskets, in turn, reduce real exchange rate volatility. The intuition for this result is simple. Since real exchange rates are commonly measured as the ratio of price levels P_i across countries (denominated in a common currency), a shock to the price of one country's output shifts the relative price level between itself and more proximate countries less than it shifts the relative price levels between itself and more distant countries. Hau (2002) obtains a similar cross-country prediction using a small open economy model by assuming that the share of tradable goods in preferences vary by country. Our model differs from his in two dimensions. First, Hau assumes different consumption baskets across countries, while in our setup they are endogenously determined by trading and searching costs. Second, in our multicountry framework, the bilateral pattern of real exchange rate volatility can differ across countries even though the distribution of underlying shocks to each country are identical. Third, we argue that his instrument for openness, land area, is effectively a proxy for variables that belong directly in the system of equations such as trade costs and aggregate price indexes, and is therefore not a valid instrument.

Figure 3.2 illustrates the impact that trade costs have on real exchange rate volatility in the model. In particular, it shows the relationship between intercontinental trading costs and the relative real exchange rate volatility between countries that share the same continent and between countries on different continents. We assume that the distribution of productivity shocks hitting each individual country are identical; $\sigma_m = \sigma_c = 5$; intracontinental

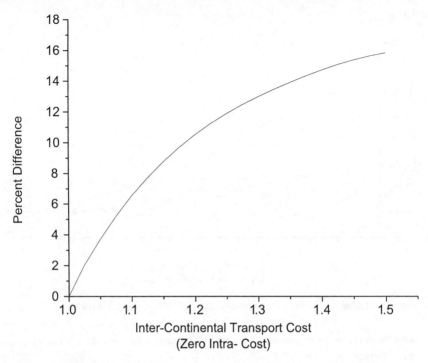

Fig. 3.2   Difference between intercontinental and intracontinental, real exchange rate volatility

trading costs $\tau_{1m} = \tau_{1c} = 1$; intercontinental trading costs are $\tau_{2m} = \tau_{2c} = \tau_2$; firms are risk neutral; and the fixed cost of entering foreign markets is sufficiently low that manufacturers export to all markets. The figure shows that with $\tau_2 > 1$, real exchange rate volatility with distant countries is larger than with proximate countries. It also shows that when the trading costs between continents increase, the intercontinental bilateral real exchange rate volatility rises relative to the intracontinental volatility. For the empirical section that follows, this means that we face a system of simultaneous equations. The OLS regressions of trade on exchange rate volatility will be biased toward finding depressing effects of real exchange rate volatility on trade, because trade itself depresses real exchange rate volatility.

But what does this other equation look like? Suppose that productivity in country e rises. At preexisting exchange rates, there is an incipient trade surplus in country e. Every country's demand shifts toward country e's output because the prices of country e's products falls. Country e's exchange rate appreciates. How much it appreciates is negatively related to how substitutable country e's output is for the output of other countries, which is determined by σ_c and σ_m. But what happens to real exchange rates? In the appendix, it is shown that the sensitivity of country i's real exchange rate

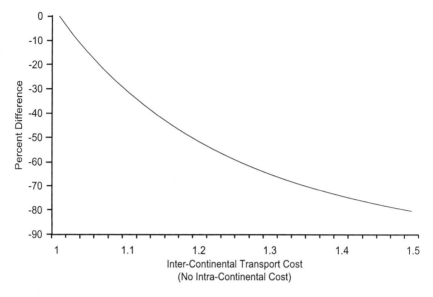

Fig. 3.3   Difference between intercontinental and intracontinental trade

with country e, in response to a small movement in country e's exchange rate, is given by:

$$(20) \qquad \frac{d\ln(P_i/P_e)}{d\ln s_e} = \frac{M_{ei} + C_{ei}}{GDP_i} - \frac{M_{ee} + C_{ee}}{GDP_e},$$

where $M_{ei}(C_{ei})$ is the dollar value of manufactures (commodities) produced in country e and consumed in country i. The terms on the right of equation (20) are simply the dollar value of country e's goods sold in countries i and e, respectively, divided by aggregate income in those countries. How much the real exchange rate moves depends on the difference in the importance of country e's goods in country i's and country e's consumption baskets. The more that country e exports to country i, the more similar their consumption baskets will look. This is consistent with figures 3.2 and 3.3; the less trade there is between countries, the greater the volatility of their real exchange rate. Trade in both manufactures and commodities is important. Without a closed-form solution, we assume that the way that exports from e to i affect bilateral real exchange rate volatility between e and i is given by:

$$(21) \qquad \ln V_{ei} = \gamma + \beta\left(\ln\frac{M_{ei} + C_{ei}}{GDP_i} - \ln\frac{M_{ee} + C_{ee}}{GDP_e}\right).$$

3.4   Empirical Model

We base our empirical specification in equations (10), (19), and (21). In order to better assess the identification structure suggested by the model, we first present this system of equations in its most general format. We include importer-exporter and time fixed effects to account for the direct effect of bilateral trade costs, and model the proportion of manufacturers that export to foreign markets, f_{ei}, as a simple linear function of expected exchange rate volatility between countries e and i. Thus we obtain the following system:

$$(22) \quad \ln \frac{M_{eit}}{M_{e'it}} = \gamma_{ei}^m + \delta_t^m + \alpha^m \ln \frac{V_{eit}}{V_{e'it}} + \theta^m \ln \frac{S_{et}\theta_{et}}{S_{e't}\theta_{e't}} + \varepsilon_{ee'it}^m,$$

$$(23) \quad \ln \frac{C_{eit}}{C_{e'it}} = \gamma_{ei}^c + \delta_t^c + \alpha^c \ln \frac{V_{eit}}{V_{e'it}} + \theta^c \ln \frac{S_{et}\theta_{et}}{S_{e't}\theta_{e't}} + \varepsilon_{ee'it}^c,$$

$$(24) \quad \ln \frac{V_{eit}}{V_{e'it}} = \gamma_{ei}^v + \delta_t^v$$
$$+ \beta \left(\ln \left[\frac{M_{eit} + C_{eit}}{M_{e'it} + C_{e'it}} \right] - \ln \left[\frac{M_{eet} + C_{eet}}{GDP_{et}} \right] + \ln \left[\frac{M_{e'e't} + C_{e'e't}}{GDP_{e't}} \right] \right)$$
$$+ \theta^v \ln \frac{S_{et}\theta_{et}}{S_{e't}\theta_{e't}} + \varepsilon_{ee'it}^v.$$

The first identification assumption suggested by the model in the previous section is that $\alpha^c = 0$. This assumption suggests that commodity trade is unaffected by exchange rate volatility. Producers of commodity products are always ready to export their product, only today's price levels matter for how much they export. This assumption is not testable as our model is exactly identified. The second identification assumption, implicit in equation (24) suggests that the impact of trade on exchange rate volatility is the same regardless of the product being traded (we relax this assumption later as a robustness check). We also assume that our model is rich enough such that $E(\varepsilon^m\varepsilon^c) = E(\varepsilon^c\varepsilon^v) = 0$. These four assumptions allow us to identify the coefficients of interest, (α^m, β) without making any assumption about $E(\varepsilon^m\varepsilon^c)$. We estimate the system using generalized method of moments (GMM), imposing these restrictions. Commodity trade is in effect being used as an instrument for the function of trade in equation (24); the only way commodity trade affects real exchange rate volatility is through its effect in making consumption bundles more similar. With equation (24) identified, GMM uses the estimated residual $\hat{\varepsilon}_{ee'it}$ as an instrument for $\ln(V_{eit}/V_{e'it})$ in equation (22). This residual is a shock to real exchange rate volatility that is not caused by trade.

This system is general enough to understand the biases introduced by other identifying procedures. In particular, estimating equation (22) while ignoring the existence of equation (24) introduces the following simultaneity bias to the estimate of α_m:

$$(25) \qquad E\,\hat{\alpha}_m - \alpha_m = \frac{\beta}{1 - \alpha_m\beta}\,\frac{\sigma^2_{\varepsilon m}}{\sigma^2_{d\overline{V}}},$$

where $d\overline{V} = \overline{V}_{eit} - \overline{V}_{e'it}$ and $\overline{V}_{eit}$ is the real exchange rate volatility variable purged of the fixed effects and exogenous variables. In the case where $\beta < 0$ and $\alpha < 0$, then $|\alpha| > |\alpha|$, which implies that the estimate of the effect of trade on exchange rate volatility overestimates the true effect when the reverse causality channel is assumed away. If, in addition, the econometrician is lax in controlling for bilateral trade costs, it can easily be shown that the simultaneity bias gets exacerbated by omitted variables bias, because these trade costs depress trade and the omitted costs will be positively correlated with real exchange rate volatility. In this situation, adding additional proxies for trade costs may reduce the omitted variables bias, but may have no effect on the simultaneity bias. We argue that this is precisely what happens in Rose (2000) and Frankel and Rose (2002). Note how in Frankel and Rose (2002) the estimated impact of currency unions declines as they better control for a broad conception of trade costs. Better controlling for trade costs is necessary to reduce omitted variable bias, but does nothing to address simultaneity bias. Hau's (2002) instrument for openness, land area, is a proxy for trade cost and price index variables that belong in the system; hence, land area will be correlated with the error term in his regression.

We adapt the model to estimate the relationship between exchange rate regimes and trade. The underlying idea is very similar to the exchange rate volatility case. Countries are more likely to bind their exchange rate to that of their major trading partners, which may have the effect of promoting trade between those countries. We use the methodology described earlier to identify how trade affects the exchange rate regime and how that exchange rate regime affects trade. In this case, $\ln V_{eit}$ is replaced by a simple indicator variable indicating the presence of a currency union or a currency board (CU_{eit}), or a fixed exchange rate (F_{eit}). This adaptation is open to the criticism that if the monetary authority is interested in promoting trade and realizes that volatility has no impact on commodity trade, it may seek to peg the exchange rate with large manufacturing-trade partners. This criticism can be addressed by reducing the weight given to commodity trade in equation (24).

3.5   Trade and Real Exchange Rate Data

Rauch (1999) provides a categorization of SITC Revision 2 industries according to three possible product types following an extensive search for published reference prices: differentiated, reference priced, and commodity. The Rauch classification is widely used in empirical international trade studies, but has not been updated to cover more recent trade classifications. The lack of a reference price distinguishes differentiated products from the rest. Those industries with reference prices can be further divided into those whose reference prices are quoted on organized exchanges (commodities) and those whose reference prices are quoted only in trade publications (reference priced). The classification is fixed; products do not migrate from one classification to the other. Most elaborate manufactures usually belong to fairly broad SITC classifications, and get classified as differentiated products even if they are effectively reference priced (for example, computer memory chips). The trade data consists of annual flows of exports from a given country to different importing countries. For instance, lead (SITC 685) is listed on an organized exchange and, therefore, treated as a commodity while footwear (SITC 851) is not and is treated as a differentiated product. Bilateral trade data for each SITC industry is available for a large number of developed and developing countries during the period 1970 to 1997. The data consists of annual flows of exports from a given country to different importing countries. Table 3A.1 shows the share of each type of product for different regions and time periods. A summary of the sample used in the estimation is listed in table 3A.1 in the appendix.

Another essential part of the estimation is to obtain a measure of exchange rate volatility. We use monthly data on real exchange rate series from the *International Financial Statistics* (*IFS*) to compute standard deviations. We detrend these series using a Hodrick-Prescott filter and take standard deviations of the filtered data in five-year periods.[13] Table 3A.1 also shows the descriptive statistics of these series. The additional data needed for the main specifications are taken from the World Development Indicators, except for export prices $s_e \theta_e$, which are computed using detailed unit export price data in U.S. trade statistics described in Feenstra (1997) and Feenstra, Romalis, and Schott (2002) after extracting product-by-year fixed effects.

We source data on currency unions and currency boards from Frankel and Rose (2002). The chapter also uses data on other fixed exchange rate regimes. The basic reference for classification of exchange rate regimes is the International Monetary Fund's Annual Report on Exchange Arrangements and Exchange Restrictions (AREAER).[14] This classification is a de jure classification that is based on the publicly stated commitment of the authorities in the country in question. The IMF report captures the notion of a formal commitment to a regime, but fails to capture whether the actual

13. We identify the trend from the monthly log real exchange rate data using a smoothing parameter of 1,000,000. Our volatility measure is the standard deviation of the detrended series over the previous five years. For robustness checks, the detrended series is further decomposed into short-term volatility and medium-term volatility, by smoothing these deviations using a smoothing parameter of 400.

14. The AREAER classification consists of nine categories, broadly grouped into pegs, arrangements with limited flexibility, and more flexible arrangements, which include managed and pure floats. This description is based on the AREAER (IMF 1996).

policies were consistent with the stated commitment. Since we mainly use bilateral data in the chapter, we use the currency to which a country is pegged to create a fixed exchange rate regime dummy that takes the value of one if one country's currency is pegged to the other country's currency, or if two countries are pegged to the same currency. While a de jure classification like the IMF's captures the formal commitment to a regime, it fails to capture whether the actual policies were consistent with this commitment. For instance, de jure pegs can pursue policies inconsistent with their stated regime and require frequent changes in the nominal exchange rate, making the degree of commitment embedded in the peg, in fact, similar to a float. The problems that arise from a pure de jure classification have prompted researchers to use different criteria to classify regimes. Reinhart and Rogoff (2002) classify exchange rate regimes using information about the existence of parallel markets combined with the actual exchange rate behavior in those markets. Levy-Yeyati and Sturzenegger (2000) analyze data on volatility of reserves and actual exchange rates. A similar bilateral fixed exchange rate dummy is constructed from the Reinhart and Rogoff and Levy-Yeyati and Sturzennegger database. We source data on currency unions and currency boards from Rose (2000) and Frankel and Rose (2002).

3.6   Results

The main results of the chapter are reported in tables 3.1, 3.2, and 3.3. The first two columns of table 3.1 present OLS estimates of equations (22) and (24). A 10 percent increase in volatility depresses differentiated product trade by 0.7 percent, while a 10 percent increase in trade reduces exchange rate volatility by 0.3 percent. The next two columns present GMM estimates of equations (22) and (24). The OLS estimate of the effect of volatility on trade is reduced by 70 percent. This reduction is because the model attributes much of the correlation between trade and volatility to the effect that trade has in depressing volatility. A 10 percent increase in the intensity of a bilateral trading relationship reduces the volatility of the associated exchange rate by 0.3 percent. Although the estimate is statistically significant, the magnitude of the effect does not at first appear to be that large. But, it must be remembered that the typical bilateral trading relationship is very small (the median was under $8 million in 1997, whereas the median GDP was $32 billion), while the typical real exchange rate is quite volatile (typically 11 percent from its trend). A trading relationship that is 1 percent of GDP greater than the median trade relationship implies that the volatility of the bilateral real exchange rate associated with the intense trading partner is 12 percent smaller than with the less intense partner. Though most trade relationships are much smaller than this, intense relationships of this size or greater are very numerous, especially between proximate countries. For example, the Canada-United States trade relationship in 1997 is equal to

Table 3.1   Exchange rate volatility and trade

	Log differentiated product trade (1) OLS	Log real exchange rate volatility (1) OLS	Log differentiated product trade (1) GMM	Log real exchange rate volatility (1) GMM	Log differentiated product trade (2) OLS	Log real exchange rate volatility (2) OLS	Log differentiated product trade (2) GMM	Log real exchange rate volatility (2) GMM
Model Estimation technique								
Right-hand side variable								
Log real exchange rate volatility	-0.077 (0.012)		-0.032 (0.015)		-0.059 (0.012)		-0.015 (0.015)	
Log total trade		-0.034 (0.005)		-0.033 (0.008)		-0.022 (0.005)		-0.033 (0.008)
Log export price level	-0.595 (0.056)	-0.165 (0.026)	-0.588 (0.056)	-0.165 (0.026)	-0.699 (0.064)	0.041 (0.025)	-0.701 (0.064)	0.038 (0.025)
Log product real GDP					X	X	X	X
Log product real GDP/capita					X	X	X	X
Log exporters' real GDP					X	X	X	X
Log exporters' real GDP/capita					X	X	X	X
Importer-exporter fixed effects	X	X	X	X	X	X	X	X
Year fixed effects	X	X	X	X	X	X	X	X
Observations	47,521	47,521	47,521	47,521	47,521	47,521	47,521	47,521

Notes: Each variable has been differenced as follows: from log differentiated product imports of country *i* from country *e* we have subtracted log differentiated product imports of country *i* from the United States. The reason, derived in the model, is to eliminate country *i* specific effects. All variables are equivalently differenced. Standard errors corrected for heteroscedasticity and autocorrelation are reported in parentheses. X indicates that the explanatory variable has been included as a control in the regression, but due to the differencing employed in the regression specification, the estimated regression coefficient has no obvious economic meaning and has been suppressed.

23 percent of the GDP using our measure: U.S. exports to Canada equal 21 percent of Canada's GDP, while Canadian exports to the United States equal 2 percent of the U.S. GDP. Our results predict that this intense relationship reduces the volatility of the United States dollar-Canadian dollar (USD-CAD) real exchange rate by 38 percent, compared with the typical exchange-rate pair. The estimated effect of trade on exchange rate volatility in table 3.1, columns (5) through (8), is barely changed by the addition of more explanatory variables that often appear in gravity models of trade, though the estimated effect of volatility on trade declines.

Table 3.2 presents estimates from the adaptation of our identification strategy to estimating the effect of currency unions and currency boards on trade. In our sample there are very few instances of a change in currency union or currency board status, so we drop the fixed effects for each importer-exporter relationship and instead include exporter fixed effects and importer fixed effects. Extension of the data to more recent years would be helpful here due to EMU. The OLS result is again presented in column (1), with the typically large estimate that a currency union increases trade by 250 percent, consistent with Rose (2000), Frankel and Rose (2002), and Glick and Rose (2002). Columns (2) and (3) present the GMM estimates. We find that controlling for reverse causality reduces the estimate of the currency union effect to 25 percent; the estimate is one-tenth the size of the OLS estimate and just as precise. Almost all of the correlation between trade and the presence of a currency union or a currency board is attributed to the fact that countries are much more likely to adopt the exchange rate of a major trading partner. The addition of explanatory variables that are often used to explain trade in the presence of currency unions does not change the basic story. The OLS estimates are always above 50 percent, the GMM estimates are always small, ranging between 10 and 25 percent, with very little loss in precision relative to their OLS counterparts. The OLS estimates are usually outside 95 percent confidence intervals for the GMM estimates.

Table 3.3 presents estimates from the adaptation of our identification strategy to estimating the effect of fixed exchange rates on trade. The fact that many countries have changed their exchange rate regime allows us to reintroduce fixed effects for every importer-exporter relationship. The coefficient on the fixed exchange rate variable is only identified because countries have changed their exchange rate regime. All estimates, be they OLS or GMM, suggest only modest effects of fixed exchange rates on trade. The GMM estimates for the two de facto measures of exchange rate regime both suggest that a fixed exchange rate regime increases differentiated product trade by 6 percent.

3.6.1   Robustness Checks

We check the robustness of our results to a number of changes to our empirical model. Table 3.4 reports sensitivity of our results to alternative mea-

Table 3.2   Currency unions, currency boards, and trade

	Left-hand side variable								
Model	Log differentiated product trade (1)	Log differentiated product trade (1)	Currency union or currency board (1)	Log differentiated product trade (2)	Log differentiated product trade (2)	Currency union or currency board (2)	Log differentiated product trade (3)	Log differentiated product trade (3)	Currency union or currency board (3)
Estimation technique	OLS	GMM	GMM	OLS	GMM	GMM	OLS	GMM	GMM
Right-hand side variable									
Currency union/board	1.246 (0.206)	0.219 (0.214)		1.282 (0.230)	0.185 (0.212)		0.423 (0.169)	0.094 (0.201)	
Log total trade			2.35E-03 (5.51E-04)			2.51E-03 (5.53E-04)			1.29E-03 (7.51E-04)
Log export price level	1.877 (0.108)	1.879 (0.108)	-2.07E-03 (3.68E-03)	2.280 (0.121)	2.282 (0.121)	-1.81E-03 (4.33E-03)	2.267 (0.102)	2.268 (0.102)	1.47E-03 (4.06E-03)
Log product real GDP				X	X	X	X	X	X
Log product real GDP/capita				X	X	X	X	X	X
Log exporters' real GDP				X	X	X	X	X	X
Log exporters' real GDP/capita				X	X	X	X	X	X
Log distance							X	X	X
Preferential trade agreement							X	X	X
Common language				X	X	X	X	X	X
Common land border				X	X	X	X	X	X
Exporter fixed effects	X	X	X	X	X	X	X	X	X
Importer fixed effects	X	X	X	X	X	X	X	X	X
Year fixed effects	X	X	X	X	X	X	X	X	X
Observations	48,808	48,808	48,808	48,808	48,808	48,808	48,808	48,808	48,808

Notes: Each variable has been differenced as follows: from log differentiated product imports of country i from country e we have subtracted log differentiated product imports of country i from the United States. The reason, derived in the model, is to eliminate country i specific effects. All variables are equivalent differenced. Standard errors corrected for heteroscedasticity and autocorrelation are reported in parentheses. X indicates that the explanatory variable has been included as a control in the regression, but due to the differencing employed in the regression specification, the estimated regression coefficient has no obvious economic meaning and has been suppressed.

Table 3.3   Fixed exchange rate regimes and trade

	Left-hand side variable								
Exchange rate regime data	Log differentiated product trade	Log differentiated product trade	Fixed exchange rate	Log differentiated product trade	Log differentiated product trade	Fixed exchange rate	Log differentiated product trade	Log differentiated product trade	Fixed exchange rate
	IMF	IMF	IMF	RogoffDF	RogoffDF	RogoffDF	LYS	LYS	LYS
Estimation technique	OLS	GMM	GMM	OLS	GMM	GMM	OLS	GMM	GMM
Right-hand side variable									
Fixed exchange rate	0.017	−0.037		−0.002	0.064		0.114	0.069	
	(0.022)	(0.026)		(0.023)	(0.031)		(0.015)	(0.019)	
Log total trade			1.35E-02			−6.68E-03			1.65E-02
			(4.59E-03)			(−2.65E-03)			(4.69E-03)
Log export price level	−0.648	−0.649	−0.012	−0.751	−0.750	−0.013	−0.747	−0.734	0.300
	(0.061)	(0.061)	(0.019)	(0.063)	(0.063)	(0.007)	(0.063)	(0.063)	(0.021)
Log product real GDP	X	X	X	X	X	X	X	X	X
Log product real GDP/capita	X	X	X	X	X	X	X	X	X
Log exporters' real GDP	X	X	X	X	X	X	X	X	X
Log exporters' real GDP/capita	X	X	X	X	X	X	X	X	X
Preferential trade agreement	X	X	X	X	X	X	X	X	X
Importer-exporter fixed effects	X	X	X	X	X	X	X	X	X
Year fixed effects	X	X	X	X	X	X	X	X	X
Observations	45,061	45,061	45,061	48,791	48,791	48,791	45,568	45,568	45,568

Notes: Each variable has been differenced as follows: from log differentiated product imports of country *i* from country *e* we have subtracted log differentiated product imports of country *i* from the United States. The reason, derived in the model, is to eliminate country *i* specific effects. All variables are equivalently differenced. Standard errors corrected for heteroscedasticity and autocorrelation are reported in parentheses. X indicates that the explanatory variable has been included as a control in the regression, but due to the differencing employed in the regression specification, the estimated regression coefficient has no obvious economic meaning and has been suppressed.

Table 3.4 Sensitivity to different volatility measures

	Left-hand side variable											
Exchange volatility Measure	Log differentiated product trade	Log real exchange rate volatility	Log differentiated product trade	Log real exchange rate volatility	Log differentiated product trade	Log real exchange rate volatility	Log differentiated product trade	Log real exchange rate volatility	Log differentiated product trade	Log real exchange rate volatility	Log differentiated product trade	Log real exchange rate volatility
Measure	Long	Long	Long	Long	Medium	Medium	Medium	Medium	Short	Short	Short	Short
Estimation technique	OLS	OLS	GMM	GMM	OLS	OLS	GMM	GMM	OLS	OLS	GMM	GMM
Right-hand side variable												
Log real exchange rate volatility	−0.016 (0.006)		−0.011 (0.008)		−0.027 (0.009)		−0.001 (0.001)		−0.134 (0.015)		−0.071 (0.020)	
Log total trade		−0.014 (0.008)		−0.012 (0.014)		−0.014 (0.006)		−0.032 (0.010)		−0.039 (0.005)		−0.037 (0.008)
Log export price level	−0.700 (0.064)	0.079 (0.044)	−0.701 (0.064)	0.080 (0.044)	−0.699 (0.064)	0.097 (0.032)	−0.701 (0.042)	0.092 (0.032)	−0.711 (0.064)	−0.086 (0.027)	−0.707 (0.064)	−0.071 (0.020)
Log product real GDP	X	X	X	X	X	X	X	X	X	X	X	X
Log product real GDP/capita	X	X	X	X	X	X	X	X	X	X	X	X
Log exporters' real GDP	X	X	X	X	X	X	X	X	X	X	X	X
Log exporters' real GDP/capita	X	X	X	X	X	X	X	X	X	X	X	X
Importer-exporter fixed effects	X	X	X	X	X	X	X	X	X	X	X	X
Year fixed effects	X	X	X	X	X	X	X	X	X	X	X	X
Observations	47,521	47,521	47,521	47,521	47,521	47,521	47,521	47,521	47,521	47,521	47,521	47,521

Notes: Each variable has been differenced as follows: from log differentiated product imports of country *i* from log differentiated product imports of country *i* from country *e* we have subtracted log differentiated product imports of country *i* from the United States. The reason, derived in the model, is to eliminate country *i* specific effects. All variables are equivalently differenced. Standard errors corrected for heteroscedasticity and autocorrelation are reported in parentheses. X indicates that the explanatory variable has been included as a control in the regression, but due to the differencing employed in the regression specification, the estimated regression coefficient has no obvious economic meaning and has been suppressed.

sures of exchange rate volatility. We construct four measures to capture volatility at different frequencies by adjusting the smoothing parameters used in the Hodrick-Prescott filters. The data is filtered to isolate very low-frequency movements that we term "long-run" volatility, very high-frequency movements that we term "short-run" volatility, and all other movements that we term "medium-run" volatility. The estimates based on short-run volatility are higher than the other estimates. Trade is both more sensitive to short-run volatility and has a greater effect in dampening short-run volatility.

Table 3.5 performs our basic regression for different regions. In particular, we are interested if our results depend on whether the exporting country is developed or developing. All of the depressing effect of volatility on trade comes from developing country exporters. Developed country exporters are not adversely affected by exchange rate volatility. This suggests that developing country exporters are more risk-averse or are less able to hedge the real exchange rate risk. For both groups of exporters, trade depresses the volatility of the exchange rate.

Table 3.6 reports the effect of adding information on capital controls and capital flows to each equation. Gross private capital flows sourced from the World Development Indicators is the sum of gross private capital flows as a percentage of the GDP for the exporting and the importing country. Capital control data sourced from the IMF's AREAER is the sum of the dummy variables indicating the presence or absence of capital controls in the exporting and importing countries. The results barely change.

Figures 3.4, 3.5, 3.6, and 3.7 illustrate the effect of reducing the relative effect of commodity trade in reducing real exchange rate volatility or in affecting the likelihood of entering into a currency union. This is done by introducing a parameter β_c to equation (21) describing how trade affects volatility and the equivalent equations describing the formation of exchange rate regimes:

$$(26) \qquad \ln V_{ei} = \gamma + \beta \left(\ln \frac{M_{ei} + \beta_c C_{ei}}{GDP_i} - \ln \frac{M_{ee} + \beta_c C_{ee}}{GDP_e} \right).$$

This new parameter has to be imposed since the model is otherwise unidentified. As this parameter is reduced from the value of 1 used in all prior regressions, the model attributes even more of the correlation between trade and volatility or currency union to the effect that trade has in depressing volatility or leading to a currency union. Exchange rate volatility and currency unions appear to have little impact on trade.

3.7   Conclusion

Most of the studies of the effect of exchange rate volatility on trade assume that the volume of trade has no impact on exchange rate volatility, thus assuming away an endogeneity problem. We present evidence that this

Table 3.5   Developing vs. developed country exporters

	Log differentiated product trade	Log real exchange rate volatility	Log differentiated product trade	Log real exchange rate volatility	Log differentiated product trade	Log real exchange rate volatility	Log differentiated product trade	Log real exchange rate volatility
	Left-hand side variable							
Exporter	Developing	Developing	Developing	Developing	Developed	Developed	Developed	Developed
Estimation technique	GMM	GMM	GMM	GMM	GMM	GMM	GMM	GMM
Right-hand side variable								
Log real exchange rate volatility	-0.053		-0.037		0.036		0.071	
	(0.019)		(0.019)		(0.020)		(0.020)	
Log total trade		-0.028		-0.020		-0.042		-0.088
		(0.009)		(0.009)		(0.028)		(0.029)
Log export price level	-0.615	-0.101	-0.884	0.109	-0.496	-0.057	0.218	0.109
	(0.070)	(0.030)	(0.080)	(0.031)	(0.072)	(0.068)	(0.095)	(0.087)
Log product real GDP		X	X	X		X	X	X
Log product real GDP/capita		X	X	X		X	X	X
Log exporters' real GDP		X	X	X		X	X	X
Log exporters' real GDP/capita		X	X	X		X	X	X
Importer-exporter fixed effects	X	X	X	X	X	X	X	X
Year fixed effects	X	X	X	X	X	X	X	X
Observations	27,481	27,481	27,481	27,481	20,040	20,040	20,040	20,040

Notes: Each variable has been differenced as follows: from log differentiated product imports of country i from country e we have subtracted log differentiated product imports of country i from the United States. The reason, derived in the model, is to eliminate country i specific effects. All variables are equivalently differenced. Standard errors corrected for heteroscedasticity and autocorrelation are reported in parentheses. X indicates that the explanatory variable has been included as a control in the regression, but due to the differencing employed in the regression specification, the estimated regression coefficient has no obvious economic meaning and has been suppressed.

Table 3.6 — Robustness to inclusion of capital controls and capital flows

Model/data estimation	Log differentiated product trade	Log real exchange rate volatility	Log differentiated product trade	Log real exchange rate volatility	Log differentiated product trade	Log differentiated product trade	Currency union or currency board	Log differentiated product trade	Log differentiated product trade	Fixed exchange rate	Log differentiated product trade	Log differentiated product trade	Fixed exchange rate
Left-hand side variable	Volatility	Volatility	Volatility	Volatility	CU	CU	CU	RogoffDF	RogoffDF	RogoffDF	LYS	LYS	LYS
Technique	OLS	OLS	GMM	GMM	OLS	GMM	GMM	OLS	GMM	GMM	OLS	GMM	GMM
Right-hand side variable													
Log real exchange rate Volatility	−0.040 (0.013)												
Currency union/board			0.008 (0.016)		0.356 (0.173)	0.080 (0.212)							
Fixed exchange rate								0.021 (0.023)	0.061 (0.032)		0.109 (0.016)	0.051 (0.019)	
Log total trade		−0.020 (0.005)		−0.037 (0.009)			1.20E-03 (8.63E-04)			−4.39E-03 (2.83E-03)			2.21E-02 (5.00E-03)
Log export price level	−0.581 (0.066)	−0.002 (0.030)	−0.582 (0.066)	0.008 (0.016)	2.174 (0.109)	2.174 (0.109)	6.00E-06 (4.68E-03)	−0.623 (0.064)	−0.622 (0.064)	−3.26E-02 (7.14E-03)	−0.704 (0.065)	−0.688 (0.065)	2.83E-01 (2.24E-02)
Log product real GDP	X	X	X	X	X	X	X	X	X	X	X	X	X
Log product real GDP/capita	X	X	X	X	X	X	X	X	X	X	X	X	X
Log exporters' real GDP	X	X	X	X	X	X	X	X	X	X	X	X	X
Log exporters' real GDP/capita	X	X	X	X	X	X	X	X	X	X	X	X	X
Log distance					X	X	X						
Preferential trade agreement					X	X	X						
Common language					X	X	X						
Common land border					X	X	X						
Gross private capital flows	X	X	X	X	X	X	X	X	X	X	X	X	X
Capital controls	X	X	X	X	X	X	X	X	X	X	X	X	X
Importer-exporter fixed effects	X	X	X	X				X	X	X	X	X	X
Exporter fixed effects					X	X	X						
Importer fixed effects					X	X	X						
Year fixed effects	X	X	X	X	X	X	X	X	X	X	X	X	X
Observations	39,979	39,979	39,979	39,979	41,265	41,265	41,265	41,258	41,258	41,258	40,304	40,304	40,304

Notes: Each variable has been differenced as follows: from log differentiated product imports of country i from country e we have subtracted log differentiated product imports of country i from the United States. The reason, derived in the model, is to eliminate country i specific effects. All variables are equivalently differenced. Standard errors corrected for heteroscedasticity and autocorrelation are reported in parentheses. X indicates that the explanatory variable has been included as a control in the regression, but due to the differencing employed in the regression specification, the estimated regression coefficient has no obvious economic meaning and has been suppressed.

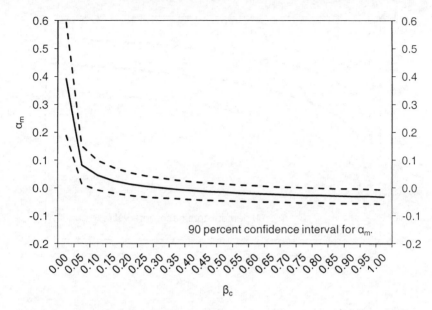

Fig. 3.4   Exchange rate volatility and trade

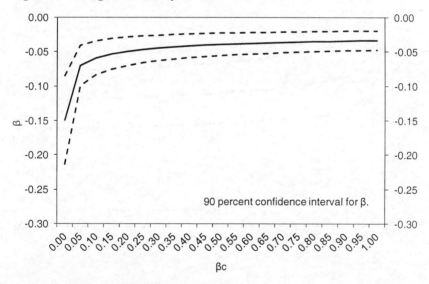

Fig. 3.5   Trade and exchange rate volatility

problem is severe. We develop a model in which both directions of causality are considered, and that allows us to structurally identify the impact of exchange rate volatility on trade. We exploit our identification structure by using disaggregate product trade data for a large number of countries for the period 1970 to 1997. We find that deeper bilateral trading relations dampen

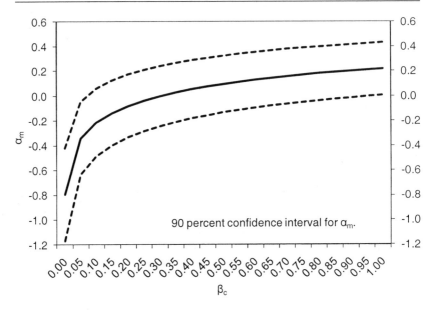

Fig. 3.6   Currency unions and trade

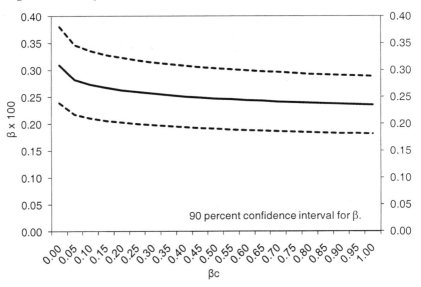

Fig. 3.7   Trade and currency unions

real exchange rate volatility and are much more likely to lead to a currency union. In fact, our empirical model attributes most of the correlation between trade and volatility to the effect that trade has in depressing volatility. It is this effect that had been assumed away in the previous literature. The chapter finds some evidence that real exchange rate volatility depresses trade in differentiated goods. The size of the effect is fairly small and unevenly distributed. A doubling of real exchange rate volatility decreases trade in differentiated products by about 2 percent. Developing country exports of manufactures may be much more greatly affected due to a combination of greater exchange rate volatility and greater sensitivity of their exporters to that volatility. We find that controlling for reverse causality, the estimates of the effect of currency unions on trade are much smaller than OLS estimates and similarly precise. Currency unions enhance trade by 10 to 25 percent rather than the 300 percent estimates previously obtained.

Appendix

Derivation of equation (20). The log of the price index for country i is:

$$(27) \qquad \ln P_i = [b \ln P_{im} + (1 - b) \ln P_{ic}],$$

where P_{im} is defined in equation (15) and P_{ic} is defined in equation (8). Differentiating:

$$(28) \qquad \frac{d \ln P_i}{d \ln s_e} = s_e \left[\frac{b}{P_{im}} \frac{dP_{im}}{ds_e} + \frac{(1 - b)}{P_{ic}} \frac{dP_{ic}}{ds_e} \right].$$

Substituting out dP_{im}/ds_e and dP_{ic}/ds_e:

$$(29) \qquad \frac{d \ln P_i}{d \ln s_e}$$

$$= s_e \left[\frac{b}{P_{im}} P_{im}^{\sigma_m} n f_{ei} \left(\frac{\sigma_m}{\sigma_m - 1} s_e \theta_e \tau_{eim} \right)^{1-\sigma_m} s_e^{-1} + \frac{1-b}{P_{ic}} P_{ic}^{\sigma_c} \tau_{eic}^{1-\sigma_c} s_e^{-\sigma_c} \right].$$

Substituting using equations (6) and (14):

$$\frac{d \ln P_i}{d \ln s_e} = b n f_{ei} \frac{p_{ei,y}^{1-\sigma_m}}{P_{im}^{1-\sigma_m}} + (1 - b) \frac{p_{ei}^{1-\sigma_c}}{P_{ic}^{1-\sigma_c}}.$$

The first term on the right side of equation (30) is the proportion of country i's income spent on manufactured goods produced in country e, while the second term is the proportion spent on commodities from country e. For small shocks to s_e, the price index in country i changes in line with the share of country e's goods in country i's consumption basket. Equation (20) follows from our definition of the real exchange rate as the ratio of two price indexes.

Table 3A.1   Descriptive statistics

Exporter from	Number of pairs	Share of exports in differentiated products	Share of exports in reference products	Share of exports in commodity products	Real exchange rate volatility (medium-term) (%)	Real exchange rate volatility (short-term) (%)	IMF fixed exchange rate regime pairs (1) (%)	Rogoff-Reinhart fixed exchange rate regime pairs (1) (%)
				1970s				
Africa	4,260	0.17	0.17	0.66	7.0	4.6	11.7	3.7
N. America	1,191	0.59	0.20	0.21	6.1	3.5	0.4	0.3
C. America and S. America	6,977	0.11	0.15	0.73	8.1	6.0	20.5	9.7
Asia	4,921	0.60	0.17	0.23	7.6	4.6	14.4	3.6
Europe	9,081	0.65	0.24	0.12	5.7	3.8	3.5	6.1
All	26,430	0.58	0.21	0.21	6.9	4.6	11.6	5.9
				1980s				
Africa	5,332	0.17	0.18	0.66	13.6	7.0	3.7	1.8
N. America	1,341	0.63	0.20	0.17	10.1	4.8	0.0	0.0
C. America and S. America	8,327	0.20	0.17	0.63	15.2	8.2	10.4	1.2
Asia	7,085	0.73	0.11	0.17	10.2	5.0	2.5	0.1
Europe	10,820	0.66	0.21	0.13	10.8	5.1	3.5	0.6
All	32,905	0.62	0.19	0.19	12.2	6.2	4.9	0.8
				1990s				
Africa	7,514	0.24	0.23	0.53	11.1	7.6	2.8	1.1
N. America	1,346	0.70	0.18	0.12	8.1	5.1	0.0	0.0
C. America and S. America	9,143	0.41	0.20	0.39	11.8	8.0	1.4	0.2
Asia	8,346	0.76	0.10	0.14	8.5	5.2	1.0	0.4
Europe	12,197	0.71	0.20	0.09	8.8	5.7	1.1	1.4
All	38,546	0.69	0.17	0.13	9.8	6.5	1.4	0.8

Notes: Pairs are included only if real exchange rate volatility data is available. For exchange rate regimes, not all number of pairs have data.

References

Alesina, A., R. Barro, and S. Tenreyro. 2003. Optimal currency areas. *NBER Macroeconomic Annual 2002,* volume 17. Cambridge, MA: MIT Press.

Bacchetta, P., and E. van Wincoop. 2000. Does exchange rate stability increase trade and welfare? *American Economic Review* 90 (5): 1093–109.

Barro, R., and S. Tenreyro. 2007. Economic effects of currency unions. *Economic Inquiry* 45 (1): 1–23.

Bini-Smaghi, L. 1991. Exchange rate variability and trade: Why is it so difficult to find any empirical relationship? *Applied Economics* 23:927–36.

Engel, C., and J. H. Rogers. 1996. How wide is the border? *American Economic Review* 86 (5): 1112–25.

Ethier, W. 1973. International trade and the forward exchange market. *American Economic Review* 63 (3): 494–503.

Feenstra, R. C. 1997. U.S. exports, 1972–1994, with state exports and other U.S. data. NBER Working Paper no. 5990. Cambridge, MA: National Bureau of Economic Research, April.

Feenstra, R. C., J. Romalis, and P. K. Schott. 2002. U.S. imports, exports, and tariff data, 1989–2001. NBER Working Paper no. 9387. Cambridge, MA: National Bureau of Economic Research, December.

Frankel, J. A., and A. Rose. 2002. An estimate of the effect of currency unions on trade and growth. *Quarterly Journal of Economics* 117 (2): 437–66.

Frankel, J. A., and S.-J. Wei. 1993. Trade blocs and currency blocs. NBER Working Paper no. 4335. Cambridge, MA: National Bureau of Economic Research, April.

Ghosh, A. R., A-M. Gulde, J. Ostry, and H. Wolf. 1997. Does the nominal exchange rate regime matter? NBER Working Paper no. 5874. Cambridge, MA: National Bureau of Economic Research, January.

Glick, R., and A. K. Rose. 2002. Does a currency union affect trade? The time series evidence. *European Economic Review* 46 (6): 1125–51.

Hau, H. 2002. Real exchange rate volatility and economic openness: Theory and evidence. *Journal of Money, Credit and Banking* 34 (3): 611–30.

Helpman, E., and P. Krugman. 1985. *Market structure and foreign trade.* Cambridge, MA: MIT Press.

Hooper, P., and S. Kohlhagen. 1978. The effect of exchange rate uncertainty on the prices and volume of international trade. *Journal of International Economics* 8:483–511.

International Monetary Fund. 1970–1997. *Annual report on exchange arrangements and exchange restrictions, volumes 1970 to 1997.* Washington, DC: IMF.

———. 1996. *Annual report on exchange arrangements and exchange restrictions, volume 1996.* Washington, DC: IMF.

Klein, M. W. 1990. Sectoral effects of exchange rate volatility on United States exports. *Journal of International Money and Finance* 9 (3): 299–308.

Krugman, P. 1980. Scale economies, product differentiation, and the pattern of trade. *American Economic Review* 70 (5): 950–59.

Levy-Yeyati, E., and F. Sturznegger. 2005. Classifying exchange rate regimes: Deeds vs. words. *European Economic Review* 49 (6): 1603–35.

Micco, A., E. Stein, and G. Ordoñez. 2003. The currency union effect on trade: Early evidence from EMU. *Economic Policy* 18 (37): 317–56.

Mundell, R. A. 1961. A theory of optimal currency areas. *American Economic Review* 51 (4): 657–65.

Obstfeld, M., and K. Rogoff. 1995. The mirage of fixed exchange rates. *Journal of Economic Perspectives* 9 (4): 73–96.

———. 2002. Global implications of self-oriented national monetary rules. *Quarterly Journal of Economics* 117 (2): 503–35.

Persson, T. 2001. Currency unions and trade: How large is the treatment effect? *Economic Policy* 16 (33): 433–48.

Rauch, J. E. 1999. Networks versus markets in international trade. *Journal of International Economics* 48:7–35.

Reinhart, C. M., and K. S. Rogoff. 2004. The modern history of exchange rate arrangements: A reinterpretation. *Quarterly Journal of Economics* 119 (1): 1–48.

Romer, D. H. 1993. Openness and inflation: Theory and evidence. *Quarterly Journal of Economics* 108:870–903.

Rose, A. K. 2000. One money, one market: Estimating the effect of common currencies on trade. *Economic Policy* 15 (30): 7–46.

Taussig, F. W. 1924. *Principles of economics,* volume 1. New York: Macmillian.

Tenreyro, S. 2007. On the trade impact of nominal exchange rate volatility. *Journal of Development Economics* 82 (2): 485–508.

Viaene, J. M., and C. G. de Vries. 1992. International trade and exchange rate volatility. *European Economic Review* 36:1311–21.

Comment   Chaiyasit Anuchitworawong

Previous research has investigated the relationship between exchange rate volatility and international trade. The literature in this area dated back several decades and the issue has been recently and rigorously reexamined, given some improvements in analytical methods, and the quantity and quality of data used to explore the relationship. Most existing studies focus on the effect of exchange rate volatility on trade, despite the fact that there are two major lines of research that differently identify the direction of relationship between the two. The main line of causality runs from exchange rate volatility to international trade, as well as the other way around, which is motivated by the early and most influential paper by Mundell (1961) on the theory of optimal currency areas, which suggested that trade flows reduce exchange rate volatility. If one adds the two strands of literature together, it becomes obvious that the exchange rate process is not exogenously given, but may, in fact, be endogenous to the level of international trade among other factors.

Most of the past studies were based on models in which the direction of causality was assumed to run from exchange rate volatility to trade, implying that the exchange rate process is driven by exogenous shocks. The findings also varied widely depending on the data and empirical methodologies being

Chaiyasit Anuchitworawong is a research specialist at the Thailand Development Research Institute.

used. The most surprising result should be drawn from Rose (2000), who found strikingly high trade creation effect of currency union membership, and by extension, of a more stable exchange rate, implying that the currency union reduces exchange rate volatility, and thus increases trade flows. A number of other studies also suggest that exchange rate volatility dampens levels of international trade, while certain papers show no significant effects or even indicate negative association. However, on the theoretical front, there are several specific assumptions that underlie the relationship between trade and exchange rate volatility. This further casts doubts on the conclusiveness of empirical evidence. More importantly, many of the existing studies did not seriously account for the endogeneity issue. It is not until recently that only few theoretical and empirical studies take into account the opposite direction of causality (Hau 2002; Tenreyro 2003).

This chapter by Broda and Romalis also tackles the endogeneity issue between exchange rate volatility and trade mentioned earlier, but approaches the problem differently. Although the authors are not the first to address the reverse-causality problem between volatility and trade, the novelty of their chapter lies in the development of a multicountry model, with four countries and two sectors based on the theory of international trade to explicitly investigate the relationship between exchange rate volatility and international trade flows. Their model is the first attempt to consider both directions of causality between trade and exchange rate volatility, and to structurally derive the empirical identification of the system of equations to test the effect of trade on exchange rate volatility, and the other way around. Furthermore, the authors use the disaggregated data for a large number of developed and developing countries during 1970 to 1997, and incorporate the difference in trading and searching costs between differentiated and homogenous products, arguing that the omission of these transaction costs in the analysis will exacerbate the extent of omitted variable bias.

The authors use theory nicely to structure the problem, and then with the aid of a reasonable econometric method of GMM to examine the issue empirically and quantitatively. Empirically, the authors find strong support to the model prediction that the exchange rate volatility reduces trade while an increase in the volume of trade decreases the volatility. Overall, the chapter tends to suggest that the endogeneity problem should be an important element that makes the impact of exchange rate volatility on international trade found in other studies overestimated. Accounting for the reverse causality issue, the effect of exchange rate volatility and currency union on trade in differentiated products is substantially reduced when using the GMM estimation method.

Although the authors provide several interesting empirical results based on the system of equations suggested by the model, one can raise a number of issues for further discussion. A few assumptions were made in the model setting. However, certain assumptions may be relaxed to make the model more realistic. First, I am quite concerned about the assumption that trade is always balanced. Although the authors argue that it is necessary to have some long-run trade balance condition in the model, one should note that it is not true in practice. For example, trade statistics in 2004 showed that the United States had by far the greatest trade imbalance. Its trade deficit with China was about one-third of its total deficit in manufactures, while China's surplus with the United States was larger than its overall trade surplus in manufacturers. However, China was running sizable manufacturing trade deficits with many of its neighbors in the Asia Pacific region, Japan in particular (Dekle, Eaton, and Kortum 2007). In sum, there is enormous room for large bilateral imbalances even in a world with overall balance. If bilateral trade imbalances are large for the sample countries in their study, the results may be biased. It may be essential to show whether the assumption can be relaxed with minimal effects on the theoretical results of the model.

The chapter also focuses on the market entry decision of exporting firms and further assumes no price rigidities in the model, implying that there is no role of price rigidities to the exchange rate. Although prices are likely to be flexible in the long run, one should note that there exists short-run market rigidities, particularly on the downward side. The study by Carlton (1986) suggests that prices for many transactions remain rigid for periods exceeding one year. There has also been the tendency for nominal rigidities to increase over time, particularly in developed economies. Hanes and James (2003) found that there is evidence of some manufacturing wage rigidity in the United States beginning in the late nineteenth century, which appears to have persisted into the twentieth century. Since the prices are not freely adjusted in short periods, this may bring about inefficient allocation of resources.

In the presence of price rigidities, firms set export prices before demand and exchange rate shocks are realized. As a consequence, firms encounter with greater price risk when invoices are denominated in foreign currency. Such uncertainty will affect the optimal pricing rule. Under a fixed exchange rate regime, productivity shock with normal price rigidities tends to have many more spillovers onto the real exchange rate volatility, while it is less affected under a flexible regime where certain mechanisms are in place to help offset an adverse shock. Moreover, in the presence of price rigidities, countries are likely to be more specialized under flexible exchange rates than under fixed exchange rates. Since the chapter includes only a small fraction of fixed exchange regime pairs in the sample set, and there exist short-term price rigidities in practice, the chapter should be carefully interpreted because exchange rate variability in a flexible exchange rate regime other than the fixed regime may create sectoral adjustment to shocks for firms located in the net-exporting countries, and cause further disturbance for firms producing the same goods in the net-importing country, resulting in more specialization in activities the countries can do the best, which allows the patterns of interindustrial and intraindustrial trade to change. In addition to the differences in the countries' consumption baskets that are claimed in the chapter to affect real exchange rate movement, real exchange rates commonly measured as the ratio of price levels across countries also depend on the international specialization pattern (Bravo-Ortega and Giovanni 2005).

With respect to exchange rate uncertainties that are not resolved before the decisions are made, the chapter should therefore put some concern on the level of financial market development—whether actual hedging instruments as a substitute to invoicing strategies are present and actively utilized in the countries to reduce or eliminate exposure to exchange rate variations. Also, the central banks' intervention in the foreign exchange markets to smooth exchange rate variability should be considered another important element that affects the extent of exchange rate volatility.

The chapter takes into account the composition of trade—commodity and manufactured goods—by assuming that the exchange rate volatility solely affects trade in differentiated manufactured goods, meaning that commodity trade is unaffected by exchange rate volatility ($\alpha_c = 0$). However, the exchange rate volatility may, in fact, affect the level of trades, varying across sectors. There are many reasons other than the degree of homogeneity, such as the level of competition, the production scale, accessibility to hedging instruments, storability, and so forth. In the literature, exchange rate uncertainty has a more pronounced impact on agricultural trade compared with trade in chemicals and other manufactured goods (Cho, Sheldon, and McCorriston 2002), positively affects poultry exports to Thailand (Langley et al. 2000), and negatively affects vegetable and fruit flows among the Organization for Economic Cooperation and Development (OECD) countries (Karemera et al. 2010). In sum, the effect is rather commodity-specific and not uniform across individual commodities. Given that countries are striving to move toward or become specialized in producing and exporting specific products, it is interesting to also test the impact of volatility on specific individual products.

Another general comment that should be noted is the consequence of rapid economic globalization during the past few decades. The chapter does include preferential trade agreement (PTA) between each pair of countries as a dummy variable in almost all tables, but not in table 3.1, to control for the trade impact of PTA. However, it might be a poor proxy for preferential trade because the level of trade in tariff lines and tariff rates between PTA partners where preferences are imposed are likely to matter more.

The important implication from this study seems to suggest that exchange rate stabilization through, for instance, the adoption of currency or monetary union membership can help boost international trade. In contrast to the findings found in the past studies, the magnitude of the impact of exchange rate volatility on trade flows has been substantially scaled down. Although the authors confirm the trade-enhancing effect of the membership, the chapter is silent in demonstrating that the benefits of entering into membership must be weighed against the costs.

References

Bravo-Ortega, C., and J. D. Giovanni. 2005. Remoteness and real exchange rate volatility. IMF Working Paper no. WP/05/1. Washington, DC: International Monetary Fund, January.

Carlton, D. W. 1986. The rigidity of prices. *American Economic Review* 76 (4): 637–58.

Cho, G., I. M. Sheldon, and S. McCorriston. 2002. Exchange rate uncertainty and agricultural trade. *American Journal of Agricultural Economics* 84:931–42.

Dekle, R., J. Eaton, and S. Kortum. 2007. Unbalanced trade. NBER Working Paper no. 13035. Cambridge, MA: National Bureau of Economic Research, April.

Hau, H. 2002. Real exchange rate volatility and economic openness: Theory and evidence. *Journal of Money, Credit, and Banking* 34 (3): 611–30.

Hanes, C., and J. A. James. 2003. Wage adjustment under low inflation: Evidence from U.S. history. *American Economic Review* 93 (4): 1414–24.

Karemera, D., S. Managi, L. Reuben, and O. Spann. 2010. The impacts of exchange rate volatility on vegetable trade flows. *Applied Economics:* 1–10.

Langley, S. V., M. Guigale, W. H. Meyers, and C. Hallahan. 2000. International financial volatility and agricultural commodity trade: A primer. *American Journal of Agricultural Economics* 82:695–700.

Mundell, R. A. 1961. A theory of optimal currency areas. *American Economic Review* 51 (4): 657–65.

Rose, A. 2000. One money, one market: Estimating the effect of common currencies on trade. *Economic Policy* 30:7–45.

Tenreyro, S. 2003. On the trade impact of nominal exchange rate volatility. Federal Reserve Bank of Boston. Working Paper.

Comment   Mark M. Spiegel

There are many studies in the literature that have identified a large effect of exchange rate volatility on the volume of trade. For example, Frankel and Rose (2002) found a 300 percent increase in trade volume as a result of joint membership in a monetary union. This result has been challenged in a number of papers, some of which have reduced the magnitude of the effect, but the qualitative result of an economically important impact of joint membership in a monetary union has held up empirically.

Broda and Romalis take this stylized fact as their starting point, noting that these studies typically take the exchange rate process as exogenous,

Mark M. Spiegel is vice president for International Research and director of the Center for Pacific Basin Studies at the Federal Reserve Bank of San Francisco.

implying that there is no reverse causality running from the volume of trade to exchange rate volatility. However, they argue that theory would suggest that increased trade would be expected to mitigate exchange rate volatility. They introduce a model where proximate countries engage in more bilateral trade and, as a result, have more similar consumption baskets. This directly implies that their real exchange rate volatility is reduced.

They also utilize their model as a vehicle for identification of the impact of increased trade on exchange rate volatility, as real exchange rate volatility impacts trade in different goods differently in their model. In particular, they assume that changes in real exchange rate volatility do not affect commodity trade volumes.

They then confirm empirically that increased trade does reduce real exchange rate variability. They obtain point estimates in their specification that suggests that trade volumes 1 percent larger are associated with a substantial 12 percent decline in bilateral real exchange rate volatility. They get weaker results for effect of exchange rate volatility on trade. Overall, they find that controlling for reverse causality reduces the effect of real exchange rate volatility on trade from 300 percent to 10 to 25 percent.

They obtain these results through a very simple theoretical model. The model has four countries i, two on each continent. Countries on the same continent are assumed to be more proximate. There is one factor of production, L, which is inelastically supplied. Trade is always balanced, and each country receives a country-specific labor productivity shock, θ_i^{-1}. All consumers have identical Constant Relative Risk Aversion (CRRA) preferences over consumption of manufactures, M, and commodities, C, with b share of income spent on M.

Commodity C is a composite good. Each country produces a different commodity, which is identical within countries and produced by perfectly competitive firms using a constant returns to scale (CRS) technology where one unit of output produces θ_i units of L. Commodity C is produced according to a constant elasticity of substitution (CES) function, where the elasticity of substitution between two commodities is equal to

$$C = \left(\sum_{i=1}^{4} (q_i^D)^{(\sigma_c-1)/\sigma_c} \right)^{\sigma_c/(\sigma_c-1)}.$$

The manufacturing sector produces a set of differentiated products with economies of scale and monopolistic competition. Active manufacturing producers pay a per-period cost, $\alpha_1 \omega_i$, and a marginal cost of production equal to $\omega_i \theta_i$. Demand for manufacturing products is also assumed to be CES with an elasticity of substitution equal to $\sigma_m > 1$,

$$M = \left(\sum_{v \in V} (q_v^D)^{(\sigma_m-1)/\sigma_m} \, dv \right)^{\sigma_m/(\sigma_m-1)}.$$

There is no foreign direct investment, so M is sold only through exports.

In order to sell in a market, exporters must pay a "market development" fee equal to $\alpha_2 \omega_i$. The cost of transporting x_v units from e to i then satisfies

$$XC_{ei}(x_v^S) = \omega(\alpha_2 + x_v^S \theta_e).$$

Trade in both manufactures and commodities are subject to iceberg costs, which are higher for shipments on the other continent. For example, producers must ship τ_{1m} for one unit of m to arrive in another country on the same continent, but must ship τ_{2m} for one unit of m to arrive on another continent, where $\tau_{1m} < \tau_{2m}$. The iceberg cost specification for exports of commodity C are similar.

In equilibrium, commodity C is priced at marginal cost, while producers charge a constant markup for manufacturing that is higher for exports to the other continent because of increased transport costs. Solving the model, the authors demonstrate that only a fraction of manufacturers will choose to pay the market development cost and become exporters to each country. They then demonstrate that the value of exports of M from one country to another will be dependent on the share of firms that pay the fixed market development cost to export to the foreign country.

They then apply this result to the impact of real exchange rate volatility. In equilibrium more proximate countries have more similar consumption bundles. As a result, productivity shocks affect relative price levels less for more proximate countries. Increased trade costs exacerbate this discrepancy. It follows that OLS regressions of trade on exchange rate volatility, similar to those found in the literature, will be biased because they ignore this channel.

Finally, the authors take this prediction to the data. As an identification strategy, they assume that commodity trade is unaffected by exchange rate volatility, while trade in all goods have the same effect on exchange rate volatility. Then, with the usual assumptions that their specification is well-behaved, they estimate using GMM and compare their results with the benchmark of OLS methodology found in the literature.

Their OLS benchmark specification implies that a 10 percent increase in exchange rate volatility decreases trade in M by 0.7 percent, while a 10 percent increase in trade decreases exchange rate volatility 0.3 percent. However, their GMM results suggest that the effect of volatility on trade is decreased by 70 percent. This reduces the estimated currency union effect on trade from 250 percent to a much more plausible 25 percent.

Let me turn to some comments. First, I really liked this chapter, particularly the simple and intuitive model. It motivates an endogenous channel for the reverse effect of trade influencing exchange rate variability. The model makes use of the differences in the impacts of exchange rate volatility on commodities and differentiated products to obtain identifying restrictions that the authors then carefully take to the data. All in all, a quality piece of work that yields the important result that the estimated impact of currency unions on trade is far lower than the values found in the literature.

However, this is not the first paper to address the endogeneity issue. As noted by the authors, Frankel and Wei (1993) instrumented for reverse causality using the standard deviation of relative money supplies. They also find that reduced exchange rate variability has a small impact on the level of trade. Similarly, Persson (2001) uses treatment effects for the impact of joining a currency union, while Tenreyro (2007) uses proximity to a "monetary anchor" country as proxies for exchange rate variability. Again, both find minimal impact from nominal exchange rate variability on the volume of trade flows, similar to the results in this chapter.

I am most concerned about the similarity of this chapter to that of Hau (2002). As in this chapter, Hau models the consumption bundle as a function of openness. The channel is somewhat different in his paper, as more closed economies have a lower share of tradables in their consumption bundle, resulting in increased real exchange rate volatility. Hau then takes his model to the data and confirms that economically open economies have lower real exchange rate volatility. Overall, the qualitative stories and results appear quite similar to that in this chapter. The authors are careful to cite all of this existing literature, but the lack of novelty in the empirical results implies to my mind that the primary contribution of the chapter is the new model and the identification strategy used in the empirics.

When taking the model to the data, I am also concerned that the determinants of the share of manufacturers that go abroad is posited to be solely a function of relative exchange rate volatility. Even according to the strict specification in the model, the share of manufacturers that go abroad is also a function of transport costs. Now, the chapter does condition on exporter-importer fixed effects, but relative transport costs may differ empirically across commodities.

The broader literature also focuses on firm heterogeneity. There is extensive evidence that firms that export are larger and more productive. One would think that the empirical specification would attempt to account for likely differences in such characteristics beyond controlling for exporter and importer fixed effects. Are these sources of heterogeneity likely to be less time-varying than real exchange rate variability?

I also think that the imposition of a constant share of expenditure on M and C is a little restrictive. In reality, there are likely to be some opportunities to substitute between the two classes of commodities. For example, recent skyrocketing oil prices coincided with large increases in the price of fuel-efficient vehicles. If these commodities are sufficiently substitutable, the identification vehicle used could be compromised.

There are also likely to be independent channels for exchange rate variability to adversely affect trade volumes, other than the exchange rate variability channel stressed in the chapter. For example, one must also acknowledge that even though prices are likely to be flexible in the long run, there are likely to be persistent short-run price rigidities. This is outside the scope of the model, but trade is usually invoiced in some currency, and in each period some party will likely bear the risk of that invoicing. This is true even if the risk is put off to a third party. The cost of inducing an alternate party to bear this risk will also likely be increasing the severity of exchange rate volatility. As such, exchange rate volatility is likely to affect the ability to invoice in a single currency, and thereby affect economic decisions, including the pattern of trade.

I would also point out that the effects of joining a currency union may go beyond the effect of reduced exchange rate volatility. There are macroeconomic policy rules typically associated with membership in a currency union, most famously those associated with the Maastricht Treaty rules for eligibility for the European Monetary Union. Common monetary union members may also be in other associations (again the European example comes first to mind), that require policy harmonization in other dimensions; for example, labor and financial regulatory policies. These alternative channels may also increase trade volumes, leading to a possible bias to the currency union coefficient if we attribute the currency union effect to be solely a function of reduced exchange rate variability.

References

Hau, H. 2002. Real exchange rate volatility and economic openness: Theory and evidence. *Journal of Money, Credit, and Banking* 34 (3): 611–30.

Frankel, J., and S.-J. Wei. 1993. Trade blocs and currency blocs. NBER Working Paper no. 4335. Cambridge, MA: National Bureau of Economic Research, April.

Frankel, J. A., and A. K. Rose. 2002. An estimate of the effect of currency unions on trade and growth. *Quarterly Journal of Economics* 117 (2): 437–66.

Persson, T. 2001. Currency unions and trade: How large is the treatment effect? *Economic Policy* 16 (33): 433–48.

Tenreyro, S. 2007. On the trade impact of nominal exchange rate volatility. *Journal of Development Economics* 82 (2): 485–508.

4

The Consumption Terms of Trade and Commodity Prices

Martin Berka and Mario J. Crucini

4.1 Introduction

Movements in a nation's terms of trade are widely viewed as important for understanding the sources of business cycle fluctuations, the dynamics of the trade balance, and economic welfare. Backus, Kehoe, and Kydland (1994) emphasize the role of productivity movements across the United States and Europe, with each assumed to specialize in a manufactured product. In their model, an increase in domestic productivity expands output at home relative to output abroad and the terms of trade deteriorates. Simply put: a large country expanding the supply of the traded good it produces must (in equilibrium) drive down the relative price of its products on world markets. The importing country's terms of trade improves, a positive spillover. Backus and Crucini (2000) add a third region to this model; a region that specializes in oil production. When the oil region cuts back production, the relative price of oil rises, improving the terms of trade of oil producers. Output falls in the United States and Europe because oil is an intermediate input in the production of manufactured goods. The business cycle implications of this model are consistent with empirical work by Hamilton (1983) showing that oil price increases are leading indicators of U.S. recessions. Mendoza

Martin Berka is senior lecturer in economics at Massey University. Mario J. Crucini is associate professor of economics at Vanderbilt University and a research associate of the National Bureau of Economic Research.

We have benefited from the comments of our discussants Mark Spiegel and Roberto S. Mariano as well as the editors, Andrew Rose and Takatoshi Ito. Mario Crucini gratefully acknowledges the financial support of the National Science Foundation (SES-0524868). Both authors are thankful to Martin Young, Head of Department, Economics and Finance at Massey University, for supporting the visit that facilitated this collaboration.

(1995) studies the terms of trade and business cycles in an extensive cross-country panel using a partial equilibrium business cycle model where terms of trade movements are exogenous. In his theoretical setting, terms of trade shocks are analogous to lotteries with the sign and magnitude of the payout dependent upon a country's pattern of specialization across an array of internationally traded goods.

Three features handicap the practical value of most theoretical models of the terms of trade, including those mentioned previously. First, the models have too few countries. In the two-country model, it must be true that at least one of the two trading partners is large enough to alter its terms of trade. In practice, countries with this amount of market power are in the minority. Even more problematic is the fact that the terms of trade of the two countries are perfectly negatively correlated with one another since one is the inverse of the other. In contrast, the terms of trade of net oil importers tend to correlate positively with each other and negatively with those of oil exporters, particularly during periods of volatile oil prices. Second, the models have too few goods. Adding countries that specialize in production means adding goods as well. This makes the aggregate terms of trade a blunt instrument for identifying the underlying sources of terms of trade movements. This is why the empirical literature tends to focus on less-aggregated measures of the terms of trade, at a minimum: energy and nonenergy components. Third, most international trade is firm-to-firm or intrafirm (e.g., a multinational purchasing parts from a foreign subsidiary) involving intermediate inputs. In contrast, consumers purchase most of the items they consume from retailers in local markets. It may be more appropriate to think of producers and consumers interacting in segmented markets that are part of a larger equilibrium process.

This chapter conducts a forensic analysis of the sources of terms of trade variation of thirty-eight countries, over the period 1990 to 2005. What makes our analysis forensic is the use of microprice data from the Economist Intelligence Unit (EIU) to parse the variance of the aggregate terms of trade into the contributions of individual goods. The microprice data in conjunction with trade shares helps us isolate the source of a nation's terms of trade variation in the space of goods. Knowledge of trade shares and economic clout of countries or regions in export markets provides indirect evidence on the national origins of terms of trade shocks (Organization of Petroleum Exporting Countries [OPEC]'s role in the oil market, for example).

The use of retail prices in our terms of trade construct is nonstandard. It is intended to distinguish between relative prices of traded goods faced by a nation's consumers from the more conventional definition using trade prices at the border. We refer to these constructs as the *consumption terms of trade* and the *production terms of trade,* respectively. Conceptually, the consumption terms of trade is the relative price that motivates shifts in consumption demand between the home export and imports, while the production terms of trade is the relative price that influences resource allocation across the export- and import-competing sectors.

If producers and consumers face the same prices for imported and exported goods, the consumption and production terms of trade are equal and a common *terms of trade* prevails. Improvements in the terms of trade motivate domestic producers to shift resources toward the production of exports and away from imports, with consumption shifting in the opposite direction. When the terms of trade in consumption differs from the terms of trade in production, the consumption, production, and trade balance implications are altered in fundamental ways. Yet, before these implications can be understood, we need to know how much the consumption and production terms of trade differ and understand the underlying sources of those differences.

The analysis begins with the study of commodity-level retail price inflation and price level inflation for the world as a whole. This is accomplished by averaging U.S. dollar prices of individual goods and services across as many cities as available in the Economist Intelligence Unit retail price survey, the source of our consumer price data. The standard deviations of these commodity-level inflation rates range from a low of 3.7 percent to a high of 11 percent; the median is about 5 percent. Averaging these global price inflation rates across goods and services provides our world inflation estimate, which turns out to have a correlation of 0.88 with the official Organization for Economic Cooperation and Development (OECD) U.S. dollar world inflation rate. This high correlation is surprising given that the EIU sample typically comprises only one city per country, and uses a different consumption basket than official estimates. It is also reassuring in the sense that the estimate appears not to be systematically biased by these differences. Next, a variance decomposition of world inflation is performed where the contribution of each good's inflation to aggregate world inflation is estimated. Prices with relatively high variation and positive comovement with other prices in the basket will contribute more to aggregate inflation variability for the same reasons that high beta stocks contribute more than their portfolio weight to the variance of a stock price index. Individual items are found to contribute vastly different amounts to price level variability. Some of the usual suspects show up at the upper end of the distribution, such as fuels, but individual food items often display annual changes not unlike that of fuel. Qualitatively, what we see is analogous to what is already known at the national level: food and energy prices are more volatile than the typical item found in the consumption basket.

The world price series at the microeconomic level form the basis of our benchmark computations of the *consumption terms of trade at world prices*. Using microdata on trade flows, we construct import and export price indices by weighting world prices (constructed from the EIU microdata) by national import and export trade shares. The ratio of the export price index to the import price index is the terms of trade estimate. The consumption terms of trade is somewhat less volatile than the production terms of trade in levels. However, this difference is nil in growth rates, when averages across the panel of thirty-eight countries are taken. As is true of the production terms of trade, the variability of the consumption terms of trade differs vastly across countries, from a low of about 1 percent in Australia to a high of about 10 percent in Korea (in levels). Countries with high production terms of trade variability tend to have high consumption terms of trade variability in log-levels, but this is not true of growth rates. The correlation of the two measures within a country averages 0.3 for log-levels and 0.4 for growth rates. The two measures, then, are conceptually and empirically distinct.

Decompositions of the aggregate consumption terms of trade into microeconomic sources of variation at the good level is telling. The bulk of the variability for most countries in the sample is accounted for by oil, automobiles, and medicine. The role of oil in the production terms of trade has been extensively studied in the existing literature; the evidence here suggests that this feature extends to the consumption level. The fact that one need not go beyond a few key items to account for virtually all of the terms of trade variance is a more novel finding. Focusing on oil, automobiles, and medicine accounts for much of the secular swing in the consumption terms of trade over the 1990 to 2005 period in our panel. Interestingly, oil moves in an idiosyncratic fashion relative to other world prices, helping to further distinguish its role beyond its very skewed trade shares internationally.

Movements in key world prices allow a classification of thirty of the thirty-eight countries into two groups, ten countries with U-shaped terms of trade profiles (seven of these are oil exporters), and twenty countries with inverted U-shaped patterns (all are oil importers). With few exceptions, patterns outside these two groups and subtle differences within the groups are elucidated by looking at differences in the relative importance of oil, automobiles, and medicine. Ireland, for example, experiences virtually continuous improvements in the consumption terms of trade due to the pull of medicine prices on the export side serving as an effective counterweight to the drag of oil prices on the import side.

The analysis highlights the fact that what determines the marginal contribution of a good to terms of trade variability is a country's net trade share in that good or sector. Due to the extensive volume of intraindustry trade among most industrialized countries, the bulk of terms of trade risk associated with world price movements is mostly hedged via balanced trade. Isolating the sources of variation, then, requires the variance decomposition method developed here that hinges on the use of microprice data.

The final section of the chapter constructs the *consumption terms of trade at local prices* using local retail prices to measure the import and export prices rather than world prices. The trade weights remain the same as in the benchmark case. This allows the law of one price (LOP) deviations to influence the terms of trade. As one would expect, the terms of trade using local prices is typically more volatile than when world prices are used. However, the difference is surprisingly modest because the LOP deviations that distinguish world prices from local prices tend to average out across goods. The redistribution of the attribution of terms of trade variance across goods, while notable, is also modest. Mostly, the contribution of oil falls while that of medicine rises. This shift makes intuitive sense since international LOP deviations are plausibly larger for medicine than oil. This is not to say that LOP deviations are unimportant in a more general sense. Our focus on the terms of trade means we ignore most of the service sector entirely. The prices of services are known to exhibit larger and more persistent deviations from the LOP than are the prices of traded goods. It may also be true that the LOP deviations for services fail to average out across items to the extent found among traded goods, contributing to greater volatility in the aggregate real exchange rate than the consumption terms of trade.

4.2 The Terms of Trade

Consider the *production terms of trade* constructed as a constant-share-weighted average of the logarithms of export and import prices.

$$(1) \qquad q_{j,t}^p = \sum_{i=1}^{M} \gamma_{ij} p_{ij,t}^x - \sum_{i=1}^{M} \omega_{ij} p_{ij,t}^m,$$

where $p_{ij,t}^x$ is the free-on-board price of good i exported from country j, at date t and $p_{ij,t}^m$ is the price inclusive of insurance and freight imported into country j. These prices are denominated in U.S. dollars throughout the chapter. The export and import shares are γ_{ij} and ω_{ij}, respectively, and are assumed to satisfy: $\Sigma_{i=1}^{M} \gamma_{ij} = \Sigma_{i=1}^{M} \omega_{ij} = 1$. The i index is used on both the import and export side to account for the fact that countries may import and export the same good, or at least goods that are difficult to distinguish given the published data. The summation should be thought of as being over the union of all goods appearing on the export and import side of the nation's income and product accounts, with many goods entering with a zero trade weight on one side of the trade balance or the other.

Our primary interest is a more novel concept, the *consumption terms of trade*. The trade weights remain the same, but prices at the border are replaced with retail prices. The benchmark is the case in which the LOP holds across retail markets in all countries, for each good, in which case the *consumption terms of trade* is given by:

$$(2) \qquad q_{j,t}^c = \sum_{i=1}^{M} (\gamma_{ij} - \omega_{ij}) p_{i,t},$$

where $p_{i,t}$ will be computed as the average U.S. dollar price of good i, across all locations. For obvious reasons, this is defined as the *consumption terms of trade at world prices.* Note the strong implication of the assumption of common prices in all locations. The consumption terms of trade of each country is simply a different geometric weighted average of a common vector of world prices. Put differently, the world price vector forms a common basis for determining all price indices and relative prices of interest. The key insight of this level of detail is that goods in which a country has balanced trade will not contribute to the variance of the terms of trade. For example, if a country imports oil and exports coal, commodities that produce energy demanded by consumers, energy is not going to be a large part of what determines variation in that nation's terms of trade if the country has balanced trade in energy.

In the penultimate section of the chapter, this measure is compared to the *consumption terms of trade at local prices.*

$$(3) \qquad \tilde{q}^c_{j,t} = \sum_i (\gamma_{ij} - \omega_{ij}) p_{ij,t}.$$

Note that the trade shares are the same as before, but the prices are now retail prices paid by final consumers in country j, not world average prices. Note that while the exports and imports of good i have the same price in the home retail market, the retail prices of these same goods may differ across countries for various reasons.

The two measures of the terms of trade may be easily contrasted, as follows:

$$(4) \qquad \tilde{q}^c_{j,t} = q^c_{j,t} + \sum_i (\gamma_{ij} - \omega_{ij}) q_{ij,t},$$

where $q_{ij,t} = (p_{ij,t} - p_{i,t})$. In other words, the consumption terms of trade of country j at local prices equals the consumption terms of trade of country j at world prices, plus the net-trade-share-weighted average of the LOP deviations of country j where those deviations are computed relative to the world average price of each good, i.

4.3   The Data

The source of the retail price data is the Economist Intelligence Unit Worldwide Survey of Retail Prices. The sample period runs from 1990 until 2005 and spans 123 cities and 301 goods and services. As these data have now been quite extensively used elsewhere, our description is brief.[1] The value of these data in this application is that the basket contains the same items in all cities, which contrasts significantly with the practice of National Statistical Agencies, where the focus is on the goods typically consumed in a particular city. While one implication of this is that we may not match the

---

1. See, for example, Crucini and Shintani (2008), Frankel, Parsley, and Wei (2005), and Rogers (2007).

official Consumer Price Index (CPI) inflation of a city, an advantage is that we are not averaging prices of different goods across locations, which would not provide a meaningful estimate of worldwide commodity level inflation at the microeconomic level. The supplemental data we use includes very disaggregated import and export shares and official terms of trade data.

To ensure reasonably broad coverage of the consumption basket, only locations with at least 200 retail prices are included in the analysis. This restriction limits our sample to 82 of the 123 available cities, including 55 cities in 28 OECD countries and 27 non-OECD locations. These include thirteen cities in the United States, five in Australia and Germany, four in Canada, and two each in Japan, Spain, France, Italy, Switzerland, and New Zealand. The non-OECD locations include five cities in three oil-exporting countries, nine Asian and Latin American countries each, and three African countries.

Products whose prices are used in the construction of our terms of trade measure account for 21.1 percent of the expenditure found in the U.S. CPI basket. Given that the consumption share of tradables in the U.S. CPI is only about 31.8 percent, these products account for 66 percent of the tradables in the U.S. consumption basket. In terms of CPI subindices, coverage rates are: 93 percent for clothing, 72 percent for alcoholic beverages, 70 percent for food at home, 61 percent for transportation goods, 40 percent for personal care products, 24 percent for household furnishings, and 19 percent for recreation goods.

Our trade shares are drawn from the United Nations (UN) Comtrade database; specifically, the six-digit 2002 Harmonized System of import and export volumes in U.S. dollars for the year 2007. Each good in the EIU retail price survey is matched to one of these six-digit trade volumes. The sample includes members of the OECD, China, Brazil, Russia, India, several major oil exporting countries, and Asian exporters. Among these countries, our retail price data cover an average of 19 percent of imports and 18 percent of exports (we do not include re-exports or re-imports). The primary reason these numbers are not higher is that much of international trade is in intermediate goods, whereas retail purchases are mostly final goods. The import coverage ratios reach up to 30 percent for Greece, but are as low as 6 percent for Singapore, which seems due to the paucity of electronic goods in the EIU survey in the latter case. The export coverage ratios range between 77 percent for Saudi Arabia and 3.5 percent for Singapore.

4.4   World Inflation

Recall that our estimate of the *consumption terms of trade at world prices* requires estimates of world price series by good. The commodity-level inflation estimates are inflation rates, in U.S. dollars, of a particular good, i, $\Delta p_{i,t}$, averaged across all available cities in the EIU sample, indexed by j,

$$(5) \qquad \Delta p_{i,t} = N^{-1} \sum_{j=1}^{N} \Delta p_{ij,t}.$$

The number of locations varies somewhat across goods. We restrict the sample of locations to those with at least 200 price observations.

Aggregate world inflation (again, in the units of the numeraire currency, the U.S. dollar) is the average across commodities of these inflation rates,

$$(6) \qquad \Delta p_t = \frac{1}{84} \sum_{i=1}^{84} \Delta p_{i,t}.$$

The use of equal weights may be justified theoretically by the zero degree homogeneity of demand functions, in which case the interpretation is that our aggregate price level is a numeraire, not a price index.

Figure 4.1 presents the inflation series for each of the eighty-four goods used to estimate world inflation while figure 4.2 presents the aggregate inflation rate, the left-hand side of the expression. The common inflation factor across goods is obvious from a visual inspection of figure 4.1, further confirmed by the fact that the median correlation of inflation at the good and aggregate level is a remarkable 0.92.

World inflation averaged 1.7 percent over the sample period (1991 to 2005). Two years exhibited significant deflation, 1997 (–6.0 percent) and 2000 (–7.6 percent), while inflation was very high in 1994 (6.9 percent), 2003 (8.6 percent), and 2005 (6.8 percent). The correlation of this inflation measure with the official estimate of OECD inflation in U.S. dollars is 0.88.

To more fully understand the role of individual prices in the evolution of the aggregate inflation rate, we use the portfolio-inspired variance decomposition used by Crucini and Landry (2009) to study the microeconomic sources of aggregate real exchange rate variation. The variance of aggregate inflation may be expressed in terms of the covariance of aggregate inflation and good-level inflation:

$$(7) \qquad \text{var}(\Delta p_t) = \frac{1}{84} \sum_{i=1}^{84} \text{cov}(\Delta p_{i,t}, \Delta p_t).$$

Dividing through by the variance of aggregate inflation gives the variance decomposition:

$$(8) \qquad 1 = \frac{1}{84} \sum_{i=1}^{84} \beta_i.$$

The decomposition centers the distribution of the contributions of good-level inflation to aggregate inflation variability, the average beta, at unity. Thus, the average good contributes its weight to the total variance, 1/84. Goods with betas exceeding unity contribute more than the average good, while goods with betas less than unity contribute less. Since beta can be negative, a commodity may reduce aggregate inflation variability. The inter-

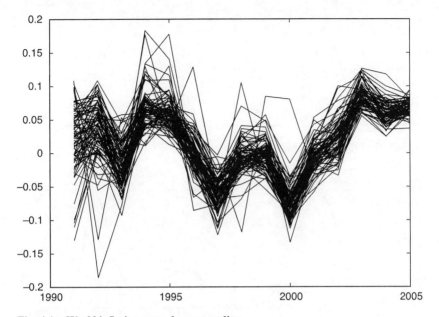

Fig. 4.1   World inflation rates, by commodity

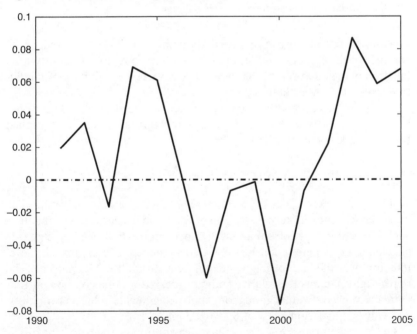

Fig. 4.2   Average (across goods) world inflation

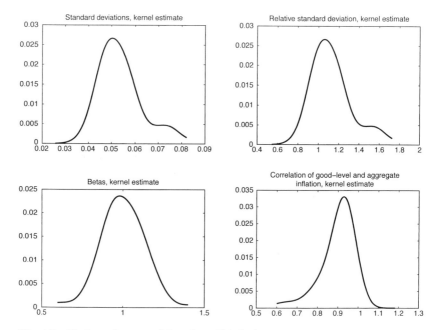

Fig. 4.3   **Variance decomposition of world inflation**

pretation is that adding such a price to the commodity basket will reduce the variance of the aggregate inflation rate. As it turns out, no commodity-level inflation in the microsample has a negative covariance with the world inflation level—the lowest beta is 0.56.

The betas may alternatively be expressed in terms of the standard deviation of commodity-level inflation relative to aggregate inflation multiplied by the sample correlation of the two:

$$(9) \qquad \beta_i = \frac{\sigma_i}{\sigma} \, \text{corr}(\Delta p_{i,t}, \Delta p_t).$$

Figure 4.3 plots kernel density estimates relating to this decomposition. The upper-left chart is the kernel estimate of the standard deviation of inflation across goods; it ranges from about 3.75 percent to about 8.68 percent (see also table 4.1). There is considerable central tendency of commodity-level inflation near the level of aggregate inflation variability, 4.75 percent. The upper-right panel is the relative standard deviation, one component that influences how individual goods contribute to aggregate inflation variability. The values range from a low of 0.79 to a high of 1.83.

The lower-left panel is the estimated distribution of the betas, the distribution of the contributions of commodity-level inflation to the variance of aggregate inflation. These average to 1 by construction, but vary considerably across goods, from a low of 0.56 for oil to a high of 1.45 for lettuce. It

Table 4.1   **Inflation variance decomposition**

Moment	Min	Mean	Median	Max
σ_i	3.75	5.40	5.26	8.68
β_i	0.56	1.00	0.99	1.45
σ_i/σ	0.79	1.14	1.12	1.83
$\text{corr}(\Delta p_{i,t}, \Delta p_t)$	0.35	0.89	0.92	0.99

may seem surprising that oil contributes the least to world inflation variability, given the attention oil prices draw in discussions of monetary policy. The conventional wisdom that oil is among the most variable prices is valid, even at the retail level: it ranks fourth among the eighty-four commodities in our inflation construct. What sets oil apart is that it has the lowest correlation with the aggregate inflation level of any commodity in our sample, at 0.35. The median correlation of good-level inflation with aggregate inflation is 0.92. The final chart is a kernel estimate of the correlation of commodity-level inflation with the aggregate inflation rate.

4.5   The Consumption Terms of Trade

Recall that the *consumption terms of trade at world prices* is defined as:

$$(10) \qquad q_{j,t}^c = \sum_{i=1}^{84} (\gamma_{ij} - \omega_{ij})p_{i,t}.$$

Figures 4.4 and 4.5 present a comparison of our estimate of the U.S. consumption terms of trade and the conventional production terms of trade, as well as the import and export price indices used in the construction of each. Because the official data is available quarterly but our retail price data is annual, we present a figure with the original official data as well as a version where we take quarterly averages to make them more comparable to our estimates. Each figure contains four charts: the left-most charts are the terms of trade, the differences between the two lines in the right-hand charts, which contain the import and export price indices.

The U.S. consumption terms of trade displays a distinctive secular swing from 1990 to 2005. This is true of ten of the twelve cases for which we have both measures of the terms of trade (not shown). The most frequent pattern, found in six of twelve cases (Finland, France, Italy, Korea, Netherlands, and the United States), is an inverted U-shape, with terms of trade improvements followed by deterioration. Four are reversed, U-shaped patterns (Australia, Canada, Denmark, and New Zealand), with the terms of trade deteriorating during the first half of the sample and then improving in the second half. Two terms of trade measures exhibit virtual continuous improvement (Switzerland and the United Kingdom). We will explore these striking similarities in the next section.

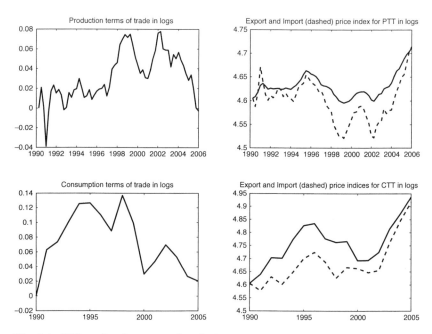

Fig. 4.4   U.S. production terms of trade (quarterly) and consumption terms of trade (annually), 1990 to 2005

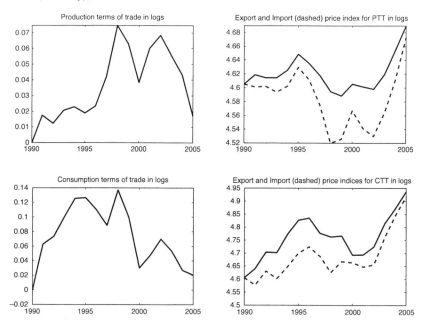

Fig. 4.5   U.S. production terms of trade and consumption terms of trade annually, 1990 to 2005

Table 4.2   Production and consumption terms of trade (world prices)

Country	Log-levels			Growth rates		
	σ_{q^p}	σ_{q^c}	$\rho_{q^p q^c}$	$\sigma_{\Delta q^p}$	$\sigma_{\Delta q^c}$	$\rho_{\Delta q^p \Delta q^c}$
Australia	9.40	1.09	0.28	4.79	0.68	0.28
Canada	3.94	1.29	0.80	2.93	0.98	0.74
Denmark	2.67	2.03	0.17	0.95	1.58	0.43
Finland	3.51	4.04	0.46	2.52	3.11	0.30
France	1.21	3.17	0.07	1.36	2.60	0.38
Italy	2.92	3.24	−0.11	2.84	2.76	0.53
Korea	16.05	9.09	0.56	3.06	6.45	0.75
Netherlands	1.72	3.00	−0.32	0.58	3.09	0.31
New Zealand	4.31	2.95	0.00	2.79	1.91	0.26
Switzerland	3.41	3.10	0.57	2.34	1.23	0.19
United Kingdom	3.02	1.30	0.77	1.78	0.62	0.02
United States	2.27	4.16	0.22	1.72	3.43	0.71
Averages	4.54	3.21	0.29	2.30	2.37	0.41

Turning to the production terms of trade, the relative price of exports to imports using prices at the border, the patterns share similarities and differences to the consumption terms of trade. The distinctive U-shapes and inverted U-shapes are largely gone. Denmark, the Netherlands, New Zealand, Switzerland, and the United Kingdom show general terms of trade improvements. Canada and Australia maintain some of their original U-shaped paths. Finland, Korea, and Italy have deteriorating terms of trade over much of the sample. The picture for France is ambiguous, due to low variability. The United States has a somewhat inverted U-shape (see figure 4.4 or 4.5), but the timing is different from what the consumption terms of trade shows.

Table 4.2 reports standard deviations of log-level and growth rates for both terms of trade measures, as well as their contemporaneous correlation. The production terms of trade tend to be more volatile than the consumption terms of trade, though this difference largely disappears in the move to growth rates, where the average standard deviation in the production terms of trade is 2.3, compared to 2.4 for the consumption terms of trade. Thus, the differences between the two is not merely less volatile prices at the retail level than at the border. The two measures move weakly together in log-levels, where the correlation is about 0.3, on average, and somewhat more strongly in growth rates, where the correlation is 0.4, on average.

Since the production and consumption terms of trade are different conceptually, it is not clear that a high correlation between them is to be expected. Moreover, the construction of the consumption terms of trade uses average international retail prices, while the production terms of trade uses prices at the customs point of entry or exit of each country. Given that deviations from the LOP have been widely documented in the literature, this is another source of difference between the two measures. The role of LOP deviations is evaluated in the penultimate section of the chapter. The question we turn to next is: what is generating the trends and fluctuations in the consumption terms of trade? As was noted earlier, there appear to be a few common secular trends shared by certain groups of countries. It will be interesting to see if those common features are driven by trade patterns and particular properties of a few key international prices, such as the price of oil.

4.5.1   Variance Decomposition

The variance of a nation's terms of trade satisfies the following equation:

$$(11) \qquad \mathrm{var}(q_{j,t}^c) = \frac{1}{84} \sum_{i=1}^{84} (\gamma_{ij} - \omega_{ij}) \mathrm{cov}(q_{j,t}^c, p_{i,t}).$$

Dividing both sides by the variance of the terms of trade gives the variance decomposition:

$$(12) \qquad 1 = \frac{1}{84} \sum_{i=1}^{84} (\gamma_{ij} - \omega_{ij}) \beta_{i,j}.$$

The betas are effectively the coefficients from a regression of the commodity-level price on the consumption terms of trade $\beta_{i,j} = \mathrm{cov}(q_{j,t}^c, p_{i,t})/\mathrm{var}(q_{j,t}^c)$.

The analysis starts by pulling back to the broadest picture, pooling all goods and locations. Figure 4.6 plots two kernel density estimates, one for the net trade share and the other for the betas. These two distributions contain all of the elements needed to decompose the variance of the terms of trade.

The net trade shares lie almost exclusively between plus and minus 5 percent. Recall that these are normalized so that for each country the import shares (and export shares) sum to unity. The net trade shares for oil are extreme outliers, averaging 40 percent across countries, while various categories of cars have an absolute net trade share that averages about 30 percent. Not surprisingly, these items will exert a disproportionately large influence on the terms of trade.

The beta distribution lies mostly between plus and minus three, with a strong central tendency toward the mean of about 0.25. Since the contribution to variance is the product of the net trade share and beta, values in the tail of the distribution are what dominate the variance decomposition of the terms of trade. To see this more clearly, it is productive to look to the details of the distribution of products of the net import share and beta: $(\gamma_{ij} - \omega_{ij}) \beta_{i,j}$.

Figure 4.7 plots the contributions to variance, the product of the net trade share and beta, for each commodity and country in our sample. Since there are eighty-four commodities and thirty-eight countries, there are 3,192 values plotted in this figure. The upper panel orders the contributions by

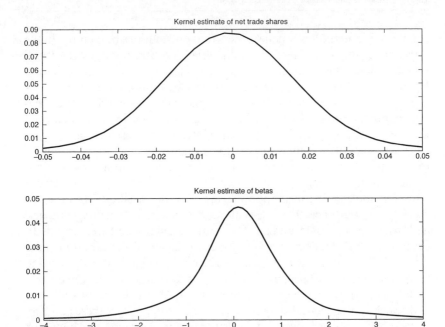

Fig. 4.6   Kernel estimates of net share shares (top chart) and betas (bottom chart), pooling all goods and countries

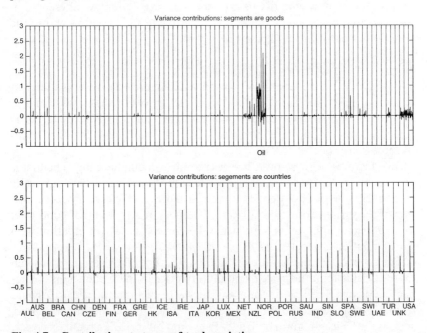

Fig. 4.7   Contributions to terms of trade variation

Notes: Top chart orders contributions by good (1 to 84), with vertical segment marking goods. Bottom chart is the same information, but with vertical segments marking countries (as labeled).

commodity, and the lower panel orders the contributions by country. In the upper panel, the vertical lines mark the variance contributions by good with points between the lines denoting a country-specific variance contribution for that good. In the lower panel, the vertical lines mark variance contribution by country with points between the lines denoting good-specific variance contributions for that country. The variance contributions organized by country will sum to unity within each interval by construction.

The clusters of extreme values in the upper chart identify commodities that contribute considerably more to terms of trade variation than the typical item. To see this more clearly, Figure 4.8 focuses on the seven most important contributors to consumption terms of trade variability. In order of ascending importance, they are: pullovers; boneless beef; luxury, compact, and large cars; medicine; and oil. The contribution from oil averages 0.6. In other words, oil alone accounts for about 60 percent of the variation in the terms of trade when we average across our thirty-eight nations. Medicine accounts for about 12 percent of terms of trade variation, the three automobile categories combined are comparable at 11 percent, while pullovers and boneless beef each account for about 2 percent. To place these numbers in perspective, the next twenty items in the ranking combine to account for the same percentage as medicine. The reader should keep in mind that the composition of influences differs across countries, which is masked by the cross-country averaging discussed here. The cross-country differences in the contribution of each commodity is visible in the variation within the commodity partitions of figure 4.8.

4.5.2   Goods Prices and the Terms of Trade

Based on the variance analysis (displayed in figure 4.8), it seems sufficient to focus on the time paths of the U.S. dollar prices of the items found to be most influential in the evolution of the aggregate consumption terms of trade: oil, automobiles, and medicine. Figure 4.9 plots the U.S. dollar prices of these five goods.

Two features of these price histories are worth emphasizing. The first is that oil prices have a large idiosyncratic component; the other four series track each other very closely. This is consistent with the earlier decomposition of the variance of world inflation. The median correlation of good-level and aggregate inflation is 0.92, while the correlation of oil inflation with world inflation is a mere 0.35.

The second striking feature of figure 4.9 is that oil prices are not much more variable than the typical commodity price in these data. This is a reflection of two facets of our analysis. First, the fact that we use prices paid by final consumers rather than prices determined in commodity exchanges such as the Chicago Board of Trade. Thus our "oil" price is a retail fuel price, not the price of a barrel of crude petroleum. The former is much less volatile than the latter at annual frequencies, in most time periods. Second, we use

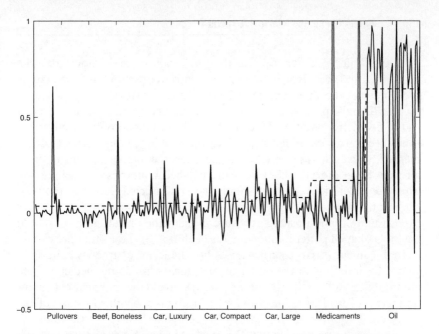

Fig. 4.8   Contribution to terms of trade variance, ordered by commodity, seven most influential goods

Notes: Dashed line marks cross-country average variance contribution by good.

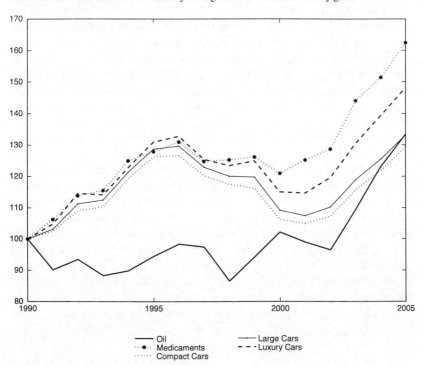

Fig. 4.9   Nominal, U.S. dollar, price indices of key traded commodities

microdata that highlights the fact that the retail prices do move around a great deal, and the aggregate CPI index tends to obscure this by averaging away much of the idiosyncratic variation. Thus, retail prices are much more volatile than the price level, which is more familiar to macroeconomists.

The distinctive paths of these prices along with their dominate contribution to the terms of trade variance for the median country, already documented, suggests a convenient link between the aggregate consumption terms of trade and a few key prices. In a nutshell, countries with net positive exposure to oil (net exporters) should have an inverted U-shaped terms of trade path, following the path of oil's price, while those with a net negative exposure in oil and positive exposure in medicine or automobiles should have a U-shaped pattern, following the evolution of these other prices.

To document this as clearly as possible, the terms of trade is built up in stages, beginning with the oil terms of trade, then adding medicine, then automobiles, and finally, everything else, to arrive at the aggregate consumption terms of trade. Figures 4.10 and 4.11 do precisely this for each of the thirty-eight countries in our sample. Figure 4.10 focuses on the eight oil exporters in our panel: Canada, Denmark, Mexico, Norway, Russia, Saudi Arabia, United Arab Emirates, and the United Kingdom. Figure 4.11 focuses on the thirty oil net importers.

The terms of trade for oil is, by definition, just the path of oil prices at the retail level (with 1990 = 0, the base year), scaled by the net trade share in fuel.[2] Thus, the dashed lines in all figures are either perfectly positively correlated with the world price of oil (for net exporters) or perfectly negatively correlated with the world price of oil (for net importers). If this was the complete picture, net exporters would experience a secular decline in their terms of trade followed by a secular rise due to oil's price movements—a U-shaped pattern. For net importers, we would see an inverted U-shaped terms of trade profile. Moreover, the dashed lines (oil terms of trade) and the solid black lines (overall terms of trade) would be the same.

While this is, of course, an oversimplification, it is the case that oil dominates the secular movements in almost every case, with net exporters of oil having U-shaped terms of trade (figure 4.10) and net importers of oil tending toward an inverted U-shaped terms of trade (figure 4.11). The pattern among net importers of oil is more complex than this stylized description, partly because their trade patterns are more complex on both the export and import side. Oil exporters, in contrast, tend to be concentrated on the export side and less concentrated on the import side. For them, complexity lies on the import side of the ledger, for the most part.

In most of the oil importing countries, the terms of trade in oil is the lower envelope of the other terms of trade constructs. What prevents the

2. The net fuel share is zero for Hong Kong, Iceland, and Luxembourg. Thus, for these three the oil terms of trade is constant, reflecting a perfect hedge.

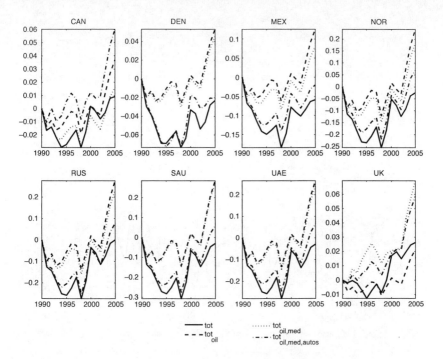

Fig. 4.10 Oil exporters: Consumption terms of trade decomposition

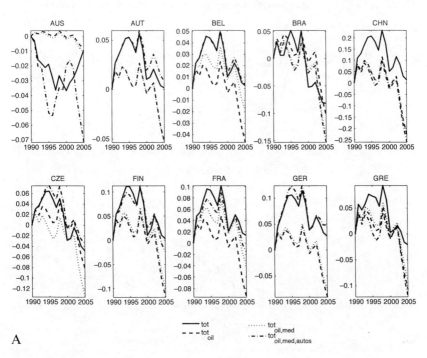

A

Fig. 4.11, Panel A Oil importers: Consumption terms of trade decomposition

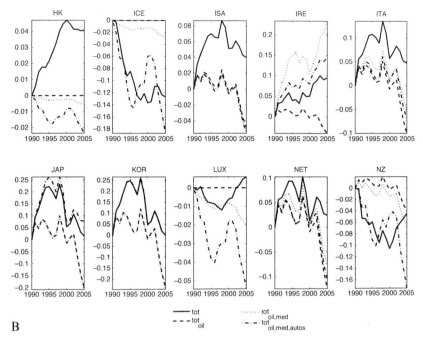

B

Fig. 4.11, Panel B   Oil importers: Consumption terms of trade decomposition

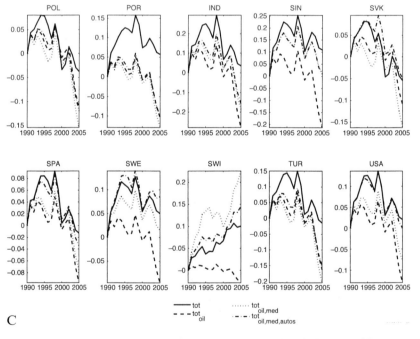

C

Fig. 4.11, Panel C   Oil importers: Consumption terms of trade decomposition

overall terms of trade from behaving similarly is that other items are fueling improvements at the same time oil is sapping the fuel. Perhaps the clearest examples of this is Ireland (figure 4.11, panel B), where oil prices contribute to terms of trade deterioration over the last third of the sample, but this is completely swamped by the improvements in the terms of trade in medicine. Moreover, during the first third of the sample, medicine and oil prices are moving in the same direction, reinforcing the improving trend in Ireland's terms of trade. Automobiles, a net import, are a drag on Ireland's terms of trade more significant even than oil (comparing the dashed lines of panel B). However, medicine is sufficient to keep the Irish terms of trade rising on trend for almost the entire sample period.

Korea is an even clearer case in point as a major oil importer and automobile exporter. Only two lines are visible; medicine and other goods play no role (this is not to say other goods are individually unimportant, as they may average out across goods). Automobile price increases buoyed Korea's terms of trade until the last third of the sample when oil prices rose relative to automobile prices. Israel is a case where oil is a significant terms of trade drag, but automobiles and medicine are not helpful in accounting for the terms of trade. Here, exploration of the sources of variation would need to go beyond these three items.

4.5.3   The Consumption Terms of Trade at Local Prices

Up to this point, we have maintained that the LOP price holds for retail prices. However, a large literature emphasizes that LOP deviations are large and persistent, particularly so when consumer prices are the focus. The *consumption terms of trade at local prices* allows for these deviations:

$$(13) \qquad \tilde{q}_{j,t}^{c} = \sum_{i}(\gamma_{ij} - \omega_{ij})p_{ij,t}.$$

Figure 4.12 presents a scatterplot of $\tilde{q}_{j,t}^{c}$ against $q_{j,t}^{c}$ pooling all cities and time periods. The asterisks are levels while the open dots are changes. The correlation of the two is 0.59 in levels and 0.45 in changes, when all locations and time periods are pooled together. As expected, the variability of the terms of trade is generally higher when local prices are used, as is evident in the increase in time series variance from 3.28 to 5.62 for the median country in levels and from 2.69 to 4.68 for growth rates.

Allowing for LOP deviations matters for some countries more than others. To see the heterogeneity across countries, table 4.3 reports the correlation of the two terms of trade measures for each country. The median correlation is 0.60, which turns out to be Finland; the range of correlations is very wide, from –0.62 for Hong Kong to 0.91 for the United States. When we examine the decomposition of the variance across goods, the reasons for the differences at the aggregate level will become clear.

Toward this end, consider how the variance of the terms of trade gets

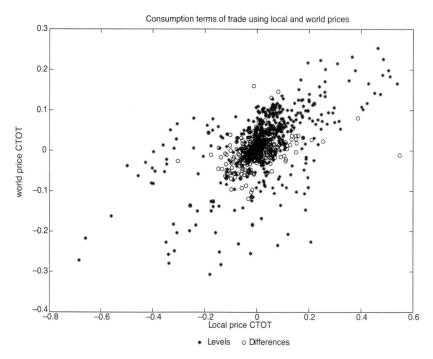

Fig. 4.12   Consumption terms of trade using local and world prices

distributed across goods based on our methodology. Taking the variance decomposition for the consumption terms of trade at local prices less the variance decomposition for the consumption terms of trade at world prices gives:

$$0 = M^{-1} \sum_{i=1}^{M} (\gamma_{ij} - \omega_{ij})(\tilde{\beta}_{i,j} - \beta_{i,j}),$$

where $\tilde{\beta}_{i,j} = \text{cov}(\tilde{q}_{j,t}^c, p_{ij,t})$ and $\beta_{i,j} = \text{cov}(q_{j,t}^c, p_{i,t})$—the β's from the variance decompositions of the two measures of the terms of trade. Since both measures use the same weights, the shift in the allocation of variance across goods boils down to a comparison of β's across goods. Goods with $\tilde{\beta}_{i,j} > \beta_{i,j}$ will have their role in the variance decomposition elevated in the move to local prices, while those with the opposite sign will be demoted in relative importance.

The fact that relatively few goods account for the bulk of the variation of the consumption terms of trade at world prices is also true for the consumption terms of trade at local prices. Table 4.4 reports the contribution to variance of the twelve most important goods for both measures of the terms of trade. The two lists have eleven common goods. Moving from world prices to local prices causes the variance contribution of oil to fall by about

Table 4.3   **Comparisons of consumption terms of trade at world and local prices**

Country	Log-levels			Growth rates		
	σ_{q^c}	$\sigma_{\bar{q}^c}$	$\rho_{q^c,\sigma_{\bar{q}^c}}$	$\sigma_{\Delta q^c}$	$\sigma_{\Delta\bar{q}^c}$	$\rho_{\Delta q^c,\Delta\bar{q}^c}$
Australia	1.09	2.81	−0.23	0.68	1.47	0.31
Austria	1.98	2.49	0.29	1.42	3.41	0.39
Belgium	1.60	1.68	0.26	1.23	1.96	0.54
Brazil	4.60	15.92	0.86	2.76	8.70	0.46
Canada	1.29	1.55	0.59	0.98	1.84	0.69
Denmark	2.03	3.34	0.71	1.58	2.42	0.56
Finland	4.04	5.16	0.62	3.11	4.67	0.62
France	3.17	4.90	−0.34	2.60	4.70	0.40
Germany	3.33	2.38	0.91	2.49	1.90	0.69
Greece	3.68	8.80	0.47	2.84	6.95	0.81
Hong Kong	1.51	4.12	−0.62	0.37	1.63	0.50
Ireland	2.76	9.90	0.70	1.49	6.55	0.62
Italy	3.24	4.01	0.29	2.76	2.03	0.65
Japan	7.79	10.10	0.32	5.47	5.14	0.69
Luxembourg	0.55	2.72	−0.58	0.27	1.19	−0.35
Mexico	4.54	12.14	0.66	3.52	7.61	0.51
Netherlands	3.00	6.31	0.79	3.09	5.69	0.48
New Zealand	2.95	6.08	−0.08	1.91	4.99	−0.07
Norway	8.04	7.52	0.37	6.39	8.08	0.38
Poland	4.11	12.94	0.53	2.92	7.40	−0.14
Portugal	3.80	6.90	0.79	2.94	3.14	0.73
Saudi Arabia	9.62	31.73	0.54	7.57	21.02	0.34
Singapore	6.12	13.45	0.68	5.63	11.13	0.55
Spain	3.56	2.63	0.81	2.58	2.88	0.68
Sweden	3.22	3.66	0.63	2.63	2.82	0.75
Switzerland	3.10	3.70	−0.21	1.23	3.27	0.11
United Arab Emirates	8.72	14.16	0.88	7.02	7.72	0.65
Turkey	5.68	12.24	0.86	4.28	10.10	0.65
United Kingdom	1.30	2.71	0.65	0.62	2.25	0.15
United States	4.16	6.79	0.91	3.43	5.77	0.92
Median	3.28	5.62	0.60	2.69	4.68	0.55
Maximum	9.62	31.73	0.91	7.57	21.02	0.92
Minimum	0.55	1.55	−0.62	0.27	1.19	−0.35

10 percent, from 0.61 to 0.51, while the contribution of medicine rises by 11 percent, from 0.13 to 0.24. This is consistent with LOP deviations tending to be larger for medicine than oil.

The last part of the analysis revisits the question of the correlation between the production terms of trade and the consumption terms of trade, now allowing for LOP deviations. Table 4.5 shows that the consumption terms of trade is now consistently more variable than the production terms of trade (eight of thirteen countries). The two are less correlated than what was found using world prices, possibly due to larger deviations from the LOP at the retail stage than at the border.

Table 4.4   **Microeconomic drivers of the consumption terms of trade**

Good	Net trade share $\gamma_{ij} - \omega_{ij}$	At world prices $\beta_{i,j}$	var_{share}	At local prices $\widetilde{\beta}_{i,j}$	$\widetilde{var}_{share}$
Oil	−0.16	−0.04	0.61	−0.60	0.51
Medicine	0.04	0.37	0.13	0.20	0.24
Large car	−0.01	0.30	0.06	0.26	0.04
Boneless beef	0.01	0.28	0.02	0.98	0.03
Wine	*	0.35	*	0.18	0.03
Pullovers	0.01	0.30	0.02	0.62	0.03
Footwear	*	0.29	0.01	0.43	0.02
Car compact	0.01	0.28	0.03	0.32	0.02
Fresh fish	0.01	0.21	*	0.36	0.01
Cheese	0.01	0.33	*	0.47	0.01
Creams	*	0.31	*	0.41	0.01
Pork chops	*	0.16	*	0.53	0.01
Apples	*	0.16	*	−0.22	*
Tomatoes canned	*	0.11	*	0.56	*
Pots	*	0.17	*	−0.13	*
Cigarettes	*	0.42	0.01	0.81	−0.01

Note: The cells report cross-country average values.
*Significant at less than 1 percent level.

Table 4.5   **Production and consumption terms of trade (local prices), 1990–2005**

Country	Log-levels σ_{q^p}	$\sigma_{\tilde{q}^c}$	$\rho_{q^p,\tilde{q}^c}$	Growth rates $\sigma_{\Delta q^p}$	$\sigma_{\Delta \tilde{q}^c}$	$\rho_{\Delta q^p, \Delta \tilde{q}^c}$
Australia	9.40	2.81	0.73	4.79	1.47	0.04
Canada	3.94	1.55	0.51	2.93	1.84	0.55
Denmark	2.67	3.34	−0.35	0.95	2.42	−0.04
Finland	3.51	5.16	0.17	2.52	4.67	0.21
France	1.21	4.90	0.25	1.36	4.70	0.09
Italy	2.92	4.01	−0.51	2.84	2.03	0.33
Netherlands	1.72	6.31	−0.41	0.58	5.69	−0.00
New Zealand	4.31	6.08	−0.17	2.79	4.99	−0.44
Switzerland	3.41	3.70	0.08	2.34	3.27	−0.06
United Kingdom	3.02	2.71	0.62	1.78	2.25	−0.09
United States	2.27	6.79	0.51	1.72	5.77	0.80
Averages	3.49	4.31	0.13	2.24	3.55	0.13

4.6   Discussion

Our findings regarding the importance of oil are reminiscent of the analysis of Backus and Crucini (2000), who documented the extraordinary extent to which oil dominated the variation in the terms of trade of major industrialized countries from the 1970s to the middle of the 1980s. The thrust of their analysis was to show how business cycle comovement evolved as the importance of oil shocks relative to total factor productivity shocks changed across historical periods and affected importers differently than exporters.

Figure 4.13 displays the quarterly data used in their paper, along with the relative price of oil in U.S. terms. By the latter, we mean the U.S. dollar spot price of crude petroleum divided by the U.S. consumer price index. In the figure, the oil price is normalized so that its standard deviation matches the standard deviation of the average of the terms of trade across all the countries in the sample (the lower-right chart displays this average terms of trade variable).

The standard deviation of the average terms of trade for the group is about 5.5 percent, while the standard deviation of the relative price of oil is an astounding 74 percent. Japan has the highest terms of trade variation at 21 percent, while Switzerland's is the most stable at 3.6 percent. Differencing both the terms of trade and the relative price of oil leave the basic implication unchanged, oil plays a large role, mostly because it has enormous variation relative to the terms of trade. The ratio of standard deviation of oil to that of the terms of trade, in levels or growth rates, is about ten.

We view our preliminary findings as pointing to a broader role than was previously thought for a small set of goods to dominate a nation's terms of trade variation. Uncovering this feature of the data would have been daunting without the novel variance decomposition employed here. The fact that oil dominates in a broad cross-section is consistent with prior work on oil and the terms of trade. The notion that individual items other than oil may

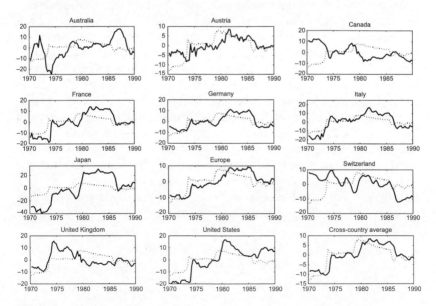

Fig. 4.13   Historical national terms of trade for major industrialized nations and the relative price of oil in U.S. terms

dominate within the cross-section of countries is novel. Moreover, it also suggests the value of organizing countries on the basis of their net export shares and a larger set of commodities than focused upon here. In focusing on the average country or group of countries, we have likely missed some important microdrivers of national terms of trade histories. It would also be interesting to consider how the influential set has evolved over time and across countries, analogous to how oil's role has been historically punctuated. Unlike oil and other commodities where comparative advantage is largely endowed, manufacturers and, increasingly, services, play a large role in trade and are likely to be more geographically footloose.

The empirical differences between the consumption and production terms of trade are compelling, though it is too early in the research program to say how they relate to the broader literature on markups and distribution costs. If the consumption terms of trade is fundamentally different than the production terms of trade, the trade balance adjustment process on the demand and supply side needs to be elaborated. The common use of one elasticity to relate prices to the trade balance condition is likely muddling consumption and production elasticities and two relative prices (the consumption and production terms of trade) rather than one.

Our results are subject to a number of important caveats. First, the Economist Intelligence Unit sample, while comprehensive, certainly does not cover the universe of consumption items and misses intermediate goods that are used by firms and not used by consumers. This, combined with the need to reconcile final goods with trade shares, leads inevitably to some errors and omissions in prices and trade weights. Second, the short sample also prevents us from backcasting our analysis before 1990, when the EIU survey was first developed. We hope to deal with some of these issues in future work, such as using the Penn World Table data to push the sample back in time. Finally, the comparisons with the official, or production terms of trade as we call it, is a crude starting point. We lack microprices at the border to conduct an analogous variance decomposition of the official terms of trade into its microeconomic determinants. Such an exercise will likely assign an important role for price variation of different brands in the terms of trade. That is, the hedging argument implicit in our use of the net trade share interacted with a single price (either the world price or the local price) becomes an imperfect hedge in the realistic cases in which the U.S. dollar inflation rates of, say, imported Mercedes and exported Infinity sedans are less than perfectly correlated. Much remains to be done.

References

Backus, D., and M. Crucini. 2000. Oil prices and the terms of trade. *Journal of International Economics* 50 (1): 185–213.

Backus, D., P. Kehoe, and F. Kydland. 1994. Dynamics of the trade balance and the terms of trade: The J-curve? *American Economic Review* 84 (1): 84–103.

Crucini, M. J., and A. Landry. 2010. Accounting for real exchange rates using microdata. Vanderbilt University. Unpublished manuscript.

Crucini, M., and M. Shintani. 2008. Persistence in law-of-one-price deviations: Evidence from micro-data. *Journal of Monetary Economics* 55 (3): 629–44.

Frankel, J., D. Parsley, and S.-J. Wei. 2005. Slow passthrough around the world: A new import for developing countries? NBER Working Paper no. 11199. Cambridge, MA: National Bureau of Economic Research, March.

Hamilton, J. 1983. Oil prices and the macroeconomy since World War II. *Journal of Political Economy* 91 (2): 228–48.

Mendoza, E. 1995. The terms of trade, the real exchange rate and economic fluctuations. *International Economic Review* 36 (1): 101–37.

Rogers, J. 2007. Monetary union, price level convergence and inflation: How close is Europe to the USA? *Journal of Monetary Economics* 54 (3): 785–96.

Comment   Roberto S. Mariano

In this chapter the authors apply a variance decomposition analysis based on microprice data to study the consumption terms of trade and the production terms of trade in various countries. The analysis starts with the study of retail price inflation and price level inflation for the world as a whole. This is done by averaging U.S. dollar prices of individual goods and services across cities covered in the EIU retail price survey. A variance decomposition of world inflation follows next—to estimate the contribution of each good to aggregate world inflation variability.

While variance decomposition analysis is a statistical tool that is well-developed and applied in the statistics and finance literature, this chapter is one of the first to utilize this methodology to undertake this study of consumption terms of trade and commodity prices. Furthermore, the level of disaggregation that the authors have chosen allows them to address detailed issues at the individual good/service level and by country. The authors adequately lay out the motivation and the basics of the approach in numerous sections of the chapter. One minor additional detail that would be useful is more information on just how the kernel density estimates of the betas and the individual good standard deviations are calculated in figure 4.3 (section 4.4).

Roberto S. Mariano is professor of economics and statistics and dean of the School of Economics at Singapore Management University, and professor emeritus of economics and statistics at the University of Pennsylvania.

The world price series at the micro level form the basis of the computations in the chapter for the consumption and production terms of trade. Import and export price indices are constructed from microdata on trade flows by weighting world prices (calculated from the EIU database) by national import and export trade shares. The ratio of the export price index to the import price index then serves as the estimate of the terms of trade.

The evidence in the chapter shows that consumption terms of trade and the production terms of trade are empirically distinct—with the former being less volatile than the latter in levels. The correlation of the two measures within a country averages 0.3 for log levels and 0.4 for growth rates.

Variance decomposition of the aggregate consumption terms of trade into microeconomic sources of variation at the good level shows that the bulk of the variability for most countries in the sample is accounted for by oil, automobiles, and medicine. The role of oil in the production terms of trade is pretty well-documented in the literature; the results in the chapter indicate that the role extends to the consumption level as well. The more novel finding in the chapter is the concentration of variance in so few items; in particular, automobiles and medicine. The movements in key world prices also allow the authors to classify most of the countries under study into two groups—those with inverted U-shaped terms of trade profiles (twenty oil-importing countries), and those with U-shaped patterns (ten countries, mostly oil exporters).

Considering their results as preliminary findings, the authors make the following conclusions. Their findings point to a broader role for a small set of goods to dominate a nation's terms of trade variation than was previously thought. The fact that oil dominates in a broad cross-section is consistent with prior work on oil and the terms of trade. The notion that individual items other than oil may dominate within the cross-section of countries is novel. This further suggests the value of organizing countries on the basis of their net export shares along a wider commodity space than oil and the few additional items focused upon in the chapter. As the authors point out, a more detailed study can be undertaken to consider how the influential set has evolved over time and across countries. This would indeed be a natural extension of the analysis that is reported in the chapter, in particular, taking into account correlations that exist over time and across countries. Finally, the authors feel that the empirical differences between the consumption and production terms of trade are compelling—but further investigation is needed to relate this result to broader related literature.

The authors conclude by pointing out a number of important caveats regarding their use of a common set of international prices to construct the consumption terms of trade, the lack of coverage in the EIU sample of intermediate goods used by firms and not by consumers, and the possibility of using other data sources such as the Penn World Table.

Comment   Mark M. Spiegel

The literature has long acknowledged that fluctuations in the terms of trade can have substantial effects. Mendoza (1995) estimates that terms of trade shocks can account for nearly one-half of observed variability in GDP. Moreover, Mendoza (1997) has shown that the variability of the terms of trade can affect savings decisions, and thereby influence long-term rates of economic growth.[1] This result implies that the welfare benefits from reducing macroeconomic uncertainty stemming from terms of trade fluctuations may be larger than the modest implications often suggested in the literature (e.g., Cole and Obstfeld 1991). As such, proper measurement of the intensity of various forms of terms of trade fluctuations is of primary interest. However, these studies fail to address the issue that terms of trade fluctuations faced by consumers are likely to differ from the commonly measured producer terms of trade fluctuations.

This chapter moves to fill this gap by introducing a concept that they label the "consumption terms of trade." They define the consumption terms of trade as the relative prices faced by home consumers for their export basket to the domestic price of their import basket. In contrast, the producer terms of trade that is commonly examined in the literature is defined as the set of relative prices faced by producers when making their export decisions. There are a variety of reasons why these two concepts need not be identical. For example, if firms price to market, consumers will face different prices than producers face in trade.

The chapter begins by examining the consumption terms of trade under the assumption that the law of one price holds. Retail price data is obtained from the Economist Intelligence Unit (EIU) worldwide survey of retail prices. The products used in the construction of the consumption terms of trade represent only 21.1 percent of the U.S. consumption basket, but 66 percent of tradables.

Using this data, the authors first conduct a variance decomposition of retail inflation versus overall price inflation, where worldwide inflation is calculated as the average inflation in goods and services by commodities. Their results using the EIU data correlate well with the OECD world inflation rate, with a correlation coefficient of 0.88.

They then calculate each good's contribution to overall inflation variability. Goods that exhibit either high variability or high degrees of comovement

Mark M. Spiegel is vice president for International Research and director of the Center for Pacific Basin Studies at the Federal Reserve Bank of San Francisco.

1. Among terms of trade shocks, the prominent role played by fluctuations in commodity values is well-documented. In particular, Hamilton (1983) finds that terms of trade fluctuations largely manifest themselves through energy price fluctuations.

with other goods are found to be more influential in determining overall inflation levels, analogous to "high beta" stocks that are more closely correlated with market equity portfolios. Indeed, they estimate such a beta measure, where betas exceeding one have greater than average contributions to inflation variability, while those with betas below one are less influential than average. They find that some goods, particularly food and energy, are particularly influential. Intuitively, the degree of influence a change in the price of a good would have on the variance of the terms of trade would be proportional to that good's net trade share and its covariance with the overall terms of trade.

To calculate the consumption terms of trade, they weight world goods prices at the retail level by national import and export trade shares, taking the pattern of trade as given and ignoring deviations from purchasing power parity. The consumption terms of trade is then the ratio of the calculated export price index to the import price index.

Using this measure, the chapter obtains a number of interesting results. First, the variation in the production terms of trade exceeds that in the consumption terms of trade, although this relationship does not hold for growth rates. Second, they find that the variability of the consumption terms of trade itself varies widely, from a low of about 1 percent in Australia to a high of 10 percent for Korea. Finally, the measured consumption terms of trade is distinct from the measured production terms of trade. These two measures are positively correlated, but with a correlation coefficient of only about 0.3 (0.4 in growth). This supports the argument that the consumption terms of trade is a distinct phenomenon from the commonly measured production terms of trade.

The authors then decompose the terms of trade into the contributions of individual goods, finding that the bulk of the observed variability in the consumption terms of trade comes from a small set of goods. In particular, they find that oil, automobiles, and medicine are notably influential. Moreover, while automobiles and medicine tend to move with the overall bundle, oil is particularly idiosyncratic relative to other goods.

Over the course of the sample, they identify two groups of countries that display U-shaped and inverse U-shaped patterns in their consumption terms of trade. The group identity of each country is primarily determined by whether it is an oil importer or exporter. One of the reasons for the strong influence of oil is that countries are fairly diversified in their production of other commodities, with net trade share for most commodities falling within the range of plus or minus 5 percent. This results in relatively balanced trade in those commodities and provides a hedge against shocks to the terms of trade. As discussed earlier, these goods that exhibit relatively balanced trade are unlikely to be influential over the variance of the terms of trade. In contrast, the net trade shares for oil and autos are much larger, 40 percent and

30 percent respectively, leaving these goods with much explanatory power in the determination of the variability of the consumption terms of trade.

The role played by oil in the determination of terms of trade variability is uniquely remarkable. Oil is found to explain over 60 percent of the variance in the terms of trade, despite the fact that oil does not display uniquely high variability. Instead, the exceptional role for oil stems from its idiosyncratic price patterns. Since oil prices follow idiosyncratic patterns historically, they end up being exceptionally influential, despite the fact that the univariate variability of oil prices is not remarkable. In contrast, retail gasoline prices do display a large amount of variability.

The authors then repeat their variance decomposition exercise for world inflation. Surprisingly, oil is found to have a low beta relative to world inflation, due primarily to its low correlation with world inflation, estimated by the authors at 0.35.

Turning to some comments, first and foremost, I would say that we learn a lot from this chapter. The authors make a compelling case that the behavior of the consumption and production terms of trade are quite different, leaving the consumption terms of trade a unique phenomenon worthy of study on its own. Since theory suggests that households would respond to the consumption terms of trade, using the production terms of trade as a proxy might lead to misleading conclusions.

We also obtain some surprising results from the variance decomposition exercises. In particular, it is surprising how low oil's contribution is to the variability of world inflation, given its extraordinarily large contribution to the variability of the consumption terms of trade. As discussed earlier, the surprising result is attributable to oil's weak correlation with overall inflation, but this would not be observable in the absence of the decomposition.

Finally, the goods decomposition reveals that a relatively small set of goods in addition to oil, particularly autos and medicine, account for almost all of the variability in the consumption terms of trade. While it was generally understood that oil had an exceptional impact, the result that the remaining variability is attributable largely in the movements of a small set of other goods is novel.

However, I also have some misgivings that should be addressed. First, the bulk of the analysis is conducted under the assumption that the law of one price holds. In practice, we observe substantial and long-lasting deviations from purchasing power parity, as in Crucini and Shintani (2008), who find that deviations from the law of one price have half-lives of eighteen months.

It therefore stands to reason that deviations from the law of one price (LOP) could influence the chapter's findings. For example, deviations from the law of one price may be one of the reasons why the chapter finds a weak correlation between the production and consumption terms of trade, as the production terms of trade are measured with domestic prices and the consumption terms of trade are measured with international prices. Also, might deviations from the LOP influence the reported variability measures? In particular, by taking averages of goods price changes might we be underestimating the variability of the consumption terms of trade?

Fortunately, the current version of the chapter addresses this issue by calculating the terms of trade at local prices. However, the results indicate that the local price terms of trade differ markedly from that used in the rest of the chapter. For example, the median correlation between the two series by country is 0.6. This leaves us uncertain about the robustness of reported other results to allowing for deviations from the LOP. In addition, the observed variability of the local price consumption terms of trade is higher, supporting our conjecture that the use of averages of goods price changes led to underestimation of the variability of the consumption terms of trade.

However, it should be acknowledged that qualitatively the main results appear similar. In particular, the authors find that the approximately 10 percent decline in the contribution of oil to the variability of the local price consumption terms of trade results in an 11 percent increase in medicine, leaving the conclusion that a small set of goods determine the variability of the consumption terms of trade intact.

Another misgiving I have with the exercise is that the trade bundle is assumed to be invariant to price changes. In the past, we have seen episodes where substantial adjustments were made to price changes; for example, subsequent to major oil price increases. At some level, this raises the question of what the terms of trade measure truly represents, as one needs to take some stand on the composition of the production and consumption bundles to conduct this kind of exercise. Also, this assumption might push the results in the opposite direction of the bias introduced into the measure of variability of the consumption terms of trade by the LOP assumption, as not allowing for changes in the consumption bundle is likely to bias the perceived variability upwards if consumers switch toward products exhibiting reduced prices.

However, I would finish with two "big picture" questions: First, is this additional terms of trade measure important, in the sense that making this distinction will substantively alter our understanding of macroeconomic phenomena? Using the single terms of trade measure, Hamilton (1983) already concluded that oil prices were very influential. Suppose that we just used the production terms of trade. We would be properly measuring the production terms of trade by definition, but, of course, the measured consumption terms of trade might be off.

I wonder how far off we would be in predicting the impact of terms of trade variability on the variability of consumption. Recall that countries are close to being hedged in most commodities. There might, however, be scope for substantive differences between, say, oil prices and consumer petroleum products, which appear to be more variable. It seems that some kind of horse race is in order.

Finally, can we push the comparison to that of core inflation more forcefully? It seems that the influential commodities are analogous to the important impacts observed by food and energy in inflation. However, we know that food and energy are typically excluded from core inflation measures that policymakers prefer to use because they detract from our ability to predict medium-term inflation.

Similarly, might there be cases where we are less interested in commodities that are influential only in the short run? That is, might we better use a "core" terms of trade volatility measure? For example, agents may smooth changes in terms of trade that are not perceived to extend at least to the medium-term. Might oil be downweighted in such a measure as well?

References

Cole, H. L., and M. Obstfeld. 1991. Commodity trade and international risk sharing. *Journal of Monetary Economics* 28:3–24.

Crucini, M. J., and M. Shintani. 2008. Persistence in law of one price deviations: Evidence from micro-data. *Journal of Monetary Economics* 55 (3): 629–44.

Hamilton, J. D. 1983. Oil and the macroeconomy since World War II. *Journal of Political Economy* 91:228–48.

Mendoza, E. G. 1995. The terms of trade, the real exchange rate, and economic fluctuations. *International Economic Review* 36 (1): 101–37.

———. 1997. Terms-of-trade uncertainty and economic growth. *Journal of Development Economics* 54:323–56.

III

"Pass-Through" of Commodity Prices to the General Price Level

5

Pass-Through of Oil Prices to Japanese Domestic Prices

Etsuro Shioji and Taisuke Uchino

5.1 Introduction

This chapter studies the effects of oil prices on domestic prices using the Japanese data. Recent dramatic surge and fall of crude oil prices have renewed interest in their effects on domestic economies. In the literature, many authors have documented (in many cases using the U.S. data) weakening impacts of oil prices on the domestic economy. For example, Hooker (1996) finds that impacts of oil prices on U.S. gross domestic product (GDR) and U.S. unemployment have diminished since the mid-1970s. Hooker (2002), which is more relevant for the current analysis, finds that the impact of oil prices on U.S. domestic inflation has been weakened significantly since around 1980. De Gregorio, Landerretche, and Neilson (2007) apply a Hooker-type approach to a number of industrialized as well as

Etsuro Shioji is a professor in the Graduate School of Economics at Hitotsubashi University. Taisuke Uchino is a researcher in the Global Centers of Excellence (COE) program, and the Research Unit for Statistical and Empirical Analysis in Social Sciences, Hitotsubashi University.

A part of this chapter is based on research we have conducted at the Research and Statistics Department of the Bank of Japan. We would like to thank members of the Department, especially Kazuo Monma, Munehisa Kasuya, and Masahiro Higo for helpful comments and discussions on our research. We also thank Takatoshi Ito for insightful suggestions at an early stage of this research. We are grateful to participants of the 20th East Asian Economic Seminar (Hong Kong, June 26–27, 2009), especially the discussants Donghyun Park and Yuko Hashimoto, as well as the organizers (Andrew Rose and Takatoshi Ito) for many invaluable comments that have led to substantial improvement of the chapter. We also would like to thank two anonymous referees for their insightful comments. Shioji thanks the "Understanding Inflation Dynamics of the Japanese Economy" project of Hitotsubashi University for financial assistance, and Uchino thanks the Hitotsubashi University Global COE Grant "Research unit for statistical and empirical analysis in social sciences."

developing countries and confirm his findings. They also estimate rolling vector autoregression (VARs) for those countries and again confirm declines in oil price pass-through. Blanchard and Gali (2007) also estimate rolling VARs for the United States. They also estimate regular VARs for the United States and other industrialized countries, splitting the sample at 1984. They arrive at similar conclusions as the previous authors.[1] Causes behind these changes have also attracted attention of macroeconomists. As Blinder and Rudd (2009) summarize succinctly, three possible candidates have been widely considered. First is increased credibility of monetary policy. Second is greater wage flexibility. Third is changing industrial structure after the two oil crises; that is, the substitution effects: firms have shifted away from energy-using technology to energy-saving technology.[2]

In this chapter, we study the Japanese data using time series analysis technique and confirm the tendency of declining pass-through of oil prices to domestic prices, for the period 1980 to 2000. We find that the main driving force behind this was different from any of the previous three. Investigation of the Japanese input-output (I-O) tables reveals that changes in the cost structure alone go a long way toward explaining the declining pass-through. In that sense, at a first glance, our results might seem consistent with the third hypothesis mentioned before. But a further analysis indicates that the main reason behind the changing cost structure was not the substitution effects or changes in relative *quantities*: it was rather changes in the relative *prices* that played a more important role. Put simply, as oil became cheaper, it became less and less important in the overall cost structure (due partially to a relatively low degree of substitution between oil and nonoil inputs), and thus the pricing behaviors of the firms became less responsive to its prices. The real factor or the substitution effect did play some role, mainly in the short

1. However, they find inexplicable impulse response results for Japan.
2. Blanchard and Gali (2007) construct a New Keynesian dynamic stochastic general equilibrium (DSGE) model that incorporates all three elements. Their simulations show that all three have contributed to declining pass-through of oil prices. Kilian (2008) mentions two other candidates: one is a U.S.-specific reason (structure of the automobile industry), which is less relevant here. The other is a difference in the fundamental causes behind different episodes of oil price surges: it is hypothesized that the oil price increase in the 2000s was a consequence of a worldwide demand increase rather than a supply shock. For inflation, however, it is not clear if demand-driven oil price increase should have either stronger or weaker effects on domestic prices. De Gregorio, Landerretche, and Neilson (2007) argue that a positive demand shock would tend to appreciate currencies of commodity importing countries, thus mitigating the effects of higher oil prices. De Gregorio, Landerretche, and Neilson (2007) also offer an additional candidate for the cause of the pass-through decline: under a low inflation environment, firms change prices less frequently and, as a consequence, oil price increases are not easily passed through to domestic prices. Another important hypothesis is that oil prices were not so influential to begin with: it was another shock that occurred around the same time period that had much impact on the economy (the most notable candidate is an excessively tight monetary policy). Refer to, for example, Bernanke, Gertler, and Watson (1997). Blinder and Rudd (2008), on the other hand, support the supply-shock view of the "Great Inflation" of the 1970s and the 1980s.

run, but its role in the long-term decline in the pass-through rate was relatively minor (with some exceptions, such as the electricity sector).[3] We also document the importance of taking into account features of the Japanese oil-related taxation system.

This chapter is a sequel to Shioji and Uchino (2009). In that paper, we estimate a series of VARs with oil prices, the exchange rate, and various indicators of domestic prices, splitting the entire sample period into two subperiods: the first is the period February 1976 to December 1989, and the second is from January 1990 to January 2009. It is reported that, as a general tendency, pass-through of both oil prices and the exchange rate tend to decline between the two periods. Then, those results are compared to the results of our study on the Japanese input-output table, though we use only information from the I-O tables only for the years 1980, 1985, 1990, 1995, and 2000 in that paper.

This chapter extends the previous analysis in three important respects. First, the VAR analysis in the previous paper does not reveal how the pass-through rate evolved over time. Note that, if changes in the cost structure were the main reason behind its decline, we might expect it to happen gradually over time, rather than experiencing a onetime structural break. To pursue this issue further, in this chapter we estimate time-varying parameter (or TVP-) VARs (refer to, for example, Kim and Nelson [1999]). It is expected that this approach will help detect timing of structural changes, and thus give us more hint on the causes behind the decline in the pass-through rate. Like in Shioji and Uchino (2009), we compare the time series estimation results with predictions from the input-output table analysis, to see how much of the observed changes in the pass-through rate can be explained by cost structure related reasons. The second feature of this chapter is that we conduct a detailed analysis of the Japanese input output table for the 2000s (years 2000 to 2010). Particularly, we pay a close attention to the mid- to late 2000s; that is, the period of a dramatic rise and a fall of oil prices.

The rest of the chapter is organized as follows. In section 5.2, we revisit evidence from the simple VARs with split samples, for the sake of comparison with our TVP-VAR results. Section 5.3 presents the results based on the TVP-VARs, and in section 5.4, we compare them with the results of the input-output table results for the period 1980 to 2000. In section 5.5, we turn our attention to the recent periods of volatile oil price movements. Section 5.6 concludes.

---

3. Among previous studies, Blanchard and Gali (2007) estimate oil shares in both consumption and production, based on the shares of oil and related products in overall *nominal* value added of the U.S. economy. They compute these shares separately for 1973 and 1997, and use them for their simulations. In that sense, they do not distinguish between relative quantities changes and relative price changes.

5.2   Evidence from Regular VARs

Japan imports over 99 percent of crude oil it uses from abroad, and is thus considered to be vulnerable to its price changes. Figure 5.1 plots three variables. First is the World Crude Oil Price Index ("OIL" for short). This variable is defined in U.S. dollars. We use the International Financial Statistics' (IFS's) "World Petroleum: Average Crude Price" monthly averages, all the way up to October 2008. As we could not obtain this data for the period November 2008 through May 2009, we supplement this with the data on North Sea Brent Spot, which are also monthly averages. Second is the Import Price Index for Crude Oil ("IPI" for short). This variable is denominated in the Japanese yen. It is taken from the Bank of Japan (BOJ)'s *Price Indexes Quarterly*. Third is Japan's Corporate Goods Price Index (overall average, "CGPI" for short), which corresponds to the wholesale price index in many other countries. The data source is the same as IPI. The figure spans the entire sample period of our analysis, namely from January 1975 to May 2009. The variables are normalized so that their values in January 1990 are all equal to 100. In figure 5.1, note that, despite the surge in the U.S. dollar price of crude oil (namely OIL) in the second half of the 2000s, its *yen* price (namely IPI) does not surpass its peak in the 1980s until late 2007. This is because the dollar-yen exchange rate changed in favor of the yen between those two periods.

It is often stated that the pass-through rate of oil prices to the domestic

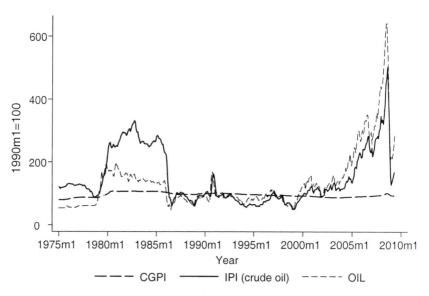

Fig. 5.1   Evolution of OIL, IPI, and CGPI, January 1990 = 100
Source: Bank of Japan and International Financial Statistics (IFS).

prices in Japan has declined in recent years. To see if this claim is verified, we estimate VARs with OIL, IPI, and Japanese domestic prices. In Shioji and Uchino (2009), we estimate VARs with multiple indices of domestic prices: some prices that represent the "upstream" of the production process, such as CGPI, as well as "downstream" prices such as CPI. This approach is in line with Ito and Sato (2008), who study exchange rate pass-through in Asian economies using VARs with multistage domestic prices. Here, instead, we estimate a series of three variables VARs, which includes just one index of domestic prices at a time. The reason is that, when estimating time varying parameter VARs (which will be introduced later), we found that we quickly run out of computer memory if we include four variables or more, with twelve lags. This choice also precludes inclusion of other potential determinants of domestic prices but, as we show in an appendix that is available upon request, our VAR results are robust to inclusion of one more variable, such as industrial production, the exchange rate, and the interest rate.

All the data is monthly. The first sample period is from February 1976 to December 1989 (often referred to as the "first half"), and the second sample period is from January 1990 to May 2009 (often referred to as the "second half").[4] Throughout this chapter (including the TVP-VAR part), the lag length is set to equal twelve. We take natural logarithms of all the variables and take their first differences. Reported impulse responses are all cumulative responses (that is, they are the responses of the log level of each variable) to one standard deviation shocks. The impulse response calculations are based on Cholesky decomposition, with OIL treated as the "most" predetermined, and IPI as the second. Although the exchange rate does not appear explicitly (unlike in Shioji and Uchino [2009]), it is implicitly included in our estimation. Note that OIL is in U.S. dollars while IPI is in the Japanese yen. Hence, the difference between the two reflects the dollar-yen exchange rate fluctuations, among other things. An advantage of this approach is that it allows us to control for other factors that influence the difference between OIL and IPI, such as changes in transportation costs and margins charged by shipping firms. To save space, we report only cases that correspond to an OIL shock, and show its own responses (i.e., responses of OIL to OIL) and responses of IPI and domestic price indices. Figure 5.2 reports the case in which the domestic price index is CGPI total. In all the panels reported in this section, the left-hand side figure is for the first half, and the right-hand side is the second half. Also, the dashed lines represent the 95 percentile bands. Panel (A) corresponds to the response of OIL to an OIL shock. Panel (B) is the response of IPI to OIL, and (C) is the response of CGPI to OIL. Note that the scales in Panels (B) and (C) are set in the same way as in (A) for

---

4. Our choices regarding the beginning of the first half and the last month of the second half are dictated by the data availability (at the time we started this research). The choice of where to break the sample is somewhat arbitrary, except that it roughly corresponds to the beginning of Japan's so-called "lost decade."

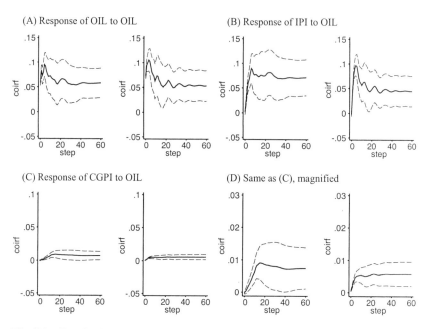

Fig. 5.2   Regular VAR with CGPI, first half (February 1976–December 1989, left) and second half (January 1990–May 2009, right)

the sake of comparison. But this makes the graphs in (C) too small. For that reason, in Panel (D), we present the same graph as in (C) but with a different scale. Note, first, that the sizes of the responses of OIL to an "own shock" are not that different between the first half and the second half (Panel (A)). This means that we can study changes in the magnitudes of pass-through primarily by looking at the responses of domestic prices.[5] Panel (B) shows that, within six months to one year, changes in the worldwide oil prices are passed onto import prices to Japan, almost fully. Panel (C) shows that the response of CGPI to OIL was small compared with its own response, even during the first half, and that it declined further in the second half (which is more evident in the magnified graphs in (D)).

One of the possible shortcomings of using the overall CGPI is that it is constructed as the weighted average of prices of goods sold at various stages of production. This means that the same oil can be counted many times: as a raw material, as a part of an intermediate input (such as naphtha, ethylene,

5. To illustrate this point, consider the following counterfactual example: suppose that the responses of CGPI to OIL are of about the same size between the two periods, but the response of OIL to itself in the second half is twice as large as that in the first half. In such a case, it is reasonable to conclude that the pass-through rate of OIL to CGPI was halved in the second half. This example suggests importance of looking at the sizes of "own responses" in drawing economic conclusions.

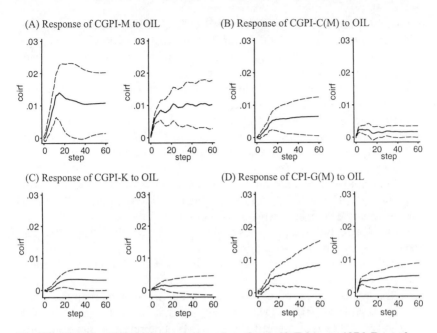

Fig. 5.3   Regular VAR with alternative prices, first half (February 1976–December 1989, left) and second half (January 1990–May 2009, right)

and polyethylene), and as a part of a final product (such as plastic hoses). To minimize this problem, we redo the analysis utilizing the information on CGPI "by stage of demand and use" published by the Bank of Japan. That is, overall CGPI is decomposed into the intermediate goods part and the final goods part. In panel (A) of figure 5.3, we use the average CGPI for intermediate products (domestically produced) only, which is denoted as "CGPI-M", and report its responses to OIL for the first half as well as the second half. Next, in panels (B) and (C) of the same figure, we further decompose CGPI for final goods between consumer goods and capital goods, as their responses are quite different. In panel (B), we use CGPI for consumer goods, restricted to manufacturing products. This means excluding agricultural and mining products, though their shares in consumer goods are quite limited (electricity, gas, and water are excluded from the beginning). We do this for the sake of comparison with CPI, which will appear in panel (D). This series is called "CGPI-C(M)" ("M" for manufacturing).[6] In panel (C),

6. The 1975 base index for CGPI-C(M) is not available, although the CGPI of overall consumption goods (hereafter CGPI-C) is available. The difference is that CGPI-C includes agricultural goods: we do have information on CGPI of those goods, but their weight in CGPI-C is not reported. In order to deal with this problem, we eliminate the effect of agricultural goods prices from CGPI-C, assuming that their weight for the 1975 base index is the same as that in the 1980 base index.

we use CGPI for capital goods, denoted as "CGPI-K." It is also interesting to compare the results for CGPI with those for CPI, to see how price changes at wholesale levels are reflected in those at retail levels. A direct comparison is difficult, however, as the two cover very different ranges of products. Most notably, CPI includes not only goods but also services. To make the comparison as meaningful as possible, in panel (D) we report results for CPI for manufactured goods, denoted as "CPI-G(M)", and compare the results with those for CGPI-C(M), in panel (B). For CGPI-C(M), CGPI-K, and CPI-G(M), we detected seasonality and influences of consumption tax rate changes. For those variables, we deseasonalize them by the Census X-11 method prior to the estimation, and also include two dummy variables, corresponding to the introduction of the consumption tax rate in April 1989 and the tax rate change in April 1997, in our estimation.

Going through different panels of figure 5.3, we see that the general tendency for declining pass-through applies to those alternative measures of domestic prices as well. We can also see that the pass-through rate tends to decline as we move downstream from CGPI-M to CGPI-C(M) and CGPI-K, with the former being more sensitive to oil price changes than the latter. Comparing panels (B) and (D), we can see that the responses of CGPI-C(M) are smaller than those for CPI-G(M). The result seems quite puzzling, because wholesale prices, which are more "upstream," are expected to be more sensitive to oil price changes than retail prices, which are more "downstream." We shall come back to this issue in the next section.

5.3   Evidence from TVP-VARs

5.3.1   Evidence for Aggregate Prices

As we have already argued, regular VARs with subsamples are not necessarily helpful in detecting timing and speed of structural changes. In this section, we employ a time varying parameter VARs (TVP-VARs) to overcome these shortcomings. Refer to the appendix at the end of the chapter for the details of the empirical method employed here. Very briefly, our method is an application of the Kalman filter, and only the reduced-form VAR coefficients are allowed to change over time.

In this section, we continue with our study on aggregate domestic prices. As in the previous section, we estimate a series of TVP-VARs with three variables, namely OIL, IPI, and a measure of domestic prices.[7] In figure 5.4, we show an example in which we use CGPI as the domestic price index. These

---

7. Both the VAR and the TVP-VAR approaches treat OIL as an endogenous variable. It might be more appropriate to model it as exogenous to the Japanese economy. We tried estimating a TVP-VARX model with OIL, IPI, and CGPI (total), in which OIL is regarded as an exogenous variable. The estimated pass-through rates were virtually the same as the ones reported later. For this reason, in the chapter, we report results from standard TVP-VARs.

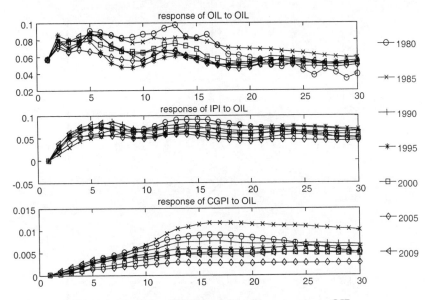

Fig. 5.4   TVP-VAR results for CGPI total: Impulse responses to OIL

are impulse responses, evaluated in January of years 1980, 1985, 1990, 1995, 2000, 2005, and 2009, of each variable to an OIL shock. We can observe that the responses of CGPI shifted upward during the 1980s, moved down sharply at the beginning of the 1990s, and then continued to decline gradually until the mid-2000s. There is a slight shift upward in 2009.

While the regular impulse responses in figure 5.4 are undoubtedly informative, it is difficult to grasp the big picture from here. This is especially so because we wish to compare the responses of the domestic price index (CGPI here) with the "own responses" at each point in time. Next, we try to summarize the vast information provided by the estimation in a little more succinct way. In figure 5.5, we report time series evolution of the estimated "pass-through rates." With respect to an OIL shock, it is defined in the following way:

(Pass-through rate of OIL at time horizon s in period t)
= (impulse response of domestic price to an OIL shock at horizon s in period t) / (impulse response of OIL to an OIL shock at horizon s in period t).

We present the results in three-dimensional graphs. On the vertical axis, we put the estimated pass-through rate as just defined. On the axis titled "year," we put time period (we show results for January of each year). On the axis labeled "horizon," we put the time horizon; that is, the number of months after the shock hits. Along the time period dimension, we start all the figures

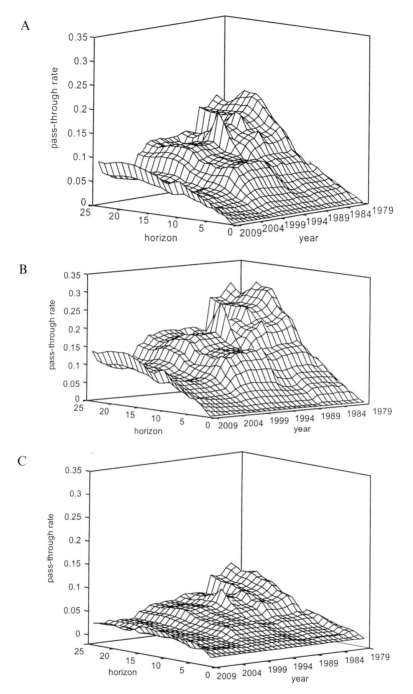

Fig. 5.5   Estimated pass-through rates for aggregate price indices: *A*, CGPI Total; *B*, CGPI-M; *C*, GPI-C(M); *D*, CGPI-K; *E*, CPI-G(M); *F*, Comparison of CGPI-C(M) and CI-G(M)

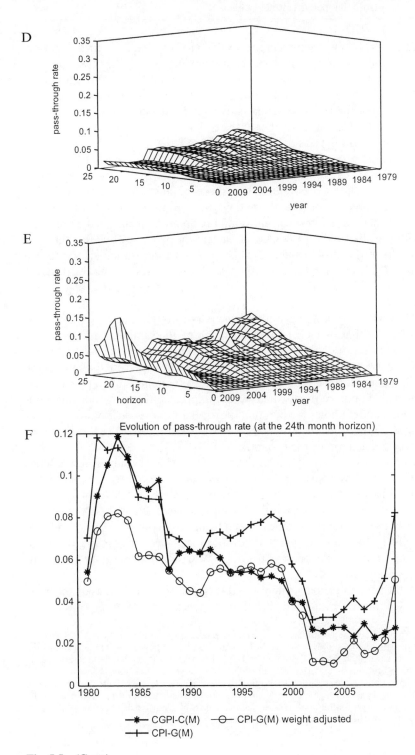

Fig. 5.5 (Cont.)

from 1979. This is because, in the TVP-VARs, the first few years of estimation results tend to be influenced by initial values set by the researcher.

In figure 5.5, panel (A), we calculate the estimated pass-through rate of OIL to CGPI total. We observe that the pass-through rate goes up at the beginning of the 1980s and comes down gradually but fast in the latter half of the 1980s. It declines further at the end of the 1990s and there is a small increase toward the end of our sample period.

In figure 5.5, panels (B), (C), (D), and (E), we report the pass-through rates for CGPI-M, CGPI-C(M), CGPI-K, and CPI-G(M), from three variable TVP-VARs that incorporate each of those variables in place of CGPI. For the latter three, we deseasonalize them prior to the estimation and regress each of them on the two consumption tax dummies mentioned before, and use the residual in the TVP-VAR. In each of the panels, we find that the basic patterns of the pass-through rate changes over time are similar to those in panel (A). The magnitudes of the pass-through rates among the different CGPI variables are in the order of CGPI-M > CGPI > CGPI-C(M) > CGPI-K.

However, we observe again that the pass-through rate for CPI-G(M) is larger than that of CGPI-C(M) for much of the sample, contrary to our prior expectation. This could be due to different weights attached to durable goods between the two indices: the weight is about 10 percent for CPI-G(M), while it is about 30 percent for CGPI-C(M). As we report in an appendix that is available upon request, when we decompose consumer goods into non-durables and durables, we find that the former is more sensitive to oil prices than the latter. Therefore, the puzzling result could be due to the difference in the composition of the two indices.[8]

In order to examine this hypothesis, we construct a counterfactual series of CPI-G(M) by adjusting the weight for durable goods to be equal to that of CGPI-C(M), and reestimate the three variable TVP-VARs. In figure 5.5, panel (F), we report the evolution of the estimated pass-through rate at the twenty-fourth month horizon derived from this hypothetical price index in the line with circles. We find that, for the most part of the sample, this pass-through rate is lower than that for CGPI-C(M). This result is consistent with our hypothesis.[9]

Although our primary interest in this chapter is in variations of the pass-through rates over time, it is also of interest to see how the levels of the pass-

8. Some argue that these differences are related to a statistical problem that might exist in the Japanese household survey on which the calculation of the CPI's weights is based (Shiratsuka 2005). It is widely recognized, not only in Japan, that the weight of household durables consumption are possibly underreported in household surveys (see ILO 2004, chapter 4).

9. Exceptions are in the latter half of the 1990s and around the year 2009. The difference in the estimated pass-through rates between the two is relatively small for the former period. The difference is larger for the last part of our sample: a possible cause is a deregulation of the retail market for gasoline (refer to the discussion in section 5.3.3).

through rates in Japan compare with those of other countries, especially in Asia. Jongwanich and Park (2008) conduct VAR analyses of oil price pass-through for various countries in Asia, for the late 1990s and the 2000s, and report their estimated pass-through rates, defined in the same way as in our study. Their estimated rate for Producer Price Index (PPI) is high for Indonesia (around 0.22), Malaysia (0.16), Singapore (0.16), and, to some extent, the People's Republic of China (PRC) (0.14). Korea, Thailand, and the Philippines are intermediate cases with about 0.07. The rate is much lower for India and Vietnam. In figure 5.5, panel (A), the pass-through rate for CGPI for the same period varies between 0.06 and 0.12 at the twenty-fourth month horizon, which places Japan below Indonesia, PRC, and so forth, and closer to Korea and Thailand. This may not be so surprising: Japan, for an industrialized country, has had a high share of manufacturing, especially heavy manufacturing such as automobiles. Even if each plant is energy efficient, it is still possible that the country as a whole is rather energy intensive. Before jumping to a conclusion, however, we would have to further investigate comparability of the data between Japan and those countries.

5.3.2   Evidence from Plastic

The previous subsection revealed declining tendencies of pass-through of oil prices to Japanese aggregate prices. This, however, could be due to a mixture of two causes: declines in responsiveness of prices of oil-related products to oil prices, and increases in the shares of nonoil-related products (and also services, in the case of the Consumer Price Index [CPI]). To extract the former effects from the data, we now turn our attention to industry-level price data and focus on products that are very oil intensive. In this subsection, we take up plastic and related products. Distilling crude oil at oil refineries produces "naphtha," among other things, and cracking naphtha in petrochemical steam crackers yields so-called "basic petrochemical products" (ethylene, propylene, benzene, etc.), and they are used to produce various types of "plastic" (polyethylene, polypropylene, etc.). Then plastic is supplied for various purposes, including production of so-called "plastic products" (such as plastic hoses). Here, we study how the pass-through rates of crude oil prices to those products at each of these stages evolved over time.

In figure 5.6, we report results from a series of three-variable TVP-VARs, with crude oil (OIL), IPI of Naphtha, and one of the product-level domestic price indices: that is, CGPI of Naphtha, CGPI of Basic Petrochemical Products, CGPI of Plastic, or CGPI of Plastic Hose. The last one is used as a representative of Plastic Products.[10] In this subsection, we use IPI of Naphtha in place of crude oil: this is because domestic prices of naphtha are

---

10. It was difficult to find many CGPI series for plastic products that go back all the way to the year 1975: we could identify only four. We use Plastic Hose as a representative example.

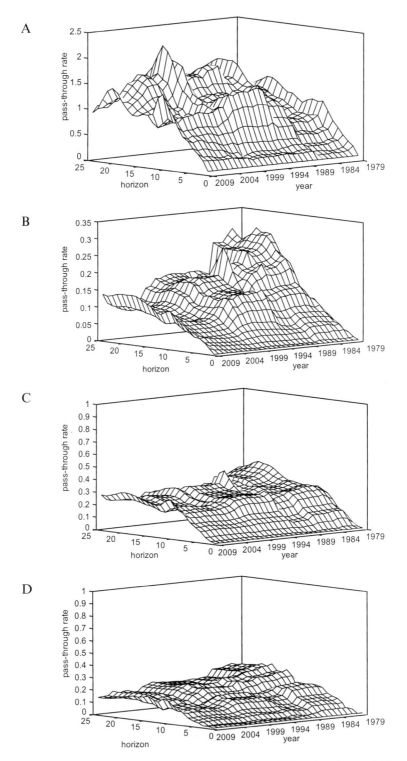

Fig. 5.6   Estimated pass-through rates for plastic and related products: *A,* Naphtha (CGPI); *B,* Petrochemical (CGPI); *C,* Plastic (CGPI); *D,* Plastic Hose (CGPI)

determined in reference to prices of imported naphtha.[11] First, note that, as we move down the panels—that is, as we move toward downstream of production stages—the estimated pass-through rate tends to decline, as one would expect. Next, we see the same general pattern that we saw in the aggregate prices: the pass-through rate increases sharply at the beginning of the 1980s, declines in the latter half of the 1980s, again toward the end of the 1990s, and we see slight increases in some cases toward the end of the sample period. The only exception to this general tendency is naphtha. The estimated pass-through rate seems too high, often exceeding 1 (note that the scale of the vertical axis is different for panel (A) only), and the pattern of the time variation is unclear. This could be because, as mentioned earlier, prices of domestically-produced naphtha are determined by some nonmarket rule.

5.3.3   Evidence from Gasoline

Next, we turn to the case of gasoline. Again, we estimate a three-variable TVP-VAR, with OIL, IPI of crude oil, and CPI of gasoline. To control for disruptive effects of a temporary reduction and a subsequent increase in the gasoline tax rate in 2008, we first regress log differences of gasoline prices on the March 2008 dummy and the April 2008 dummy. Then the residuals are included in our TVP-VAR estimation. We report the estimated pass-through rates in figure 5.7, panel (A). We observe that the level of the pass-through rate is lower compared with, for example, naphtha. Its tendency to decline over time, before starting to increase again in the late 2000s, is similar to the previous results.

As gasoline is one of few oil-intensive items that appear in both CGPI and CPI, it is of interest to study how the results differ between the two. In figure 5.7, panel (B), we compare the evolution of their estimated pass-through rates at the twenty-fourth month horizon. As expected, the pass-through rate is higher for CGPI of gasoline than its CPI counterpart for much of the sample. However, somewhat surprisingly, toward the end of the sample, the order is reversed. One possible cause of this is the deregulation of the retail market for gasoline. According to Japan Fair Trade Commission (2004), a series of deregulation put gasoline stations under strong competitive pressures. This might have made retail gasoline prices sensitive to various factors affecting oil prices. On the other hand, the supplier side of gasoline to those stations remains oligopolistic.[12]

---

11. To be more precise, this custom started formally in 1982, when the Ministry of International Trade and Industry decided that domestic prices of naphtha should be determined by adding certain margin to prices of imported naphtha, and that the price should be revised every quarter (rather than monthly).

12. Some participants at the Twentieth East Asian Seminar on Economics suggested using the gasoline tax reduction in March 2008 (and the subsequent tax hike in the following month) as a natural experiment to study how cost changes are transmitted to wholesale and retail prices. We think this incident was quite different in its nature from most of the oil price increases in history in one important aspect: the tax reduction was fully expected to be very temporary

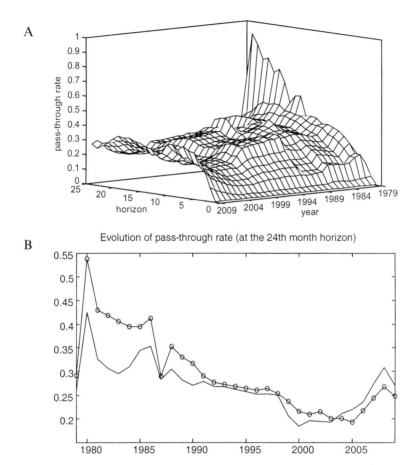

A

B

Evolution of pass-through rate (at the 24th month horizon)

-⊖-CGPI for gasoline   —— CPI for gasoline

Fig. 5.7   Estimated pass-through rate for gasoline: *A*, Estimated pass-through for Gasoline (CPI); *B*, Estimated pass-through rates, Gasoline (CGPI) and Gasoline (CPI)

5.3.4   Evidence from Electricity

Finally, we turn to the case of electricity. In this case, we estimate a three-variable TVP-VAR: with OIL; IPI of "crude oil, coal, and natural gas," and CGPI of electric power. We include natural gas, and so forth, in our definition of IPI here, because even thermal power plants use not only oil but also

---

from the beginning. As a consequence, this policy induced tremendous intertemporal substitution of gasoline usage, both before and after the tax rate changes. We think it is difficult to make inference about the effects of oil price changes, which are typically more persistent, by studying this event.

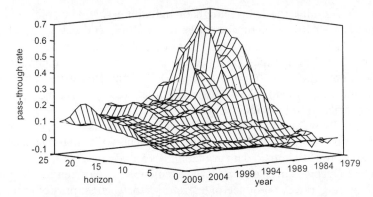

Fig. 5.8   Estimated pass-through rate for electricity

coal and natural gas.[13] The CGPI of electric power is deseasonalized by the Census X-11 Method. We report the estimated pass-through rates in figure 5.8. We can observe continuous declines in the pass-through rate, starting in the early 1980s and lasting throughout much of the sample period, until it starts to increase again toward the end of the sample.

To summarize this section, we have seen that the declines in the pass-through rates at the aggregate level are not simply a result of shrinking shares of oil-related products. Even at the level of those products, we can find declines in the pass-through rates. In the next section, we study implications from the input-output tables to see if this can be explained from changes in the cost structure of oil-related production.

5.4   Cost Structure and Pass-Through Rates: What Do the Input-Output Tables Predict? The 1980 to 2000 Period

5.4.1   Data and Methodology

In Japan, frequent changes in rules and methodology (such as classification of goods and services) make a long-run comparison of input-output structure difficult. Fortunately, the Research Institute for Economy, Trade, and Industry (RIETI) provide detailed input-output tables for years 1980, 1985, 1990, 1995, and 2000 that are directly comparable between each other (see http://www.rieti.go.jp/jp/database/d01.html [in Japanese only]). They provide tables in both nominal units and real (constant 1995 price) units. Each of the tables contains 511 rows (industries that provide inputs) and 398 columns (industries that use those inputs). Most notably, "crude oil"

13. In fact, oil has come to play a relatively minor role. We shall discuss this matter further in the next section.

appears as a single row item (though, on the column side, it is combined with natural gas). Also, different types of Petroleum Products, such as "gasoline," "naphtha," "fuel oil A," and "fuel oil B&C," all appear as separate items on the row side (though they are all combined into one on the column side). This is important, as different types of Petroleum Products receive very different tax treatments. We make suitable assumptions to expand the tables into matrices of dimensions 511 times 511.[14]

Naturally, we are also interested in the period after 2000. The next section employs more recent I-O tables, which are much smaller than the ones just explained (due to limited data availability), to study the 2000s.

The I-O tables can be used to derive predictions on a percentage response of the average price of products of a certain sector when the price of imported goods (say, of another sector) increases by 1 percent. The input-output analysis with N sectors (with trade) has the following basic structure:

$$\mathbf{x} = A\mathbf{x} + \mathbf{d} + \mathbf{e} - M(A\mathbf{x} + \mathbf{d}),$$

where $\mathbf{x}$ is the vector of output ($N \times 1$), A is the input coefficient matrix, $\mathbf{d}$ is the vector of domestic final demand ($N \times 1$), $\mathbf{e}$ is the vector of exports ($N \times 1$), and M is the matrix of import coefficients. The matrix M is a diagonal matrix whose ith diagonal element is the ratio of the imports of the ith sector to the sum of intermediate inputs from the ith sector to all the sectors plus the domestic final demand to this sector's output. From here, it is possible to derive the following pricing equation:

$$\Delta\mathbf{p} = [(I - (I - M)A)^{-1}]' \cdot A'M' \cdot \Delta\mathbf{p}^m,$$

where $\Delta\mathbf{p}$ is the vector of the rate of domestic price change in each sector and $\Delta\mathbf{p}^m$ is the vector of the rate of price change of imported goods in each sector. For example, suppose that the crude oil sector is the Jth sector and that we wish to study the impact of 1 percentage increase in imported crude oil price. Then we set the Jth element of the vector $\Delta\mathbf{p}^m$ to be 1 and all the other elements to be 0. Then each element of $\Delta\mathbf{p}$ would indicate the predicted percentage increase in the domestic prices of goods in each sector, under the assumption of flexible prices (complete pass-through at

14. The numbers of columns and rows do not coincide basically because certain row industries are combined into single column industries. In such cases, in principle, we assume that each row industry that belongs to the same column industry group has the same input structure. There are only very minor exceptions in which the correspondence between the row industries and the column industries is not perfect. For Petroleum Products, it is important to consider the fact that different types of products are subject to very different tax schemes. For this reason, we take the following approach. From the input-output table for each year, we obtain the total amount of indirect taxes paid by the whole Petroleum Products sector. From tax revenue statistics of the Ministry of Finance, we obtain the shares of taxes imposed on each type of Petroleum Product. We allocate indirect taxes to each of the subsectors according to those shares. The rest of the cost structure is assumed to be the same across those subsectors. We consider this to be a reasonable assumption, as all of those products are by-products of a single distillation process.

each production stage) and zero substitution. In essence, the previous equation provides a way to compute "oil contents" of the cost of production for each sector, which takes into account the complex input-output structure of the economy.

In this chapter, we utilize both nominal and real I-O tables to derive those predictions. The current prices table will predict the impact of an increase in oil prices given the current cost structure of each industry. The constant price table, on the other hand, will give a hypothetical prediction on what would happen if only the real cost structure changed between the current year and the benchmark year (due to, for example, substitution between oil and other types of materials), while maintaining the same relative price structure. It turns out that differences in predictions from those two types of tables are quite informative.

5.4.2   Plastic, 1980 to 2000

We start with product level analysis here. Figure 5.9, panel (A), uses the *nominal* I-O tables to derive the predicted responses of Naphtha; Basic Petrochemical Products (ethylene, propylene, benzene, etc.); Thermoplastic Resin (a type of plastic: polyethylene, polypropylene, etc.); and Plastic Products. Solid lines with cubes show the predicted percentage responses of those prices when the price of imported crude oil increases by 1 percent. Dashed lines with triangles show the predicted responses when imported prices of both crude oil and petroleum products increase by 1 percent, simultaneously. This calculation is necessary because currently Japan imports much of naphtha it needs from abroad (which was not the case in 1980). Solid lines with circles show what happens when prices of all the imported goods increase simultaneously by 1 percent. Figure 5.9, panel (B), performs an analogous study using the *real* I-O tables (1995 constant prices).

The contrast between panels (A) and (B) is striking. While the nominal I-O table predicts sharp declines in the price responsiveness over time, the real I-O table does not predict any systematic tendency. The fact that the real I-O table does not predict much decline suggests that there was not much of a real substitution away from the use of oil during this period. We had expected a decline in the importance of oil, at the very least in the comparative sense, as we had originally thought the importance of services such as distribution and finance would have increased over time: apparently, that did not happen. Yet the nominal I-O table tells a very different story. The difference comes from the fact that, during this period, there were substantial declines in prices of imported oil, naphtha, and other imports. To summarize, although there was very little substitution between quantities of different types of input, the relative importance of oil still declined substantially, basically because it became cheaper. As the lower price of oil reduced its share in overall nominal production costs, prices of those products became much less responsive to fluctuations in oil prices.

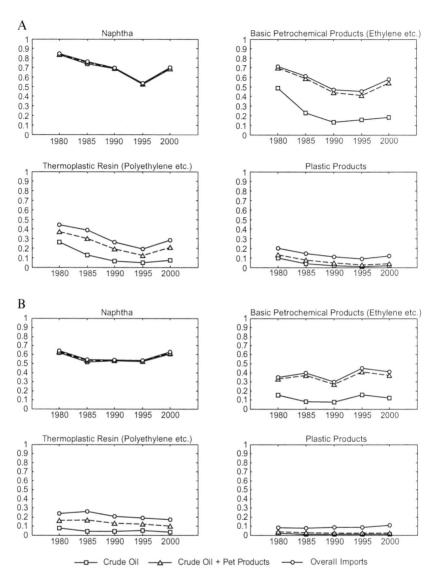

Fig. 5.9   Predicted responses of plastic and related products to OIL (etc.): *A,* Predictions from nominal I-O tables; *B,* Predictions from real I-O tables (1995 constant prices)

How do these predictions in figure 5.9, panel (A), compare with the actual estimation results in figure 5.6? Comparing the two panel by panel (looking at the long-run estimated pass-through rates at the twenty-four months horizon in each panel of figure 5.6), we learn that the cost-related factors that appear in figure 5.9, panel (A), are enough (in some cases, more than enough) to explain the declines in the estimated pass-through rates. Our conclusion for these sectors is that the pass-through rates of oil declined because oil became cheaper and thus became less important in overall costs for those sectors.

5.4.3   Gasoline, 1980 to 2000

Studying the case of gasoline in Japan requires a caution, as it is subject to heavy taxation.[15] What is important is that those taxes are *per-unit* taxes (or specific duties) as opposed to ad valorem taxes. Taxes therefore do not go up when oil prices increase. In the period of high oil prices, the share of those taxes in overall gasoline prices is relatively low. Gasoline prices will move nearly one-for-one with oil prices. When oil prices are lower, the share of taxes—the portion that does not respond to oil price fluctuations—in overall gasoline prices is higher. Gasoline prices are thus expected to be less responsive to oil price changes. Pass-through rates of oil prices are thus expected to change endogenously with the level of oil prices. This could at least partially explain the declining pass-through rate we saw in figure 5.7.

In fact, we estimate that, as of 1980, indirect taxes were equal to about 29.6 percent of total output value of gasoline. In 2000, this ratio was up to as high as 53.8 percent.

To study the magnitude of this effect, in figure 5.10, panel (A), we first compute predicted response of gasoline prices to oil prices from the nominal I-O tables, under the actual cost structure (line with cubes). Note that those predictions are fairly close to the actual estimated pass-through rates (reported in figure 5.7) for the medium and long runs. Next, we redo the calculation under the counterfactual assumption that the indirect taxes did not exist (or the taxes move proportionately with prices), and the results appear in the line with triangles. Lastly, we redo the analysis by assuming that not only domestic taxes but also tariffs did not exist (or they also move proportionately with prices), and the results appear in the lines with circles.

Comparing those lines reveals that the presence of those taxes is greatly mitigating the responsiveness of gasoline prices to oil prices. More importantly, the presence of those taxes made the responsiveness to decline substantially between 1980 and 2000. Without those taxes and tariffs, the responsiveness would have decreased by relatively small percentages. Figure 5.10, panel (B), does analogous calculation based on the real I-O table. We see that, without the effects of nominal price levels and taxes and tariffs, the responsiveness would have remained nearly constant, and high. We conclude that the declining pass-through rates in figure 5.7 could possibly be explained entirely by those two effects.

15. Also, diesel and jet fuel are heavily taxed in Japan. On the other hand, naphtha and heavy fuel oil are, relatively speaking, lightly taxed. This necessitates careful treatment of indirect taxes that we explained in the previous section.

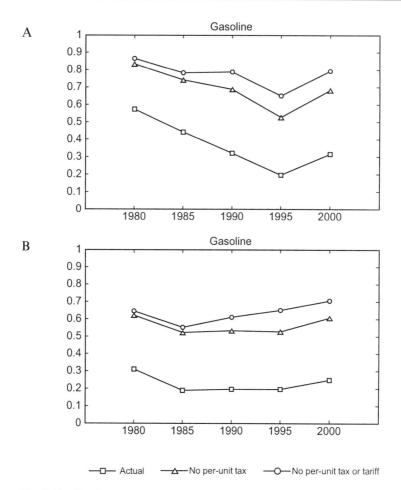

Fig. 5.10   Predicted responses of gasoline to OIL: *A*, Predictions from nominal I-O tables; *B*, Predictions from real I-O tables (1995 constant prices)

5.4.4   More on the Importance of Taxes: Diesel and "Type A Fuel," 1980 to 2000

To further investigate the importance of the presence of taxes in pass-through of oil prices, we next consider two types of petroleum products, diesel and so-called "type A fuel." Those two are almost identical in their physical nature. The difference is that diesel is heavily taxed. From the I-O tables, we estimate that the ratio of indirect taxes to diesel production was 20.0 percent for 1980 and 40.6 percent in 2000. On the other hand, type A fuel is very lightly taxed. As a consequence, usage of this type of fuel is restricted mainly to agriculture and fishery. According to our argument in the previous subsection, we should observe higher pass-through rates for type A fuel.

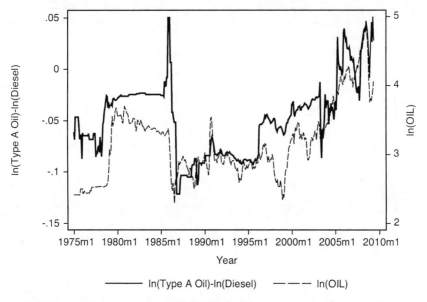

Fig. 5.11   Evolution of price differentials between type A fuel and diesel (solid line) and oil prices (dashed line), all the prices are in logs

In figure 5.11, we show the difference between prices of those two types of products (in logarithms), along with crude oil prices. It is evident that the two are highly correlated. This is an indication that type A fuel responds more strongly to fluctuations in oil prices; that is, their pass-through rates are higher.

Next, we estimate regular three variable VARs with OIL, IPI (of crude oil), and either type A fuel or diesel. Figure 5.12 shows impulse responses of type A fuel (solid line) and diesel (dashed line) to OIL for the first half of the sample (left panels) and the second half (right panels). We confirm our hypothesis that, as type A fuel is lightly taxed, it tends to be more responsive to oil price changes.

5.4.5   Electricity, 1980 to 2000

We next turn to the case of electricity. There are two electricity-related entries in the I-O table, namely electricity for business uses and self uses. We derive the predicted responses for both of them, and the results are shown in figure 5.13, panel (A), for the nominal table and panel (B) for the real table. We study the case in which only crude oil prices increase (solid lines with cubes), the case in which oil and natural gas prices increase simultaneously by 1 percent (dashed lines with triangles), and the case in which prices of all the imported goods increase at the same time (solid lines with circles). The nominal tables predict substantial declines in pass-through rates of oil. The estimated pass-through rates in figure 5.8 are close to predictions that

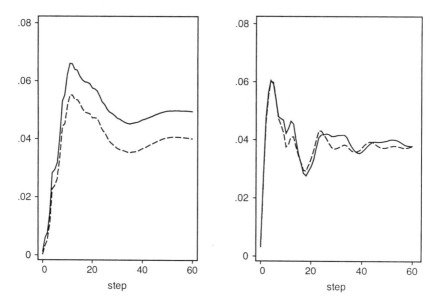

Fig. 5.12   Impulse responses to OIL of type A fuel (solid lines) and diesel (dashed lines), first half (left) and second half (right)

appear in the solid line with circles in the electricity for self use case. What is noteworthy about this sector is that, even in the predictions from the real tables, we observe some declines in the predicted responsiveness, though the declines are much smaller compared with the predictions from the nominal tables. The decline is most evident for "crude oil" in the "electricity for self use" case. It is also likely that increasing use of imported coal and construction of nuclear power plants have contributed to the general tendency. Evidently, some part of this decline, since 1990, is the emergence of natural gas as an alternative to using oil. Hence, we conclude that, for this sector, real substitution played a minor but nonnegligible role.

Another feature of the electricity industry is that prices were under strict regulations previously, but a series of deregulation took place during our sample period. This would have contributed to increase the pass-through rate. But such an increase does not seem to show up in a noticeable manner either in figure 5.8 or in 5.12.

5.4.5   Overall Consumer Goods Prices, 1980 to 2000

Through the I-O analysis in this section, we have found some important elements that could explain declining pass-through of oil prices. The most notable factor has been the relative price factor, or the relative price of oil itself. Input substitution showed up as a minor (but nonnegligible) factor for electricity. Also, the analysis for gasoline has pointed out importance of the

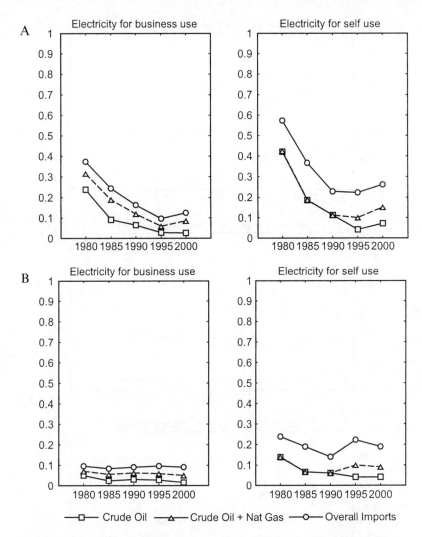

Fig. 5.13 Predicted responses of electricity to OIL (etc.): *A,* **Predictions from nominal I-O tables;** *B,* **Predictions from real I-O tables (1995 constant prices)**

tax structure. Are they important in accounting for declines in pass-through rates in overall prices as well? To answer this question, we apply the same procedure we have employed so far to all the sectors in manufacturing simultaneously. Then we take weighted averages of their predicted responses, where the weights are based on the amount consumed by households. This is an effort to derive predictions about how manufactured consumer goods prices, or CGPI-C(M), would respond to oil prices. The results are in figure 5.14. Panel (A) uses the nominal tables. Panel (B) uses the real tables. Panel

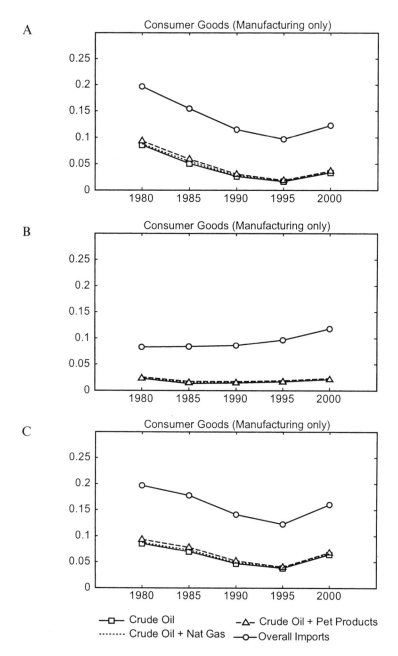

Fig. 5.14 **Predicted responses of manufactured consumer goods prices to OIL (etc.):** *A,* **Predictions from nominal I-O tables;** *B,* **Predictions from real I-O tables;** *C,* **Predictions from nominal I-O tables with no taxes or tariffs on petroleum products**

Table 5.1   **Comparisons between TVP-VAR estimates and predictions from I-O tables for consumer goods**

	TVP-VAR estimates, 12th month (1982–2002)	TVP-VAR estimates, 24th month (1982–2002)	Prediction from NOMINAL I-O tables (1980–2000)	Prediction from REAL I-O tables (1980–2000)
Percentage decline in pass-through rates	−69.0%	−78.6%	−61.3%	−7.1%

Note: Manufacturing only: percentage declines in estimated versus predicted pass-through rates to oil prices.

(C) uses the nominal tables, under the hypothetical assumption that there are no per-unit taxes or tariffs on Petroleum Products (such as gasoline, diesel, and jet fuel).

Predictions from panel (A) fit very well with the evolution of the estimated pass-through rates for CGPI-C(M) that appears in figure 5.5, panel (A). This leads us to suspect that changing cost structure could go a long way toward explaining observed declines in pass-through between 1980 and 2000. Comparison between panels (A) and (B), on the other hand, seems to indicate that the real side story plays only a minor role in the structural change that lowered pass-through during this period: we observe only slight declines in the predicted responsiveness to imported oil, petroleum products (basically naphtha), and natural gas. This indicates that, once again, the main factor behind the change was the relative price factor: as oil became cheaper, it became less relevant in the cost structure.

To give more formal and quantitative support to the aforementioned impressions, in table 5.1 we contrast our TVP-VAR estimates for the pass-through rates for CGPI-C(M), which appear in figure 5.5, panel (C), with predictions from both nominal and real I-O tables for manufactured consumer goods that appear in figure 5.13, panels (A) and (B). All the numbers are percentage declines in pass-through rates, either estimated or predicted. The first column indicates that the estimated pass-through rate at the twelfth month horizon declined, between January 1982 (its peak in figure 5.5, panel (C)) and 2002 (its bottom), by 69 percent. Likewise, the second column indicates that the estimates at the twenty-fourth month horizon declined by 78.6 percent. The third column indicates that the predicted pass-through rate from the nominal I-O table declined, between 1980 and 2000, by 61.3 percent. Hence, changes in cost structure, namely the relative price changes and relative quantity changes combined, can account for between 78 percent and 89 percent of the declines in the estimated pass-through rate, leaving only about 11 percent to 22 percent for the other factors to explain. The fourth column indicates that the predicted pass-through rate from the real I-O table declined by just 7.1 percent. Thus, the relative quantity factor played a minor role in this long-term decline in the pass-through rate.

We should acknowledge that our results do not eliminate the possibility that there was some other important factor that contributed to the declining pass-through, whose effect was largely offset by yet another factor that happened to work in the opposite direction. Nevertheless, to be able to support such a view, one would first have to specify what this force that was working in the other direction was, and this is, in our view, not an easy task.

It is also important to note that our results do not entirely deny the importance of the real factor or the relative quantity factor. We have already seen that it was quite important in the electricity sector. Figure 5.13, panel (B), indicates that the relative quantity factor was also important in the period 1980 to 1985: during this short period, the predicted pass-through rate from the real I-O table declines by as much as 40.7 percent, and this accounts for all of the decline in the prediction from the nominal I-O table. This suggests that, in reaction to the sudden increase in oil prices in the early 1980s, Japanese households and firms shifted away from oil-intensive products and inputs, temporarily. After oil prices declined in the late 1980s, however, there was some unwinding of this effect. As a result, the relative quantity effect does not contribute much to the long-run trend of declining pass-through.

Finally, panel (C) of figure 5.13 is similar to panel (A), but the decline in the predicted responsiveness to oil prices for the 1990s is milder. In fact, between 1980 and 2000, it declines by only 24.5 percent, compared to 61.3 percent in table 5.1. This confirms the importance of the presence of taxes that are imposed per volume.

5.5   Predictions from the I-O Tables, 2000 to 2007

In this section, we shift our focus to the 2000s, especially toward the end of this period. At the time of this writing, detailed input-output tables were available only up to the year 2006, which is not sufficient for our purpose. We have decided to employ basic input-output tables provided by the Ministry of Economy, Trade, and Industry, with only seventy-three sectors, which were available for years 2000 and 2003 to 2007. In these tables, "crude oil" is no longer a separate sector but is combined with natural gas. Also, all the Petroleum Products subsectors are merged into one. We expand them by making suitable assumptions to decompose a single Petroleum Products sector into nine subsectors.[16] As in the previous section, we compute

16. On the row side, for years 2004 to 2006, we have information from detailed I-O tables with 511 row sectors, and we can directly utilize information provided by these tables to decompose a single row into nine separate ones. For year 2003, we assume that the shares of each subproduct of Petroleum Products used in different sectors, in *real* units, were the same as in year 2004. We then use deflators provided for 511 sectors in each year's I-O table to convert them into nominal units. For year 2007 we utilize information from the 2006 detailed table to conduct a similar approximation. On the column side, we apply a procedure analogous to the one explained in the previous section.

predicted responsiveness of sectoral prices to prices of imported oil and natural gas.

Figure 5.15 presents the results. Panel (A) is for plastic and related products, (B) is for gasoline, (C) is for electricity, and (D) is for the weighted average of manufactured consumer goods. All of these are based on the nominal I-O tables. Lastly, panel (E) is similar to panel (D) except that it is based on the real I-O table.

Note that in all cases, with the exception of gasoline,[17] the nominal I-O tables predict increases in the responsiveness. This is natural, from what we have seen so far: as oil prices increase, the share of oil and related products in overall production cost returns to be large, and thus their prices are expected to become more sensitive to oil prices. We have seen that our TVP-VAR results indicate, in most cases, increases in the estimated pass-through rates of oil during this period: in that sense, they are consistent with the predictions from the I-O tables. However, the magnitudes are very different. Note that the nominal I-O tables predict swift and sharp increases in oil price sensitivities: for the average of manufactured consumer goods prices, predictions on oil price pass-through in figure 5.14, panel (D), increases by 58.1 percent between 2000 and 2007. On the other hand, according to numbers underlying figure 5.5, panel (C), the estimated pass-through rate at the twenty-fourth month horizon increased between 2002 (its bottom) and 2007 by only 15.7 percent, and even for the period between 2002 and 2009, the rate of increase was 32.4 percent.

What accounts for the discrepancies between the TVP-VAR results and the predictions from the nominal I-O tables? We can think of several possible explanations. First, our TVP-VAR estimation uses the fixed weight Laspeyres price indices:[18] the data for the post-2005 period uses the year 2005 weights. Thus, the rapidly increasing nominal weights of oil-related products after 2005 are not reflected in those indices. Hence, our estimation could have underestimated the true extent of the increase in the pass-through rate, which was caused by the oil price increase in this period. The second hypothesis is that, around 2000, there was a factor that pushed down the pass-through rate in Japan. One possible cause would be that the Bank of Japan's monetary policy stance suddenly gained enhanced credibility around this period. This is not totally impossible: amendment of the Bank of Japan Law in 1998 gave greater independence to Japan's central bank.[19] Another possible reason is that, due to deregulation, the labor market became more

---

17. The predicted responsiveness of gasoline is large in 2000 because our estimated tax revenue from gasoline tax for this year was small. We suspect this is related to changes in tax treatment of diesel, which is a close substitute for gasoline, that happened around this time.

18. Chained price indices were not available for long enough time periods.

19. It should also be remembered, however, that this period was a difficult time for the central bank policy. Due to the zero bound on the nominal interest rate, there was not much room to lower the interest rate. The still sluggish economy implied that rate hikes, even small ones, would have been politically vastly unpopular.

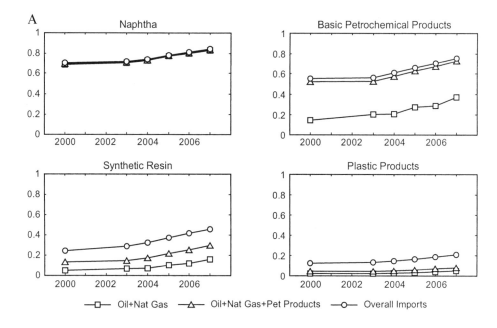

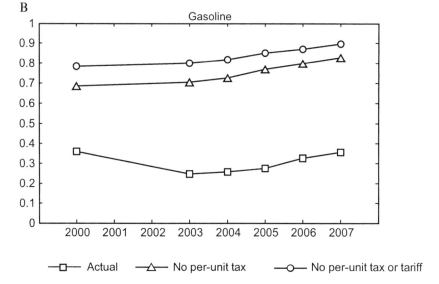

Fig. 5.15 Predicted responses for the 2000s: *A*, Plastic and related products, based on nominal I-O tables; *B*, Gasoline, under actual and hypothetical tex systems, based on nominal I-O tables; *C*, Electricity, based on nominal I-O tables; *D*, Overall manufactured consumer goods prices, based on nominal I-O tables; *E*, Overall manufactured consumer goods prices, based on real I-O tables

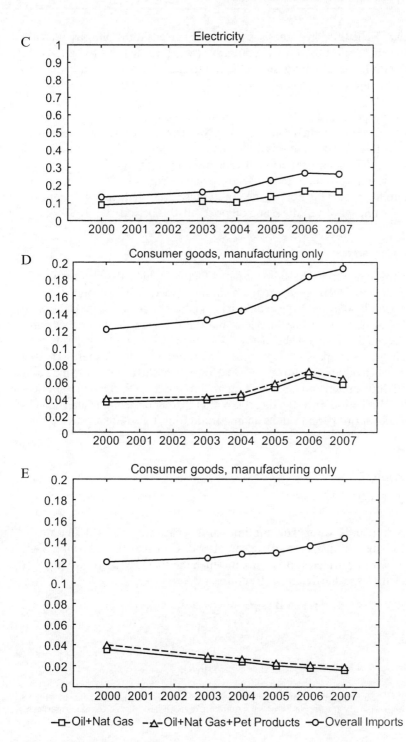

Fig. 5.15 (Cont.)

flexible.[20] The third hypothesis is that firms perceived the oil price increase during this period to be very temporary (which turned out to be the case eventually), thus did not wish to respond to such a shock. Further analyses of this period would be needed to investigate the plausibility of each of the hypotheses.

Finally, panel (E) indicates that the relative quantity factor contributed greatly to reduce predicted pass-through of oil prices. This is consistent with our previous finding that this factor was important for the short period of 1980 to 1985. In a short period of exceptionally high oil prices, households and firms adjust quite rapidly to reduce dependence on oil-intensive products and inputs. This kind of flexibility has certainly helped alleviate the negative impact of rapidly rising oil prices of this period.

5.6   Conclusions

In this chapter, we have investigated factors behind the declining pass-through rate of oil prices to Japanese domestic prices. We have found that, for the period 1980 to 2000, the main driving force behind the decline is the price level of oil itself. As oil became a less important cost item for firms, they naturally decided to respond less to its price changes. Consistently with this view, we find increasing pass-through rates in many of our TVP-VAR results for the 2000s, when oil prices were on the rise. However, at this point, those increases seem a little muted and delayed compared to the sharp increase in oil prices during this period. Investigating this matter further once more data becomes available for this period will be an important topic for future research.

Appendix
TVP-VAR

In this appendix, we explain our time varying parameter (TVP-) VAR methodology based on Kim and Nelson (1999). Consider the following VAR model with K variables and L lags, in which the coefficients are varying over time with a specific dynamic structure.

(A1) $$\mathbf{y}_t = x_t \boldsymbol{\beta}_t + e_t, \qquad t = 1,2,3,\ldots,T,$$

(A2) $$\boldsymbol{\beta}_t = \boldsymbol{\beta}_{t-1} + \upsilon_t,$$

(A3) $$e_t \sim i.i.d. N(0,R),$$

20. On the other hand, the rapid aging of the Japanese society increased the share of workers with high seniority at workplaces, which might have reduced flexibility of the labor market.

and

(A4) $$\upsilon_t \sim i.i.d. N(0, Q),$$

where the vector x_t consists of lagged dependent variables. In this specification, we assume that the coefficient vector follows a random walk, but Kim and Nelson (1999) allow a more general VAR(1) specification. The dimensions of the vectors and matrices are as follows:

$$x_t : (K \times (K \times L + 1)); \; y_t : (K \times 1); \; \beta_t : ((K \times L + 1) \times 1); \; R : (K \times K);$$
$$\text{and } Q : ((K \times L + 1) \times (K \times L + 1)).$$

We consider estimating this model by the Kalman filter. Note that, in implementing this estimation, we need to specify the matrices Q and R, known as "hyper-parameters." We introduce the following notations.

$\beta_{t|s}$: expectation of β_t, conditional on information available in period s.
$P_{t|s}$: variance-covariance matrix of β_t, conditional on information available in s.
$y_{t|s} = E(y_t \mid \Psi_s) = x_t\beta_{t|s}$: forecast of y_t given information available in period s.
$\eta_{t|s} = y_t - y_{t|t-1}$: prediction error.
$f_{t|s} = E(\eta_{t|s}^2)$: conditional variance of the prediction error.

Given the information available up to period $t-1$, the prediction rules for period t are written as follows:

$$\beta_{t|t-1} = \beta_{t-1|t-1}, \; P_{t|t-1} = P_{t-1|t-1} + Q, \text{ and } f_{t|t-1} = x_t P_{t|t-1} x_t' + R.$$

Define the prediction errors in period t as:

$$\eta_{t|t-1} = y_t - y_{t|t-1} = y_t - x_t\beta_{t|t-1}.$$

Then the updating rules are given by

(A5) $$\beta_{t|t} = \beta_{t|t-1} + K_t\eta_{t|t-1},$$

and

(A6) $$P_{t|t} = P_{t|t-1} - K_t x_t P_{t|t-1}$$

where

(A7) $$K_t = P_{t|t-1}x_t'f_{t|t-1}^{-1} \text{ (Kalman gain)}.$$

In our estimation, the initial values $\beta_{0|0}$ and $P_{0|0}$, as well as the hyper-parameters Q and R, are chosen in the following manner. We first estimate a reduced-form VAR using the entire sample. The initial coefficient vector $\beta_{0|0}$ is set to be equal to the estimated coefficient vector from this estimation, and $P_{0|0}$ is set to be equal to h_0 times the estimated variance covariance matrix of the coefficients. Denote the variance covariance matrix of the estimated coefficients as $\hat{Q}$ and the residual variance covariance matrix as $\hat{R}$. Then we impose the following relationships:

(A8) $$Q = h_Q \cdot \hat{Q},$$

and

(A9) $$R = h_R \cdot \hat{R},$$

where both h_Q and h_R are positive constants. This restriction greatly reduces the number of parameters to be chosen by the researcher.

We set $h_0 = 10$ in all the estimations reported in the text.[21] For h_Q and h_R, we try several different values and choose a combination that minimized the likelihood:

(A10) $$l(\theta) = -\frac{1}{2} \sum_{t=1}^{T} \ln((2\pi)^n |f_{t|t-1}|) - \frac{1}{2} \sum_{t=1}^{T} \boldsymbol{\eta}'_{t|t-1} f_{t|t-1}^{-1} \boldsymbol{\eta}_{t|t-1}.$$

In practice, we tried four different values (0.01, 0.025, 0.05, and 0.1) for h_Q, and three different values (0.9, 1, and 1.1) for h_R (for the latter, the value of 1 was usually preferred by the likelihood criterion).

References

Bernanke, B. S., M. Gertler, and M. Watson. 1997. Systematic monetary policy and the effects of oil price shocks. *Brookings Papers on Economic Activity* 1:91–142.
Blanchard, O. J., and J. Gali. 2007. The macroeconomic effects of oil shocks: Why are the 2000s so different from the 1970s? NBER Working Paper no. 13368. Cambridge, MA: National Bureau of Economic Research, September.
Blinder, A. S., and J. B. Rudd. 2008. The supply-shock explanation of the Great Stagflation revisited. NBER Working Paper no. 14563. Cambridge, MA: National Bureau of Economic Research, December.
———. 2009. Oil shocks redux. VOX website. Available at: http://www.voxeu.org/index.php?q=node/2786.
De Gregorio, J., O. Landerretche, and C. Neilson. 2007. Another pass-through bites the dust? Oil prices and inflation. Bank of Chile Working Paper no. 417.
Hooker, M. A. 1996. What happened to the oil price-macroeconomy relationship? *Journal of Monetary Economics* 38 (October): 195–213.
———. 2002. Are oil shocks inflationary? Asymmetric and nonlinear specifications versus changes in regime. *Journal of Money, Credit, and Banking* 34 (May): 540–61.
International Labor Office. 2004. *Consumer price index manual: Theory and practice.* United Nations: International Labour Organization.

21. It is customary to choose a relatively large number for this parameter, so that the results are not very sensitive to the initial values. We avoid reporting results for the first five years of the sample, namely 1975 to 1979, in an effort to further minimize the effects of those initial values.

Ito, T., and K. Sato. 2008. Exchange rate changes and inflation in post-crisis Asian economies: Vector autoregression analysis of the exchange rate pass-through. *Journal of Money, Credit, and Banking* 40:1407–38.

Japan Fair Trade Commission. 2004. Research note on the state of gasoline distribution (in Japanese). Tokyo: JFTC.

Jongwanich, J., and D. Park. 2008. Inflation in developing Asia: Pass-through from global food and oil price shocks. Working Paper, Asian Development Bank.

Kilian, L. 2008. The economic effects of energy price shocks. *Journal of Economic Literature* 46 (4): 871–909.

Kim, C.-J., and C. R. Nelson. 1999. *State-space models with regime-switching: Classical and Gibbs-sampling approaches with applications.* Cambridge, MA: MIT Press.

Shioji, E., and T. Uchino. 2009. Kawase reto to genyu kakaku hendo no pasu suru ha henka shitaka (Have pass-through of the exchange rate and oil prices changed?). Bank of Japan Working Paper Series no. 09-J-8.

Shiratsuka, S. 2005. Waga kuni no shouhisha bukka shisuu no keisoku gosa (Measurement errors in the Japanese Consumer Price Index). *Bank of Japan Review* no. 2005-J-14.

Comment   Yuko Hashimoto

This chapter examines the responsiveness of Japanese price indices to fluctuations in crude oil prices using various econometric methodologies. Shioji and Uchino find that the continued decline in the pass-through rate of oil prices to Japanese prices can mainly be explained by changes in cost structures in the Japanese manufacturing industry. That is, a decrease in oil prices has lowered the share of oil prices in the total cost and thus Japanese domestic prices have become seemingly less sensitive to fluctuations in oil prices. The authors conclude that this cheaper oil "price" effect explains more of the declining pass-through rate than the "quantity" effect, which captures a substitution between oil-related goods and nonoil related goods (i.e., consumers switch to nonoil goods when oil prices rise sharply and therefore retail prices are not affected as much from the oil price hike). This finding is consistent with the estimation exercise for the sample period up to May 2009 in that the recent oil price surge has clearly pushed up the pass-through rate to Japanese price indices. The authors also show that the existence of taxes has contributed to lower the gasoline and diesel price responses to oil price fluctuations. In other words, for a high oil import-dependent country like Japan, these taxes, among others, have also helped mitigate oil price shocks on retail prices and further maintain domestic price levels as relatively stable.

This chapter is very well written. The authors derive conclusions and

Yuko Hashimoto is an economist at the International Monetary Fund.

interpretations based on careful empirical examinations that are conducted over time and along the downstream of various products, using VAR, TVP-VAR, and I-O table analyses. This chapter has a huge potential to serve as material for policy discussions. Here I would like to add one suggestion for future work, probably for a completely new paper.

The authors could enrich the chapter, for example, with more in-depth analysis on Japanese firms' reaction to a supply shock based on figure 5.5. This figure shows very interesting facts: the responses of CPI-G(M) (CPI for manufacturing good) to an oil price shock at the end of sample period of 2009 are larger than responses of other intermediate products' prices. On the surface, this is not consistent with a presumption of a declining pass-through rate along with the product downstream. Usually, the pass-through rate from oil price shocks becomes smaller as weights of nonoil components (intermediate goods and nonoil items) in a price index become larger. And it is apparent in figure 5.5 that, until 2008, the pass-through rate becomes smaller for a price index of downstream products. However, only for 2009 estimations, the pass-through rate of CPI-G(M) shows a bigger jump than that of other "upper" stream price indices. Why? One possible story is the Calvo pricing; prices have been adjusted first at the retail sales level because of the uncertainty in the oil price movement in early 2009. It was unpredictable at that time how long the oil price surge would continue and to which extent the price would increase, so manufacturing industry/retail sectors did not incorporate this external shock into their prices for a while, otherwise they would lose price competitiveness (given that other firms and shops did not raise prices). However, as the oil price hike continued, these shops and firms had incurred losses and, finally, attempted to absorb this external shock by price changes. This drastic price change could have been reflected more sharply in the retail levels. So, one of the extensions of this chapter could draw implications about Japanese oil-related companies' behavior by examining reactions to an unperceived and (believed) temporally oil price shock—probably by passing it on to consumers.

Comment   Donghyun Park

I read this chapter with a great deal of interest because in 2008 I wrote a joint paper on the pass-through of the global oil and food price shocks to domestic consumer prices in nine countries in developing Asia: namely, China, India, Indonesia, Korea, Malaysia, Philippines, Singapore, Thailand, and

Donghyun Park is principal economist in the Economics and Research Department at the Asian Development Bank.

Vietnam (Jongwanich and Park 2008). We estimated a vector autoregression (VAR) model and applied a recursive Cholesky orthogonalization to identify the primitive shock in the VAR. This approach is used to model the dynamic interrelationship between the price variables in the distribution chain. The ordering and choice of variables is motivated by the idea that prices are revised at each of three different stages (i.e., imports, production, and consumption) which together make up a stylized distribution chain of goods. The model controls for external shocks and aggregate demand pressures. The model was based on McCarthy (1999), Bhundia (2002), and Duma (2008), but was extended to include food prices.

The central finding of our paper was that in developing Asia the pass-through of global food and oil price shocks to domestic prices has been limited. While there are differences across countries, the clear overall pattern is that consumers bear the cost of only a relatively small part of the increase in global food and oil prices. Our analysis implies that the various obstacles to pass-through have been strong enough in the case of developing Asian countries to seriously dilute the impact of global commodity prices on domestic inflation. In particular, the fuel and food subsidies provided by many Asian governments create a sizable wedge between global market prices and domestic prices. Furthermore, our results suggest that Asian producers are reluctant to pass on higher input costs to consumers, at least in the short run. In short, government policy and producer behavior can explain the limited pass-through in Asia.

Turning to Shioji's and Uchino's chapter itself, I thought the it was well-organized, well-written, and rigorous in terms of its empirical methodology. In particular, the major strength of the chapter is that it uses two types of analyses that complement each other very well to answer two central questions—whether there has been a significant change in the extent to which oil prices are passed through to domestic prices and, if so, what is the underlying driver of that change. First, the authors estimate a VAR model to evaluate how the pass-through rate of oil prices has evolved over time and further estimate a time-varying parameter VAR (TVP-VAR) model. The issue of central interest is whether the pass-through of oil prices to domestic prices has declined over time, and the authors' evidence clearly indicates that it has. Second, the authors look at predictions from input-output tables to study how the changing cost structure of Japanese firms affects the decline in the pass-through. A comparison of the TVP-VAR results and the I-O analysis results indicates that structural change in the cost structure explains much of the decline in the pass-through. The changing cost structure is, in turn, due primarily to the cost of lower oil prices rather than a shift from oil-intensive technology to a less oil-intensive technology.

Another major contribution of the chapter is that, in terms of the underlying sources behind the decline in the pass-through of oil prices to domestic prices, it disentangles the responsiveness of the prices of oil-related products to oil prices from increases in the share of nonoil-related products. To do so, the authors collect price data on highly oil-intensive products and examine the responsiveness of their prices to oil prices. For example, if the prices of the oil-intensive products do not respond at all to oil prices, then a higher share of nonoil-related products is likely to explain the decline in the pass-through. Plastic is a classic example of an industry that uses oil as a raw material. An additional advantage of plastic exploited by the authors is that it involves several stages of production, from crude oil to intermediate petrochemical goods to final plastic goods. Oil intensity declines with each additional stage of processing, so pass-through should be greater for products from earlier stages than later stages, and this is indeed what the evidence suggests. At a broader level, the evidence indicates that the pass-through for oil-intensive products has declined over time, just as it has for aggregate prices. This implies that the lower pass-through of aggregate prices is driven to a large extent by lower pass-through of oil-intensive products rather than smaller share of oil-related products.

I would now like to make a few constructive suggestions for improving the chapter. First, while I realize that the central objective is to analyze the evolution of oil price pass-through over time, a discussion of the pass-through coefficients themselves would be useful and interesting. As it stands, the chapter fails to provide any interpretation or discussion about the magnitude of the estimated pass-through coefficients. In particular, are the estimated pass-through coefficients in Japan relatively high or low in the international context? That is, are those coefficients higher or lower than the coefficients for other countries reported in the literature? In particular, is the pass-through higher or lower than in other countries? A comparison with other developed countries, in particular the United States, and other oil-importing Asian countries would be especially illuminating. To the extent that the pass-through in Japan is noticeably high or low in the international context, a discussion of the underlying explanation would be instructive. My conjecture is that Japan's pass-through is relatively low due to superior efficiency in use of oil.

Second, the chapter would do well to provide a more in-depth discussion of the impact of government policies on the pass-through. In the case of developing Asia, the presence of sizable government subsidies goes a long way toward explaining the limited pass-through of global oil prices to domestic consumer prices, even in the face of oil shocks which has led to sharp escalation of oil prices. The authors rightfully point out that in the case of Japan the tax system exerts a major negative impact on the pass-through of oil prices to domestic prices, but the authors can perhaps provide some quantitative estimates of the reduction in the pass-through due to the tax system. Also, some discussion of the differential impact of the tax system on producer prices and consumer prices is warranted. Some oil-related products (e.g., gasoline), may be used primarily by consumers, while others may be used primarily by producers, so that taxes on such products will have a bigger impact on the pass-through to consumer prices.

Third, at a general level, it would be better to distinguish more clearly between aggregate producer prices and aggregate consumer prices in the discussion of results. In our analysis of pass-through in developing Asia, we find that pass-through is significantly higher for producer prices than for consumer prices. This suggests that producers are reluctant to pass on higher oil prices to consumers when they view such higher prices as temporary. In fact, along with government subsidies for consumers, the failure of producers to pass on higher costs to producers is one of the two major reasons for the low pass-through to consumer prices. The study would benefit from exploring the extent to which Japanese producers pass on higher oil prices to consumers.

Fourth, the VAR model used in the empirical analysis fails to adequately control for the other determinants of inflation. Oil prices are certainly a potentially significant determinant of inflation but there are many other potential determinants. In particular, aggregate demand pressures arising from expansionary monetary policy and other demand shocks are not controlled for in the model. The omission of other inflation drivers may compromise the robustness of the main finding—a decline in the oil price pass-through over time. In our analysis of developing Asia, we proxy aggregate demand by the output gap, which is the gap between actual and potential output or the level of output consistent with nonaccelerating inflation. Actual output is real GDP while potential output is proxied by the trend of real GDP, derived from the Hodrick-Prescott filter. Inflation may be subdued due to weak aggregate demand even though oil prices are rising, and this would show up as low pass-through even though there may be no change in the pass-through.

Lastly—and this is the biggest concern I have with the chapter—I am not clear about how the I-O analysis by the authors enables us to conclude that the underlying driver behind the lower pass-through of oil prices is the cheaper price of oil itself rather than substitution between oil-intensive technology and less oil-intensive technology. For one, the authors need to elaborate upon how the striking contrast between panels (A) and (B) of figure 5.9—that is, the nominal I-O table predicts sharp decline in price responsiveness over time whereas the real I-O table does not show such tendency—illustrates that changes in the cost structure were largely due to lower oil prices rather than real substitution away from the use of oil. Intuitively, given Japan's position as a leader in green technology and environmental protection, it is difficult to believe that such substitution did not play a major role in the declining pass-through. Efficiency in the use of oil—that is, the amount of oil required to produce 1 unit of output—would provide a simple robustness check on the chapter's interpretation of the contrast between panels (A) and (B) of figure 5.9. In particular, a substantial improvement in the efficiency of oil use over time would imply that structural shifts such as the rising share of services in GDP and the shift toward greener technology within manufacturing played a major role in the shift toward a less oil-intensive structure.

Overall, the chapter is a major contribution to the oil price pass-through literature. It is the most rigorous and comprehensive analysis of the extent of the pass-through in Japan at both the aggregate and sector levels. The analysis is enriched by the use of data from both upstream and downstream oil-related products. Nevertheless, it would be further strengthened from incorporating my relatively minor suggestions for improvement.

References

Bhundia, A. 2002. An empirical investigation of exchange rate pass-through in South Africa. IMF Working Paper no. WP/02/165. Washington, DC: International Monetary Fund.

Duma, N. 2008. Pass-through of external shocks to inflation in Sri Lanka. IMF Working Paper no. WP/08/78. Washington, DC: International Monetary Fund.

Jongwanich, J., and D. Park. 2008. Inflation in developing Asia: Demand-pull or cost-push? Economics and Research Department (ERD) Working Paper Series no. 121. Asian Development Bank, September.

McCarthy, J. 1999. Pass-through of exchange rates and import prices to domestic inflation in some industrialized economies. BIS Working Paper no. 79. Basel: Bank for International Settlements.

6

The Effects of Oil Price Changes on the Industry-Level Production and Prices in the United States and Japan

Ichiro Fukunaga, Naohisa Hirakata, and Nao Sudo

6.1 Introduction

There is a large body of empirical literature on the effects of oil price changes on the U.S. economy; their magnitudes, transmission mechanisms, and historical changes have been investigated. However, the underlying causes of oil price changes have not been seriously considered until recently. The way oil price changes affect the economy may be very different depending on where the changes fundamentally come from. In particular, global factors such as rapid growth in emerging economies and the integration of global supply chains seem to have become increasingly important for oil price changes themselves and their transmission mechanisms.

Moreover, much remains unknown about the effects of oil price changes in countries other than the United States. Some recent empirical international comparative studies show that the magnitudes of the effects of oil price changes differ greatly even among oil-importing countries. In particular, Japan is different in the sense that oil price increases have little, or even a positive, effect on real economic activity.[1]

Ichiro Fukunaga is director of the Research and Statistics Department at the Bank of Japan. Naohisa Hirakata is deputy director of the Research and Statistics Department at the Bank of Japan. Nao Sudo is deputy director of the Institute for Monetary and Economic Studies at the Bank of Japan.

This chapter was prepared for the 20th Annual East Asia Seminar on Economics, Hong Kong, June 26–27, 2009. The authors are grateful to their discussants, Francis Lui and Warwick McKibbin, the organizers, Takatoshi Ito and Andrew Rose, and other participants for helpful comments and discussions. The authors would also like to thank seminar participants at the Institute for Monetary and Economic Studies, Bank of Japan. Views expressed in this chapter are those of the authors and do not necessarily reflect those of the Bank of Japan.

1. Recent studies, including those of Blanchard and Galí (2007) and Jiménez-Rodríguez and Sánchez (2004), show that the effects of oil price changes in Japan are exceptionally different from other oil-importing countries.

In this chapter, we investigate the underlying causes of oil price changes and their transmission mechanisms in the United States and Japan. We decompose oil price changes into their component parts and estimate the dynamic effects of each component on industry-level production and prices in both countries using identified vector autoregression (VAR) models. Our models incorporate two major extensions to the standard models used in previous studies. First, instead of treating oil price changes as exogenous shocks, we identify the underlying demand and supply shocks to the global oil market. Second, we use industry-level data as well as aggregate data to investigate the transmission mechanisms of oil price changes in more detail.[2] Our models have three-block structures comprising the global oil market block, the domestic macroeconomy block, and the domestic industry block. To our knowledge, this is the first attempt to investigate the effects of structural shocks to the global oil market on industry-level production and prices.[3]

In identifying structural shocks to the global oil market, we closely follow Kilian (2009), who proposes a structural decomposition of the real price of oil into the following three components: oil supply shocks; shocks to the global demand for all industrial commodities (global demand shocks);[4] and demand shocks that are specific to the global oil market (oil-specific demand shocks). These three structural shocks that all tend to raise the oil price have very different effects on domestic economic activity. While an unexpected disruption of oil supply and an unexpected increase in oil-specific demand tend to reduce domestic industrial production, an unexpected increase in global demand raises domestic production. One of the main reasons why the surge in oil prices from 2002 seems to have had a smaller effect on real economic activity than did the oil price increases of the 1970s is that the recent oil price surge and economic expansion were simultaneously driven by the global demand shocks.[5]

Examining the industry-level effects of oil price changes facilitates under-

2. We focus on manufacturing industries for which lengthy periods of monthly time-series data are available. The quarterly gross domestic product (GDP) data that include nonmanufacturing industries are not compatible with the short-run restrictions on our structural VAR models.

3. Kilian and Park (2009) briefly analyze the effects of structural shocks to the global oil market on industry-level stock returns using a two-block VAR model.

4. Kilian (2009) refers to this component as an "aggregate demand shock." We do not use this term because it can be confused with domestic aggregate shocks in our model.

5. Blanchard and Galí (2007) offer other explanations for the smaller effects: the smaller share of oil in production, greater labor market flexibility, and improvements in monetary policy. Rather than consider these structural changes, we focus on changes in the nature of the shocks to the global oil market. As mentioned in the appendix, estimating our models for shorter sample periods does not greatly change most of the impulse responses to the identified shocks, except those to the oil supply shocks. Hirakata and Sudo (2009) point out that reduced oil supply variation and the associated correlation with total factor productivity may be more important than structural changes for explaining the smaller effects of oil price changes on real economic activity.

standing of their transmission mechanisms. Lee and Ni (2002) estimate the effects of exogenous oil price shocks using U.S. industry-level data and find that oil price shocks act mainly as supply shocks for oil-intensive industries—such as petroleum refineries—and act mainly as demand shocks for many other industries.[6] They distinguish between demand and supply shocks depending on whether production and prices move in the same or opposite directions in response to the shocks. Our estimation results for the domestic industry block reveal that whether oil price changes act as supply shocks or demand shocks for each industry depends on what kind of underlying shock drives the oil price changes, as well as on industry characteristics such as oil intensity. For most industries in the United States, the global demand shocks act mainly as positive demand shocks, and the oil-specific demand shocks act mainly as negative supply shocks.[7] The oil supply shocks act mainly as negative supply shocks for oil-intensive industries and act mainly as negative demand shocks for less oil-intensive industries, as Lee and Ni (2002) found for exogenous oil price shocks.

Comparing the United States and Japan also enhances our understanding of the transmission mechanisms of oil price changes. In Japan, relative to the United States, the oil supply shock has weaker negative or statistically insignificant effects, the global demand shock has stronger positive effects, and most importantly, the oil-specific demand shock has positive rather than negative effects on the production of many industries. These findings seem to confirm the results of recent studies showing that the effects of oil price increases on Japan's economy are small or even positive and very different from those of other oil-importing countries. The positive response of production to the oil-specific demand shock might be the result of global demand shifts, especially in automobiles, toward more oil-efficient products made in Japan. In this sense, unlike in the United States, the oil-specific demand shocks act mainly as demand shocks rather than supply shocks for many industries in Japan.

The remainder of the chapter is organized as follows. Section 6.2 describes our empirical framework and the identified structural shocks to the global oil market. In section 6.3, we briefly discuss the estimation results for the domestic macroeconomy blocks for the United States and Japan. Section 6.4 reports the estimation results for the domestic industry blocks of both countries for each industry. In section 6.5, we briefly survey the transmis-

---

6. Lee and Ni (2002) use Hamilton's (1996) "net oil price increase" as an oil price variable. Hooker (1996), in his reply to Hamilton (1996), casts doubt on the theoretical and empirical validity of using this variable to represent oil price shocks to the macroeconomy and argues that the use of cross-sectional data on industries, regions, or countries is required for a better understanding of the effects of oil price changes.

7. The global demand shocks and the oil-specific demand shocks are demand shocks to the global oil market and do not necessarily act as demand shocks to domestic aggregate or industrial markets. For instance, the global demand shocks may include nonoil sector productivity shocks that act as supply shocks to oil-importing countries' domestic markets.

sion mechanisms of oil price changes and interpret our estimation results in more detail. We also consider the background of the differences between the results for the United States and Japan. Section 6.6 concludes. The appendix summarizes the estimation results under several alternative assumptions and specifications of the model to check the robustness of our main results.

6.2   Empirical Framework

6.2.1   The Structural VAR Model

Our VAR models comprise the global oil market block, the domestic macroeconomy block, and the domestic industry block. Following Lee and Ni (2002), we impose block recursive restrictions so that the identified shocks to the global oil market are the same for each country and the identified macroeconomic shocks are the same for each industry. In other words, domestic variables do not affect global oil market variables, and industry-level variables do not affect aggregate variables.[8] An identified VAR model has the following form:

$$A_0 X_t = A_0 c + A_0 B(L) X_t + u_t$$

or

$$A_0 \begin{pmatrix} X_{1t} \\ X_{2t} \\ X_{3t} \end{pmatrix} = A_0 \begin{pmatrix} c_1 \\ c_2 \\ c_3 \end{pmatrix} + A_0 \begin{pmatrix} B_{11}(L) & 0 & 0 \\ B_{21}(L) & B_{22}(L) & 0 \\ B_{31}(L) & B_{32}(L) & B_{33}(L) \end{pmatrix} \begin{pmatrix} X_{1t} \\ X_{2t} \\ X_{3t} \end{pmatrix} + \begin{pmatrix} u_{1t} \\ u_{2t} \\ u_{3t} \end{pmatrix},$$

where X_{1t} is an N_1 dimensional column vector of global oil market variables; X_{2t} is an N_2 dimensional column vector of domestic aggregate variables; X_{3t} is an N_3 dimensional column vector of domestic industry-level variables; c_1, c_2, and c_3 are vectors of constants. Variable $B(L)$ is a block recursive matrix of polynomials of the lag operator L. Moreover, we assume that A_0 is a lower triangular matrix such that the reduced-form residuals can be decomposed into the structural shocks, u_t. The covariance matrix of the structural shocks, $E(u_t u_t')$, is given by an identity matrix of dimension $N(= N_1 + N_2 + N_3)$.

We use monthly data from 1973:1 to 2008:12 (that is, from January 1973 to December 2008).[9] The lag length of the VAR is 12. Following Kilian

---

8. This assumption may be too strong if movements in domestic economy in an individual country and linkages among countries have large impacts on the global oil market or if movements in an individual industry and linkages among industries have large impacts on the domestic aggregate economy. However, we impose these restrictions to enable comparison of impulse responses in different countries and different industries to the same structural shock to the global oil market. As mentioned in the appendix, allowing domestic aggregate variables to affect global oil market variables makes little difference to our estimation results.

9. Kilian (2009) also uses monthly data from 1973:1. Consistent data on the global oil market before 1973 are difficult to obtain.

(2009), we consider oil supply shocks, shocks to the global demand for all industrial commodities, and demand shocks that are specific to the global oil market as structural shocks to the global oil market. Correspondingly, we use the following three variables in the global oil market block ($N_1 = 3$): world crude oil production; the industrial production of the Organization for Economic Cooperation and Development (OECD) countries plus major six nonmember economies (hereafter, world industrial production);[10] and West Texas Intermediate spot crude oil prices.[11] The last two variables differ from those used by Kilian (2009).[12] We use the nominal price of oil rather than the real price because the deflator is endogenous with respect to the domestic macroeconomy, which would violate our assumption of a block recursive structure.[13] For the domestic macroeconomy block, we only use aggregate industrial production ($N_2 = 1$). For the domestic industry block, we use industrial production and producer prices ($N_3 = 2$).[14] We take first differences in the logs of all variables. The data on industrial production in each block and producer prices are seasonally adjusted. The ordering of the variables in the VAR is as described before.[15] The reduced-form VAR is estimated consistently by the method of ordinary least squares.

6.2.2   Structural Shocks to the Global Oil Market

We follow Kilian (2009) to identify the structural shocks to the global oil market. The oil supply shocks are innovations to global oil production that are assumed not to respond to innovations to the demand for oil within the same month. The global demand shocks are innovations to world industrial production that cannot be explained by the oil supply shocks. The oil-specific demand shocks are innovations to the oil price that cannot be explained by either the oil supply shocks or the global demand shocks. The oil-specific demand shocks are supposed to reflect changes in precautionary demand arising from uncertainty about future oil supply, and may also reflect changes in speculative demand. Although we use slightly different data from those used by Kilian (2009), our estimation results for the global oil market block are similar to his. Figure 6.1 plots the historical evolution

10. This index can be downloaded from OECD websites. The six nonmember economies are Brazil, China, India, Indonesia, the Russian Federation, and South Africa.

11. Data for before 1982 are posted prices.

12. Kilian (2009) uses an original measure of global real economic activity based on dry cargo freight rates and the U.S. refiner acquisition cost of imported crude oil deflated by the U.S. Consumer Price Index (CPI) (both in natural logs). The data on world crude oil production used by Kilian (2009) are the same as those we use.

13. Hamilton (2008) and Rotemberg and Woodford (1996) point out this problem. We do not use the refiner acquisition cost of imported crude oil for the same reason.

14. We use the Index of Industrial Production published by the Federal Reserve Board and that published by the Japanese Ministry of Economy, Trade, and Industry. For prices data, we use the Producer Price Index from the U.S. Bureau of Labor Statistics and the Corporate Goods Price Index from the Bank of Japan.

15. As mentioned in the appendix, changing the ordering in the domestic industry block so that prices rather than production come first makes little difference to the estimation results.

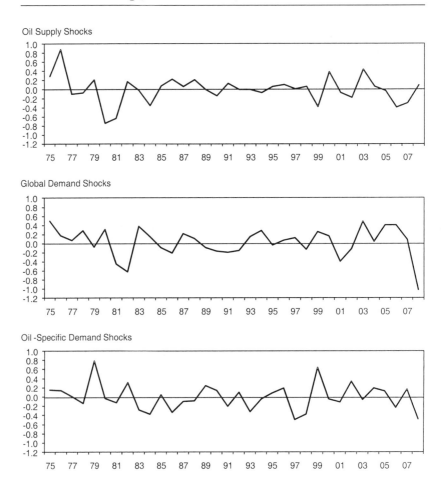

Fig. 6.1   Historical evolution of the structural shocks

(annual averages) of the structural shocks implied by our model. As shown by Kilian (2009), there was no unanticipated disruption of oil supply in 1978 or 1979 but there were disruptions in 1980 and 1981 associated with the Iran-Iraq War. Positive shocks to the global demand have been repeated since 2003 and a large negative shock occurred in 2008. The occurrence of the oil-specific demand shocks has been constant throughout the sample period.

The cumulative responses of the three variables in the global oil market block to one-standard-deviation structural shocks identified earlier are shown in figure 6.2. The oil supply shock has been normalized to represent a negative shock to oil production, whereas the other shocks have been normalized to represent positive shocks such that all shocks tend to raise the oil price. One-standard-error bands computed from a bootstrap method are

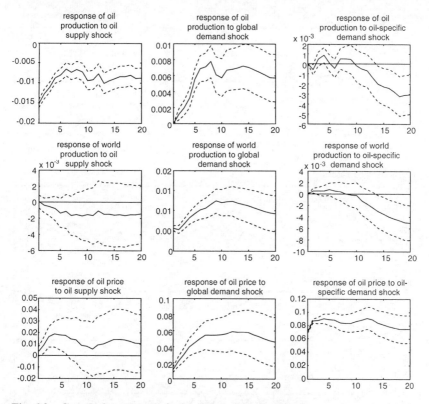

Fig. 6.2   Cumulative responses in the global oil market block

indicated by dashed lines. Of the three shocks, the oil-specific demand shock has the largest and most persistent effect on the oil price. It sharply raises the oil price on impact, which remains high for a long time. The global demand shock also has a large and persistent effect, causing a gradual increase in the oil price that lasts for about a year (twelve months). The oil supply shock has only a small and transitory effect, causing a gradual increase in the oil price that lasts for about four months. Whereas an unexpected global demand increase is associated with increases in oil production and world industrial production, an unexpected oil-specific demand increase is associated with decreases, following a ten-month lag, in oil production and world industrial production. An unexpected disruption of oil supply is also associated with a decrease in oil production and its effect on world industrial production is statistically insignificant. These results imply that the effects of the three shocks on the oil price differ in magnitude and persistence. Moreover, the effects of oil price changes on oil production and world industrial production are very different depending on what kind of underlying shock drives the oil price changes.

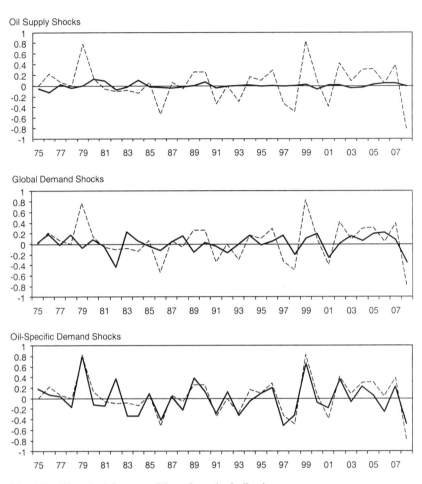

Fig. 6.3   Historical decomposition of nominal oil price

Figure 6.3 plots a historical decomposition of the oil price into the contribution of the structural shocks. The annual rate of change (difference in logs) in the oil price is indicated by the dashed line in each panel.[16] The oil supply shocks made a small contribution to nominal oil price movements, which is consistent with the finding of Kilian (2009) for the real price of oil. Most changes in the nominal oil price before 2000 were driven by the oil-specific demand shocks. Rapid temporary changes, such as the sharp fall following the collapse of the Organization of the Petroleum Exporting

16. Since the model contains a constant term, the sum of the contribution of the three shocks is not equal to the rate of change in the oil price. The same applies to the historical decompositions in figures 6.5 and 6.7.

Countries (OPEC) cartel in late 1985 and the spike after Iraq's invasion of Kuwait in 1990 (which are not obvious from the annual figures), were also attributable mainly to the oil-specific demand shocks. Meanwhile, the persistent surge in the oil price from 2002 and the sharp fall in 2008 were driven by the global demand shocks as well as by the oil-specific demand shocks.

6.3   Macroeconomic Effects of Oil Price Changes

In this section, we briefly discuss the estimation results for the domestic macroeconomy block in our models for the United States and Japan and compare them. The domestic macroeconomy block includes only one variable, aggregate industrial production. The shock to this block captures all domestic aggregate disturbances not driven by the structural shocks identified in the global oil market block. Because our main concern in this chapter is the industry-level effects of oil price changes and how these effects compare in the United States and Japan, we model the domestic macroeconomy block as simply as possible.[17]

6.3.1   Effects on Aggregate Production in the United States

Figure 6.4 shows the cumulative responses of aggregate industrial production in the United States to one standard deviation of the three structural shocks identified in the global oil market block and the domestic aggregate shock. The three structural shocks to the global oil market, which all tend to raise the oil price, have very different effects on domestic macroeconomic activity. Whereas the oil supply shock and the oil-specific demand shock reduce industrial production, the global demand shock raises production for about ten months. Whereas the decrease in production caused by the oil supply shock lasts for about ten months, the decrease caused by the oil-specific demand shock accelerates around ten months after the shock. The domestic aggregate shock raises production gradually and persistently.

Figure 6.5 plots a historical decomposition of U.S. aggregate industrial production into the contribution of the three global shocks and the domestic aggregate shock. The annual rate of change in U.S. industrial production is indicated by the dashed line in each panel. Changes in U.S. industrial production were driven mainly by the global demand shocks and the domestic aggregate shocks. Because U.S. production accounts for a large share of world production, it seems natural that the global demand shocks make a substantial contribution to U.S. production. It is nonetheless remarkable that movements in U.S. production in the 2000s (that is, 2000 to 2010) have been driven mainly by the global demand shocks despite the fact that the

17. As mentioned in the appendix, we tried an alternative specification of the domestic macroeconomy block that includes the short-term nominal interest rate and the real effective exchange rate in addition to aggregate industrial production. This extension of the domestic macroeconomy block, however, made little difference to our estimation results.

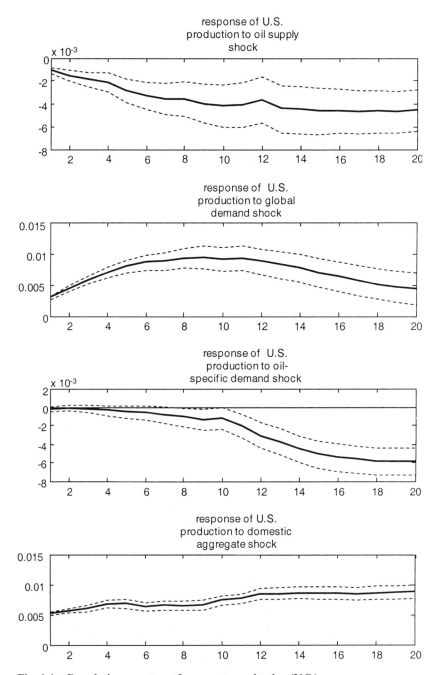

Fig. 6.4   Cumulative responses of aggregate production (U.S.)

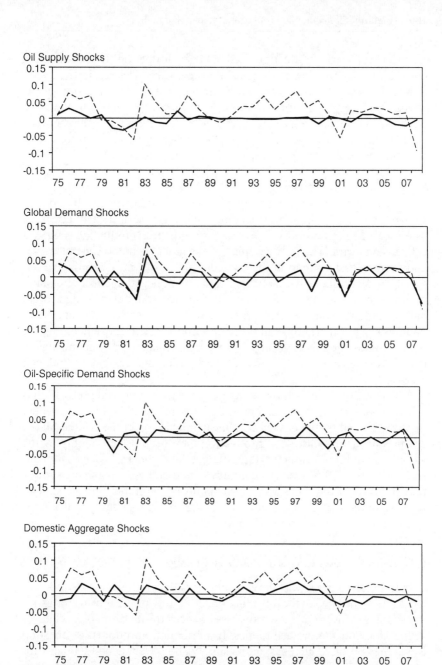

Fig. 6.5 Historical decomposition of aggregate production (U.S.)

U.S. share of world production declined over this period. By contrast, the contribution of the domestic aggregate shocks has declined in the 2000s, although they made a substantial contribution to U.S. expansion in the 1990s. Because the oil price and industrial production move in the same direction in response to the global demand shocks, the relationship between them seems to have changed in the 2000s, when movements in these two variables have been driven by the global demand shocks.

6.3.2   Effects on Aggregate Production in Japan

The cumulative responses of Japan's aggregate industrial production are shown in figure 6.6. They are rather different from those of the United States. The effect of the oil supply shock on Japan's industrial production is statistically insignificant. The positive effect of the global demand shock is larger and more persistent than in the United States. Most importantly, the oil-specific demand shock has a positive, rather than negative, effect on Japan's production, at least in the short run. Production starts decreasing around half a year (six months) after a positive oil-specific demand shock. These findings suggest that, unlike in other oil-importing countries including the United States, the effects of oil price increases in Japan are either negligibly negative or even positive. The effect of the domestic aggregate shock in Japan is larger than in the United States.

A historical decomposition of Japan's aggregate industrial production is shown in figure 6.7. The annual rate of change in Japan's industrial production is indicated by the dashed line in each panel. As in the United States, changes in Japan's industrial production have been driven mainly by the global demand shocks and the domestic aggregate shocks. Whereas the contraction of the 1990s was driven mainly by the domestic aggregate shocks, the expansion of the 2000s was driven mainly by the global demand shocks. Relative to the U.S. case, the domestic aggregate shocks have made a large contribution to Japan's industrial production.

6.4   Industry-Level Effects of Oil Price Changes

In this section, we report the estimation results for the domestic industry block. As mentioned in the introduction, our motivation for using industry-level data is to investigate the transmission mechanisms of oil price changes in the U.S. and Japan's economies. In particular, an important question is whether oil price changes act as supply shocks or demand shocks for each industry. Before reporting the estimation results, we briefly summarize basic statistics on the industrial structures of the United States and Japan, which may characterize the supply and demand sides of the transmission mechanisms. We discuss the implications of the estimation results in detail in section 6.5.

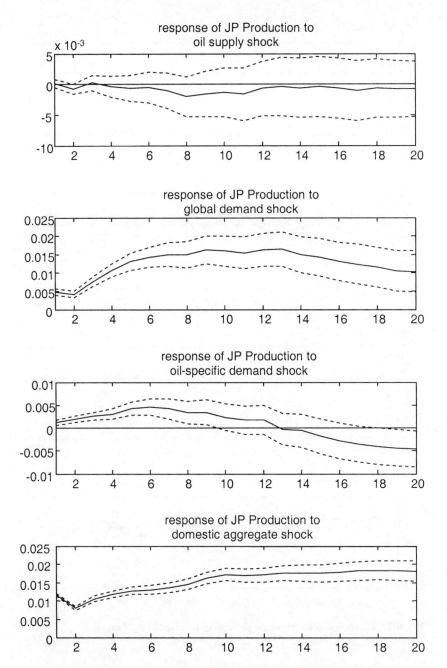

Fig. 6.6   Cumulative responses of aggregate production (Japan)

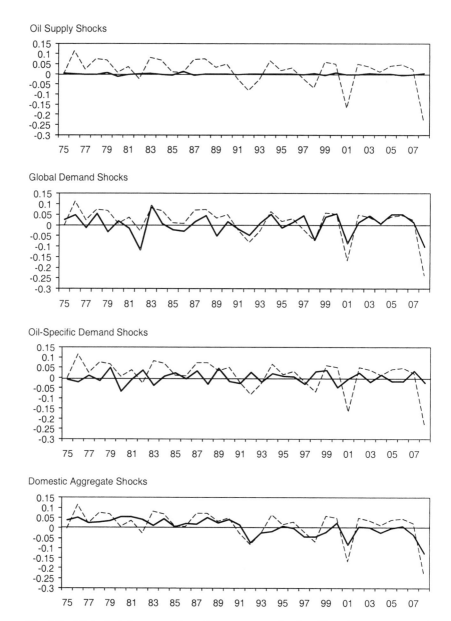

Fig. 6.7 Historical decomposition of aggregate production (Japan)

6.4.1   Basic Statistics on Industrial Structures

Table 6.1 shows the value-added shares of industrial production for the twelve industries in the United States and Japan selected for the present study. Although the total share of our selected industries accounts for only around 40 percent of U.S. aggregate manufacturing production, they include key industries for the transmission of oil price changes, such as petroleum refineries and automotive products, as discussed in section 6.5. Because we must match industry-level data on production and prices, we cannot select broadly defined (three-digit North American Industry Classification Sys-

Table 6.1   **Value-added share of production**

	U.S.	
Industry	Share in 2006 (%)	Share in 1973 (%)
Fabricated metal product	5.5	6.7
Chemical materials	5.4	4.4
Machinery	5.0	8.6
Petroleum refineries	3.9	1.3
Automotive products	3.3	3.5
Plastics and rubber products	3.2	2.9
Paper	2.6	3.1
Nonmetallic mineral product	2.3	2.7
Furniture and related product	1.5	1.6
Wood product	1.4	2.1
Iron and steel products	1.4	3.1
Electrical equipment	0.6	1.1
12-industry total	36.3	41.3

	Japan	
Industry	Share in 2005 (%)	Share in 1975 (%)
Electric machinery and equipment	18.4	11.0
Transportation equipment	16.9	11.8
General machinery and equipment	13.2	12.8
Chemicals and related products	11.8	9.5
Iron and steel products	6.0	6.6
Metal products	5.7	5.0
Plastic products	3.8	2.8
Ceramic, stone, and clay products	2.9	5.7
Pulp, paper, and related products	2.4	3.5
Nonferrous metals and products	2.1	1.9
Precision instruments	1.0	1.6
Petroleum and coal products	1.0	2.9
12-industry total	85.2	75.3

Sources: Industrial Production, Federal Reserve Board. Indices of Industrial Production, Japanese Ministry of Economy, Trade, and Industry.

tem [NAICS]) industries. For Japan, where the total value-added share of our selected industries is around 80 percent, data on both production and prices for broadly defined industries are available, although lengthy time-series data at the highly disaggregated industry level are not available. For instance, petroleum refineries are included in "petroleum and coal products" and automotive products are included in "transportation equipment." Table 6.1 also shows that some industries' shares changed considerably during our sample period. For instance, in the United States, from 1973 to 2006, chemical materials and petroleum refineries increased their shares, whereas fabricated metal products and machinery decreased their shares. In Japan, from 1975 to 2005, shares for the electrical machinery and transportation equipment increased, whereas the share for the ceramic, stone, and clay products decreased.

We consider two industry characteristics: oil intensity and export dependence. The former relates to the cost share of oil in production and is a key characteristic for the supply channel in the transmission of oil price changes, as discussed in section 6.5. The latter relates to the export share of shipments and is a key characteristic for the effects of the global demand shocks. We measure these characteristics for both countries based on the 2000 Japan-U.S. input-output table from Japan's Ministry of Economy, Trade, and Industry.

Table 6.2 shows the cost share of oil in each industry in both countries.[18] The oil intensity of the petroleum and coal products (which includes petroleum refineries) is particularly high in both countries. Oil intensity is also relatively high in ceramics, stone, and clay products, chemical products, steel and steel products, and nonsteel metals and products. We term these industries "oil-intensive industries" and refer to the others as "less oil-intensive industries." Based on the twelve-industry average, Japan is less oil-intensive than the United States.

Table 6.3 shows the export share of shipments in each industry in both countries. The export dependences of precision instruments, electric machinery, general machinery, and transportation equipment (which includes automotive products) are particularly high in both countries. These industries are termed "export-dependent industries." Based on the twelve-industry average, Japan is more export-dependent than the United States.

6.4.2   Effects of Oil Supply Shocks on
         Industry-Level Production and Prices

Figures 6.8 through 6.21 illustrate the estimated cumulative responses of production and prices of the twelve selected industries in the United States and Japan to one standard deviation of the three structural shocks identified in the global oil market block. In figures 6.10 through 6.21, each

---

18. The figures show the input cost shares of "mining" and "petroleum and coal products."

Table 6.2   Oil intensity (cost share of mining and petroleum and coal products)

Industry	Share in 2000 (%)
U.S.	
Petroleum and coal products	68.5
Ceramic, stone, and clay products	6.2
Chemical products	6.2
Steel and steel products	5.5
Nonsteel metals and products	2.8
Pulp, paper, and wooden products	0.7
Plastic, rubber, and leather products	0.5
Other metal products	0.3
Transportation equipment	0.3
General machinery	0.2
Electric machinery	0.1
Precision instruments	0.1
12-industry average	6.4
Japan	
Petroleum and coal products	40.6
Ceramic, stone, and clay products	9.7
Nonsteel metals and products	7.3
Steel and steel products	6.4
Chemical products	4.8
Pulp, paper, and wooden products	1.2
Other metal products	0.5
Plastic, rubber, and leather products	0.4
General machinery	0.3
Precision instruments	0.3
Transportation equipment	0.3
Electric machinery	0.2
12-industry average	4.0

Sources: The 2000 Japan-U.S. input-output table, Japanese Ministry of Economy, Trade, and Industry.

response is accompanied by one-standard-error bands computed from a bootstrap method. The graphs for the selected industries are presented in order of oil intensity. Note that the scales of the responses are different for different industries. For cross-industry comparisons, we show the magnitudes of the twelve-month cumulative responses for all the selected industries in the United States in figure 6.8 and those in Japan in figure 6.9. In addition, in tables 6.4 and 6.5, we summarize the signs of the peak responses within twenty months to each shock in the United States and Japan, respectively, following Lee and Ni (2002).[19] These tables enable us to identify the main

19. Rather than plot the cumulative responses of first-difference series to *permanent* level shocks as we do, Lee and Ni (2002) plot the responses of level variables to temporary level shocks. Therefore, our responses have different interpretations, particularly in the long run, from theirs.

Table 6.3   **Export dependence (export share of shipments)**

Industry	Share in 2000 (%)
U.S.	
Electric machinery	30.2
Precision instruments	29.6
General machinery	26.3
Transportation equipment	20.4
Nonsteel metals and products	17.3
Chemical products	17.2
Plastic, rubber, and leather products	9.6
Pulp, paper, and wooden products	6.6
Steel and steel products	6.4
Ceramic, stone, and clay products	6.4
Other metal products	6.3
Petroleum and coal products	5.7
12-industry average	14.9
Japan	
Precision instruments	33.9
Transportation equipment	33.4
Electric machinery	33.1
General machinery	27.9
Steel and steel products	17.0
Chemical products	15.6
Nonsteel metals and products	15.3
Plastic, rubber, and leather products	8.6
Ceramic, stone, and clay products	6.9
Other metal products	3.8
Pulp, paper, and wooden products	2.1
Petroleum and coal products	1.6
12-industry average	17.1

Sources: The 2000 Japan-U.S. input-output table, Japanese Ministry of Economy, Trade, and Industry.

effects of each structural shock for each industry. If production and price move in the same (opposite) direction after a shock, the dominant effect of that shock is on the demand (supply) side.

First we examine the responses of production and prices to the oil supply shock in the United States, as shown in figures 6.10 and 6.11. In most industries in the United States, an unexpected disruption of oil supply causes a gradual decline in production that lasts for about a year. The production of petroleum refineries declines on impact and then continues to decline gradually and persistently. The responses of prices vary across industries. An unexpected oil supply disruption significantly raises the price of petroleum refineries and reduces the prices of wood product and electrical equipment. It tends to raise the prices of oil-intensive industries and tends to reduce the prices of less oil-intensive industries, although these effects for many

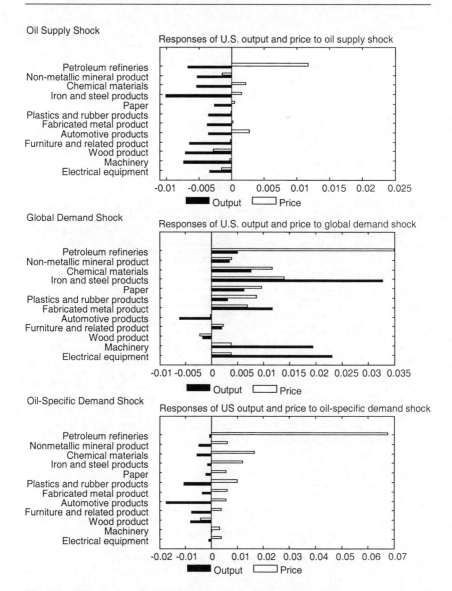

Fig. 6.8   Magnitudes of twelve-month cumulative responses (U.S.)

industries are only partially (in limited periods) statistically significant. This implies that the oil supply shocks act mainly as supply shocks for oil-intensive industries and act mainly as demand shocks for less oil-intensive industries. This finding is similar to that obtained by Lee and Ni (2002) for exogenous oil price shocks.

The responses of production and prices to the same shock in Japan are

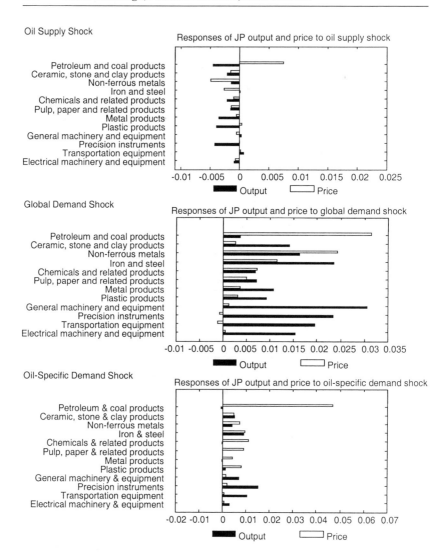

Fig. 6.9   Magnitudes of twelve-month cumulative responses (Japan)

shown in figures 6.12 and 6.13. An unexpected disruption of oil supply gradually decreases petroleum and coal production, which includes production of petroleum refineries, and this lasts for about a year. There are declines in production of many other industries, but only partially statistically significant. Disruption of oil supply gradually increases prices of petroleum refineries, and this also lasts for about a year. There are price falls in other oil-intensive industries such as ceramic, stone, and clay products and iron and steel products, but only partially statistically significant.

Table 6.4   **Signs of peak responses (U.S.)**

Oil supply shock

Industry	Peak effect on output	Peak effect on prices	Oil supply shock effects
Petroleum refineries	–*	+*	Decrease in supply
Nonmetallic mineral product	–*	–	Decrease in demand
Chemical materials	–*	+*	Decrease in supply
Iron and steel products	–	+*	Decrease in supply
Paper	–*	0	
Plastics and rubber products	–*	0	
Fabricated metal product	–*	0	
Automotive products	–*	+*	Decrease in supply
Furniture and related product	–*	0	
Wood product	–*	–*	Decrease in demand
Machinery	–*	0	
Electrical equipment	–	–*	Decrease in demand

Global demand shock

Industry	Peak effect on output	Peak effect on prices	Global demand shock effects
Petroleum refineries	+*	+*	Increase in demand
Nonmetallic mineral product	+*	+*	Increase in demand
Chemical materials	+*	+*	Increase in demand
Iron and steel products	+*	+*	Increase in demand
Paper	+*	+*	Increase in demand
Plastics and rubber products	+*	+*	Increase in demand
Fabricated metal product	+*	+*	Increase in demand
Automotive products	Mixed	+*	
Furniture and related product	Mixed	+*	
Wood product	Mixed	–*	
Machinery	+*	+*	Increase in demand
Electrical equipment	+*	+*	Increase in demand

Oil-Specific Demand Shock

Industry	Peak effect on output	Peak effect on prices	Oil-specific demand shock effects
Petroleum refineries	–*	+*	Decrease in supply
Nonmetallic mineral product	–*	+*	Decrease in supply
Chemical materials	–*	+*	Decrease in supply
Iron and steel products	–*	+*	Decrease in supply
Paper	–*	+*	Decrease in supply
Plastics and rubber products	–*	+*	Decrease in supply
Fabricated metal product	–*	+*	Decrease in supply
Automotive products	–*	+*	Decrease in supply
Furniture and related product	–*	+*	Decrease in supply
Wood product	–*	–*	Decrease in demand
Machinery	–*	+*	Decrease in supply
Electrical equipment	–*	+*	Decrease in supply

Notes: "+" and "–" represent peak positive and negative responses; "*" means that the peak responses are significant; "0" means the peak responses are negligible. "Mixed" means that the positive and negative responses are of similar magnitudes.

Table 6.5   **Signs of peak responses (Japan)**

Oil supply shock

Industry	Peak effect on output	Peak effect on prices	Oil supply shock effects
Petroleum and coal products	−*	+*	Decrease in supply
Ceramic, stone, and clay products	−*	−*	Decrease in demand
Nonferrous metals and products	−	−	Decrease in demand
Iron and steel products	0	−*	
Chemicals and related products	−	0	
Pulp, paper, and related products	−*	−	Decrease in demand
Metal products	−*	−	Decrease in demand
Plastic products	−*	+*	Decrease in supply
General machinery and equipment	0	0	
Precision instruments	−*	0	
Transportation equipment	0	0	
Electric machinery and equipment	−*	0	

Global demand shock

Industry	Peak effect on output	Peak effect on prices	Global demand shock effects
Petroleum and coal products	+*	+*	Increase in demand
Ceramic, stone, and clay products	+*	+*	Increase in demand
Nonferrous metals and products	+*	+*	Increase in demand
Iron and steel products	+*	+*	Increase in demand
Chemicals and related products	+*	+*	Increase in demand
Pulp, paper, and related products	+*	+*	Increase in demand
Metal products	+*	+*	Increase in demand
Plastic products	+*	+*	Increase in demand
General machinery and equipment	+*	+*	Increase in demand
Precision instruments	+*	−*	Increase in supply
Transportation equipment	+*	−*	Increase in supply
Electric machinery and equipment	−*	−	Increase in demand

Oil-specific demand shock

Industry	Peak effect on output	Peak effect on prices	Oil-specific demand shock effects
Petroleum and coal products	Mixed	+*	
Ceramic, stone, and clay products	+*	+*	Increase in demand
Nonferrous metals and products	Mixed	+*	
Iron and steel products	+*	+*	Increase in demand
Chemicals and related products	Mixed	+*	
Pulp, paper, and related products	Mixed	+*	
Metal products	Mixed	+*	
Plastic products	Mixed	+*	
General machinery and equipment	+*	+*	Increase in demand
Precision instruments	+*	+*	Increase in demand
Transportation equipment	+*	+*	Increase in demand
Electric machinery and equipment	Mixed	−	

Notes: "+" and "−" represent peak positive and negative responses; "*" means that the peak responses are significant; "0" means the peak responses are negligible. "Mixed" means that the positive and negative responses are of similar magnitudes.

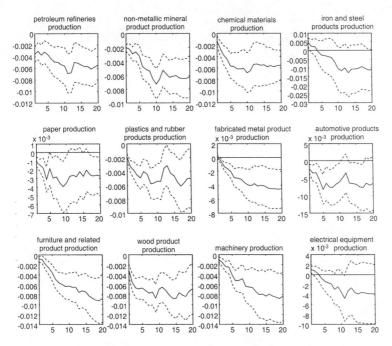

Fig. 6.10 Cumulative responses of production to oil supply shock (U.S.)

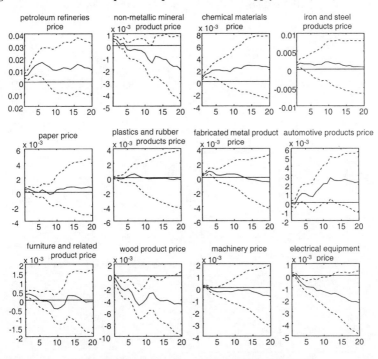

Fig. 6.11 Cumulative responses of prices to oil supply shock (U.S.)

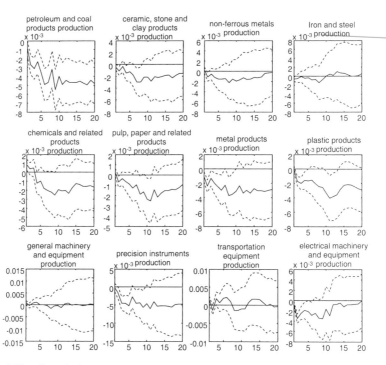

Fig. 6.12   Cumulative responses of production to oil supply shock (Japan)

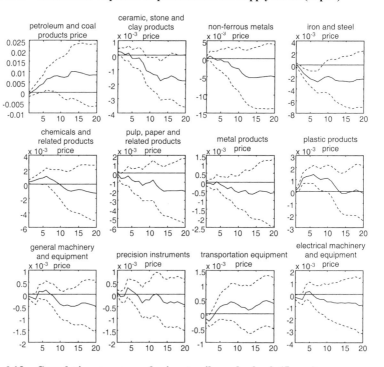

Fig. 6.13   Cumulative responses of prices to oil supply shock (Japan)

The effects on prices of less oil-intensive industries are mostly statistically insignificant. Overall, the oil supply shocks act mainly as supply shocks for petroleum refineries but have insignificant effects on many other industries in Japan.

6.4.3   Effects of Global Demand Shocks on Industry-Level Production and Prices

Figures 6.14 and 6.15 illustrate the responses of production and prices to the global demand shock in the United States. An unexpected expansion in the global demand for all industrial commodities gradually increases the production of most industries. Whereas increases in the production of some export-dependent industries such as machinery and electrical equipment last for about a year, the increases in many other industries last for only a few months or half a year. In particular, automotive products, furniture and related product, wood product, and some oil-intensive industries including petroleum refineries, experience only transitory increases in production. At the same time, a positive global demand shock gradually and persistently increases the prices of most industries. The price increase in petroleum refineries is the largest among the industries. Prices in many less oil-intensive industries also increase, but by less than do those in oil-intensive industries. These results imply that the global demand shocks act mainly as demand shocks, at least in the short run, for most industries. Note that these global demand shocks act as positive demand shocks for many industries, in contrast to the oil supply shocks, which act as negative demand shocks for less oil-intensive industries.

The responses of production and prices to the same shock in Japan are shown in figures 6.16 and 6.17. As in the United States, a positive global demand shock gradually increases production of most industries in Japan. Whereas the increases in production of some oil-intensive industries such as petroleum and coal products last for only about half a year, production increases in many less oil-intensive and export-dependent industries last for about a year, and the effects are larger than those in oil-intensive industries. Compared with the United States, the global demand shocks have persistent effects on production in a wider range of industries, which include transportation equipment. At the same time, a positive global demand shock gradually and persistently raises the prices of many industries, particularly oil-intensive industries. By contrast, prices of some less oil-intensive industries such as precision instruments and transportation equipment fall, at least in the short run. As in the United States, the global demand shocks act mainly as demand shocks for most industries in Japan. However, the magnitude and persistence of the effects in some industries differ greatly from the corresponding effects in the United States.

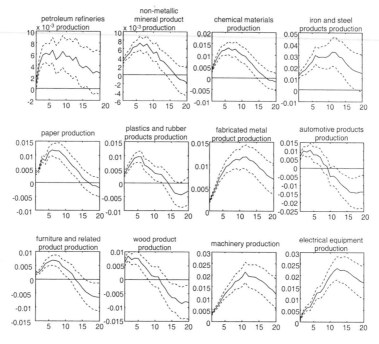

Fig. 6.14 **Cumulative responses of production to global demand shock (U.S.)**

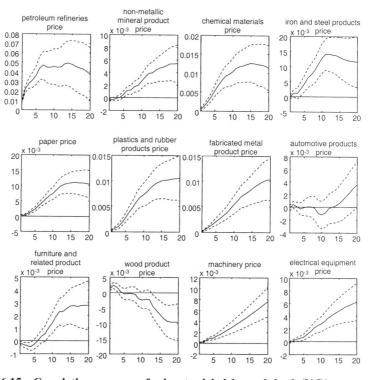

Fig. 6.15 **Cumulative responses of prices to global demand shock (U.S.)**

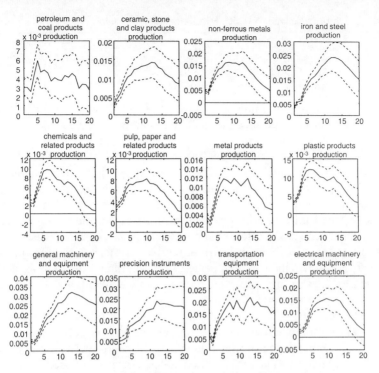

Fig. 6.16 **Cumulative responses of production to global demand shock (Japan)**

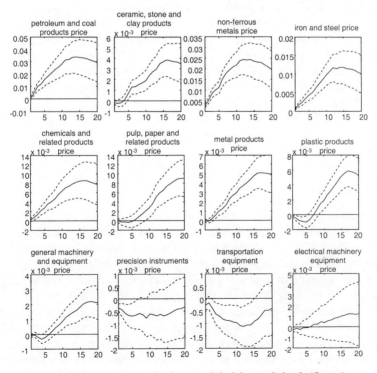

Fig. 6.17 **Cumulative responses of prices to global demand shock (Japan)**

6.4.4   Effects of Oil-Specific Demand Shocks
on Industry-Level Production and Prices

Figures 6.18 and 6.19 illustrate the responses of production and prices to the oil-specific demand shock in the United States. An unexpected increase in demand that is specific to the global oil market gradually and persistently reduces the production of most industries, with a half-year lag. The decrease in automotive production is the largest, and generally production declines are relatively large in less oil-intensive industries. At the same time, a positive oil-specific demand shock persistently increases the prices of most industries. In petroleum refineries, prices increase on impact and then continue to rise until around a year after the shock, which is the largest increase among the industries. Prices in many less oil-intensive industries, including automotive products, also increase, but generally by less than those in oil-intensive industries. These results imply that the oil-specific demand shocks act mainly as supply shocks for most industries.

Lastly, the responses of production and prices to the same shock in Japan are shown in figures 6.20 and 6.21. Of the three structural shocks, the responses to the oil-specific demand shock differ most between the United States and Japan. Unlike in the United States, a positive oil-specific demand shock raises rather than reduces production of most industries in Japan, at least in the short run. Whereas production increases in oil-intensive industries are small and transitory, those in some less oil-intensive and export-dependent industries, such as general machinery, precision instruments, and transportation equipment, last for about a year. Therefore, the oil-specific demand shocks have similar effects on production to the global demand shocks, although the latter have much larger effects. At the same time, a positive oil-specific demand shock gradually and persistently raises the prices of most industries. Unlike in the United States, the oil-specific demand shocks act mainly as demand shocks rather than supply shocks for many industries in Japan.

6.5   Discussion

The estimation results for the domestic industry block in section 6.4 reveal that whether the oil price changes act as supply shocks or demand shocks for each industry depends on what kind of underlying shock drives the oil price changes. It also depends on each industry's characteristics: that is, oil price changes tend to act more as supply shocks for oil-intensive industries and tend to act more as demand shocks for less oil-intensive industries, as shown by Lee and Ni (2002). However, our results imply that the global demand shocks act mainly as demand shocks for most industries, including oil-intensive industries, and that the oil-specific demand shocks act mainly as supply shocks for most industries, including less oil-intensive industries in the United States. Considering this key finding, we briefly survey the

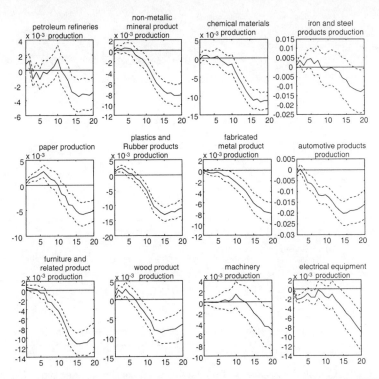

Fig. 6.18   Cumulative responses of production to oil-specific demand shock (U.S.)

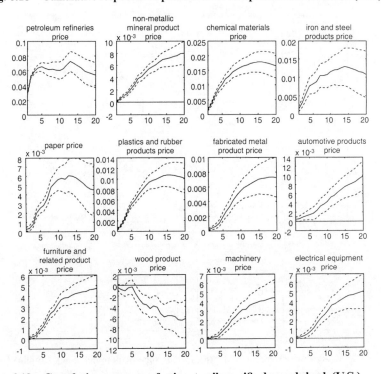

Fig. 6.19   Cumulative responses of prices to oil-specific demand shock (U.S.)

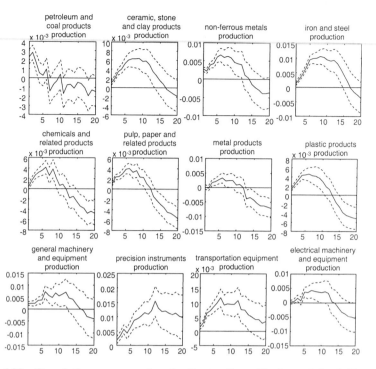

Fig. 6.20　Cumulative responses of production to oil-specific demand shock (Japan)

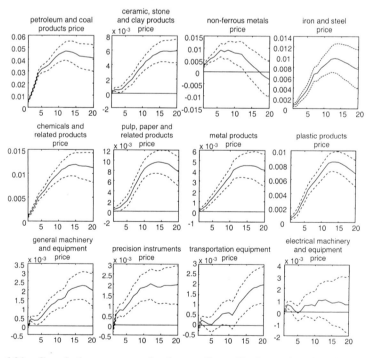

Fig. 6.21　Cumulative responses of prices to oil-specific demand shock (Japan)

transmission mechanisms of oil price changes and interpret our estimation results in more detail. The three structural shocks to the global oil market identified in our model are transmitted to each industry through various channels, some of which are familiar and others less familiar in the literature.[20]

Another key finding is that the transmission mechanisms differ considerably between the United States and Japan. In particular, the oil-specific demand shocks in Japan act mainly as demand shocks rather than supply shocks for many industries. Following discussion of the transmission mechanisms, we consider the background of the differences between the United States and Japan.

6.5.1 Transmission Mechanisms of Oil Price Changes

Oil price changes have been viewed traditionally as cost shocks or productivity shocks to oil-importing countries, and many studies focus on the supply side of their transmission mechanisms.[21] When an oil price hike pushes up production costs, producers reduce their use of oil, which may lower the productivity of capital and labor. This cost channel or supply channel of transmission operates mainly in oil-intensive industries. According to our estimation results, the magnitudes of the price responses to any kind of structural shock to the global oil market are relatively large in oil-intensive industries, particularly petroleum refineries. However, production responses in oil-intensive industries are not particularly large. The effect of an oil-specific demand shock in the United States on production of oil-intensive industries is smaller than that of less oil-intensive industries such as automotive products. The production of oil-intensive industries increases rather than decreases in response to a positive global demand shock, which moves in the same direction as prices. Because the economy-wide cost share of oil is low, it is reasonable to suppose that the direct effect of the cost channel by itself cannot explain the whole impact of oil price changes on economic activity.[22]

Another important channel of the transmission is on the demand side of the economy. Kilian (2008) categorizes the effects of oil price changes on consumption expenditure into a discretionary income effect, a precautionary savings effect, an uncertainty effect, and an operating cost effect.[23] The

---

20. The survey is limited to mechanisms relating to our estimation results. Because our models do not explicitly consider either monetary policy shocks or endogenous responses of monetary policy to oil price changes, we ignore the relationship between oil prices and monetary policy.

21. For instance, Bruno and Sachs (1985) extensively study the supply side of the transmission mechanisms of oil price changes.

22. Hamilton (2008) discusses the empirical relevance of the cost channel in his survey of the mechanisms through which the effects of oil price changes are transmitted to the macroeconomy.

23. Oil price changes also affect firms' investment expenditures, but these effects are considered small by Kilian (2008).

first two effects, which operate through consumers' present and expected future incomes, relate to a wide range of goods and services, whereas the other two effects relate only to consumer durables. The uncertainty effect of oil price changes causes consumers to postpone irreversible purchases of consumer durables, and the operating cost effect causes consumers to refrain from purchasing oil-using durables, particularly automobiles. According to our estimation results, the U.S. automotive industry exhibits the largest production decrease following a positive oil-specific demand shock. This implies that the oil-specific demand shocks act as demand shocks as well as supply shocks for the U.S. automotive industry, though the negative effect on prices through the demand channel is not as strong as the positive effect on prices through the supply channel. Note that all the aforementioned effects of oil price increases reduce consumption expenditure; that is, they act as negative demand shocks. By contrast, the global demand shocks identified in our model act mainly as positive demand shocks. This is because, by construction, these shocks incorporate positive shocks to the income of U.S. or other countries' residents who purchase U.S. products. More precisely, however, the global demand shocks act as both positive and negative demand shocks that offset each other: the positive effects operate through positive income shocks and the negative effects operate through the oil price increases induced by the same shocks. According to our estimation results, a positive global demand shock raises U.S. automotive production only slightly and temporarily, relative to other less oil-intensive industries such as machinery and electrical equipment. This is because the negative effect that operates through the oil price increase in the automotive industry is stronger than in other less oil-intensive industries.

If oil price changes intensively affect a certain sector of the economy, whether through the supply or demand channel, sectoral shifts of resources between the affected sector and less affected sectors are likely to occur. In the process of such sectoral shifts, some resources might be unemployed by any sector because of frictions in capital and labor markets, which may further depress aggregate economic activity and amplify the negative effects of oil price changes. This reallocation effect has been discussed by many researchers, including Hamilton (1988) and Davis and Haltiwanger (2001). Our estimation results, however, do not provide clear evidence of significant resource reallocation across industries either for the United States or Japan. Although the magnitudes of the production responses to each type of shocks differ considerably across industries, the directions of the responses are the same for most industries.

Meanwhile, some of our results imply demand shifts across countries. The production increases in export-dependent industries, such as machinery and electric equipment, that follow a positive global demand shock tend to be larger and more persistent than those of less export-dependent industries, both in the United States and Japan. This is because, as mentioned before, the global demand shocks partly reflect changes in the incomes of foreign residents who purchase domestic products. Moreover, demand shifts from U.S. products to Japanese products might constitute an explanation for the significant difference in the effects of the oil-specific demand shocks between the two countries, as discussed in the next subsection. These global transmission channels of oil price changes have received relatively less attention in the literature.[24]

6.5.2   Differences between the United States and Japan

Based on the previous discussion, we consider the background of the differences between our estimation results for the United States and Japan. For Japan, in many industries, the production responses to the oil supply shock are weaker or statistically insignificant, and those to the global demand shock are stronger than those of the United States. These differences are explained by the fact that Japan's economy is less oil-intensive and more export-dependent than the United States, as shown in section 6.4.1.

The biggest difference is in the effects of the oil-specific demand shocks. For many industries in Japan, production as well as prices increase rather than decrease in response to a positive oil-specific demand shock. Therefore, the oil-specific demand shocks act mainly as positive demand shocks, similarly to the global demand shocks. This implies the existence of some oil-specific factors, which cannot be explained by the global demand shocks, causing global demand shifts toward Japanese products. One possibility is the oil efficiency of Japanese products. In particular, Japanese automotive manufacturers have produced smaller and more oil-efficient cars than have U.S. manufacturers since the 1970s. By causing a massive demand shift toward small cars, the oil crisis of the 1970s damaged U.S. carmakers, who produced only large cars, as documented by Bresnahan and Ramey (1993), among others. At the same time, Japanese carmakers sharply raised their market shares in the United States.[25] These demand shifts have continued until recently. Figure 6.22 shows that the market share of Japanese cars in the United States started rising again when gasoline prices increased around 1999. In 2004 to 2006, Japanese cars were still more fuel efficient than U.S. cars, as shown in figure 6.23. These demand shifts might constitute an explanation for why U.S. and Japanese automotive production differ in their responses to the oil-specific demand shocks; among our selected industries, automotive production differs the most between the United States and

24. Some large-scale multicountry macroeconomic models, including "G-Cubed model" (McKibbin and Wilcoxen 1998) and the International Monetary Fund's (IMF's) "Global Economy Model (GEM)" (Pesenti 2008), consider the global transmission channels of oil price changes.

25. There are many empirical studies on the U.S. automobile market. For instance, Goldberg (1998) examines the effects of the Corporate Average Fuel Economy Standards enacted in 1975 on automobile sales, prices, and fuel consumption, considering demand shifts toward more fuel-efficient vehicles.

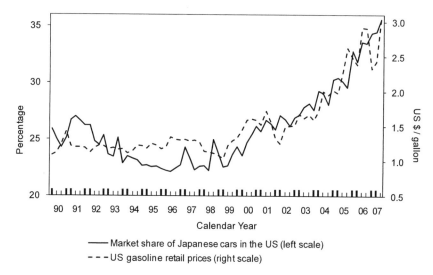

Fig. 6.22   Market share of Japanese cars in United States

Source: Research and Statistics Department, Bank of Japan (2007).

Japan. Moreover, the demand for automotive products induces production of many other industries such as steel and precision instruments. Although the value-added share of passenger cars (excluding buses and trucks) in Japanese industrial production is only about 8.5 percent, the economy-wide impacts of demand shifts toward Japanese cars may be substantial.

6.6   Concluding Remarks

In this chapter, we decomposed oil price changes into their component parts following Kilian (2009) and estimated the dynamic effects of each component on industry-level production and prices in the United States and Japan using identified VAR models. Our results reveal that the way oil price changes affect each industry depends on what kind of underlying shock drives the oil price changes as well as on industry characteristics. We also found that the transmission mechanisms differ considerably between the United States and Japan.

Our results imply that global demand shifts across countries are important factors for oil price changes themselves and their transmission mechanisms. We considered the global demand shocks as underlying causes of oil price changes and discussed the effects of global demand shifts toward more oil-efficient products. For a better understanding of the transmission mechanisms, it would be worth investigating differences in the effects of oil price changes among countries other than the United States and Japan. Moreover, developing open-economy dynamic stochastic general equilibrium models

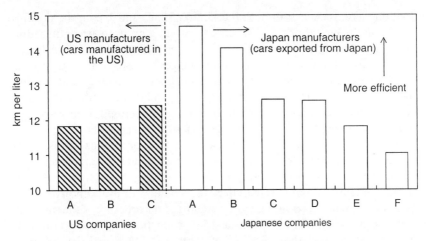

Fig. 6.23   Average fuel consumption of cars sold in United States
Source: Research and Statistics Department, Bank of Japan (2007).
Notes: Fuel consumption is calculated for each company as 2004 to 2006 averages. Fuel consumption of different vehicle types are averaged using their sales volume as weights.

that incorporate the global oil market is also a promising way of deepening our understanding and would enhance the interpretation of empirical results on the effects of oil price changes.

Appendix
Robustness Checks

In this appendix, we summarize the estimation results under several alternative assumptions and specifications of the model to check the robustness of our main results.[26]

First, we changed the sample period of estimation, while keeping the model unchanged. Although we focus on changes in the nature of the shocks rather than structural changes as an explanation for the weakening effects of oil price changes on real economic activity (as stated in footnote 5), it is possible to estimate our models for shorter sample periods and check whether structural changes occurred during the full sample period. We divided the sample period into the two subperiods, 1973:1 to 1983:12 and 1984:1 to 2008:12, following Blanchard and Galí (2007) in choosing the break point. In the later subperiod, the negative effects of the oil supply shocks on pro-

---

26. The detailed results of the robustness checks will be available upon request.

duction were weakened in both the United States and Japan, the positive effects of the global demand shocks on production were strengthened in Japan, and the effects of the oil-specific demand shocks were little changed in both countries. Therefore, structural changes occurred only in the effects of oil price changes caused by the oil supply shocks (and the global demand shocks in Japan), which historically made a small contribution to oil price movements (as shown in figure 6.3). Overall, the directions of the responses to the three structural shocks were little changed in each industry.

Second, we partially relaxed the block recursive restrictions and assumed that domestic aggregate variables could affect global oil market variables. Third, we included in the domestic macroeconomy block the short-term nominal interest rate and the real effective exchange rate in addition to aggregate industrial production.[27] Lastly, we changed the ordering of the variables in the domestic industry block (industrial production and producer prices) so that prices rather than production come first. We found that all these changes made little differences to our main results.

References

Blanchard, O. J., and J. Galí. 2007. The macroeconomic effects of oil shocks: Why are the 2000s so different from the 1970s? NBER Working Paper no. 13368. Cambridge, MA: National Bureau of Economic Research, September.
Bresnahan, T. F., and V. A. Ramey. 1993. Segment shifts and capacity utilization in the U.S. automobile industry. *American Economic Review* 83 (2): 213–18.
Bruno, M., and J. Sachs. 1985. *Economics of worldwide stagflation.* Cambridge, MA: Harvard University Press.
Davis, S. J., and J. Haltiwanger. 2001. Sectoral job creation and destruction responses to oil price changes. *Journal of Monetary Economics* 48 (3): 465–512.
Goldberg, P. K. 1998. The effects of the corporate average fuel efficiency standards in the U.S. *Journal of Industrial Economics* 46 (1): 1–33.
Hamilton, J. D. 1988. A neoclassical model of unemployment and the business cycle. *Journal of Political Economy* 96 (3): 593–617.
———. 1996. This is what happened to the oil price–macroeconomy relationship. *Journal of Monetary Economics* 38 (2): 215–20.
———. 2008. Oil and the macroeconomy. In *The new Palgrave dictionary of economics,* 2nd ed., ed. S. N. Durlauf and L. E. Blume. Houndmills, UK: Palgrave Macmillan.
Hirakata, N., and N. Sudo. 2009. Accounting for oil price variation and weakening impact of the oil crisis. IMES Discussion Paper no. 2009–E–1. Institute for Monetary and Economic Studies, Bank of Japan.
Hooker, M. A. 1996. This is what happened to the oil price–macroeconomy relationship: Reply. *Journal of Monetary Economics* 38 (2): 221–2.

27. The short-term nominal interest rate we use is the federal funds rate for the United States and overnight call rate for Japan. We use the real effective exchange rates published by the Federal Reserve Board and those published by Bank of Japan.

Jiménez-Rodríguez, R., and M. Sánchez. 2004. Oil price shocks and real GDP growth: Empirical evidence for some OECD countries. ECB Working Paper no. 362. European Central Bank, Frankfurt am Main.

Kilian, L. 2008. The economic effects of energy price shocks. *Journal of Economic Literature* 46 (4): 871–909.

———. 2009. Not all oil price shocks are alike: Disentangling demand and supply shocks in the crude oil market. *American Economic Review* 99 (3): 1053–69.

Kilian, L., and C. Park. 2009. The impact of oil price shocks on the U.S. stock market. *International Economic Review* 50 (4): 1267–87.

Lee, K., and S. Ni. 2002. On the dynamic effects of oil price shocks: A study using industry level data. *Journal of Monetary Economics* 49 (4): 823–52.

McKibbin, W., and P. Wilcoxen. 1998. The theoretical and empirical structure of the G-Cubed model. *Economic Modelling* 16 (1): 123–48.

Pesenti, P. 2008. The global economy model: Theoretical framework. *IMF Staff Papers* 55 (2): 243–84.

Research and Statistics Department, Bank of Japan. 2007. Recent developments of Japan's external trade and corporate behavior. BOJ Reports & Research Papers (Ad Hoc Themes). Bank of Japan.

Rotemberg, J. J., and M. Woodford. 1996. Imperfect competition and the effects of energy price increases on economic activity. *Journal of Money, Credit, and Banking* 28 (4): 549–77.

Comment   Francis T. Lui

Fukunaga, Hirakata, and Sudo's chapter provides a useful analysis of how shocks in oil prices affect production and prices at industry and aggregate economy levels. Changes in oil prices have been regarded in the real business cycles (RBC) literature as a major source of productivity shocks that can cause business cycles. The findings of this chapter therefore may have interesting implications for RBC models. They also remind us that the particular transmission mechanism of the effects of oil price changes matters a lot and that different economies may respond to these shocks in different ways.

The methodology of the chapter consists of using an identified VAR model with three sets of variables. They are

X_{1t} = global oil market variables
  = (world crude oil output, world industrial output, spot crude oil price)
X_{2t} = domestic aggregate variable
  = (aggregate industrial production)
X_{3t} = domestic industry-level variables
  = industry production, producer price)

Francis T. Lui is a professor of economics at the Hong Kong University of Science and Technology.

The block recursive matrix in the estimated model ensures that the X_{1t} variables depend on their lags, the X_{2t} variables depend on their own lags and those of X_{1t}, and the X_{3t} variables depend on its own lags and those of X_{1t} and X_{2t}. By adopting this approach, the chapter can analyze how the shocks in the X_{1t} variables are transmitted to the X_{2t} and X_{3t} variables.

While this approach is reasonable, one can nevertheless raise a number of issues. First, as stated before, the actual data used for the X_{1t} variables are world crude oil output, industrial output of major economies, and spot crude prices. However, the chapter interprets the shocks to these variables as oil supply shocks, global demand shocks, and oil-specific demand shocks, respectively. This interpretation is questionable. Here we only have a quantity variable, a demand shifter, and a price variable. They are not sufficient for identifying the supply and demand functions separately. Thus, interpreting changes in these variables as supply and demand shocks in the oil market could be misleading.

Second, the block-recursive nature of the VAR model implies that the "global" variables in X_{1t} do not depend on the "domestic" variable X_{2t} or X_{3t}. But the United States and Japan are the two largest economies in the world. World industrial output must therefore be affected by the industrial outputs in the United States or Japan in some significant ways. In the newly added appendix, the authors state that they have partially relaxed the block recursive restrictions by incorporating the feedbacks from the United States and Japan to the global oil market. They claim that the main results remain robust. This is a good attempt, but some readers may want to know some measures of the quantitative differences.

Third, the chapter interprets a shock as a demand shock when it causes price and quantity to move in the same direction and as a supply shock when it causes price and quantity to move in opposite directions. Changes in price and quantity could be the results of simultaneous movements in supply and demand. All we can say in this context is that supply shock dominates demand shock, or vice versa.

Fourth, the chapter claims that there is no clear evidence indicating sizable resource reallocation across industries both in the United States and Japan. However, it also reports that the magnitudes of the responses of production to each kind of shocks differ considerably across industries. Why cannot this phenomenon be interpreted as resource reallocation across industries?

The chapter has several interesting results. First, oil-specific "demand" shocks are shown to have different implications for the United States and Japan. This seems to be true irrespective of whether the oil price shocks are demand or supply shocks. Second, unanticipated oil price increases have a negative impact on the U.S. economy both at the aggregate and industry levels. Third, the impact of an increase in oil price on Japan's aggregate economy could be positive or insignificant. However, the impact on oil-intensive industries there is positive.

The second result is easily anticipated. The third one is surprising, but is in fact reasonable. Japan is good at producing energy-efficient products. An increase in oil price may benefit Japan because this may induce even more people to purchase energy-efficient Japanese products such as cars or intermediate products used for producing them. This result may inspire government policy-making, especially at times of economic crisis.

Another point we should note is that outputs in United States and Japan during the sample period seem to be driven by world demand and domestic aggregate demand. This may mean that productivity changes or other supply-side factors are unimportant. It would be premature for us to arrive at this conclusion, because the model itself cannot distinguish supply shocks from demand shocks.

Comment   Warwick J. McKibbin

This chapter explores the causes and impacts of oil price changes in the United States and Japan. It also focuses on the transmission of global oil shocks within these economies at the macroeconomic and industry levels. The introduction of the chapter talks about the scarcity of studies on the impact and causes of oil price shocks but this discussion is really about the studies that have used the vector autoregression (VAR) methodology. There is a large literature using large-scale macroeconometric models, computable general equilibrium models (e.g., the G-Cubed model of McKibbin and Wilcoxen [1999]), and energy models in academic journals such as *Energy Journal and Climate Change,* which explore the causes and impacts of oil price shocks. It is true that these approaches use a different methodology, but more widespread citation would be worthwhile.

The basis of the empirical part of the chapter is two independent VAR models. One model is for the United States and a separate model is for Japan. Each model has a global oil market, a domestic macroeconomic variable, and domestic industry-level variables. The disaggregation into industry-level detail is a contribution of the chapter.

Identification is critical in VAR models. Most of my comments focus on how identification is imposed in the chapter. The authors impose restrictions so that the global energy markets are not affected by feedback from the macroeconomic or industry variables. Similarly, the macroeconomic variables are affected by the global oil market but not by industry variables. Finally, the industry variables are affected by themselves and the global oil market

Warwick J. McKibbin is director of the Research School of Economics and of the Centre for Applied Macroeconomic Analysis (CAMA) at the Australian National University.

and macroeconomic variables. The two country VARs are completely independent from each other.

Given the identification of the model, both global oil markets give the same answer to the decomposition of shocks between oil supply shocks, global demand shocks, and oil-specific demand shocks. These shocks can then be used to explore how oil shocks feed through the United States and Japanese economies.

The authors find that the persistence and magnitude of changes in oil prices depends primarily on the nature of the shock to the oil market. They find that oil-specific demand shocks have the largest and most persistent effect on the oil price. Oil supply shocks have only temporary and insignificant effects on industrial production. They also find that global oil shocks have very different effects on Japan and the United States.

One set of issues regards the identification restrictions. It is hard to imagine that the two largest economies in the world do not affect the global oil market, yet there is no link back between responses in the country models on the global macroeconomic variable included in the energy market equations. Yet this is the assumption imposed by the specification of the VARs. This could be tested by relaxing the zero restrictions on the macroeconomic variables and the oil markets. However, if this was done then the equivalence of the oil markets would break down because the shocks presumably would be different in the U.S. model versus the Japanese model. This, then, suggests that both country models should be incorporated into a single VAR model, but degrees of freedom problems then arise and an approach like the Global VAR model of Dees et al. (2007) would be required.

It is also important how variables are ordered in terms of identification in the VAR model. It would be worth extending the approach of this chapter to explore the new sign restriction methodology such as by Fry and Pagan (2007).

Another issue regarding identification is the variables that are given zero restrictions in the macroeconomic parts of the VAR. In particular, exchange rates, inflation, and interest rates are excluded from the VAR (i.e., given zero restrictions), yet most macroeconomic VAR models find these variables are important. If the oil shocks propagate through the economy via changes in these variables then there may be a serious misspecification error. This might explain some of main differences between the transmission of shocks in the United States relative to Japan in the chapter. In particular the real exchange rate in Japan responds strongly to change in oil prices in the G-Cubed and macroeconometric models and therefore its omission from the VAR might be a problem. For example, suppose that an oil price rise depreciates the Japan real exchange rate, causing exports of manufacturing goods to rise and therefore stimulate industrial production (as found in the G-Cubed model). It might appear that oil has no impact on industrial production in Japan when in fact it does have a negative impact via input costs but a positive impact via exports. The general equilibrium story is very important for understanding the transmission story. The current specification excludes this understanding.

A further issue is the assumption that macroeconomic or aggregate variables drive industry outcomes whereas industry variables do not affect aggregate outcomes. This is hard to reconcile with the results from multisectoral macroeconomic models such as G-Cubed, where macroeconomic and sectoral adjustments are simultaneously determined. It is also a little surprising because the macro variable used is industrial production, which is the sum of the industry production data.

Another issue is the primacy given to oil prices rather than energy prices. We know from the oil price shocks of the 1970s and the more recent run up in oil prices from 2004 to 2008 that the prices of all energy sources (gas, coal, etc.) moved in a similar manner. It may be that not taking into account the more general energy sources could miss some key aspects of the transmission of oil shocks to the major economies.

Overall, there are some interesting extensions in this chapter to the standard approaches of estimating the effects of oil price shocks in the global economy. It is not surprising, and indeed is encouraging, that the model finds the same results as Killian (2009). The decomposition of oil shocks is probably robust to the specification issues raised in these comments but some of the results for the transmission through the economy need further exploration by relaxing the identification restrictions in ways outlined in these comments.

References

Dees S., F. Di Mauro, H. Pesaran, and V. Smith. 2007. Exploring the international linkages of the Euro area: A global VAR analysis. *Journal of Applied Econometrics* 22 (1): 1–38.

Fry, R., and A. Pagan. 2007. Some issues in using sign restrictions for identifying structural VARS. National Centre for Econometric Research Working Paper no. 14.

Killian, L. 2009. Not all oil price shocks are alike: Disentangling demand and supply shocks in the crude oil markets. *American Economic Review* 99 (3): 1053–69.

McKibbin, W., and P. Wilcoxen. 1999. The theoretical and empirical structure of the G-Cubed model. *Economic Modelling* 16 (1): 123–48.

Price Pass-Through, Household Expenditure, and Industrial Structure
The Case of Taiwan

Biing-Shen Kuo and Su-Ling Peng

7.1 Introduction

The pass-through caused by global commodity prices has substantial impacts on the Taiwan economy and has resulted in shifts in household expenditure patterns and the industrial structure. Globalization links the world through a network of increasingly close relationships, and causes each economy to be intertwined with the world market. The pass-through caused by global commodity prices is also evidence of this situation. Taiwan is a unique small open economy that is lacking in natural resources.[1] Since Taiwan behaves as a price-taker in international markets, the price pass-through effect caused by changes in global commodity prices has a substantial impact on the domestic economy.

Price pass-through can convulse an economy. Not only may it give rise to incentives to innovation and investment in technology as well as reflect market efficiency, but it may also inevitably worsen the income distribution, and fuel speculation.

The degrees of price pass-through in food and energy appear to differ in the levels of economic development.[2] Taiwan's economy has taken off since

Biing-Shen Kuo is professor in the department of international business at National Chengchi University. Su-Ling Peng is an associate research fellow in the Center for Economic Forecasting, Chung-Hua Institution for Economic Research.

See online appendix for this chapter at: http://www.nber.org/data-appendix/ito_09-1/EASE20ch7appendix.pdf.

1. Taiwan has to import about 99.9 percent of its crude oil. The value of imports of crude oil far exceeded Taiwan's trade surplus (25.2 billion in U.S. dollars) in 2007.

2. According to the IMF (2008), the estimated coefficients for twenty-five advanced economies and twenty-one emerging economies show that food-related price pass-through in advanced economies was found to be higher than in developing economies, whereas energy-related price

Table 7.1   The economic performance of Taiwan during the price fluctuations

Period (average)	Per capita GNP (US$)	Household expenditure on food-related items (%)	Household expenditure on energy-related items (%)	2nd ind. GDP/GDP (%)	Oil price (WTI)[a]
1972–1974	722	49.2	19.9	40.9	19.6
1979–1981	2,360	40.9	23.1	43.2	109.0
1989–1991	8,451	28.9	30.4	38.7	72.3
1999–2001	13,935	24.1	29.7	28.9	82.9
2004–2007	16,275	24.0	29.2	27.4	194.8
2008	17,524	24.0	28.0	25.0	328.5

Source: Own calculations based on DGBAS and AREMOS data sets.

Note: The GDP in Taiwan has increased fourfold since 1972 and the industrial structure has been upgraded.

[a]Oil price is denoted by the Texas Spot price index, which is obtained from the IFS.

the 1970s. Taiwan's per capita gross national product (GNP) was about $393 in 1970, and reached $17,524 in 2008 while her household expenditure patterns and industrial structure have been radically transformed, as shown in table 7.1. Household expenditure patterns have been changing in Taiwan with the proportion of expenditure on food dropping from 50 percent in 1970 to about 24 percent in 2008. The expenditures on food-related goods and energy-related items[3] are accorded a weight of 52 percent over the disposable income of the lowest 20 percent of households.[4] The higher the price pass-through effect, the more adverse is its effect on low-income households.[5]

The ratio of the secondary industry gross domestic product (GDP) to total GDP was around 36 percent in 1970, and reached 46 percent in 1980. Yet, the ratio of the secondary industry GDP to total GDP gradually fell to about 25.0 percent in 2008, being caused by Taiwan's expansion plans in the service sector in the past twenty years as well as low production costs in China, which has attracted many of Taiwan's manufacturing businesses. It needs to be asked if pass-through effects will result in distinct impacts as an economy is transformed and its household expenditure patterns and industrial structure are transformed as in Taiwan?

---

pass-through was found to be lower in developing economies. The sample was obtained from the IMF (2008).

3. The food-related goods include food, beverages, and tobacco. The energy-related goods and services comprise rent, water, electricity, gas, and other fuels.

4. The expenditures on food, rent, water, electricity, gas, and other fuels account for less than 40 percent of disposable income for the highest 20 percent of households, according to the "Survey on Household Income and Expenditure in Taiwan," published in 2007.

5. According to the Organization for Economic Cooperation and Development (OECD) and the Food and Agriculture Organization (FAO 2008), the weights of the food-related prices relative to the consumer price index are around 39.3 percent in developing economies and 16.2 percent in the developed economies, respectively.

As for the factors that might affect the extent of price pass-through, some studies have focused on institutional factors such as Imbs (2006) and Balakrishnan et al. (2009), who placed emphasis on financial integration, while some have focused on the relationship between monetary policy and exchange rate orientation with pass-through, such as Engel (2009), Ito and Sato (2008), the International Monetary Fund (IMF 2008), Monacelli (2005), and so on. According to the IMF (2008), more than 80 percent of emerging and developing economies around the world still maintain heavily-managed exchange rate regimes in order to anchor inflationary expectations more easily, but this also restricts the ability of monetary policy to respond.[6]

Taiwan is an export-oriented economy. The central bank of Taiwan has also carefully managed the exchange rate regime and thereby facilitated merchandise exports even though Taiwan has adopted a managed independently floating exchange rate policy since the mid-1980s. The influence of the monetary side on price pass-through has been restricted. Besides, the household expenditure patterns and transformation of the industrial structure have been more important than inflation to Taiwan's economy since the 1990s, owing to Taiwan's businesses having moved to China, which has evidently speeded up the transformation of the industrial structure.

Moreover, due to the constraints on data availability, both the United Nations and the IMF have omitted Taiwan's statistics; there are also no empirical results for Taiwan in studies such as De Gregorio, Landerretche, and Neilson (2007); IMF (2008); and Jongwanich and Park (2008). We thus focus on Taiwan as a case study both to make up for this omission and to serve as a source of reference for other economies.

We focus our analysis more on the inner structural and distribution effects in Taiwan. Based on the data availability and the features of the Taiwan economy, we look at this issue by placing emphasis on the relationship between a commodity's price pass-through with distribution effects on the real side and focus on consumers and producers.

As a result, while the price pass-through coefficients for food follow global trends, the coefficients for energy-related prices are higher in terms of domestic prices to core Consumer Price Index (CPI), which may result from the industrial structure factors in energy-related industries and government policies. However, shifts in the energy-related products that help make up the household expenditures are only slight because the supply of energy-related services is inelastic, and they are heavily subsidized. The impacts of commodity price shocks on the industrial structure are also reduced, resulting from the technology innovations in food processes, energy-saving improvements, and a reduction in energy-dependency.

We start with a fundamental analysis of Taiwan's price transmission

6. See the IMF (2008, 105–06).

channel and engage in empirical estimation to calculate the degree of price pass-through. Then we use the results to analyze the characteristics of the Taiwan economy and compare them with global trends. Then by adopting various scenarios we go further down to the demand side and the supply side in order to consider the economic outlook for Taiwan to see how the global commodity price fluctuations impact both consumers and producers.

7.2   The Commodity Price Pass-Through in Taiwan

7.2.1   The Transmission Mechanisms and Empirical Procedures for Price Pass-Through

The fluctuations in global commodity prices have impacts on the business cycles of small economies. As for Taiwan, the annual growth rates of the CPI were higher during the oil crisis in 1973 and the energy crisis in 1979. Nevertheless, the fluctuations in the prices of food-related items that were used in the calculation of the CPI were relatively moderate compared with the fluctuations in the prices of oil-related items that were used in the calculation of the CPI from the 1980s onward. This kind of situation was similar to the global trend.

Figure 7.1 depicts the transmission channels and empirical procedures for the fluctuations in global commodity prices transmitted to Taiwan's domestic prices and their impacts on Taiwan's economy. The fluctuations in the global commodity prices affect the domestic prices by means of the trade sectors and domestically-produced processes, and result in changes in relative prices. They may influence consumers' choices and reflect shifting household expenditure patterns. Thus, the various kinds of goods and services should be adjusted over time and thus the degrees of variation might be diversified. However, the changes in relative prices are not adjusted immediately and completely for there is usually a time lag. The degrees of global price pass-through are related to the industrial structures and consumers' expenditure patterns. Hence, the fluctuations in global commodity prices will result in changes in consumer behaviors, the costs of production, and the impacts on different goods and services.

In order to calculate the pass-through effect from international commodity prices to domestic prices in Taiwan, and evaluate the impact on household expenditure patterns and the industrial structure, we have conducted an empirical study with a focus on Taiwan.

The empirical procedures involve first calculating the degree of price pass-through by means of the vector autoregression (VAR) model, then utilizing AIDS (almost ideal demand system), a consumption conversion matrix, and input-output tables to distribute the impacts of price pass-through effects to consumers and producers. To transmit the price pass-through effects to consumers and producers, we need bridges to access the linkages. The bridges

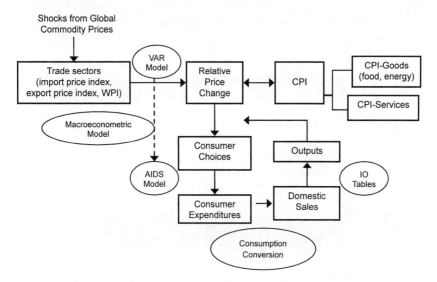

Fig. 7.1   The price transmission and empirical procedures flow chart

Note: The fluctuations in global commodity prices transmitted to Taiwan's domestic prices and their impacts on Taiwan's economy.

must capture the characteristics of the Taiwan economy and depict the interactions and transmissions of the price indexes. A macroeconometric model is an excellent solution.[7] The details of the empirical procedures are referred to in the appendices and the technical details are referred to on the web.

7.2.2   Estimating Commodity Price Pass-Through

There are two steps involved in assessing the potential impacts of the changes in the global commodity price pass-through on the core CPI in Taiwan. The first step is to link the changes in the domestic prices with the changes in global commodity prices. The second step is to link the core CPI inflation with the changes in the fuel and food prices in terms of domestic prices by controlling the changes in the Phillips curve output gap, respectively.[8]

---

7. Although a macroeconometric model is criticized for the nonstationarity of time-series data and suffers from the problems of spurious regression, a macroeconometric model can capture the characteristics of the Taiwan economy and depict the interactions and transmissions of price indexes. Besides, according to Park and Philips (1988, 1989), the traditional estimated methodology and asymptotic normality t test are still available if the residuals are I(0) and even if the model is a mix of I(1) and I(0). Furthermore, Hsiao (1997) also demonstrates that, despite variables that are integrated, the fundamental issues regarding structural equation modeling raised by the Cowles Commission remain valid and standard estimation and testing procedures can still be applied.

8. The equations used for the estimation are in a simple VAR form. The technical details are listed in the appendices, which are available in the web version.

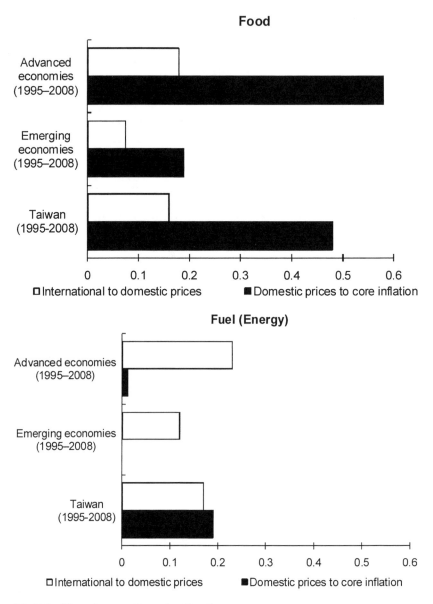

Fig. 7.2   The price pass-through estimation
Sources: Calculation based on IMF (2008). Own calculations based on estimation results.

The estimated results of the price pass-through in Taiwan are illustrated in figure 7.2 and displayed in table 7.2. The coefficient of price pass-through for food-related items in Taiwan, from global commodity prices to domestic prices, is 0.1346 and from domestic prices to core CPI is 0.1894. The IMF (2008) has stated that the estimated coefficients of price pass-through from

Table 7.2   **The price pass-through for core CPI in Taiwan**

Dependent variable		Independent variables	Sample period: 1995Q1–2008Q3
Step 1			
Domestic price (CPI_FOOD)		(a) Global commodity price—Food	0.1346
Domestic price (CPI_ENERGY)		(b) Global commodity price—Energy[a]	0.1733
Step 2			
Core CPI		(c) Domestic price (CPI_FOOD)	0.1894
		(d) Domestic price (CPI_ENERGY)	0.1921
Total price	Food	(e) = (a)*(c)	0.0255
Pass-though	Energy	(f) = (b)*(d)	0.0333

Source: Own calculations based on estimation results.
[a]In the IFS database, the world price index for energy starts from 1992Q2.

global commodity prices to domestic prices for advanced economies and developing economies are about 0.09 and 0.15, respectively, while Taiwan's lies somewhere in the middle. In addition, the estimated coefficients of price pass-through from domestic prices to core CPI in advanced economies and developing economies are about 0.18 and 0.48, respectively, while Taiwan's still lies in between.

On the other hand, the coefficient of price pass-though for energy-related items from global commodity prices to domestic prices is 0.1733, and from domestic prices to core CPI is 0.1921 for Taiwan. The IMF (2008) reported the estimated coefficients of global commodity prices to domestic prices in advanced economies and developing economies as being 0.23 and 0.12, respectively. Taiwan's is again still in between these two groups. Nevertheless, the estimated coefficients of price pass-through from domestic prices to core CPI in advanced economies and developing economies are 0.01 and almost 0, respectively. Here, Taiwan's is, however, higher than both that for advanced economies and that for developing economies, but is similar to the advanced economies (0.21) over the 1970 to 1995 period.

As figure 7.2 illustrates, the two price pass-through estimated coefficients, from international prices to domestic prices and domestic prices to core inflation in food-related items, is higher in emerging economies than in advanced economies during the period from 1995 to 2008, which indicates the influence that food-related goods price changes have on other goods (except fuel-related goods) is more price-sensitive in emerging economies.

The pass-through from international to domestic prices and from domestic prices to core inflation for fuel-related items is substantially lower in emerging economies than it is in advanced economies. We can explain that this may result from declining energy intensity, price controls in emerging economies, and energy-saving incentives, as well as high fuel taxes in advanced economies.

We define the total pass-through effects as the product of the two stages of the estimated coefficients, with the total price pass-through effects being equal to the pass-through from the global price index to the domestic price index multiplied by the pass-through from the domestic price to core CPI. The total food-related price pass-through for Taiwan lies between that for advanced economies and for developing economies, but the total energy-related price pass-through for Taiwan is found to be significantly higher than for advanced economies and developing economies during the 1995 to 2008 period. In addition, Taiwan's energy pass-through is slightly higher than the food price pass-through.

Notwithstanding that Taiwan is lacking in natural resources—such as oil, soybeans, or wheat, depending on foreign supplies—the estimated coefficients of price pass-through in Taiwan approximately follow the global trends. The exception is the price pass-through from domestic prices to core CPI for energy-related price items. The price pass-through for energy-related items is found to be slightly higher than for food-related items. We explain that this is because energy-related industries are almost public utility services and characterized by inelastic supply, and the industrial structures are either monopolies or oligopolies. Taiwan's government mostly adopts subsidy-related treatments[9] when fluctuations in energy-related prices become excessively large. Furthermore, energy shortages and a low degree of substitution in energy as well as guaranteed profits for certain companies all result in the higher price pass-through in Taiwan.

As we wondered whether the price pass-through may be different for domestic prices with export prices in the export-oriented economies such as Taiwan, we examined the price pass-through effects of global prices to import prices and export prices. We extended the work of the IMF (2008) to estimate price pass-through in the MPI (import price index) and XPI[10] (export price index). The estimated results are shown in table 7.3. The global price pass-through for the XPI was lower than it was for the MPI for both food and energy prices. We suggest that these results are attributed to Taiwan's entrepreneurial strength. The lower the XPI, the higher the world competitiveness. To benefit from international competition, Taiwan may mostly pass through the fluctuations in global commodity prices to the domestic market, but keeps the XPI more stable than it would otherwise have been.

Since there is no PPI (Produce Price Index) in Taiwan, we use the WPI (Wholesale Price Index) instead of PPI, which is composed of XPI, MPI,

9. The price control may cut down the price pass-through effects, but the subsidy may have positive effects to encourage the pass-through effects.
10. The XPI and MPI, which are denoted as price indexes, are expressed in terms of U.S. dollars, while the others are expressed in terms of New Taiwan (NT) dollars. We have added the exchange rate index to remove the effect of the exchange rate. However, the results are similar regardless of whether there is an exchange rate index or not.

Table 7.3   **The Price pass-through for other prices in Taiwan**

Dependent variable	Independent variables	Sample period: 1995Q1–2008Q3
Import Price Index (MPI)		
Food	Global commodity price—Food	0.4233
Energy	Global commodity price—Energy[a]	0.1904
Export Price Index (XPI)[b]		
Food	Global commodity price—Food	0.2252
Energy	Global commodity price—Energy[a]	0.0961
Domestic Sales Excluding Imports Price Index (DSPI)		
Food	Global commodity price—Food	0.2588
Energy	Global commodity price—Energy[a]	0.0713
WPI[c]		
Food	Global commodity price—Food	0.3004
Energy	Global commodity price—Energy[a]	0.1193

Source: Own calculations based on estimation results.
[a]In the IFS database, the world price index for energy starts from 1992Q2.
[b]There is no energy-related index in the XPI (export price index), so we cannot calculate the price pass-through for energy goods in the XPI.
[c]The WPI is composed of MPI (weighted 32.7 percent), XPI (weighted 36.5 percent), and DSPI (weighted 30.8 percent).

and DSPI (the domestic sales excluding imports price index). We compare our estimated results with core CPI and the WPI, and find the pass-through from the global commodity prices to the WPI is higher than it is to core CPI. These findings are similar to the 2008 study by Jongwanich and Park (in which Taiwan is somehow omitted), which states that the pass-through coefficients tend to be lower for consumer prices than producer prices, implying that the gap between these two price indices depends on the ability of firms to pass higher costs on to consumers. In the face of intense market competition, as the global commodity prices increase dramatically, the private producers may cut their marginal profits instead of immediately charging higher prices to consumers to keep their market shares. In addition, Taiwan's government policies such as price controls, energy-saving incentives, and other regulations might be implemented to reduce or delay the pass-through to CPI.

7.3   The Impacts of Price Pass-Through

The price pass-through might have distinct distribution impacts on the content of household expenditures and the industrial structure.[11] To evalu-

---

11. Hamilton (2009) stated that, regardless of whether oil price shocks are primarily caused by physical disruptions in supply or caused by strong demand, the consequences for the economy appear to have been very similar.

ate the distribution effects of the pass-through via the macro-econometric model of Taiwan's economy, we quantify the results from price pass-through to household expenditure patterns and the industrial structure—the impact on household expenditure patterns is treated as the demand side, while the impact on the industrial structure is represented as the supply side. To observe whether the impacts change as time passes, there are two scenarios:

1. Scenario 1: Assume the food-related price shock and energy-related price shock both occurred in 1993.[12] That is, we consider how much of an impact these had on the Taiwan economy in the 1990s as the food-related price index and energy-related price index both rose sharply in 1993.

2. Scenario 2: Assume that the food-related price shock and energy-related price shock both occurred in 2004. That is, we consider how much of an impact these had on the Taiwan economy in the twenty-first century as the food-related price index and energy-related price index both rose sharply in 2004.

7.3.1   Price Pass-Through Distribution Effects upon Consumers

When we evaluate the household expenditure patterns, we reclassify the categories of household expenditure patterns from twelve classifications to four classifications, which are referred to as "food-related expenditures" (which includes different kinds of food, beverages, and tobacco); "energy-related expenditures" (which is composed of fuel, gas, light, rent, and water charges); "entertainment-related expenditures" (which is made up of recreation, entertainment, education, and cultural services); and "other goods and services expenditures" (which includes various kinds of clothing, transport, communications, and so on).

Figure 7.3 indicates that the impacts on energy-related expenditures are smaller as shocks occur. It is known that the energy-related items are inelastic demand and the Taiwan government mostly adopts subsidy-related treatments, as the fluctuations in energy-related prices are noticeably large. As for food-related expenditures, they are for living necessities, and the elasticity of price is generally low. However, as diversities of food selections increase and the beverages, which are included in food-related items and whose ratio was around 10 percent in 2008, are more price-flexible, we think those might be the reasons why the food-related impacts are greater than the energy-related impacts. In addition, the impact on entertainment-related expenditures is the most severe—due to their being luxuries—and their income elasticity is also higher.

12. The energy index in International Financial Statistics (IFS) starts with the year 1992 and this results in the historical data covering fewer years than for the food index, which starts from the 1960s. When we set the scenario, we refer to the food index rather than the energy index. We assume that the annual growth rate of the commodity price shocks, as measured by both the food and energy indexes, rose by 80 percent of the growth rate of the food price index in 1973.

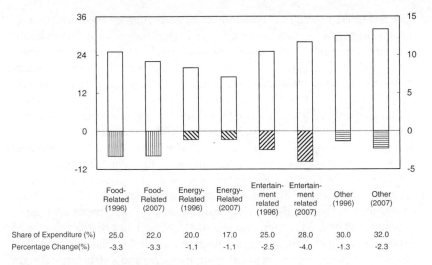

	Food-Related (1996)	Food-Related (2007)	Energy-Related (1996)	Energy-Related (2007)	Entertain-ment related (1996)	Entertain-ment related (2007)	Other (1996)	Other (2007)
Share of Expenditure (%)	25.0	22.0	20.0	17.0	25.0	28.0	30.0	32.0
Percentage Change(%)	-3.3	-3.3	-1.1	-1.1	-2.5	-4.0	-1.3	-2.3

Fig. 7.3   Price pass-through and household expenditure patterns

Source: Based on estimated results.

Notes: The upper parts are the share of each kind of expenditure over total expenditures. The lower parts are the percentage changes as commodity price shocks occur, which are based on scenario 1 and scenario 2.

7.3.2   Price Pass-Through Distribution Effects upon Producers

We employ the consumption conversion matrix to project the twelve categories of goods and services into 161 industries. The consumption conversion matrix and the input-output tables are based in the years 1996 and 2007,[13] respectively.

In general, the input-output model is excellent at describing the industrial structure,[14] and it may be the best tool that we can use to analyze the impacts of industrial shocks, which result in final demand such as household expenditures, and export-oriented and promotional policies. We apply the input-output tables to analyze and describe the price pass-through from household expenditure patterns to industrial structure that is caused by the global food and energy price shocks.

Although the input-output tables for 1996 and 2007 classify industries into 161 industries,[15] based on considerations of keeping the analysis concise, we

13. The 2007 input-output table is also extended, using 2004 as the base by means of the biproportional adjustment technique which is provided by Professor Hao-Yen Yang.

14. The frequency for the input-output tables in Taiwan is every five years. Owing to the data availability, we can only link the tables in different eras to capture the trends. If more data were available, we could have expressed them in terms of a dynamic process, but this is not possible here.

15. Although the shocks lasted for a period of more than one year, they have ceased to be felt as time passes. The variation in the real sector is close to zero in the fourth year after the shocks occurred, and the price deflators respond more quickly than the real sector. Due to the

have reclassified them into nine industries and renamed them as "agriculture and minerals"; "manufacturing—traditional industries"; "manufacturing—chemical and petroleum-related industries"; "manufacturing—heavy industries"; "construction"; "electricity, gas, and water"; "transportation, telecommunications, wholesale, and trading"; "finance, insurance, and real estate services"; as well as "other services."

The food-related goods and energy-related goods are the main intermediate inputs for "agriculture and minerals," and manufacturing industries. The manufacturing industries are described in more detail because of the differences in technology level, energy intensity, and energy efficiency. They are separated into "traditional industries," which include processed foods, beverages, tobacco, textile mill products, wearing apparel and accessories, leather and leather products, wood and wood products, paper and paper products and printed matter, and so on. "Chemical and petroleum-related industries" comprise chemicals, artificial fibers, plastic, plastic and rubber products, miscellaneous chemical manufactures, and petroleum-refining products; "heavy industries" might be treated as hi-tech industries and include iron and steel products, metallic products, machinery, electronic products, information products, communications equipment, electronic components and parts, electrical machinery, and so forth.

In table 7.4, we calculate the industrial linkage effect by means of forward linkages and backward linkages for the global commodity price shocks. In scenario 1, based on final demand, the top three industries ranked by percentage changes are "agriculture and minerals"; "electricity, gas, and water"; and "manufacturing-traditional industries", whose percentage changes are all over –2.5 percent. In scenario 2, the ranks are similar to those in scenario 1 except that the "manufacturing—traditional industries," is replaced by "electricity, gas, and water,"

"Agriculture and minerals" include food-related goods and crude oil, which suffer seriously due to the direct effects caused by the commodity price shocks. The "electricity, gas, and water" are regarded as intermediate inputs for almost all industries and their energy intensity is also higher. Therefore, the impacts are as sharp as if the shocks had occurred. "Manufacturing—traditional industries" are lower in terms of energy technology investment, and include processed food industries that are using food-related goods as intermediate inputs; therefore, the final demand is also likely to be affected.

Among the manufacturing industries, the higher the technology level, the smaller the impacts. The impacts on the "manufacturing—traditional industries," are the most critical, followed by those on "manufacturing—chemical and petroleum-related industries." Although "manufacturing—heavy industries," are relatively energy-intensive, they are also higher in

---

national incomes and input-output tables being compiled annually, we calculate their impacts by using weighted averages, and take the base years as 1996 and 2007.

Table 7.4   Simulation results in input-output tables

No. industries	1996 Base (millions)	(a) Scenario 1 (1996)	2007 Base (millions)	(b) Scenario 2 (2007)	(c) = (b) − (a)
	Final demand (percentage change [%])				
1 Agriculture and minerals	263,012	-4.952	412,417	-4.037	0.915
2 Manufacturing—traditional industries	1,213,545	-2.534	1,412,253	-2.746	-0.212
3 Manufacturing—chemical and petroleum-related industries	583,044	-0.600	1,701,082	-0.532	0.068
4 Manufacturing—heavy industries	3,232,880	-0.130	7,564,001	-0.194	-0.065
5 Construction	861,800	0.000	1,081,775	0.000	0.000
6 Electricity, gas, and water	87,044	-2.911	155,599	-2.254	0.658
7 Transport, telecom, and trading	1,483,245	0.038	2,925,416	-0.069	-0.106
8 Finance, insur., and real estate services	1,317,928	-1.576	2,745,917	-1.477	0.099
9 Other services	1,928,251	-0.792	2,975,259	-1.346	-0.554
Total	10,970,749	-0.816	20,973,719	-0.788	0.028
	Output (percentage change [%])				
1 Agriculture and minerals	488,894	-7.753	687,090	-7.331	0.422
2 Manufacturing—traditional industries	1,690,809	-2.917	1,893,071	-3.463	-0.546
3 Manufacturing—chemical and petroleum-related industries	1,662,753	-1.508	3,931,377	-1.253	0.254
4 Manufacturing—heavy industries	4,060,134	-0.439	8,596,517	-0.541	-0.101
5 Construction	1,013,445	-0.121	1,251,176	-0.152	-0.032
6 Electricity, gas, and water	366,281	-1.731	623,621	-1.652	0.079
7 Transport, telecom, and trading	2,894,714	-0.329	4,288,290	-0.458	-0.129
8 Finance, Insur., and real estate services	1,523,656	-2.092	4,175,374	-1.512	0.580
9 Other services	2,549,009	-1.092	4,496,904	-1.451	-0.359
Total	16,249,695	-1.273	29,943,420	-1.242	0.031
	Value added (percentage change [%])				
1 Agriculture and minerals	180,714	-10.893	335,824	-8.070	2.823
2 Manufacturing—traditional industries	455,928	-2.637	456,809	-3.562	-0.925
3 Manufacturing—chemical and petroleum-related industries	492,224	-1.206	883,516	-1.325	-0.119
4 Manufacturing—heavy industries	1,083,427	-0.337	1,928,870	-0.511	-0.174
5 Construction	350,008	-0.097	289,792	-0.181	-0.084
6 Electricity, gas, and water	174,621	-1.371	251,572	-1.554	-0.183
7 Transport, telecom, and trading	2,053,243	-0.307	2,611,210	-0.475	-0.167
8 Finance, Insur., and real estate services	1,051,525	-2.100	3,042,128	-1.391	0.708
9 Other services	1,714,111	-0.975	2,836,047	-1.431	-0.455
Total	7,555,801	-1.180	12,635,768	-1.303	-0.123

Source: Own calculations based on simulation results.

terms of energy efficiency and in terms of being energy-saving. Therefore, the impacts could be smaller than in the case of the traditional industries and petroleum-related industries. The services industries are also affected as commodity shocks occur by means of the industrial linkage effect. However, the impact is smaller than that of the "agriculture and minerals industries," and manufacturing industries.

By comparing the results from scenario 1 (based on 1996) with those from scenario 2 (based on 2007), in terms of final demand, the gaps that take differences in terms of percentage changes between 1996 and 2007 are extremely small. Those industries such as "agriculture and minerals"; "manufacturing—chemical and petroleum-related industries"; "electricity, gas, and water"; as well as "finance, insurance, and real estate services," for which the negative effects of price shocks have become smaller in 2007 than in 1996, almost all use food-related or energy-related items as intermediate inputs. The first three industries are all highly correlated with global commodity shocks. The reduced impacts may result from technology innovations in food processes, energy-saving improvements, and reductions in energy-dependency. The impacts on "finance, insurance, and real estate services" are also reduced; these might be correlated with the deregulation and globalization in the financial sector since the mid-1990s.

The gaps are amplified in "other services"; "manufacturing—traditional industries"; "transportation, telecommunications, wholesale, and trading"; and "manufacturing—heavy industries." The "other services," which include information services, education services, medical services, broadcasting, recreational and cultural services, and so on, and "transportation, telecommunications, wholesale, and trading," are highly related to reductions in expenditure on entertainment. The entertainment-related industries saw a bigger reduction in 2007 than in 1996.

The "manufacturing—traditional industries" and "manufacturing—heavy industries" are also deepened because their technology related to energy efficiency and energy-saving has been upgraded more slowly than the improvement in energy intensity. In addition, the traditional industries have been hollowed out to mainland China since the mid-1990s.

The impacts on the industrial structure in terms of output and value added are similar with final demand. While the results have been analyzed, the impacts on output and value added appear to be superfluous; we do not reproduce them here.

7.4   Conclusion

In order to calculate the price pass-through effect from international commodity prices to domestic prices and evaluate the impacts on household expenditure patterns and the industrial structure, we have conducted an empirical study that focuses on Taiwan.

Being a small, open, export-oriented, price-taker economy and lacking natural resources, the price pass-through effect caused by global commodity prices has a substantial impact on Taiwan's economy. In particular, Taiwan's household expenditure patterns and industrial structure have gradually been transformed and upgraded since its economy took off in 1972.

The commodity price shocks will affect the Taiwan economy by means of the price pass-through effect. How significant are the impacts? This will depend on the degree of pass-through, household expenditure patterns, and industrial structures. We apply a case study to calculate the extent to which global commodity prices are passed through to domestic prices for a small, open, price-taker, and developing economy like Taiwan in order to evaluate their impact on distribution effects such as household expenditure patterns and the industrial structure.

The price pass-through also results in distinct impacts on household expenditure patterns and industrial output by means of distribution effects. The effects of cuts in household expenditures on fuel and power and transportation and communications are slightly less pronounced than in the food-related industries, although the global price pass-through effects on domestic prices included in core CPI are similar. These findings reflect diversification in food purchases for households and the government's subsidy treatments for energy-related items.

Regarding the impacts of commodity shocks on the industrial structure, the food-related goods and energy-related goods mostly belong to the "agriculture and minerals" sectors and will be affected directly, so the impact will be most serious regardless of whether it is accounted for in final demand, output or value added. The impacts are evident in the primary industries and in secondary industries, which treat foods and energy as the main intermediate inputs. Nevertheless, the lessening of the impacts on food-related industries and energy-related industries results from technology innovations in food processes, energy-saving improvements, and the reduction in energy-dependency.

For the empirical procedures, we employ a VAR model to estimate the coefficients of price pass-through. Since the specifications of the VAR model take the possible control variables into account by means of the log-dependent variables, it may not be necessary to add more control variables if there are no specific issues of concern.

We do not emphasize the response of the pass-through to monetary policy, but have looked closely at the relationship between the pass-through and distribution effects in terms of household behavior following the shocks. In particular, the household expenditure patterns and transformation of the industrial structure have been more important than inflation to Taiwan's economy since the 1990s, resulting from Taiwan's firms moving to China, which has resulted in a rapid transformation of the industrial structure.

In taking the labor market into account, we have considered generalized Phillips curve equations in the price pass-through equations, which are treated as the supply-side effect. Furthermore, the labor market in Taiwan is characterized by almost full employment. The unemployment rate is almost always under 4.5 percent except during the bursting of the dot-com bubble in 2002 and 2003.

We focus on the relationship between structural transformation such as household expenditure patterns and the industrial structure with price pass-through effects. Since we consider the pass-through in terms of the overall effect, the estimation results for the price pass-through obtained from the VAR model should be regarded as a total effect based on the changing tax policy, exchange rate, and so on. Much more complicated modeling would be involved and more detailed data would need to be collected for the purpose of isolating each individual effect. These items may be regarded as limitations in this study.

Appendix

The Empirical Procedures for Price Pass-Through, Household Expenditure, and the Industrial Structure: The Case of Taiwan

In order to clarify the pass-through effect from global commodity prices to domestic prices, we evaluate the distribution effects of the pass-through on household expenditure patterns, which is treated as the demand side, and on the industrial structure, which is represented as the supply side.

The empirical procedures can be divided into two parts. In the first part, we follow the IMF (2008) to employ simple VAR models to estimate the coefficients of price pass-through, which are described as just mentioned. In the second part, we utilize AIDS, a consumption conversion matrix, and input-output tables to distribute the impacts of the price pass-through effects.

The VAR Model for Commodity Price Pass-Through

We modified De Gregorio, Landerretche, and Neilson (2007) and IMF (2008) to calculate the price pass-through coefficients for Taiwan. There are two steps involved. The first step traces the changes in domestic prices to the changes in global commodity prices. The first step employs simple regressions of the following form:

(A1) $$\pi_t^{domestic} = \alpha + \sum_{i=1}^{4} \beta_i \pi_{t-i}^{domestic} + \sum_{i=0}^{4} \delta_i \pi_{t-1}^{world} + \varepsilon_t.$$

Here, π is denoted as the annualized quarter-over-quarter log difference (in percent) in food or fuel prices (we also include seasonal dummies). The reported pass-through coefficients are calculated as:

(A2)   price pass-through $= \dfrac{\sum_{i=0}^{4} \delta_i}{1 - \sum_{i=1}^{4} \beta_i}$.

The second step for pass-through from domestic (food and fuel) prices to core CPI is estimated using the following generalized Phillips curve equations:

(A3) $\pi_t = \alpha + \sum_{i=1}^{4} \beta_i \pi_{t-i} + \sum_{i=0}^{4} \gamma_i (y_{t-i} - y_{t-i}^*) + \sum_{i=0}^{4} \phi_i \pi_{t-i}^{food} + \sum_{i=0}^{4} \varphi_i \pi_{t-i}^{fuel} + \varepsilon_t.$

The price pass-through can be defined as:

(A4)   food price pass-through $= \dfrac{\sum_{i=0}^{4} \phi_i}{1 - \sum_{i=1}^{4} \beta_i}$

(A5)   fuel price pass-through $= \dfrac{\sum_{i=0}^{4} \varphi_i}{1 - \sum_{i=1}^{4} \beta_i}$.

Here π stands for the annualized quarter-over-quarter log difference (in percent) in core, food, and fuel prices, while y and y^* denote the annualized quarter-over-quarter log difference (in percent) in, respectively, real and potential output[16] (the equations also include seasonal dummies). To eliminate contamination of the estimates by endogenous factors, the price pass-through from domestic commodity prices to core inflation is estimated using predicted values from the first step.[17]

The Macroeconometric Model of Taiwan's Economy

To feed the parameters for evaluating the distribution effects of the pass-through on household expenditure patterns, we employ a macroeconometric model for reference purposes. The macroeconometric model can be treated as a conduit to transfer the price pass-through effect to consumers and producers.

The features of such a macroeconometric model of the Taiwan economy are listed as follows.

16. We follow the IMF (2008) by employing the Hodrick-Prescott filtered trend to estimate potential GDP.
17. In this way, domestic food and fuel prices reflect only the variation that is due to changes in international prices and the lagged effects of domestic price developments, rather than movements in labor, transportation, and retailing costs that may have common origins with overall inflation.

First, the model provides detailed descriptions of the GDP deflator, WPI, MPI, XPI, CPI, and the private consumption deflator. For the settings of the price functions, we consider the transmission mechanism and comovement between price indices. Second, the model is demand driven.[18] Third, as for the composition of GDP on the expenditure side, each of its components has its own behavioral equations except for the government sector, which we treat as exogenous. Fourth, the household expenditures are classified into twelve categories based on the characteristics of the goods and services, which can be described in more detail.[19] Based on the transmission processes, feedback effects, and related theories, we specify and capture the variables' interactions.

Based on the transmission processes and feedback effects, we capture the variables' interactions. In the processes of selecting the behavioral functions, the independent variables are specified and recognized as their related theories. Moreover, each equation must satisfy the statistical diagnosis. The technical details are available on the web (http://www.nber.org/confer//2009/ease09/program.html).

We find that the global commodity price shocks will pass away as time passes. The changes in real GDP will be close to zero in the fifth year. The paths for the changes in the price indexes, such as the CPI, XPI, and MPI, will respond more quickly than the real sectors. They will tail off as time passes by. That is, by comparing the change and trend from real GDP (or the real sectors) with the CPI (or the price index), we learn that the price indexes respond more quickly. The price index almost responds perfectly within a period of two years. Then the negative effect tails off.

If we compare the simulation results for only the food-related price shock with only the energy-related price shock, we find that the food-related shock has a heavier impact even though the pass-through effect is higher. Owing to the energy-related price fluctuating more frequently, the government mostly adopts subsidy-related treatments. Besides, there is a gearing effect related to the domestic food-related prices. That is, it is easier for the food-related prices in the domestic market to rise than it is for them to fall. Therefore, the food-related price shock has a more serious impact on the Taiwan economy.

18. Due to the labor market being stable in Taiwan, for example, the unemployment rate is almost under 4.5 percent except in 2002 and 2003, the rigidities in the labor market are not so serious, and we have added a term representing the gap between actual output and potential output. This is denoted as $(y - y^*)$ in the price pass-through equations, which are denoted as the generalized Phillips curve equations, and is also treated as a proxy for the supply-side effect. In view of this, we model the labor market as simply as possible.

19. We have adopted the suggestions proposed by the referee to reestimate the macroeconometric model and the AIDS model using the sample periods from 1992Q2 to 2008Q3, and so the estimated equations' sample period could coincide with the simulation results. We also conducted structural break tests, such as the Chow test, and only little evidence was found for the structural break.

References

Balakrishnan, R., S. Danninger, S. Elekdag, and I. Tytell. 2009. The transmission of financial stress from advanced to emerging economies. IMF Working Paper no. WP/09/133. Washington, DC: International Monetary Fund.

De Gregorio, J., O. Landerretche, and C. Neilson. 2007. Another pass-through bites the dust? Oil prices and inflation. Working Paper no. 417. Santiago: Central Bank of Chile.

Engel, C. 2009. Pass-through, exchange rates, and monetary policy. *Journal of Money, Credit, and Banking* 41: 177–85.

Hamilton, J. 2009. Causes and consequences of the oil shock of 2007–08. *Brookings Papers on Economic Activity* (Spring): 1–68.

Hsiao, C. 1997. Cointegration and dynamical simultaneous equation models. *Econometrica* 65: 647–70.

International Monetary Fund. 2008. Is inflation back? Commodity prices and inflation. Available at: www.imf.org/external/pubs/ft/weo/2008/02/pdf/c3.pdf.

Imbs, J. 2006. The real effects of financial integration. *Journal of International Economics* 51: 296–24.

Ito, T., and K. Sato. 2008. Exchange rate changes and inflation in post-crisis Asian economies: Vector autoregression analysis of the exchange rate pass-through. *Journal of Money, Credit, and Banking* 40: 1407–38.

Jongwanich, J., and D. Park. 2008. Inflation in developing Asia: Demand-pull or cost-push? Asian Development Bank, ERD Working Paper no. 121. European Report on Development.

Monacelli, T. 2005. Monetary policy in a low-through environment. *Journal of Money, Credit, and Banking* 37 (6): 1047–66.

Organization for Economic Cooperation and Development (OECD) and the Food and Agriculture Organization (FAO). 2008. *OECD–FAO agricultural outlook 2008–2017.* OECD publication. Available at: http://www.fao.org/es/esc/common/ecg/550/en/AgOut2017E.pdf.

Park, J. Y., and P. C. B. Phillips. 1988. Statistical inference in regressions with integrated processes, part 1. *Econometric Theory* 4: 468–97.

———. 1989. Statistical inference in regressions with integrated processes, part 2. *Econometric Theory* 5: 95–131.

Comment   Cayetano Paderanga Jr.

Introduction

I would like to thank the National Bureau of Economic Research and the Hongkong University of Science and Technology for inviting me to this conference. I found this chapter quite enjoyable and informative, and I would like to commend the authors for writing a chapter with important policy implications for Taiwan and with probable applicability of the same

Cayetano Paderanga Jr. is professor of economics at the University of the Philippines.

or similar models to other countries. The lessons learned here could be tremendously useful for emerging economies.

Structure of the Chapter

The chapter creatively exploits distinct developments in economic modeling to estimate the impact of oil and commodity prices on domestic inflation and, after that, consumption and economic structure. It utilizes methods used by De Gregorio, Landerretche, and Neilson (2007) and the International Monetary Fund (2008) to trace the price pass-through from the global markets to the domestic economy. Using a three-step approach, the chapter first estimates the price pass-through using VAR regressions. Second, it uses a macroeconometric model to estimate the impact on key macro variables. Finally, it traces the impact on the whole economy and on various sectors by using the input-output tables and the consumer demand system estimated through the almost ideal demand system (AIDS).

Initial Lessons

The findings in the chapter by themselves already provide some very useful insights for other countries. For example, the authors extract some results from comparison of the price pass-through for Taiwan and compare it to those of the two polar ends in the IMF study; that is, the highest-income and the lowest-income countries, finding that Taiwan, being a midlevel income economy, also experienced a midrange price pass-through. Some of the other results of the chapter regarding the relationship of Taiwan's price pass-through to some structural features of the economy provide valuable lessons for others. I only included some possible extensions as more of wish list for others who may implement a similar exercise for their own countries.

On the Price Pass-Through

The estimation of the pass-through for Taiwan and the subsequent comparison with results of similar measurement for economies at various levels of development, in a previous study, already provide important lessons for other countries. The study finds that Taiwan is in the middle of the IMF range of countries, confirmed by analogy to stages of structural variation in income per person and food and total expenditure, that the results are reasonable. It attributes the actual estimated variation in price pass-through to the level of industrial development of Taiwan. Perhaps the addition of more control variables such as the use of relatively more flexible production technology, depth of the financial markets to hedge price volatility, macroeconomic policy interventions, or degrees of concentration in key industries to the extent possible with available data could have added even more dimensions to the lessons from the estimated pass-through coefficient. Inclusion of these relevant control variables could have an effect on the time-lag and the pattern of the estimated pass-through. The study has already shown the importance of control variables by explicitly recognizing the output-gap in the pass-through estimation from domestic price index to core CPI.

Second, on the Simulation Exercise

The study uses an econometric model estimated for the period 1987 to 2008 to estimate the impact of the price pass-through on major macroeconomic variables. Then it uses a combination of an almost ideal demand system (AIDS) estimated for 1987 to 2007 and input-output tables for 1997 and 2007 to distribute the impact to the various sectors.

One possible extension of the study would be to explicitly recognize the possibility of structural change during the period by either: (a) introducing appropriate dummy variables to capture changes in intercepts and/or slopes over the period, or (b) estimating separate macroeconometric and AIDS models for at least two separate subperiods. There seem to be enough observations to estimate these separate models (even allowing for some overlap in the middle part of the period). This could improve the precision and even provide more elaboration on the impact of the price pass-through on the industrial structure. For the input-output tables, I wonder if the study could have elicited more inferences if it explicitly recognized the changes in structure and incorporated these into the analysis along the lines of Chenery-Syrquin (1975).

References

Chenery, H. B., and M. Syrquin. 1975. *Patterns of development, 1950–1970.* London: Oxford University Press.

De Gregorio, J., O. Landerretche, and C. Neilson. 2007. Another pass-through bites the dust? Oil prices and inflation. Working Paper no. 417. Santiago: Central Bank of Chile.

International Monetary Fund. 2008. *Is inflation back? Commodity prices and inflation.* Available at: www.imf.org/external/pubs/ft/weo/2008/02/pdf/c3.pdf.

Comment   Arianto A. Patunru

This chapter by Kuo and Peng is very promising. It is one of the few that examines global commodity price pass-through into an individual country. It therefore lends itself to further elaboration and integration with other instruments to assess the country's response to global price fluctuation and its likely impacts on household and industrial behavior in the respective country. Thus far the literature on similar pass-through analysis approach has

Arianto A. Patunru is head of the Institute for Economic and Social Research, Department of Economics, University of Indonesia (LPEM-FEUI).

been dominated by cross-country examination (e.g., De Gregorio, Lander-retche, and Neilson 2007; IMF 2008). Those studies are bound to maintain certain commonalities across countries to allow for direct comparison, with the downside being the inability to go deeper into any given country. Hooker (2002) does evaluate price pass-through to the U.S. economy. However, he does not extend the analysis into examining the response of domestic house-hold and industries.

Other works in this line have actually attempted to examine global price pass-through to individual countries; however, most of them rely on stan-dard VAR approaches that are rather theory-free and therefore are limited in lending themselves to more comprehensive economic analysis.[1] Kuo and Peng, on the other hand, use a Hooker-type of Phillips curve to examine the price pass-through, as do De Gregorio, Landerretche, and Neilson and IMF. Prior to the Phillips curve estimation, following IMF, the authors also apply direct regression of lagged domestic and world prices on the current domestic price (that is, without output deviations). They then use the predicted values of domestic prices in their Phillips curve estimation in order to keep out the factors other than changes in international prices and lagged effects of domestic price development (e.g., labor movements, transportation costs, etc.).

The novelty of this chapter lies in its attempt to integrate the pass-through estimation of food and energy world prices to domestic prices with a macro-econometric model and AIDS model to see the impacts on household expen-diture and industrial structure. The authors then use input-output tables to do a series of simulation to see how the Taiwan economy would respond if the world price shocks like those of the 1970s occurred in the 1990s and 2000s.

The authors find that the global food and energy price pass-through to Taiwan lies between those of advanced and emerging economies (compared to the IMF study results). Furthermore, they find that food-related CPI and energy-related CPI have quite similar impacts on the core CPI—the former follows the global trend while the latter is higher; the global price pass-throughs to export and import prices are higher for food than for energy; the pass-through to import price is higher than that to export price; and that pass-through to WPI is higher in food but lower in energy than that to CPI. Finally, the authors also find that price impact is highest in house-

1. This is not to say that VAR is useless. On the contrary, VAR and its variants have been proved useful in the previous studies to examine *direct* effect of global price change. Blanchard and Gali (2007) combine VAR and a New Keynesian dynamic stochastic general equilibrium (DSGE) to examine oil price pass-through to the United States and other industrial countries. De Gregorio, Landerretche, and Neilson (2007) use VAR to check the robustness of their results from the Phillips curve estimation. Shioji and Uchino (chapter 5, this volume) combine VAR and time-varying parameter VAR (TVP-VAR) to assess the oil price through to Japan. In fact, checking their result robustness with VAR might strengthen Kuo and Peng's chapter.

hold's entertainment-related expenditures, followed by food-related and energy-related expenditures; and as for the production side, the higher the technology level, the smaller the global commodity price impact on manufacturing industries as price fluctuates and passes through.

These results are interesting. However, the authors spend little time explaining each of them in an integrated perspective. They assert that these results are due to the fact that Taiwan's economic development is indeed between those of advanced and emerging economies; that energy-related industries in Taiwan are either monopolies or oligopolies; that food-related industries are more domestic-oriented; that price impacts on household expenditures are consistent with the nature of the commodities (i.e., subsidy in energy-related expenditure, diversity in food selection, and entertainment being luxurious and hence highly elastic); and that export structure is more concentrated in industrial goods. These explanations are scattered and too limited to give a clear picture to readers of what the Taiwan economy is and why the results make sense. For example, the authors might want to explain further what the nature of market structure has to do with the price through coefficients. Or why export being more concentrated in industrial goods makes pass-through to import price higher than that to export price.

Furthermore, the authors might want to have more discussion on the nature of the labor market in Taiwan. It is true that their two-stage estimation might have cleared the pass-through coefficients from this factor, but considering that the broad literature (e.g., De Gregorio, Landerretche, and Neilson 2007; Blanchard and Gali 2007) put emphasis on real wage rigidity as a factor that might dampen the price effect, it calls for an address in this chapter as well. This will also be useful to give a sense of the second-round effect of global price changes. It is helpful that the authors have explained that the labor market in Taiwan is "stable" and that the rigidity in the labor market is "not so serious." However, it would be more useful if the authors gave more evidence to support these explanations. For example, the authors might have a small table of unemployment rate series corresponding to their selected sample.

The chapter is also rather silent on the role of taxes, tariffs, and monetary policies—other factors that appear quite extensively in the related literature. Especially on the issue of monetary policy, it is important to address whether the low pass-through coefficient can to some extent be attributed to more favorable inflation environment due to monetary policy, so as to confirm or disconfirm previous studies (e.g., Bernanke, Gertler, and Watson 1997; Hooker 2002; Leduc and Sill 2004; De Gregorio, Landerretche, and Neilson 2007). It will be informative if the authors explain further why they think the monetary policy's influence on the price pass-through "has been restricted." It is also unclear why the authors think that the relocation of Taiwan's business to China has speeded up the structural transformation (and that such transformation is more important than inflation to Taiwan's economy).

De Gregorio, Landerretche, and Neilson 2007 modify their Phillips curve estimation by also measuring world oil prices in domestic currencies. That way, they are able to address the role of exchange rate pass-through; they find that almost half of the inflationary effect of the 1970s oil shocks was caused by oil-induced devaluations, not the mere increase in world oil prices. It would be useful if the authors followed this approach to see whether a specific case like that of Taiwan survives this generalization.[2]

Finally, the authors might want to elaborate more on why, as they find it, price pass-through impacts more on primary industries (e.g., agriculture) and secondary industries (e.g., mineral). On the other hand, among manufacturing industries, heavy industries are "only slightly damaged." This is rather strange for, as the authors acknowledge, their energy intensities might be the highest. The authors do assert that this is because the industry's heavy use of energy is efficient relative to other industries (despite the volume) and because almost all heavy industries focus on export-oriented goods whose price pass-through are low. It would be more helpful if the authors supplied some information about energy intensity in related industries as well as the share of exports in their products.

References

Bernanke, B., M. Gertler, and M. Watson. 1997. Systematic monetary policy and the effects of oil price shocks. *Brookings Papers on Economic Activity* 1:91–116. Washington, DC: Brookings Institution.

Blanchard, O. J., and J. Gali. 2007. The macroeconomic effect of oil shocks: Why are the 2000s so different from the 1970s? NBER Working Paper no. 13368. Cambridge, MA: National Bureau of Economic Research, September.

De Gregorio, J., O. Landerretche, and C. Neilson. 2007. Another pass-through bites the dust? Oil process and inflation. Bank of Chile Working Paper no. 417.

Hooker, M. 2002. Are oil shocks inflationary? Asymmetric and nonlinear-specifications versus changes in regime. *Journal of Money, Credit, and Banking* 34 (2): 540–61.

International Monetary Fund. (IMF). 2008. Is inflation back? Commodity prices and inflation. *2008 world economic outlook.* Available at: www.imf.org/external/pubs/ft/weo/2008/02/pdf/c3.pdf.

Leduc, S., and K. Sill. 2004. A quantitative analysis of oil price-shocks, systematic monetary policy, and economic downturns. *Journal of Monetary Economics* 51 (4): 781–808.

2. The authors did use exchange rates in some of their estimations (e.g., those of export and import prices equations). However, it seems that these are not for addressing the role of exchange rate pass-through, at least in the way shown by De Gregorio, Landerretche, and Neilson (2007). In fact, it is not very clear in what currency denomination they input their world prices in the food-CPI and energy-CPI estimating equations.

IV

Macroeconomic Effects of Oil Prices

8

Oil and Macroeconomy
The Case of Korea

Junhee Lee and Joonhyuk Song

8.1 Introduction

The world oil price reached a recorded high level in the summer of 2008 following its ascent from 2002. The increase in oil price is noticeable following a long stable period of oil price movements after the second world oil crisis of 1979 and 1980. Figure 8.1 shows the Western Texas Intermediate (WTI) oil price movements and the (shaded) recessions of the Korean economy since 1970. As we glance over the figure, we find that several of the Korean economic recessions coincide with episodes of world oil price hikes, particlarly for the periods of 1973 to 1974 and 1979 to 1980.

The recent increase in the world oil price did not induce much attention concerning the possibility of causing an economic recession. This is in contrast to previous episodes of the world oil price hikes, that many studies attributed as causes of economic recessions. The recent oil price hike began to stabilize after autumn 2008. However, it still raises questions concerning the relationship between world oil price hikes and macroeconomy; such as why the recent oil price hike did not cause a serious economic recession as it did previously. The macroeconomic impacts or nature of the oil price hike might have changed from the past.

Generally, an increase in oil price will affect econmic growth adversely both through consumption and procution channels. An increase in oil price will raise the consumers' cost of living and reduce overall consumption. In addition, it will add more uncertainties to consumers' future economic out-

Junhee Lee is assistant professor at School of International Economics and Business, Yeungnam University. Joonhyuk Song is assistant professor at Economics Division of Hankuk University of Foreign Studies.

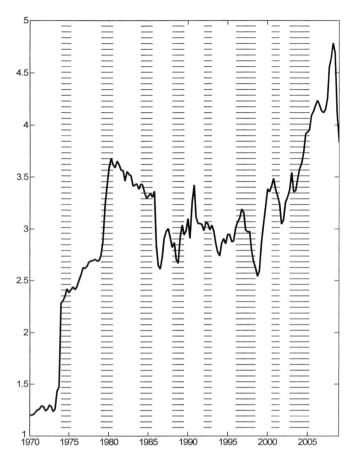

Fig. 8.1   Oil price and Korean economic recessions

looks and negatively affect the economy, as consumers will save more and spend less out of a precautionary motive facing the increased uncertainties. Hamilton (2005) stressed an indirect effect due to changes in the compositions of consumption expenditure. That is, changes in the compositions disturb sectoral allocations of resources and result in cutbacks in consumption, as well as increases in unemployment due to frictions in labor and capital markets. An increase in oil price will also affect economic growth adversely through production channels. An increase in oil price will raise production costs and increase uncertainties surrounding businesses and thus it will reduce productions.

In the past, large oil price hikes occurred following supply contractions due to geopolitical conflicts and uncertainties tied to oil-exporting countries. Hamilton (1996) showed that increases in oil prices preceded most U.S. recessions and that they were the main causes of the recessions. Using

New York Mercantile Exchange (NYMEX) crude oil futures data, Guo and Kliesen (2005) found that oil price volatilities had significant adverse effects on investment, consumption, and the unemployment rate.

The recent rise in oil price, however, can be viewed from a somewhat different perspective. In terms of the world oil market, oil demand recently increased substantially. For instance, China and India, new world economic powerhouses, have become huge consumers of crude oil. Other Asian economies have also increased their demands for crude oil as they recover from the financial crises of the late 1990s. In addition, developed countries also continued to grow during the period, supported by somewhat low interest rates. The recent hike in oil price thus might be viewed as endogenous movements along with the developments of strong oil market demands (or world economy), rather than exogenous movements stemming from supply-side contractions, as in the past.[1]

In terms of monetary policy, the recent oil price hike also reignites debates as to on which inflation measure the central bank should focus.[2] Oil price hike results in divergence between headline inflation and core inflation, which excludes energy and food inflation from headline inflation. The oil price increase may pass through to the price of nonenergy goods and services and lead to a dissociation between the headline and core inflation. The possible widening gap between two measures of inflation again raises the questions concerning the correct choice of inflation measure for conducting monetary policy.

In this chapter, we first analyze the nature of oil price hikes and their impacts on the Korean economy. We examine in detail whether the recent oil price hike is similar to or different from previous ones in terms of its origination. We further examine the impacts of the recent oil price hike on the Korean economy and compare them to previous experiences. We find the recent oil price hike originates endogenously from the demand side of world oil market, rather than exogenously from the supply side. The macroeconomic impact of the oil price hike is somewhat weakened compared to the previous oil price hikes, due to possible changes in macroeconomic structure.

We also discuss which inflation target would be more appropriate for the central bank to stabilize the economy. For this purpose, we built a dynamic stochastic general equilibrium (DSGE) model to examine the issue in a structural model. The model incorporates a Taylor-type monetary policy rule and monetary policy responds differentially to oil and nonoil prices, which correspond to noncore and core measures of inflation.

1. Kilian (2008) provide evidence that unanticipated crude oil supply shocks are far less important than shocks from the demand for crude oil.
2. Countries differ in their choice of an inflation measure for monetary policy. For example, the Bank of England and the Bank of Korea choose headline inflation as their policy target, while the U.S. Federal Reserve puts more emphasis on core inflation.

Previous literature generally tends to side with core inflation targeting rather than headline inflation targeting. Goodfriend and King (1997) suggest that monetary policy needs to focus on the sticky component of prices, rather than overall prices, implying core inflation to be the major target for conducting monetary policy. Aoki (2001) constructs a two-sector model, one with sticky price and the other with flexible price, and shows that complete stabilization of sticky price inflation is optimal in the model. Blinder and Reis (2005) provide evidences that core inflation predicts future headline inflation better than headline inflation itself.[3] Bodenstein, Erceg, and Guerrieri (2008) show that core inflation targeting in response to oil price shocks stabilize the economy better than headline inflation targeting in a DSGE model.

Conversely, Harris et al. (2009) criticize the policy recommendations from the aforementioned standard New Keynesian models in that these models assume the complete anchoring of inflation expectations. They show that longer-term consumer expectations on inflation respond to oil price shocks and suggest that the Fed should have put more weight on headline inflation. Hamilton (2008) shows that oil price shocks cannot be treated as merely transitory, discussing statistical characteristics of oil price shocks from historical data, and suggests that the central bank needs to pay more attention to the development of headline inflation including energy and food prices.

We find in an estimated DSGE model of the Korean economy that energy or oil price is relatively flexible compared to nonoil price and wage (but not completely flexible), and monetary policy would stabilize the economy better when it accommodates oil price inflation rather than fight against it.

The remainder of the chapter is organized as follows. In section 8.2, we describe basic findings from data. In section 8.3, we construct a five-variable structural vector autoregression (VAR) model and analyze the relationship between oil price and the Korean economy. In section 8.4, we present a DSGE model with oil sector and discuss monetary policy implications. Finally, section 8.5 concludes.

8.2   Data

In this section, we examine the properties of quarterly Korean data as well as world oil price; real gross domestic product (GDP), Consumer Price Index (CPI), and (real and nominal) interest rates together with world oil price (the WTI) as a preliminary step before formal analyses. We divide the data set into two subperiods, namely before and after the Korean currency crisis in 1998 and 1999 that is believed to have caused a structural break in

---

3. Cogley (2002) and Rich and Steindel (2005) also found the significant reversion of headline inflation to core inflation.

Table 8.1   **Summary Statistics**

	Pre-crisis		Post-crisis	
	Mean	Standard deviation	Mean	Standard deviation
Δ log WTI	1.45	12.08	3.08	15.64
Δ log CPI	2.39	1.96	0.76	0.44
Δ log CORE	2.06	1.75	0.70	0.31
Δ log RGDP	1.87	1.29	1.09	1.43
INTR	3.15	0.58	1.05	0.17
INTR-Δ log CPI	1.67	0.70	0.28	0.42

Notes: Measures in quarterly growth. Log difference from the previous quarter times 100.

the Korean economy.[4] The pre-crisis sample period is 1987:I to 1997:IV and post-crisis sample period is 2000:I to 2009:I. The division is also helpful to compare the effects of the recent oil price hike from the previous ones before the 1990s.

We first show the means and standard deviations of the log-difference data during the two subperiods in table 8.1. As we can see from the table, the standard deviations of the WTI and the real GDP log difference during the post-crisis period are somewhat higher than for the pre-crisis period. The standard deviations of headline and core CPI inflations and real interest rate during the post-crisis period are substantially lower than the pre-crisis period. We also report unit root tests on the variables in table 8.2. Interestingly, we find CPI-level data does not contain the unit root process and seems to be stationary during the post-crisis period from the tests, reflecting recent low inflation.

As a way to observe the dynamic impacts of oil price hikes on the macroeconomy, we provide the cumulative real GDP growth and CPI inflation during the two world oil crises and the recent oil price hike in figure 8.2. The series in figure 8.2 have four years duration each and the datings follow Blanchard and Gali (2007).[5]

The left-hand side of the figure depicts the cumulative real GDP growth and we observe that the negative effects on real GDP growth possibly induced by the oil price hike are most pronounced during the second world oil crisis, 1979:I to 1983:I. The real GDP growth shrank for almost two years before bouncing back to its trend growth. During the recent oil price hike, the real GDP growth seems to be little affected for at least one year after the

4. Much evidence supports the view that the Korean economy has experienced important and long-term changes during the periods. See Kim and Kang (2004), among others.
5. Blanchard and Galí (2007) identify four episodes of oil price shocks when the cumulative changes in (log) oil price are above 50 percent. We discard the third episode (1999:I to 2000:IV) as the period is close to the fourth period (2002:I to 2005:III).

Table 8.2   Unit root tests

| | Pre-crisis | | | | | Post-crisis | | | | |
| | PP test | | ADF test | | KPSS test | PP test | | ADF test | | KPSS test |
	ρ	t-val	ρ	t-val	LM-stat	ρ	t-val	ρ	t-val	LM-stat
WTI	-0.03	-1.63	-0.04	-1.56	-0.24	-0.20	-1.85	-0.47	-3.15	0.13
CPI	-0.02	-1.92	-0.01	-1.89	0.24	-0.20	-2.31	-0.29	-2.06	0.08
CORE	-0.01	-1.78	-0.03	-2.46	0.11	-0.01	-1.53	-0.24	-3.07	0.08
RGDP	0.00	-0.15	-0.00	-0.41	0.31	-0.15	-1.73	-0.65	-2.87	0.09
INTR	-0.21	-2.09	-0.25	-2.18	0.15	-0.07	-1.74	-0.17	-2.03	0.14
Δ log WTI	-0.86	-9.75	-0.82	-5.76	0.08	-0.54	-3.52	-0.68	-2.30	0.09
Δ log CPI	-0.45	-6.03	-0.37	-4.14	0.11	-0.96	-5.71	-0.87	-2.84	0.06
Δ log CORE	-0.33	-4.79	-0.18	-2.24	0.12	-0.47	-3.54	-0.47	-2.66	0.10
Δ log RGDP	-0.83	-8.67	-0.75	-5.15	0.07	-0.93	-5.65	-1.03	-2.96	0.09
INTR-Δ log CPI	-0.75	-5.28	-0.57	-2.59	0.11	-1.04	-6.14	-0.75	-2.49	0.11

Notes: Asymptotic critical values for LM statistics are 0.216, 0.146, and 0.199 at 1%, 5%, 10%, respectively. PP = Phillips-Perron; ADF = Augmented Dickey-Fuller; KPSS = Kwiatkowski-Phillips-Schmidt-Shin; LM = Lagrange multiplier.

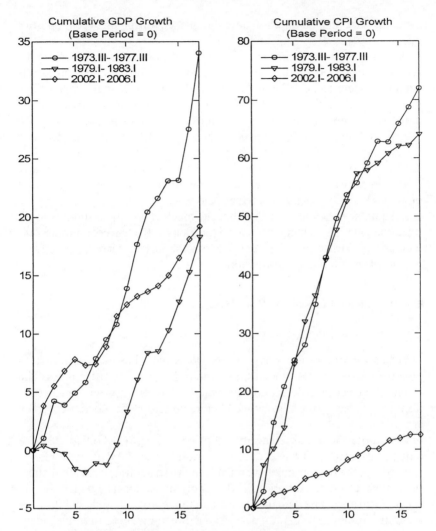

Fig. 8.2   Cumulative growth of GDP and CPI inflation

oil price hike and then it declined slightly later, but the contraction was not much pronounced.

The right-hand side of the figure illustrates the cumulative CPI inflation for the periods. The cumulative CPI inflation for the first and second oil crises look similar and the CPI inflation increased about 70 percent during both periods. However, the cumulative CPI inflation during the recent oil price hike shows different dynamics from the previous periods and the CPI inflation has risen about 12 percent over four years (i.e., 3 percent increase per annum). We may possibly conjecture that the macroeconomic effects of an oil price hike on inflation have diminished during the recent oil price hike.

As a simple way to compare the pre- and post-crisis macroeconomic responses to oil price hikes, we present nonparametric estimation results from regressing real GDP and CPI inflation on oil price in figure 8.3.[6] The left-hand side panel of the figure shows pre-crisis results and the right-hand panel shows post-crisis results. During the pre-crisis period, real GDP growth and oil price are negatively related and CPI inflation and oil price are not clearly related. During the post-crisis period, real GDP growth is almost flat to oil price changes and real GDP and oil price are not clearly related in contrast to the pre-crisis sample. In addition, CPI inflation and oil prices are not as clearly related as before.

In summary, the data indicate that the macroeconomic responses to oil price hikes may have changed in such a way that the Korean economy accommodates them better, which recently follows the Korean currency crisis from our simple preliminary examinations.

8.3   Dynamic Effects of Oil Price Hikes

8.3.1   A Structural VAR Model

In this section, we use a five-variable VAR model as our workhorse to quantify the responses of real GDP and inflation to oil price hikes. The results will be used to detect how the macroeconomic transmission mechanism of oil price hikes has changed before and after the Korean currency crisis.

We choose the log difference of oil price, export, real GDP, CPI price index, and real interest rate as our five variables for the VAR analysis. Corresponding to the five variables, we introduce five structural shocks that affect the Korean economy: oil price shock, export shock, local aggregate supply shock, local aggregate demand shock, and monetary policy shock. Because these structural shocks cannot be observed directly, we need to employ identifying restrictions to disentangle them. Our identification assumptions are based on both long-run and short-run restrictions. These will be discussed shortly. Let $\Delta z_t = [\Delta P_{o,t}, \Delta X_t, \Delta Y_t, \Delta P_t, i - \Delta P_t]'$ denote the vector of the five variables: the log difference of oil price, export, real GDP, price index, and real interest rate. We assume that Δz_t is a covariance stationary vector process suggested by the statistics in table 8.2. Each element of Δz_t is demeaned, hence it has a zero mean. The structural VAR with p lags can be expressed with the following representation

$$(1) \qquad A_0 \Delta z_t = A_1 \Delta z_{t-1} + A_2 \Delta z_{t-2} + \ldots + A_p \Delta z_{t-p} + \omega_t,$$

6. In estimation, we use a Gaussian kernel regression with optimal bandwidth, suggested by Bowman and Azzalini (1997).

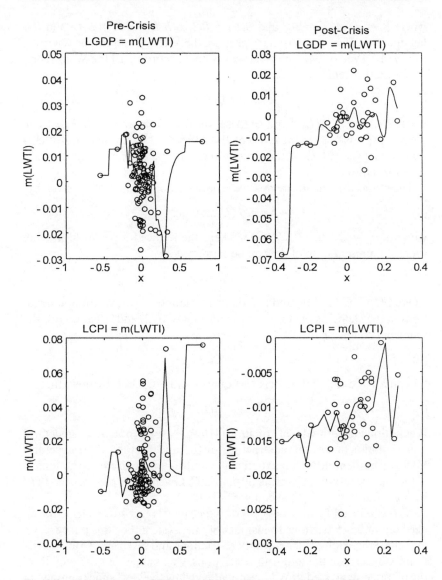

Fig. 8.3   Nonparametric GDP and inflation responses to oil price hikes

where A_0 is a 5×5 matrix restricting contemporaneous relations of the included variables; $\omega_t = [\omega_t^{OS}, \omega_t^{ES}, \omega_t^{LS}, \omega_t^{LD}, \omega_t^{MP}]'$ is a 5×1 column vector consisting of oil price shock (OS), export shock (ES), local aggregate supply shock (LS), local aggregate demand shock (LD), and monetary policy shock (MP), respectively, and $E[\omega_t] = 0$ and $E[\omega_t \omega_t'] = I_{5 \times 5}$. Alternatively, the structural VAR can be expressed as the following

$$(2) \quad \Delta z_t = B_1 \Delta z_{t-1} + B_2 \Delta z_{t-2} + \ldots + B_p \Delta z_{t-p} + C\omega_t = B(L)\Delta z_t + C\omega_t,$$

where $B_j = A_0^{-1}A_j$, $C = A_0^{-1}$ and $B(L) = B_1L + B_2L^2 + \ldots + B_pL^p$ and L is lag operator. If z_t is a stationary process, the VAR system can be rewritten as a VMA (Vector Moving Average) system according to the Wold representation theorem:

(3) $$\Delta z_t = D(L)\omega_t$$

where $D(L) = (I - B(L))^{-1}$ and $D(L)$ is invertible. Once we have $D(L)$, we can recover expressions for the levels of the different variables in terms of current and lagged values of the structural disturbances by a straightforward transformation.

The reduced-form autoregressive representation of the VAR is given by

(4) $$\Delta z_t = F(L)\Delta z_t + u_t,$$

where $E[u_t] = 0$ and $E[u_t u_t'] = \Omega$. Then, the reduced-form Wold moving average representation of Δz_t can be expressed as

(5) $$\Delta z_t = G(L)u_t,$$

where $G(L) = (I - F(L))^{-1}$ and $G(L)$ is invertible and u_t is the vector of innovations in the elements of Δz_t. Comparing equation (2) and equation (4), the following condition holds

(6) $$u_t = C\omega_t$$

for some 5×5 full rank matrix C. Equations (3), (5), and (6) imply that

(7) $$D(L) = G(L)C.$$

Premultiplying both sides of equation (4) by C^{-1}, we can obtain the structural representation of Δz_t and the structural disturbance vector ω_t. The structural VAR can be identified to the extent that we introduce sufficient restrictions to determine twenty-five elements of matrix C. Given C, we can recover $D(L)$ by post-multiplying $G(L)$ in equation (7).

As the reduced-form variance-covariance matrix has fifteen elements, we need ten more restrictions to just identify the system. For this purpose, we introduce three long-run neutrality restrictions and seven short-run restrictions. Concerning the long-run restrictions, we assume that the growth in the oil price, expressed in WTI, is not affected by the local shocks, implying $D_{1,3}(1) = D_{1,4}(1) = D_{1,5}(1) = 0$.

The short-run restrictions are composed of two groups: one limits the contemporaneous effects of shocks; the other limits the contemporaneous effects of endogenous variables. Simply put, we introduce the short-run restrictions for both the matrix C and A_0. Concerning the restrictions on the matrix C, we assume no contemporaneous effects of local shocks on oil price. These imply the following three constraints on C

(8) $$C_{1,3} = 0$$

(9) $$C_{1,4} = 0$$

(10) $$C_{1,5} = 0.$$

We finally impose linear restrictions on the relationships between the contemporaneous variables, namely restrictions on A_0: (a) contemporaneous oil price does not affect export, (b) contemporaneous interest rate does not affect real GDP, (c) contemporaneous oil price does not affect real interest rate, and (d) contemporaneous export does not affect real interest rate. The restrictions imply

(11) $$A_{0,(2,1)} = 0$$

(12) $$A_{0,(3,5)} = 0$$

(13) $$A_{0,(5,1)} = 0$$

(14) $$A_{0,(5,2)} = 0.$$

Given $A_0^{-1} = C$, these restrictions can be mapped into four nonlinear constraints on the elements of C.

8.3.2   Empirical Results

Figure 8.4 displays the cumulative impulse response functions based on VAR estimates from the pre-crisis sample period. Each column in the figure represents impulse-response functions to one standard deviation of a structural shock.

In the first column, we show the impulse response functions to an oil price shock. The shock decreases both export and real GDP immediately. The decrease in export is due to the contraction of the world economy after a hike in oil price. Similarly, the domestic real GDP decreases due to contractionary effects after the oil shock. The positive standard deviation shock decreases real GDP permanently by 0.5 percent. The CPI decreases initially but climbs steadily up after the shock, resulting in 0.2 percent increase twenty quarters after the shock. Real interest rate decreases due to the increased inflation after the shock.

The second column represents the impulse response functions to an export shock. A positive foreign export shock raises export and real GDP permanently by 2.1 percent and 0.4 percent each. The shock has limited effects on oil price. The CPI increases for seven quarters after the shock and then decreases slowly. Real interest rate decreases due to the increase in inflation but slowly moves up, resulting in a long-run rise of 0.4 percent.

The third column represents the impulse response functions to a local aggregate supply (AS) shock. The local AS shock increases domestic output and decreases CPI as a textbook aggregate demand (AD)-AS analysis predicts. The initial deflationary impact raises the real interest rate. Export decreases somewhat after the shock. This is somewhat nonstandard. We

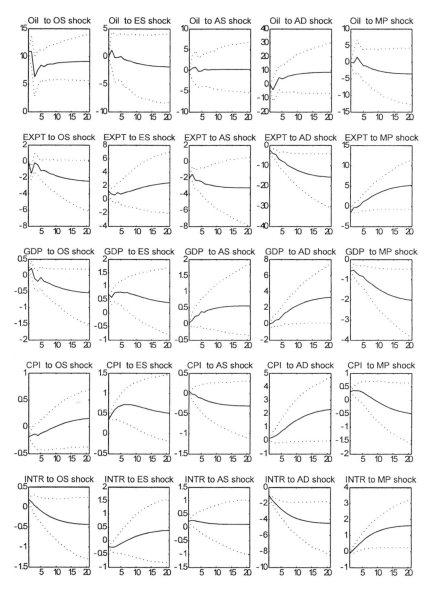

Fig. 8.4   Impulse responses, based on pre-crisis estimates

may interpret this as a switch from export to domestic absorption, given unchanged demand from abroad and increased domestic demand (output) after the shock.

The fourth column shows the impulse response functions to a local AD shock. In addition, as predicted by a standard AD-AS analysis, real GDP and CPI move up together in the same direction. The real interest rate goes down due to the increase in inflation. Export decreases somewhat given unchanged demand from abroad and increased domestic demand after the shock.

Finally, the fifth column provides the impulse response functions to a monetary policy shock. The monetary policy shock lowers real GDP and CPI as predicted. Contractionary effects of the shock reduce domestic demand and export increases accordingly. Real interest rate rises after the deflationary effect of the shock.

We next report the results from the post-crisis sample period in figure 8.5. As we discussed in the introduction, the purpose of the VAR analyses is to detect the nature of the oil shock that may originate from the supply or demand sides of the oil market. Thus, we focus on the impulse response functions to an oil price shock.

What stands out from the post-crisis sample is the impulse response function of export to an oil price shock and export increases after the shock in contrast to the pre-crisis sample. We interpret this as an oil shock in the post-crisis sample originating from the demand side of the oil market and the demand-side factor that drives the oil price up is a common factor that increases export. In the pre-crisis sample analysis, the export response to an oil price shock is negative and we interpret this as an oil price shock originating from the supply side of the oil market, and it reduces export due to its contractionary effects on the world economy. Real GDP shows similar movements in response to the oil price shock.

One might think that the different responses of real GDP and export to an oil price shock before and after the crisis stem from changed exchange rate regimes between the pre- and post-crisis period. If we review the history of the Korean foreign exchange system briefly, Korea introduced a multicurrency basket system in 1980 and the government tightly controlled foreign exchange rates until a market average exchange rate system was introduced in 1991. Since the adoption of the system, market forces played an increasingly important role in the determination of foreign exchange rates. Daily fluctuations in exchange rates were limited strictly in this system, however. After the outbreak of the crisis, Korea adopted a free floating exchange rate system and foreign exchange rates are freely determined by market forces. From this perspective, one may conjecture that an increase in oil price raises the exchange rate and spurs exports after the crisis, which would have been weak before the crisis, when exchange rates were strictly controlled by the government.

We find this argument unconvincing. We regress oil price on exchange rates and report the results in table 8.3. We find the regression coefficients are negatively (not positively) significant in the post-crisis sample, with their values ranging from –0.171 to –0.226; whereas those of the pre-crisis are distributed between –0.004 to 0.008—moreover, statistically insignificant.

These pictures can be understood as follows: the dynamic effects of the

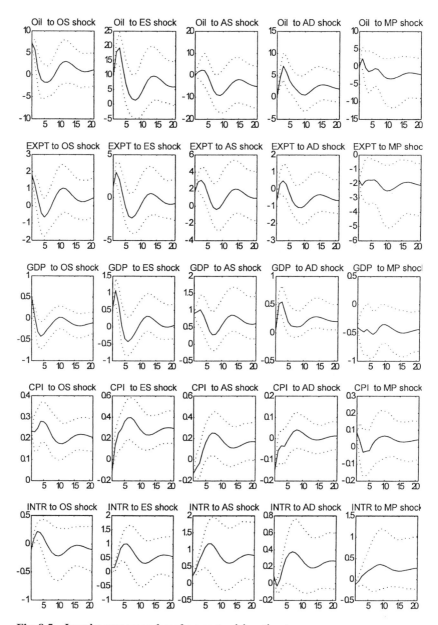

Fig. 8.5   Impulse responses, based on post-crisis estimates

oil price shock have changed after the crisis and the interactions between oil prices and macroeconomic aggregates build different patterns in the post-crisis sample period.

Turning from the impulse response functions to the other structural shocks, we report only the results in response to an AS shock to compare to

Table 8.3   Regression estimates

	Pre-crisis				Post-crisis			
	KRW/USD		REER		KRW/USD		REER	
WTI	-0.002	-0.004	0.007	0.008	-0.226	-0.241	-0.171	-0.197
	[-0.09]	[-0.17]	[0.20]	[0.22]	[-5.11]	[-4.84]	[-3.82]	[-3.98]
WTI(-1)		0.014		-0.008		0.035		0.062
		[0.56]		[-0.21]		[0.67]		[1.20]
Const.	4.576	4.446	2.175	2.158	3.505	3.204	2.650	2.111
	[3.87]	[3.71]	[1.25]	[1.23]	[1.30]	[1.16]	[0.97]	[0.77]
R^2	0.0001	0.0025	0.0006	0.0012	0.4272	0.4346	0.2943	0.3230

Notes: The t-values are reported in the parentheses. KRW/USD = South Korean won/U.S. dollar; REER = Real Effective Exchange Rate.

pre-crisis results. The impulse response functions to the rest of the structural shocks can be interpreted similarly. Figure 8.5 presents the impulse response functions to a local AS shock in the third column. The shock increases real GDP, as expected from a textbook AD-AS analysis. Although inflation decreases initially after the shock, it increases by 0.2 percent in the long run. The result is statistically insignificant, however, and we would not give much weight to it. Real interest rate increases due to the initial deflationary pressure and increased productivity. Export increases, given increased productivity after the shock.

8.3.3   Historical Simulation

To further examine the different impacts an oil price hike may have on the Korean economy before and after the crisis, we estimate dynamic correlations between real GDP and CPI in response to historical oil price shocks before and after the crisis. Thus, we first extract historical disturbances from the estimated structural VAR and eliminate all the shocks, other than oil price shocks, and then estimate the dynamic correlations. If the correlations are positive (negative), this can be interpreted as oil price shocks originating from the demand (supply) side of the oil market and having an aggregate demand (supply) nature in generating economic fluctuations.

The j-period-ahead dynamic correlation at time t can be written as follows:

$$Corr(\Delta \hat{Y}_{t+j}, \Delta \hat{P}_{t+j} | \Omega_t) = \frac{(\Delta \hat{Y}_{t+j} - E[\Delta \hat{Y}_{t+j} | \Omega_t])(\Delta \hat{P}_{t+j} - E[\Delta \hat{P}_{t+j} | \Omega t])}{\sigma(\Delta \hat{Y}_{t+j} | \Omega_t)\sigma(\Delta \hat{P}_{t+j} | \Omega_t)}$$

$$= \frac{\eta_{\Delta \hat{Y}_{t+j}} \eta_{\Delta \hat{P}_{t+j}}}{\sigma(\Delta \hat{Y}_{t+j} | \Omega_t)\sigma(\Delta \hat{P}_{t+j} | \Omega_t)}$$

where $\eta_{\Delta \xi_{t,t+j}}$ is the j-period-ahead forecasting error of $\xi (= \Delta \hat{Y}_t, \Delta \hat{P}_t)$ and Ω_t is information set up to time t. The hatted variables denote that the variables are disturbed by oil price shocks only.

Figure 8.6 presents the dynamic correlations in the pre- and post-crisis periods. In the short run, oil shocks work as demand factors; real GDP and CPI move in the same direction for both periods. However, comparing the magnitudes of the correlations, the post-crisis correlations are more than twice the pre-crisis correlations in the short run.

The difference with respect to the nature of oil price shocks between the two periods is more pronounced when medium or long-run correlations are compared. Medium or long-run correlations are around 0.4 in the post-crisis period, indicating that oil price shocks work as demand factors in the period. In contrast, medium or long-run correlations in the pre-crisis period are negative. The results imply that oil price shocks worked as aggregate supply factors in the period.

These findings, combined with the earlier impulse response analyses, lead

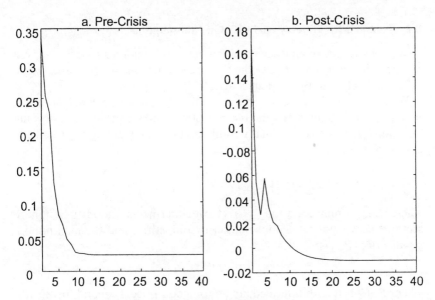

Fig. 8.6   Dynamic correlation between real GDP and CPI

to the following conclusion. The identified oil price shocks from the VAR in the pre-crisis period are mainly of aggregate supply nature and they affect domestic production adversely and raise CPI inflation by shifting the AS schedule to the left. In contrast, the oil price shocks in the post-crisis period largely work as aggregate factors and they increase export and domestic output, as well as CPI inflation, as they shift the AD schedule to the right.

In summary, the oil price changes, especially upward changes, have brought about many economic difficulties in the past. They may still be important macroeconomic factors but their impacts have been changed in recent years, as shown in our VAR evidence. We argue that the nature of oil price shocks have changed in recent years. In contrast to the previous oil price hikes, which were driven by supply disruptions, the recent oil price hike originated from an increase in the demand for oil. The demand-driven oil price hike has less, and diminished, adverse effects on the Korean economy compared to the previous oil price hikes.[7]

Thus far, we have examined the nature of oil price hikes and their macroeconomic impacts on the Korean economy with VAR analyses. We next construct a structural dynamic stochastic general equilibrium (DSGE) model to further consider economic and policy implications of the recent oil price hike. We especially consider which monetary policy rule would work better among Taylor-type rules in the face of oil price inflation based on the DSGE model.

7. See Kilian (2009) and Hamilton (2009) for related results.

8.4   Nominal Rigidities Model with Oil Consumption

We construct a small open economy nominal rigidities model, with oil and nonoil sectors, and extend the closed economy one sector models with oil usage, such as in Bodenstein et al. (2008).

We start with the production side of the nonoil sector. We denote the nonoil sector by subscript n and the oil sector by subscript o in the following equations. Firms produce final nonoil goods by aggregating intermediate goods. Namely,

$$(15) \qquad y_{n,t} = \left[\int y_{n,t}(i)^{1/\mu_n} di \right]^{\mu_n}, \qquad \mu_n \geq 1,$$

where $y_{n,t}$ is the final good and $y_{n,t}(i)$ is the ith intermediate good in the nonoil sector. The final nonoil goods market is competitive and the final nonoil goods price $(P_{n,t})$ is

$$(16) \qquad P_{n,t} = \left[\int P_{n,t}(i)^{1/(1-\mu_n)} di \right]^{1-\mu_n},$$

where $P_{n,t}(i)$ is the ith intermediate nonoil good price. Demand for the ith intermediate good is

$$(17) \qquad y_{n,t}(i) = y_{n,t} \left[\frac{P_{n,t}(i)}{P_{n,t}} \right]^{\mu_n/(1-\mu_n)}.$$

Production technology for the ith intermediate good is

$$(18) \qquad y_{n,t}(i) = z_t(n_{n,t}(i))^{\alpha_n} (o_t(i))^{\alpha_o}$$

where $n_{n,t}(i)$ is labor input, $o_t(i)$ is oil usage, and z_t is the labor augmenting technology shock. This follows the law of motion given as

$$(19) \qquad \ln z_t = z + \ln z_{z,t-1} + \zeta_{z,t}$$

$$(20) \qquad \ln \zeta_{z,t} = \rho_{\zeta_z} \ln \zeta_{z,t-1} + \varepsilon_{z,t}, \qquad \varepsilon_{z,t} \sim N(0, \sigma_z).$$

Intermediate goods producers behave as monopolistic competitors and set prices using the Calvo mechanism. Namely, they set new prices with probability $1 - \theta_n$ or adjust prices just as much as the trend inflation rate with probability θ_n in each period. Thus, the ith intermediate good producer in the nonoil sector solves

$$(21) \qquad \max_{P_{n,t}^N} E_t \sum_{s=0}^{\infty} (\beta \theta_n)^s \upsilon_{t+s} [\pi_n^s P_{n,t}^N y_{n,t+s}(i) - MC_{n,t+s}(i) y_{n,t+s}(i)]$$

subject to the demand for the ith intermediate good (see equation [17]). Variable π_n is the trend inflation rate in the nonoil sector, $P_{n,t}^N$ is the newly set price, $y_{n,t}(i)$ is the ith intermediate good, and $MC_{n,t}(i)$ is the nominal marginal cost in the nonoil sector given as

(22)
$$MC_{n,t}(i) = \frac{W_t\, n_{n,t}(i)}{\alpha_n\, y_{n,t}(i)},$$

where W_t is the nominal wage rate. The input ratio to minimize costs is

(23)
$$\frac{o_t}{n_n} = \frac{\alpha_o}{\alpha_n}\frac{W_t}{P_{o,t}}$$

where $P_{o,t}$ is the final oil good's price. In addition, υ_t is the marginal value of a dollar to the household. The first-order condition with respect to $P_{n,t}^N$ is

(24)
$$E_t \sum_{s=0}^{\infty} (\beta\theta_n)^s \upsilon_{t+s} y_{n,t+s}(i)\, [\pi_n^s P_{n,t}^N - \mu_n MC_{n,t+s}(i)] = 0.$$

The oil sector works similarly to the nonoil sector. Firms in the oil sector produce final oil goods by aggregating intermediate goods. Namely,

(25)
$$y_{o,t} = \left[\int y_{o,t}(i)^{1/\mu_o}\, di\right]^{\mu_o}, \qquad \mu_o \geq 1$$

where $y_{o,t}$ is the final good and $y_{o,t}(i)$ is the ith intermediate good in the oil sector. The final oil good price ($P_{o,t}$) is given as

(26)
$$P_{o,t} = \left[\int P_{o,t}(i)^{1/(1-\mu_o)}\, di\right]^{1-\mu_o}$$

where $P_{o,t}(i)$ is the ith intermediate oil good price. The demand for the ith intermediate good in the oil sector is

(27)
$$y_{o,t}(i) = y_{o,t}\left[\frac{P_{o,t}(i)}{P_{o,t}}\right]^{\mu_o/(1-\mu_o)}$$

Production technology for the ith intermediate good is

(28)
$$y_{o,t}(i) = z_t(cr_t(i))^{\alpha_{cr}}$$

where $cr_t(i)$ is the crude oil input imported from abroad. We abstract the labor input in the oil production for simplicity. Intermediate goods producers in the oil sector also behave as monopolistic competitors and set prices using the Calvo mechanism. The first-order condition is

(29)
$$E_t \sum_{s=0}^{\infty} (\beta\theta_o)^s \upsilon_{t+s} y_{o,t+s}(i)\, [\pi_o^s P_{o,t}^N - \mu_o MC_{o,t+s}(i)] = 0.$$

Variable $MC_{o,t}$ is the nominal marginal cost given as

(30)
$$MC_{o,t}(i) = \frac{P_{cr,t}}{z_t \alpha_{cr} cr_t(i)^{\alpha_{cr}-1}},$$

where $P_{cr,t} = S_t P_{cr,t}^*$ is the domestic crude oil price. This is the crude oil price in dollar terms, $P_{cr,t}^*$, times nominal exchange rate, S_t.

We also assume imported goods (other than crude oil) prices are sticky. Intermediate importers behave as monopolistic competitors and set prices using the Calvo mechanism. The first-order condition is

$$(31) \qquad E_t \sum_{s=0}^{\infty} (\beta \theta_m)^s \upsilon_{t+s} y_{m,t+s}(i) [\pi_m^s P_{m,t}^N - \mu_m MC_{m,t+s}(i)] = 0.$$

Variable $MC_{m,t}$ is the nominal marginal cost given as

$$(32) \qquad MC_{m,t}(i) = S_t P_t^*.$$

Next, we consider the household problem. The household i maximizes expected utility

$$(33) \qquad E_t \left[\sum_{s=0}^{\infty} \beta^s (U(c_{t+s}) - V(n_{t+s}(i))) \right]$$

subject to the budget constraint

$$(34) \qquad \begin{aligned} P_{n,t} c_{n,t} + P_{o,t} c_{o,t} + P_{m,t} c_{m,t} + B_t &\leq W_t(i) n_t(i) + \Pi_t + T_t \\ &+ (1 + R_{t-1}) B_{t-1}, \end{aligned}$$

where c_t is the final consumption good, n_t is the labor hours, B_t is the nominal savings, Π_t is the transfer from firms, T_t is the transfer from government, and R_t is the nominal interest rate. The final consumption good (c_t) is a composite of the domestically produced nonoil consumption good ($c_{n,t}$), oil consumption good ($c_{o,t}$), and imported consumption good ($c_{m,t}$) given as

$$(35) \qquad c_t(i) = \chi (c_{n,t}(i))^{1-w_o-w_m} (c_{o,t}(i))^{w_o} (c_{m,t}(i))^{w_m},$$

where $\chi = (1/w_o)^{w_o} (1/w_m)^{w_m} (1/(1-w_o-w_m))^{1-w_o-w_m}$ is a normalizing factor. The parameters w_o and w_m are the shares of the oil and imported consumption goods in total consumption. Variable $P_{n,t}$ is the domestically produced nonoil consumption good's price, $P_{o,t}$ is the oil consumption good's price, and $P_{m,t}$ is the imported good's price in the domestic currency. We drop subscript i, except for the household i's wage and labor supply assuming symmetric equilibrium.

First-order conditions, except for wage setting, are

$$(36) \qquad U_{c_n,t} = \upsilon_t P_{n,t}$$

$$(37) \qquad U_{c_o,t} = \upsilon_t P_{o,t}$$

$$(38) \qquad U_{c_m,t} = \upsilon_t P_{m,t}$$

$$(39) \qquad \frac{1}{1 + R_t} = \beta E_t \frac{\upsilon_{t+1}}{\upsilon_t}$$

where $U_{c_n,t}$, $U_{c_o,t}$, and $U_{c_m,t}$ are the derivatives of the utility function with respect to $c_{n,t}$, $c_{o,t}$, and $c_{m,t}$ respectively. We assume the utility function takes a form as

(40) $U(c_t) = \zeta_{c,t} \ln c_t, \qquad V(n_t(i)) = \zeta_{n,t} \chi_n n(i)^2,$

where $\zeta_{c,t}$ and $\zeta_{n,t}$ are the consumption preference shock and labor supply shock, respectively. They follow the laws of motion given as

(41) $\ln \zeta_{c,t} = (1 - \rho_{\zeta_c}) + \rho_{\zeta_c} \ln \zeta_{c,t-1} + \varepsilon_{c,t}, \qquad \varepsilon_{c,t} \sim N(0, \sigma_c)$

(42) $\ln \zeta_{n,t} = (1 - \rho_{\zeta_n}) + \rho_{\zeta_n} \ln \zeta_{n,t-1} + \varepsilon_{n,t}, \qquad \varepsilon_{n,t} \sim N(0, \sigma_n).$

In addition, χ_n is a normalizing factor that ensures the steady-state labor supply is one-third of available time.

Households set wages using the Calvo mechanism. Labor used for production is an aggregate of differentiated labor supply by households given as

(43) $$n_t = \left[\int n_t(i)^{1/\mu_w} di \right]^{\mu_w}, \qquad \mu_w \geq 1.$$

The wage associated with n_t is given as

(44) $$W_t = \left[\int W_t(i)^{1/(1-\mu_w)} di \right]^{1-\mu_w}.$$

Demand for the ith household's labor is

(45) $$n_t(i) = n_t \left[\frac{W_t(i)}{W_t} \right]^{\mu_w/(1-\mu_w)}.$$

In each period, household i sets a new wage with probability $1 - \theta_w$, or adjusts its wage just as much as the trend inflation rate times the trend growth rate with probability θ_w. The household wage setting problem is then

(46) $$\max_{W_t^N} E_t \sum_{s=0}^{\infty} (\beta\theta_w)^s \left[-V(n_{t+s}(i)) + \upsilon_{t+s} (\pi_c \cdot z)^s W_t^N n_{t+s}(i) \right]$$

where π_c is the final consumption good's trend inflation rate and z is the economy-wide trend growth rate. The first-order condition with respect to W_t^N is given as

(47) $$E_t \sum_{s=0}^{\infty} (\beta\theta_w)^s n_{t+s}(i) \upsilon_{t+s} \left[-\mu_w \frac{V'(n_{t+s}(i))}{\upsilon_{t+s}} + (\pi_c)^s W_T^N \right] = 0.$$

Market-clearing conditions are

(48) $$y_{n,t} = c_{n,t} + S_t x_{n,t}^*$$

(49) $$y_{o,t} = o_t + c_{o,t}$$

(50) $$n_t = n_{n,t}$$

where $x_{n,t}^*$ is the nonoil goods export in dollar terms. We abstract the oil sector export for simplicity. We define the real GDP of the economy as

$$(51) \qquad y_t = c_t + \frac{P_{n,t}}{P_{c,t}}x_t - \frac{P_{cr,t}}{P_{c,t}}cr_t - \frac{P_{m,t}}{P_{c,t}}c_{m,t}.$$

Exogenous variables—detrended log nonoil goods export in dollar terms ($\tilde{x}_{n,t}^*$), detrended log real exchange rate ($\tilde{\xi}_t$) and detrended log relative price of crude oil to foreign price level ($\tilde{\gamma}_t^*$)—follow joint process given as

$$(52) \qquad F_0 \begin{bmatrix} \tilde{x}_{n,t}^* \\ \tilde{\xi}_t \\ \tilde{\gamma}_t^* \end{bmatrix} = F(L) \begin{bmatrix} \tilde{x}_{n,t-1}^* \\ \tilde{\xi}_{t-1} \\ \tilde{\gamma}_{t-1}^* \end{bmatrix} + \varepsilon_t^*, \qquad \varepsilon_t^* \sim N(0, \Sigma^*).$$

We assume $\tilde{\gamma}_t^*$ does not contemporaneously affect the other variables in equation (52). We thus identify the effects of oil price shocks (innovations in $\tilde{\gamma}_t^*$) using a recursive ordering scheme, so that F_0 is a lower triangle matrix.[8]

Monetary policy follows a Taylor-type interest rate rule given as

$$(53) \quad R_t = \rho_R R_{t-1} + (1 - \rho_R)(\rho_{\pi_{core}} \pi_{core,t-1} + \rho_{\pi_{non}} \pi_{non,t-1} + \rho_y \tilde{y}_{t-1}) + \varepsilon_{m,t},$$

where $\tilde{y}_t$ is the output gap and $\varepsilon_{m,t} \sim N(0, \sigma_m)$. We also note that the final consumption good price ($P_{c,t}$) is given as

$$(54) \qquad P_{c,t} = P_{o,t}^{w_o} P_{m,t}^{w_m} P_{n,t}^{1-w_o-w_m}.$$

We define core CPI inflation as CPI inflation excluding oil price inflation. Then, we can define $\pi_{core,t} = (w_m \pi_{m,t} + (1 - w_o - w_m)\pi_{n,t})$ and $\pi_{non,t} = w_o \pi_{o,t}$.

We next estimate the nominal rigidities model constructed before using Bayesian methods, as in Smets and Wouters (2007). The sample period for the estimation is 2000:I to 2009:I, corresponding to the post-Korean currency crisis period.[9]

We fix some parameters by calibration and then estimate the remaining parameters by Bayesian methods. We set the subjective discount rate β as $0.98^{1/4}$. The nonoil sector production function parameters α_n and α_o are set as 0.448 and 0.062, respectively, using the shares of labor input and intermediate oil (petroleum) use in the total value-added plus intermediate oil use in the nonoil (nonpetroleum) sector, obtained from the 2005 Korean input-output table. We also set α_{cr} as 0.657, using the share of intermediate crude oil use in total value-added plus intermediate crude oil use in the oil (petroleum) sector from the input-output table. We set the price and wage markup parameters (μ_n, μ_o, μ_m, and μ_w) as 1.1 as in the literature. We calibrate the shares of oil (petroleum) and imported goods in total consumption, w_o and

---

8. The oil price shocks in equation (52) are identified in the context of the DSGE model and monetary policy assessments as in Bodenstein et al. (2008). They differ from the oil price shocks identified from the VAR analyses in the previous section to detect the differences in the nature of oil price hikes. The oil price shocks in equation (52) would resemble oil price shocks originating from the purely supply side of oil markets.

9. For the pre-crisis DSGE analysis, one may consult the working paper version of the paper, Lee and Song (2009).

w_m, as 0.021 and 0.390, respectively, using the shares of oil (petroleum) and imported goods in the GDP from the input-output table.

We use the log difference of real GDP, CPI inflation rate, CPI energy price inflation rate (as oil sector inflation rate), overnight call rate, linearly detrended log export in dollar (constructed as export in real GDP divided by the real exchange rate and then multiplied by core CPI and divided by CPI), linearly detrended log real effective exchange rate from Bank for International Settlements (BIS), and linearly detrended log WTI price divided by U.S. CPI (as the relative price of crude oil to foreign price level). We obtain the data from the Korean National Statistical Office, Datastream, and the BIS. The seven observable variables match seven structural shocks in the model and we can identify the model.

In addition, we estimate the exogenous VAR block equation (52) with the data and insert the estimated block in the model before the Bayesian estimations. We find that a VAR with lag length one is appropriate based on the Schwartz criterion.

We estimate parameters concerning price, as well as wage stickiness, shock processes, and monetary policy rule, using Bayesian methods after log-linearizing the model around the stationary steady states, as in Adolfson et al. (2007) and Smets and Wouters (2007).

We set the prior distributions of the price stickiness and wage stickiness parameters, θ_n, θ_o, θ_m, and θ_w, as uniform distributions on the interval $[0, 1]$. We set the prior distribution of the parameter concerning the weight on the nonoil inflation rate, $\rho_{\pi_{core}}$, as a normal distribution with a mean of 1.5 and a standard deviation of 0.4 and the prior distribution of the parameter concerning the weight on output gap, ρ_y, as a beta distribution with a mean of 0.125 and a standard deviation of 0.1 following the literature. We set the prior distribution of the parameter concerning the weight on the oil inflation rate, $\rho_{\pi_{non}}$, as a normal distribution with a mean of 0 and a standard deviation of 2. The zero prior mean and relatively large standard deviation reflect the lack of prior information concerning the monetary policy response toward oil price inflation. We set the prior distributions of shock persistence and monetary policy interest rate smoothing parameters, ρ_{ζ}, ρ_{ζ_z}, ρ_{ζ_n}, and ρ_R, as beta distributions with a mean of 0.7 and a standard deviation of 0.1. We set the prior distributions of all parameters concerning the shock standard deviation as an inverse gamma distribution with a mean of 0.2 and a standard deviation of 2. We also estimate the diagonal elements of Σ^* in the VAR block equation (52), which is the identity matrix by definition, and set the prior distributions of the diagonal elements of the matrix as inverse gamma distributions with a mean of 1 and a standard deviation of 2. We will denote the ith diagonal element of the matrix by Σ_{ii}^* in the following. Table 8.4 summarizes the prior distributions of the parameters.

Table 8.5 summarizes the estimated posterior distributions of the parameters. When we examine the estimated posterior distributions of the price

Table 8.4   Priors

Parameters		Type	Mean	Standard deviation
		Priors		
Nonoil price stickiness	θ_n	Uniform	0.5	$1/\sqrt{12}$
Imported goods price stickiness	θ_m	Uniform	0.5	$1/\sqrt{12}$
Oil price stickiness	θ_o	Uniform	0.5	$1/\sqrt{12}$
Wage stickiness	θ_w	Uniform	0.5	$1/\sqrt{12}$
Monetary policy nonoil inflation response	$\rho_{\pi_{core}}$	Normal	1.5	0.4
Monetary policy oil inflation response	$\rho_{\pi_{non}}$	Normal	0.0	2.0
Monetary policy output gap response	ρ_y	Beta	0.125	0.1
Interest rate smoothing	ρ_R	Beta	0.7	0.1
Aggregate tech. shock persistence	ρ_{ζ_z}	Beta	0.7	0.1
Consumption preference shock persistence	ρ_{ζ_c}	Beta	0.7	0.1
Labor supply shock persistence	ρ_{ζ_n}	Beta	0.7	0.1
Monetary policy shock standard deviation	σ_m	Inv. Gamma	0.02	2
Aggregate tech. shock standard deviation	σ_z	Inv. Gamma	0.02	2
Consumption preference shock standard deviation	σ_c	Inv. Gamma	0.02	2
Labor supply shock standard deviation	σ_n	Inv. Gamma	0.02	2
VAR cov. matrix diagonal elements	Σ_{ii}^*	Inv. Gamma	1	2

stickiness parameters, the posterior of the nonoil sector price stickiness parameter, θ_n, is estimated to be highest; its mode is 0.958. The posterior of the oil sector price stickiness parameter, θ_o, is estimated to be lowest amongst the price stickiness parameters; its mode is 0.492. We note the estimated degree of oil price stickiness differs from zero, as we can see from the tenth percentile of the posterior. The posterior mode of imported goods price stickiness, θ_m, is 0.843, between the modes of nonoil good's price stickiness and oil good's price stickiness. The posterior of the wage stickiness parameter, θ_w, is estimated to be lower than the posteriors of the price stickiness parameters; its mode is 0.210.[10]

Concerning the parameters of the monetary policy Taylor rule, the posterior mode of the monetary policy response to nonoil price inflation parameter, $\rho_{\pi_{core}}$, is 1.537, slightly higher than the prior mode. The posterior mode of the monetary policy output gap response parameter, ρ_y, is 0.003, lower than the prior mode. When we examine the posterior of the monetary policy response to oil price inflation, $\rho_{\pi_{non}}$, the mode is −0.120, the tenth percentile is −3.327, and the ninetieth percentile is 3.188. Thus, the monetary policy response toward oil price inflation is rather imprecisely estimated, including zero between the tenth and ninetieth percentile. The

---

10. The estimated wage stickiness parameter is relatively low compared to previous results, as in Adolfson et al. (2007). This might be because we do not utilize wage data in the estimation since we cannot obtain reliable Korean wage data.

Table 8.5   **Posteriors**

			Posteriors		
Parameters		Mode	Standard deviation	10th percentile	90th percentile
Nonoil price stickiness	θ_n	0.958	0.012	0.924	0.970
Imported goods price stickiness	θ_m	0.843	0.066	0.744	0.938
Oil price stickiness	θ_o	0.492	0.045	0.418	0.559
Wage stickiness	θ_w	0.210	0.053	0.136	0.325
Mon. policy nonoil response	$\rho_{\pi_{core}}$	1.537	0.313	1.268	2.320
Mon. policy oil response	$\rho_{\pi_{non}}$	−0.120	1.980	−3.327	3.188
Mon. policy output gap response	ρ_y	0.003	0.006	3.031e-6	0.015
Interest rate smoothing	ρ_R	0.698	0.091	0.563	0.833
Aggregate tech. shock per.	ρ_{ζ_z}	0.414	0.036	0.353	0.482
Cons. preference shock per.	ρ_{ζ_c}	0.835	0.046	0.710	0.883
Labor supply shock per.	ρ_{ζ_n}	0.974	0.011	0.946	0.985
Monetary policy shock standard deviation	σ_m	0.026	0.003	0.024	0.032
Aggregate tech. standard deviation	σ_z	0.352	0.065	0.268	0.475
Cons. preference shock standard deviation	σ_c	0.161	0.031	0.131	0.254
Labor supply shock standard deviation	σ_n	0.637	0.193	0.450	1.073
VAR cov. first diag. element	Σ^*_{11}	0.929	0.105	0.778	1.132
VAR cov. second diag. element	Σ^*_{22}	0.925	0.104	0.775	1.133
VAR cov. third diag. element	Σ^*_{33}	0.914	0.103	0.765	1.116
Marginal likelihood			375.9		

estimated mode represents less adverse or more accommodating policies toward oil price inflation than nonoil price inflation, as mentioned in Dhawan and Jestke (2007).

We can summarize our findings from the DSGE model based on the Korean data as follows. First, the degree of oil sector price stickiness is relatively lower than nonoil sector price stickiness, as in the literature. However, the oil sector price is not completely flexible differing to the theoretical models, as in Aoki (2001), in which optimal monetary policy is the complete stabilization of the core inflation rate. Second, the monetary policy response toward noncore CPI inflation is rather imprecisely estimated and the estimated posterior mode represents less strict policy toward noncore CPI inflation than core CPI inflation.

8.5   Monetary Policy Rules

In the following, we consider different degrees of monetary policy responses toward noncore oil price inflation in the Taylor-type rules equation (53) and examine the effects on CPI inflation and output gap volatilities

Table 8.6   **Monetary policy rules and volatilities**

Permanent tech. shocks			Preference shocks		
$\rho_{\pi_{non}}$	$S.D.(\pi_c)$	$S.D.(y)$	$\rho_{\pi_{non}}$	$S.D.(\pi_c)$	$S.D.(y)$
10th per.	0.0005	0.1491	10th per.	0.0065	0.6923
Mode	0.0005	0.1489	Mode	0.0067	0.6949
Zero	0.0005	0.1489	Zero	0.0067	0.6950
90th per.	0.0005	0.1487	90th per.	0.0068	0.6972

Labor supply shocks			Oil shocks		
$\rho_{\pi_{non}}$	$S.D.(\pi_c)$	$S.D.(y)$	$\rho_{\pi_{non}}$	$S.D.(\pi_c)$	$S.D.(y)$
10th per.	0.0413	0.5049	10th per.	0.0021	0.1575
Mode	0.0380	0.4343	Mode	0.0021	0.1582
Zero	0.0378	0.4319	Zero	0.0021	0.1582
90th per.	0.0350	0.3727	90th per.	0.0021	0.1593

Export shocks (1st shocks in VAR)			Real exchange rate shocks (2nd shocks in VAR)		
$\rho_{\pi_{non}}$	$S.D.(\pi_c)$	$S.D.(y)$	$\rho_{\pi_{non}}$	$S.D.(\pi_c)$	$S.D.(y)$
10th per.	0.0041	0.1041	10th per.	0.0022	0.1289
Mode	0.0043	0.1132	Mode	0.0022	0.1301
Zero	0.0043	0.1136	Zero	0.0022	0.1302
90th per.	0.0045	0.1231	90th per.	0.0022	0.1323

Note: S.D. = standard deviation.

in the DSGE model. It would also be necessary to consider different values for ρ_{π_o}, since its posterior distribution is imprecisely estimated.

We further consider cases separately when the model economy is perturbed by each structural shock to examine the different effects of monetary policy responses to the shocks. The other parameter values are set at their posterior modes.

We simulate the model by setting $\rho_{\pi_{non}}$ equal to –3.327, –0.120, 0.0, and 3.188, respectively. They are respectively the tenth percentile, the mode, zero response, and the ninetieth percentile of the posterior distribution of $\rho_{\pi_{non}}$. Table 8.6 reports the results.

When the model economy is simulated with oil shocks only, more accommodating policies toward oil price inflation works better, as we can reduce output gap volatilities without raising CPI inflation volatilities very much. This resembles the results from Dhawan and Jeske (2007). More aggressive monetary policies toward oil price inflation destabilize nonoil sector inflation and output through interest rate adjustments and lead to higher volatilities in overall CPI inflation and output gap.

The results for the other structural shocks are mixed. In response to technology shocks and labor supply shocks, more aggressive policy toward oil price inflation works better. In response to consumption preference shocks, more accommodating policy works better, as can be seen in table 8.6.

8.6   Conclusion

The price of crude oil has increased steadily since 2002. It started to increase very rapidly at the end of 2007. Facing the recent hike of the oil price, economists, as well as policymakers, became concerned with the difficulties the rising oil price might have on the Korean economy.

This chapter investigates the changing nature of oil price hikes and macroeconomic responses to them in the Korean economy. We also evaluate which monetary policy rule works better in the face of oil price shocks to stabilize the economy. We find that the recent run-up in oil price is induced by an increase in the demand for oil, and its effects on the Korean economy are weak from the VAR analyses. This is in contrast to the causes and effects of the previous two oil price hikes in the 1970s. In addition, we find monetary policy in Korea needs to be operated more or less accommodatingly to the oil price shocks to stabilize the economy given the shocks and frictions in the DSGE model.

Naturally, there are other possible explanations for the declining importance of oil price hikes. One may ascribe mild impacts of oil prices to the macroeconomy to declining shares of oil in consumption and production. We look into the time series for both consumption and production shares of oil but fail to find conspicuous changes in the shares. This is consistent with the findings in Kilian (2008).[11] We also investigate whether the wage inflation has shown any significant differences in the pre- and post-crisis periods, but persuasive results cannot be found, either.

References

Adolfson, M., S. Laseen, J. Linde, and M. Villani. 2007. Bayesian estimation of an open economy DSGE model with incomplete pass-through. *Journal of International Economics* 72:481–511.

Aoki, K. 2001. Optimal monetary policy responses to relative-price changes. *Journal of Monetary Economics* 48:55–80.

Blanchard, O. J., and J. Galí. 2007. The macroeconomic effects of oil shocks: Why are the 2000s so different from the 1970s? NBER Working Paper no. 13368. Cambridge, MA: National Bureau of Economic Research, September.

Blinder, A. S., and R. Reis. 2005. Understanding the Greenspan standard. In *The Greenspan era: Lessons for the future,* ed. T. M. Hoenig, 11–96. Federal Reserve Bank of Kansas City.

11. However, Blanchard and Galí (2007) find the decline in the share of oil in consumption and production results in quantitatively significant implication for the recent U.S. economy.

Bodenstein, M., C. J. Erceg, and L. Guerrieri. 2008. Optimal monetary policy with distinct core and headline inflation rates. *Journal of Monetary Economics* 55: 18–33.

Bowman, A. W., and A. Azzalini. 1997. *Applied smoothing techniques for data analysis,* Oxford Statistical Science Series 18. New York: Oxford University Press.

Cogley, T. 2002. A simple adaptive measure of core inflation. *Journal of Money, Credit and Banking* 34:94–113.

Den Haan, W. J. 1996. The comovements between real activity and prices at different business cycle frequencies. NBER Working Paper no. 5553. Cambridge, MA: National Bureau of Economic Research, May.

Dhawan, R., and K. Jeske. 2007. Taylor rules with headline inflation: A bad idea. Federal Reserve Bank of Atlanta Working Paper no. 2007-14.

Goodfriend, M., and R. King. 1997. The new neoclassical synthesis and the role of monetary policy. *NBER macroeconomics annual* 12:231–96.

Guo, H., and K. L. Kliesen. 2005. Oil price volatility and U.S. macroeconomic Activity. *Federal Reserve Bank of St. Louis Review* (November/December): 669–83.

Hamilton, J. D. 1996. This is what happened to the oil price-macroeconomy relationship. *Journal of Monetary Economics* 38:215–20.

———. 2005. Oil and the macroeconomy. In *The New Palgrave dictionary of economics,* 2nd ed., ed. S. N. Durlauf and L. E. Blume. Houndmills, UK: Palgrave Macmillan.

———. 2008. Understanding crude oil prices. NBER Working Paper no. 14492. Cambridge, MA: National Bureau of Economic Research, November.

———. 2009. Causes and consequences of the oil shock of 2007–08. NBER Working Paper no. 15002. Cambridge, MA: National Bureau of Economic Research, May.

Harris, E. S., B. C. Kasman, M. D. Shapiro, and K. D. West. 2009. Oil and the macroeconomy: Lessons for monetary policy. Unpublished Manuscript.

Kilian, L. 2008. The economic effects of energy price shocks. *Journal of Economic Literature* 46 (4): 871–909.

———. 2009. Not all oil price shocks are alike: Disentangling demand and supply shocks in the crude oil market. *American Economic Review* 99 (3): 1053–69.

Lee, J., and J. Song. 2009. Nature of oil price shocks and monetary policy. NBER Working Paper no. 15306. Cambridge, MA: National Bureau of Economic Research, September.

Rich, R., and C. Steindel. 2005. A review of core inflation and an evaluation of its measures. Federal Reserve Bank of New York Staff Report no. 236.

Smets, F., and R. Wouters. 2007. Shocks and frictions in U.S. business cycles: A Bayesian DSGE approach. *American Economic Review* 97:586–606.

Comment   Tokuo Iwaisako

Lee and Song's chapter analyzes the effect of oil shocks on the Korean economy and examines the role of monetary policy in dealing with oil

Tokuo Iwaisako is the principal economist of the Policy Research Institute, Ministry of Finance, Government of Japan, and a visiting researcher at the Institute of Economic Research, Hitotsubashi University.

shocks. In doing this, they employ two analytical tools out of the standard macroeconomists' toolbox, structural VAR and Dynamic Stochastic General Equilibrium model (DSGE). However, their analytical tools are particularly constrained in this case for two reasons. First, the Asian currency crisis in the late 1990s caused serious turmoil and significant structural changes for the Korean economy. Hence, in addition to dividing the sample around the Asian currency crisis, Lee and Song dropped the observations in 1998 and 1999. This limits the sample size for the post-Asian crisis period to less than forty observations of quarterly data. It is obviously a short sample for an application of time-series techniques.

Second, oil price movements in the 2000s (2000 to 2009) exhibit large swings relative to the post-crisis sample period. Like Japan's asset price bubble episode in the late 1980s, the existence of a large onetime fluctuation in asset prices often spoils sophisticated econometric techniques that rely on asymptotic methods. I am particularly afraid that the nature of estimated VAR system for the post-Asian crisis sample might be dominated by the effect of volatile oil price movements toward the end of the sample period, as documented in figure 8.1.

Even though the small sample size imposes serious constraints, Lee and Song have presented a worthy analysis of the issues addressed in their chapter, using the tools employed. As a conclusion to the first half of the chapter, the authors argue that the persistent increase of the oil price in the 2000s is induced by the increase in demand for oil, in contrast with the oil price fluctuations in the pre-crisis period that are mostly caused by supply-side disturbances. While this conclusion seems reasonable, their VAR analysis obviously suffers because of the limited sample size. For example, in figure 8.5, impulse response functions of most of the variables exhibit rather unusual wave shapes. I suspect that this reflects the effect of wild fluctuations of the oil price in 2008 and 2009. A related minor point is that because the authors included the interest rate variable, which is available only for the period after 1987, in their VAR analysis, their pre-crisis sample does not contain important information about the first and second oil crisis episodes. Therefore, we have to be particularly careful in interpreting the VAR results presented here.

I also have some comments on the DSGE results. First, while the relative size of the price stickiness parameters makes sense, I am not very comfortable with the fact that the estimated wage stickiness parameter (0.539) is lower than any other price stickiness parameters, even lower than oil price stickiness (0.685) in table 8.5. The result is even more surprising with pre-crisis estimates in table 8.7, with the wage stickiness parameter being 0.149 and the oil price stickiness parameter being 0.464. I hope that the authors provide some discussion about this problem.

Second, from the simulation results reported in table 8.6, the authors conclude that the monetary policy rule, which accommodates oil price inflation, generally works well, except for the case of very persistent technology shocks. However, exactly how costly is it for the Bank of Korea to deviate from the optimal policy rule? The numbers reported in table 8.6 seem to suggest that the cost might not be very large. I would like to see the authors discuss the economic significance of the numbers reported in table 8.6, as well as their implications for monetary policy in practice.

Comment   Mohamed Rizwan Habeeb Rahuman

Generally, this chapter is timely as it attempts to discern the reasons for the recent rise in oil prices and the macroeconomic impact it has on South Korea. The authors attribute the recent oil price shock (especially since 2003) on demand conditions, which is distinct in character from previous oil price shocks that were mostly supply shocks. On this point, this discussant concurs fully with the authors, and indeed, it is clear that the authors were inspired by James Hamilton's seminal works (Hamilton and Herrera 2004; Hamilton 2008, 2009) that lead to this conclusion as well.

However, I have some comments. The authors mention the inherent "battle" between headline inflation and core inflation in determining the function of oil shocks on the macroeconomy, especially in setting monetary policy. Though the chapter seems to lean toward Hamilton's contention that oil price shocks, due to their increasingly permanent nature, cannot be treated as transitory and headline inflation must be paid close attention by central banks, the authors shied away from making a clear argument. I believe a thorough discussion on this issue, and clearly stating which way the authors believe the direction should be taking, would not only strengthen the argument of demand-shock role of oil prices that this chapter wants to make, but also would serve to influence many central bankers in deciding the role of oil price shocks in setting monetary policy.

The authors inserted a clear "structural break" in the data set, separating the data set for the Korean economy between "pre-crisis" (which is 1970 to 1997) and "post-crisis" (which is 2000 to 2009). The years 1998 and 1999 were omitted, as the authors argued that these two years saw the Korean economy moving to a free-floating exchange rate system, and adopting an inflation-targeting regime. I believe this structural break could have led to a flawed data set, as the years 1998 and 1999, the years of the Asian Financial Crisis, also led to a sharp decline in oil prices (hitting the trough of US$10 per barrel in September 1998) due to negative demand shock from East Asia. Just as the authors intend to investigate the positive demand shock

Mohamed Rizwan Habeeb Rahuman is an economist at the Central Bank of Malaysia.

on oil prices on the Korean economy, the data set must include the negative demand shock on oil prices on the Korean economy experienced in those two years. This critical omission will, in the discussant's humble opinion, affect the conclusions of this chapter. I suggest the inclusion of the 1998 to 1999 data, with perhaps a dummy variable introduced to address the author's concerns on the changes in the Korean economy during the time period.

This chapter makes an extraordinary finding that the effect of the demand-led oil price increase post-crisis on GDP and inflation has been far more muted than the pre-crisis oil price increase. In other words, in pre-crisis, the oil prices and GDP growth were negatively correlated, while in the post-crisis, the effect of oil price on GDP growth is almost flat. To discover such conclusions in an oil-importing country such as Korea is surprising, and yet supports the discussant's view that oil price movements are increasingly demand-led and relate to economic growth much more strongly than in the 1970s and 1980s.

The chapter argues that if monetary policy (MP) behaves in an anti-inflationary manner toward rises in oil prices, especially if it is demand-shock driven, the resultant decline in oil price inflation would be matched (or overriden, even) by higher output gap volatility, affecting GDP growth. If MP is accomodative however, the opposite is true. I agree with the findings, but I wonder what the authors would have recommended a central bank to do, depending on the MP methodology. Again, the authors shied away from taking a stand on this issue, which considerably weakens their argument.

References

Hamilton, J. D., and A. M. Herrera. 2004. Oil shocks and aggregate macroeconomic behavior: The role of monetary policy. *Journal of Money, Credit, and Banking* 36 (April): 265–86.

Hamilton, J. D. 2008. Understanding crude oil prices. NBER Working Paper no. 14492. Cambridge, MA: National Bureau of Economic Research, November.

———. 2009. Causes and consequences of the oil shock of 2007–08. *Brookings Papers on Economic Activity* (Spring): 215–59. Washington, DC: Brookings Institution.

Oil Shocks in a DSGE Model
for the Korean Economy

Sungbae An and Heedon Kang

9.1 Introduction

The Western Texas Intermediate (WTI) crude oil price was 29.19 U.S. dollars per barrel at the third quarter of 2003 and it peaked at 139.96 dollars by the third quarter of 2008. This rapid and continual rise in oil prices over recent years posed many questions among the general public as well as economists. Since the Korean economy depends entirely on imports for its acquisition of crude oil, households, entrepreneurs, and policymakers are interested in knowing to what extent the rise in oil prices affects the economy.

There are various channels through which changes of oil prices have effects on the economy. In our model economy, an oil price shock is reflected through the oil consumption. It generates income and substitution effect because oil is included in the consumption bundle of a typical household; that is, oil is directly consumed. An oil price shock also affects a firm's decision, which results in substitution of oil input in production with capital and labor hiring. The marginal costs of production faced by firms and their pricing decisions are affected; this generates dynamic effects when prices are rigid. Also the substitution with capital in production affects decisions on the capital accumulation, and this brings along long-run effects. We do not

Sungbae An is assistant professor in the School of Economics at Singapore Management University. Heedon Kang is an economist in the Research Department of the Bank of Korea.

We thank Mario Crucini, Takatoshi Ito, Warwick McKibbin, Andrew Rose, Etsuro Shioji, Pengfei Wang, and conference participants at the 20th NBER-EASE conference in Hong Kong for helpful comments. The views expressed in this article are those of authors and do not necessarily reflect those of the Bank of Korea. Any errors or omissions are the responsibility of the authors.

Table 9.1   Oil uses: Korea (2005) (volume, percent)

	Industry	Transport	Home and commercial	Public	Other	Total
Gasoline	0.27	7.48	0.01	0.07		7.83
Kerosene	0.72	0.01	4.27	0.09	0.09	5.18
Diesel	2.52	14.64	1.08	0.47	0.02	18.73
Bunker	5.56	3.05	1.08	0.04	3.49	13.21
Naphtha	35.90					35.90
Solvent	0.58					0.58
Jet Oil		2.67		0.62		3.29
LPG	2.70	5.70	3.43	0.03	0.18	12.04
Asphalt	1.38					1.38
Lubricant	0.65					0.65
Etc.	0.81		0.41			1.22
Total	51.09	33.55	10.27	1.30	3.78	100.00

explicitly model the speculative motive of oil consumption and trading that can change the expectation formation and we assume that international oil prices are purely exogenous.

The composition of oil use in Korea is reported in table 9.1. By sector, the fuel for transportation accounts for 34 percent of oil consumption in 2005 while industrial use occupies 51 percent. Home and commercial share is 10 percent. Along the rows shares are listed by types of oil from a petroleum refinery. At a first glance we can notice that use of a certain type of oil is tightly linked to a certain sector. For example, most of gasoline and diesel are used as the fuel for transportation and kerosene is mostly used as the fuel for heating in home and commercial sector. Naphtha, solvent, asphalt, and lubricant are exclusively used in industry. Particularly we note that the naphtha occupies 36 percent of total oil use and that it is the main input for the petrochemical industry that produces plastic-related products. Because of this clear separation of oil use by type, the imported crude oil after the refinery can be categorized into direct consumption (fuels for transportation and heating) and input of production.

We present the model economy that uses oil imports either as direct consumption or an input of production. The model is a conventional New Keynesian model for a small open economy with an augmentation of oil uses. Within Bayesian estimation framework including dynamic stochastic general equilibrium-vector autoregressions (DSGE-VARs), the empirical analysis is performed based on the Korean aggregate data. The DSGE-VAR procedure developed by Del Negro and Schorfheide (2004) provides an assessment tool of DSGE model specifications. By Bayesian analysis, we first perform model comparison to check the importance of each channel that transmits an oil price shock to the economy. The model comparison is extended to VAR models whose coefficients are restricted by DSGE models a priori with various degrees of tightness. In terms of fitting the data, an optimal degree of tightness; that is, an "optimal" combination between the VAR and a DSGE model is found. We can also derive more sensible impulse responses from VARs that are in line with those from the DSGE models.

We find that the model economy produces reasonable posterior estimates of the structural parameters and works relatively well compared to impulse responses from the VAR with optimal prior weight from the DSGE model. The misspecification becomes very severe when either consumption or production motive of oil imports is ignored. From the variance decomposition analysis, we conclude that the variability of the domestic interest rate can be explained mainly by the oil price shocks transmitted to domestic oil prices. The shock to the deviation from the law of one price (LOP) in oil prices has an important role in explaining variability of most observables. The impulse response analysis shows that the oil price shock has negative impacts on most of the observables at first, but it brings in positive and hump-shaped responses in a medium run. This prolonged response is mainly due to the interplay of the substitution and income effect. The low substitution elasticities between oil and core consumption, and between oil-capital aggregate and labor input, prevent the quick adjustment. In a medium run where the rigid prices and wages are renewed, the income effect from increased demand for Home goods plays an important role. We also calculate the pass-through of oil prices into the core consumption price index using estimated DSGE and VAR models and find that the pass-through is relatively low in both cases. Finally, the deviation from the LOP in oil prices has decreased but the government accommodating tax policy played a limited role during this period. Therefore, a more elaborated model on government behavior is anticipated to investigate the pass-through of oil price shocks.

The rest of the chapter is organized as follows. Section 9.2 sets up a small open economy model with oil. Section 9.3 describes data and estimation methods including DSGE-VARs, the main tool for empirical analysis used in this chapter. Section 9.4 discusses empirical findings, and section 9.5 concludes.

9.2   The Model

Following Bouakez, Rebei, and Vencatachellum (2008) and Medina and Soto (2005), we model an economy where imported oil is either directly consumed by households or used as an input of production. Most common source of direct consumption is fuel for heating and transportation. It is also obvious that oil is used in the production. Noting that the oil use and the capital are substitutable in production, we introduce the capital unlike Medina and Soto (2005).

Households are heterogeneous in the sense that they are monopolistic labor suppliers but wage setting by each household is limited by reoptimization probability. Each household's consumption basket consists of Home and Foreign goods and oil. Firms are monopolistically competitive firms that produce differentiated goods. Just like the wage setting of households, the price-setting behavior is characterized á la Calvo (1983), which introduces nominal stickiness of output price of the economy. The government plays a passive role in this model, where it runs a balanced budget without any government spending. Monetary authority plays monetary policy based on the interest rate feedback rule. As an open economy, imports consist of oil and Foreign goods either for consumption and investment while only Home goods that are produced with oil, capital, and labor are exported. Exchange rate pass-through is perfect for import and export prices, with the exception of oil prices. Since we treat the Korean economy as a small open economy, foreign sectors are modeled as a set of exogenous processes.

9.2.1   Households

The domestic economy is populated by a continuum of monopolistically competitive households indexed by $j \in [0, 1]$. Each household supplies a differentiated labor services to firms. There exists a set of perfectly competitive employment agencies that combine the different labor services from households into an aggregate labor index H_t, defined as

$$H_t = \left(\int_0^1 H_t(j)^{\nu_L/(\nu_L-1)} \right)^{\nu_L/(\nu_L-1)},$$

where ν_L is the elasticity of substitution across different labor services. Let $W_t(j)$ denote the nominal wage set by household j. Then demand for this household's labor is

(1) $$H_t(j) = \left(\frac{W_t(j)}{W_t} \right)^{-\nu_L} H_t,$$

where the aggregate wage index W_t is given by

$$W_t = \left(\int_0^1 W_t(j)^{1-\nu_L} dj \right)^{1/(1-\nu_L)}.$$

Household j maximizes its expected lifetime utility drawn from consumption $C_t(j)$ relative to a habit stock, real money balances $M_t(j)/P_t$, and leisure:

$$\mathbf{E}_t \left[\sum_{k=0}^{\infty} \beta^k \left(\log\left(C_{t+k}(j) - \gamma h C_{t+k-1}\right) + \frac{\chi_M}{\mu} \left(\frac{M_{t+k}(j)}{\gamma^{t+k} P_{t+k}} \right)^{\mu} - \chi_H \frac{H_{t+k}(j)^{1+\tau}}{1+\tau} \right) \right],$$

where β is the discount factor, and τ is the inverse of the intertemporal substitution elasticity of hours. The habit persistence in consumption is governed by h while γ denotes the growth of the aggregate output by which it is ensured that the economy evolves along a balanced growth path. Note here that the habit stock refers to the entire economy's habit consumption rather than individual habit consumption.

The consumption bundle of household j is given as a constant elasticity of substitution (CES) aggregate of oil $O_{C,t}(j)$ consumption and nonoil core consumption $Z_t(j)$:

$$C_t(j) = [\omega_o^{1/\phi_c} O_{C,t}(j)^{1-1/\phi_c} + (1 - \omega_o)^{1/\phi_c} Z_t(j)^{1-1/\phi_c}]^{\phi_c/(\phi_c-1)},$$

where ϕ_c is the intratemporal elasticity of substitution between oil and core consumption, and ω_o denotes the share of oil consumption. Oil is directly consumed as fuel for heating and transportation. The core consumption is again defined as a CES aggregate of domestically produced goods (Home goods) $C_{H,t}(j)$, and imported goods (Foreign goods) $C_{F,t}(j)$:

$$Z_t(j) = [(1 - \omega_F)^{1/\phi_z} C_{H,t}(j)^{1-1/\phi_z} + \omega_F^{1/\phi_z} C_{F,t}(j)^{1-1/\phi_z}]^{\phi_z/(\phi_z-1)},$$

where ϕ_z denotes the intratemporal elasticity of substitution between Home and Foreign goods, and ω_F is the import share. For any given level of consumption bundle $C_t(j)$ as a result of household utility maximization behavior, household j tries to maximize the profit in purchasing such a consumption bundle. Let $P_{o,t}$ and $P_{Z,t}$ denote the prices of oil and core consumption goods, respectively. We further define P_t as the price of the composite consumption good. Then the consumption bundle is composed of oil and core consumption goods:

$$O_{C,t}(j) = \omega_o \left(\frac{P_{o,t}}{P_t}\right)^{-\phi_c} C_t(j), \qquad Z_t(j) = (1 - \omega_o)\left(\frac{P_{Z,t}}{P_t}\right)^{-\phi_c} C_t(j).$$

The core consumption goods basket $Z_t(j)$ is purchased in a similar fashion:

$$C_{H,t}(j) = (1 - \omega_F)\left(\frac{P_{H,t}}{P_{Z,t}}\right)^{-\phi_z} Z_t(j), \qquad C_{F,t}(j) = \omega_F \left(\frac{P_{F,t}}{P_{Z,t}}\right)^{-\phi_z} Z_t(j)$$

where $P_{H,t}$ and $P_{F,t}$ are the prices of Home and Foreign goods, respectively. The price of the composite consumption good P_t, namely, the consumption-based price index (CPI), can be written as

$$P_t = [\omega_o P_{o,t}^{1-\phi_c} + (1 - \omega_o)P_{Z,t}^{1-\phi_c}]^{1/(1-\phi_c)},$$

where the CPI for core consumption is given by

$$P_{Z,t} = [(1 - \omega_F) P_{H,t}^{1-\phi_z} + \omega_F P_{F,t}^{1-\phi_z}]^{1/(1-\phi_z)}.$$

Household j enters period t with domestic portfolio of Arrow securities $D_t(j)$ that pays out one unit of domestic currency in a particular state; foreign-currency bond $B_{t-1}^*(j)$ that pays one unit for sure; nominal money balances $M_{t-1}(j)$; and a stock of capital $K_{t-1}(j)$.[1] In period t, the household pays a lump-sum tax $T_t(j)$, earns income from selling labor and renting

---

1. As usual, "star" refers to foreign economy.

capital to firms, receives dividends (profits) $\Pi_t(j)$ from monopolistic firms, and adjusts the balances on domestic portfolio, foreign-currency bond, and nominal money balances. In particular, acquiring the position on foreign-currency bond entails the premium; that is, households need to pay more than the international price to purchase bonds. Now we can write the budget constraints that domestic households face each period as

$$P_t(C_t(j) + I_t(j)) + \mathbf{E}_t[Q_{t,t+1} D_{t+1}(j)] + M_t(j) + \frac{e_t B_t^*(j)}{R_t^* \Theta\left(\dfrac{e_t B_t^*}{P_{X,t} X_t}\right)}$$

$$\leq W_t(j)H_t(j) + R_t^K K_{t-1}(j) + D_t(j) + M_{t-1}(j) + e_t B_{t-1}^*(j)$$
$$+ \Pi_t(j) - T_t(j),$$

where $Q_{t,t+1}$ is the stochastic discount factor used for evaluating consumption streams, R_t^K is the nominal rental rate of capital, e_t is the nominal exchange rate, and R_t^* is the nominal international interest rate. Had it not been for the foreign bond premium, households would have paid $1/R_t^*$ as the price of the foreign bond. In reality, however, they should pay the premium $\Theta(e_t B_t^*/P_{X,t} X_t)$ to purchase the foreign bond. The functional form suggests that the premium is related to the ratio of the outstanding foreign debt to nominal value of exports, a measure for healthiness of the economy. That is, the premium increases as foreign debt ratio increases. For simplicity, we further assume that $\Theta(\cdot)$ show constant elasticity κ. In this case, the premium of foreign bond prices changes κ percent when the foreign debt ratio changes by 1 percent. The international interest rate, inverse of the foreign bond price, is assumed to follow a stochastic process. Households accumulate capital according to

$$K_t(j) = (1 - \delta)K_{t-1}(j) + I_t(j),$$

where δ is the capital depreciation rate. Since we assume that there is no adjustment cost for investment, the consumption good and the investment good are interchangeable. Under the assumption of the complete domestic asset market, households entertain the perfect risk-sharing, which implies the same level of consumption across household regardless of the labor and rental income they receive each period; therefore, we can drop the notation j from consumption and investment. The household decision problem regarding consumption, savings, and investment can be characterized by the following Euler equations:

$$\mathbf{E}_t\left[\beta\left(\frac{C_{t+1} - \gamma h C_t}{C_t - \gamma h C_{t-1}}\right)^{-1} R_t \frac{P_t}{P_{t+1}}\right] = 1$$

$$\mathbf{E}_t\left[\beta\left(\frac{C_{t+1} - \gamma h C_t}{C_t - \gamma h C_{t-1}}\right)^{-1} \Theta\left(\frac{e_t B_t^*}{P_{X,t} X_t}\right) R_t^* \frac{e_{t+1}}{e_t} \frac{P_t}{P_{t+1}}\right] = 1$$

$$\mathbf{E}_t\left[\beta\left(\frac{C_{t+1} - \gamma h C_t}{C_t - \gamma h C_{t-1}}\right)^{-1}\left(\frac{R_{t+1}^K}{P_{t+1}} + 1 - \delta\right)\right] = 1,$$

where $R_t = {}_t[Q_{t,t+1}]^{-1}$. The first and second equations are asset pricing equations regarding the real return on the purchase of domestic and foreign bonds, while the third equation is related to the return on the investment on the physical capital.

As in Erceg, Henderson, and Levin (2000) we assume that wage setting is subject to a nominal rigidity à la Calvo (1983) and Yun (1996). While each household can set the wage $W_t(j)$ of its own labor service by entertaining its monopoly power, only a fraction $(1 - \theta_L)$ of households are entitled chances for full optimization at any given period, independent of the time elapsed since the last adjustment. Thus, in each period a measure $(1 - \theta_L)$ of households reoptimizes its wage, while a fraction θ_L adjusts its wage according to a partial indexation rule:

(2) $$W_{t+k}(j) = \Gamma_{W,t}^k W_t(j),$$

where $\Gamma_{W,t}^k = (\gamma\bar{\pi}^{(1-\xi_L)}\pi_{t+k-1}^{\xi_L})\Gamma_{W,t}^{k-1}$. That is, households who cannot reoptimize wages update them by considering a weighted average of past CPI inflation π_{t-1} and the inflation target $\bar{\pi}$ set by the monetary authority.

Household j, who has the chance to reoptimize its wage at period t, chooses $\tilde{W}_t(j)$ (and $\tilde{H}_t(j)$, accordingly) to maximize the lifetime utility subject to the labor demand (1) and the updating rule for the nominal wage (2). The first-order condition can be written as

$$\mathbf{E}_t\left[\sum_{k=0}^{\infty}(\beta\theta_L)^k\left(\left(\frac{1}{\nu_L}\right)\frac{\tilde{W}_t(j)\Gamma_{W,t}^k}{P_{t+k}}(C_{t+k} - \gamma h C_{t+k-1})^{-1} - \chi_H \tilde{H}_{t+k}(j)^\tau\right)\tilde{H}_{t+k}(j)\right] = 0.$$

9.2.2   Domestic Firms

There is a continuum of monopolistically competitive Home goods-producing firms indexed by $i \in [0, 1]$. Home goods producers have identical CES production functions that use labor, capital service, and oil as inputs:

$$Y_{H,t}(i) = \zeta_{H,t}[(1 - \alpha)^{1/\phi_H}(\gamma^t N_{H,t}(i))^{1-1/\phi_H} + \alpha^{1/\phi_H}(K_{H,t}(i)^{1-\eta} O_{H,t}(i)^\eta)^{1-1/\phi_H}]^{\phi_H/(\phi_H-1)},$$

where $N_{H,t}(i)$ and $K_{H,t}(i)$ are the labor and capital input hired by firm i, $O_{H,t}(i)$ is oil used in the production of the variety i, and $\zeta_{H,t}$ represents a stationary productivity shock in the Home goods sector that is common to all firms. The aforementioned production specification requires that the oil input being combined with the capital and the unit elasticity of substitution between oil and capital is assumed. Parameter ϕ_H governs the elasticity of substitution between labor and capital-oil aggregate in production, α denotes the share of oil-capital aggregator, and η is the share of oil in oil-capital aggregator. While firms behave monopolistically in the goods market, they buy inputs competitively in the factor market. Given input prices W_t, R_t^K, and $P_{o,t}$ the cost minimization gives us

$$\frac{R_t^K}{P_{o,t}} = \frac{1-\eta}{\eta}\frac{O_{H,t}(i)}{K_{H,t}(i)}$$

$$\left(\frac{W_t}{\gamma^t P_{o,t}}\right)^{\phi_H} = \frac{1-\alpha}{\alpha}\eta^{-\phi_H}\frac{K_{H,t}(i)}{\gamma^t N_{H,t}(i)}\left(\frac{O_{H,t}(i)}{K_{H,t(i)}}\right)^{\eta=\phi_H-\eta\phi_H}.$$

That is, the oil-capital ratio and labor-capital ratio are constant across firms. Therefore, the nominal marginal cost of production is given by

$$MC_t = \frac{1}{\zeta_{H,t}}\left[(1-\alpha)\left(\frac{W_t}{\gamma^t}\right)^{1-\phi_H} + \alpha\left\{\left(\frac{P_{o,t}}{\eta}\right)^{\eta}\left(\frac{R_t^K}{1-\eta}\right)^{1-\phi_H}\right\}^{1-\eta}\right]^{1/(1-\phi_H)},$$

which implies that the marginal cost of production is the same across all firms.

Price setting is again subject to a nominal rigidity à la Calvo (1983) and Yun (1996). In each period only a fraction $(1-\theta_H)$ of firms can fully optimize their output prices. The remaining firms of fraction θ_H can only adjust the price according to a partial indexation scheme:

$$P_{H,t+k}(i) = \Gamma_{H,t}^k P_{H,t}(i)$$

where $\Gamma_{H,t}^k = (\overline{\pi}^{(1-\xi_H)}\pi_{H,t+k-1}^{\xi_H})\,\Gamma_{H,t}^{k-1}$ and $\pi_{H,t} = P_{H,t}/P_{H,t-1}$. For firms who do not have chances to reoptimize prices, the price adjustment factor is a weighted average between the past inflation of Home goods $\pi_{H,t-1}$ and the target inflation rate $\overline{\pi}$. The parameter ξ_H captures the degree of indexation in the economy. For firm i, who has the opportunity to reoptimize the output price, it chooses $\tilde{P}_{H,t}(i)$ to maximize the expected profit

$$E_t\left[\sum_{k=0}^{\infty}\theta_H^k \Lambda_{t,t+k}(\Gamma_{H,t}^k \tilde{P}_{H,t}(i) - MC_{t+k})\tilde{Y}_{H,t+k}(i)\right]$$

subject to the demand function:

$$\tilde{Y}_{H,t}(i) = \left(\frac{\tilde{P}_{H,t}(i)}{P_{H,t}}\right)^{-\nu_H} Y_{H,t}.$$

Hence, the first-order condition is

$$E_t\left[\sum_{k=0}^{\infty}\theta_H^k \Lambda_{t,t+k}\tilde{Y}_{H,t+k}(i)\left(\Gamma_{H,t}^k \tilde{P}_{H,t}(i) - \frac{\nu_H}{\nu_H-1}MC_{t+k}\right)\right] = 0.$$

Note that $\Lambda_{t,t+k}$ is the marginal value of a unit of the consumption good to households, which is treated as exogenous by the firm:

$$\Lambda_{t,t+k} = \beta^k \frac{P_t}{P_{t+k}}\left(\frac{C_t - \gamma h C_{t-1}}{C_{t+k} - \gamma h C_{t+k-1}}\right).$$

Given the price charged by a firm i, its profit is given by

$$\Pi_t(i) = P_{H,t}(i)Y_{H,t}(i) - W_t N_{H,t}(i) - R_t^K K_{H,t}(i) - P_{o,t}O_{H,t}(i).$$

9.2.3   The Foreign Economy

The foreign demand for Home goods is given by

(3)
$$C_{H,t}^* = \omega_H^* \left(\frac{P_{H,t}^*}{P_{F,t}^*} \right)^{-\phi^*} C_t^*$$

where ω_H^* denotes the import share in the consumption basket of foreign agents and ϕ^* captures the intratemporal elasticity of substitution between Foreign and Home goods in the foreign economy. The foreign consumption C_t^* is exogenously given and follows a stochastic process.

We assume the law of one price (LOP) holds for Home goods. That is, the domestic firms cannot discriminate across markets in terms of prices. This also holds for imported Foreign goods except oil:

$$P_{H,t}^* = \frac{P_{H,t}}{e_t}, \qquad P_{F,t} = e_t P_{F,t}^*.$$

We can define the real exchange rate as:

$$s_t = \frac{e_t P_{F,t}^*}{P_t}.$$

Note that the price of consumption bundle of foreign agents is dominated by $P_{F,t}^*$ rather than P_t^* because home country is assumed to be a small open economy; therefore the import share of the foreign economy ω_H^* is negligible. The domestic real price of oil is given by

(2)
$$\frac{P_{o,t}}{P_t} = s_t \frac{P_{o,t}^*}{P_{F,t}^*} \zeta_{o,t},$$

where $P_{o,t}^*$ is the foreign currency price of oil abroad. The pass-through of oil prices is incomplete in the sense that $\zeta_{o,t}$ signifies the deviations from the law of one price in the oil price. This deviation $\zeta_{o,t}$ is assumed to follow a stochastic process. The real international oil price $P_{o,t}^*/P_{F,t}^*$ also follows a stochastic process.

9.2.4   Monetary Authority

Monetary policy is described by an interest rate feedback rule of the form

$$R_t = R_t^{\rho_R} \overline{R}_{t-1}^{1-\rho_R} \exp(\epsilon_{R,t}),$$

where $\epsilon_{R,t}$ is a monetary policy shock and $\overline{R}_t$ is the nominal target interest rate. Monetary authority sets its target in responding to inflation and deviations of output growth rate from its trend:

$$\overline{R}_t = r\overline{\pi} \left(\frac{\pi_t}{\overline{\pi}} \right)^{\psi_\pi} \left(\frac{Y_t}{\gamma Y_{t-1}} \right)^{\psi_y}$$

where $\overline{r}$ is real interest rate at the steady state.

9.2.5   Aggregation and Equilibrium

We abstract from the government spending. We further assume that the government passively runs a balanced budget every period:

$$\int_0^1 (M_t(j) - M_{t-1}(j))\, dj + \int_0^1 T_t(j)\, dj = 0.$$

The goods market, the labor market, and the capital market clear

$$Y_{H,t} = \int_0^1 (C_{H,t}(j) + C^*_{H,t}(j) + I_{H,t}(j))\, dj$$

$$H_t = \int_0^1 N_{H,t}(i)\, di$$

$$\int_0^1 K_{t-1}(j)\, dj = \int_0^1 K_{H,t}(i)\, di.$$

We consider the symmetric equilibrium where households and firms make the same decision when available. Combining equilibrium conditions, the budget constraint of the government, and the aggregate budget constraint of households, we get the following dynamics of foreign bond holdings:

$$\frac{e_t B^*_t}{R^*_t \Theta\, e_t B^*_t / (P_{X,t} X_t)} = e_t B^*_{t-1} + P_{X,t} X_t - P_{M,t} M_t.$$

As noted before, imports consist of oil and Foreign goods for consumption and investment while domestically produced goods are the only export of the economy. Therefore, the aggregate nominal value of exports and imports are defined as

$$P_{X,t} X_t = P_{H,t} C^*_{H,t}$$

$$P_{M,t} M_t = s_t P_t (C_{F,t} + I_{F,t}) + e_t P^*_{o,t} O_t,$$

where X_t and M_t denote exports and imports, respectively. Total oil imports are the sum of oil for direct consumption and that for production, $O_t = O_{C,t} + O_{H,t}$. We can also write the nominal gross domestic product (GDP) as

$$P_{Y,t} Y_t = P_t (C_t + I_t) + P_{X,t} X_t - P_{M,t} M_t,$$

where $P_{Y,t}$ denotes the implicit output deflator.

9.2.6   Steady State

The model is equipped with deterministic trend. Hence, we first detrend variables to define the steady state. All price and wage variables are written as relative prices to the Home CPI P_t. Real variables with trend are to be divided by γ^t. At the steady state after detrending, all relative prices and the real wage are normalized to one for computational convenience.

9.3 Estimation Methods

This section consists of two parts. First, we briefly discuss how to estimate and evaluate the model with Bayesian approach. With the state space representation of the model, we can estimate the model within Bayesian estimation frameworks, so-called Metropolis-Hastings algorithm with Kalman filter. See An and Schorfheide (2007) for a review. Also, we introduce the DSGE-VAR framework developed in Del Negro and Schorfheide (2004) and Del Negro et al. (2007). The DSGE-VARs are useful to check how DSGE models are misspecified. This framework tries to find out the optimal weight between two approaches, DSGEs and VARs, that fit data best. Next, we explain the data used in our analysis.

9.3.1 Estimation and Evaluation of DSGE Models

To establish an estimable representation, we first log-linearize the model around its nonstochastic steady state. Several solution algorithms of the linearized rational expectations system are available; for instance, Blanchard and Kahn (1980), Uhlig (1999), and Sims (2002). With the help of the solution algorithm, the log-linearized system can be written as an autoregressive model in a vector of variables:

$$(4) \qquad s_t = \Phi^{(s)}(\theta)s_{t-1} + \Phi^{(\varepsilon)}(\theta)\varepsilon_t,$$

where s_t denotes the vector of model variables in log-deviation from steady state, and ε_t is the vector of innovations to shock processes. The coefficients $\Phi^{(s)}(\theta)$ and $\Phi^{(\varepsilon)}(\theta)$ are conformable matrices whose values are dependent on the values of DSGE model parameters θ. Given that some of the variables in s_t are not observable, we can treat (4) as the transition equation of a state space representation. Once we define a vector of observables, y_t, we can set up measurement equations:

$$(5) \qquad y_t = \Theta^{(0)}(\theta) + \Theta^{(s)}(\theta)s_t.$$

More specifically, we assume that the time period t in the model corresponds to one quarter and that the following observations are available for estimation: quarter-to-quarter per capita GDP growth rate, annualized nominal interest rate, annualized quarter-to-quarter core CPI inflation rate, annualized quarter-to-quarter hourly wage inflation, quarter-to-quarter nominal exchange rate depreciation, international oil prices relative to domestic price level, and quarter-to-quarter growth rate of oil imports. The system matrices, $\Phi^{(s)}$, $\Phi^{(\varepsilon)}$, $\Theta^{(0)}$, and $\Theta^{(\varepsilon)}$, in the state space representation, (4) and (5), are given as highly nonlinear functions of the DSGE model parameters θ.

While DSGE models are popular among the economists because of their microfoundations, the empirical performance is not so successful until Christiano, Eichenbaum, and Evans (2005) and Smets and Wouters (2003). On the contrary, VARs are widely used in empirical macroeconomics and considered as benchmarks for evaluating dynamic economies due to better fit of the data and forecasting power. Del Negro and Schorfheide (2004) and Del Negro et al. (2007) investigate possible connections between DSGE models and VARs. We first briefly mention the Bayesian approach to estimate the state space representation of DSGE models as in (4) and (5). Then we proceed further on the DSGE-VAR procedure.

The Bayesian approach is widely used in the estimation of DSGE models. The main advantage is that it has a systematic way to incorporate information that is available but at the same time tricky or even impossible to formally construct the likelihood. The likelihood information $p(Y|\theta)$ contained in the data used for estimation is extracted via Kalman filter in the state space representation, and the information that is informally available is summarized as the prior distribution $p(\theta)$. This informal information can include results from related literature that employs other data sets and models. The Bayes theorem provides the basic insight how to update the prior belief on parameters with the information contained in the data; that is, the likelihood. With well-specified prior distribution, the posterior distribution $p(\theta|Y)$ can be simulated through the Markov-chain Monte Carlo (MCMC) procedure.

Another convenient procedure in Bayesian analysis is the model selection. The posterior odd ratio is a key statistic in selecting a model among a series of competing models. We can just choose one with the highest posterior odds. With equal prior probabilities assigned to each model, the posterior odds are not different from the ratio of the marginal data densities (or the marginal likelihood, equivalently) $p(Y)$ across models. Therefore, it suffices to have a procedure to evaluate the marginal data density given the draws from the posterior distribution. This can be achieved by Geweke's (1999) modified harmonic mean estimator.

Given the state space representation of DSGE models, it is not difficult to imagine that there exists a tight link between DSGE models and VARs. That is, the cross equation relationships restricted by DSGE models can be imposed on VAR parameters; therefore we can expect a better performance of VARs with this priori restriction. Del Negro and Schorfheide (2004) introduce the DSGE-VAR(λ) procedure from this perspective. The hyper parameter λ governs the tightness of the priori restrictions from DSGE models. When the DSGE prior weight λ approaches infinity, the VAR parameters are tightly restricted by the cross equation restrictions from DSGE models. When the DSGE prior weight λ approaches zero, on the contrary, the DSGE model imposes no restriction on the VAR parameters and the estimation procedure behaves like an unrestricted VAR model. Hence, by changing the value of the hyper parameter λ we can generate a series of VAR models whose parameter restrictions based on a DSGE model have different tightness.

Another interpretation of DSGE-VARs tackles misspecification issues of

DSGE models. As noted before, DSGE models are well accepted among the economists since their modeling is based on economic theory and impulse response analysis is straightforward. However, restrictions derived from DSGE models are often too tight to match the data, and hence the empirical performance is usually far from satisfactory. Del Negro et al. (2007) point out that the data generating process of a VAR is decomposed into the DSGE model part and its possible misspecifications, and this misspecification can be modeled in a Bayesian framework. The same hyper parameter λ now refers to the degree of misspecification. As λ moves away from the infinity where only DSGE models are allowed as correct specification, the flexibility in describing the data increases. If we can find out the "optimal" value, namely $\hat{\lambda}$, it can be used to evaluate the specification of the DSGE model. In short, the larger $\hat{\lambda}$ is, the smaller is the misspecification of the DSGE model and a lot of weight should be placed on its implied restrictions.

As discussed before, we can consider a series of specifications in terms of the hyper parameter λ given a DSGE model. Noting that the best model can be selected using the posterior odds ratio in Bayesian analysis, the "optimal" weight on DSGE prior $\hat{\lambda}$ can be found by maximizing the marginal likelihood with respect to λ. When $\hat{\lambda}$ is chosen according to the posterior odds criterion, a comparison between DSGE-VAR($\hat{\lambda}$) and DSGE model impulse responses can reveal important insights about the misspecification of the DSGE model. While DSGE model impulse response is well defined, impulse responses of DSGE-VAR($\hat{\lambda}$) needs careful treatment. To obtain a proper impulse response, we should align DSGE-VAR($\hat{\lambda}$) along with structural shocks of the DSGE model. The details of this procedure can be found in Del Negro and Schorfheide (2004).

9.3.2   Data

Most of the data are obtained through KOSIS (Korean statistical information service),[2] maintained by Korea National Statistical Office and ECOS (Economic statistics system),[3] maintained by the Bank of Korea. Seasonally adjusted real GDP is divided by population fifteen years and older and its growth rate is calculated as 100 times the first difference in logs. The interest rate is the overnight call rate. The core inflation rate is calculated from core CPI as 400 times the first difference in logs. The nominal hourly wage is obtained by dividing total wage by total hours worked and its inflation is again calculated as 400 times the first difference in logs. The nominal exchange rate depreciation is calculated as 100 times the first difference in logs of the effective exchange rate published by the Bank of International Settlement (BIS). The international oil price relative to domestic price level is obtained by dividing WTI crude oil spot price by CPI and being nor-

---

2. See http://www.kosis.kr.
3. See http://ecos.bok.or.kr.

malized after taking logs. Finally, the crude oil import is obtained from Korea National Oil Corporation[4] and then seasonally adjusted by the X12 method, available from EViews. Per capita term is obtained by dividing it by population fifteen years and older, and then quarter-to-quarter growth rate is calculated as 100 times the first difference in logs. Data are available for 1993:Q2 to 2008:Q4.

9.4   Empirical Results

We begin this section by explaining the specification of prior distributions of structural parameters of the DSGE model. In the following discussion on the "optimal" DSGE prior weight, we also consider two variants of our baseline DSGE model. One lacks oil in consumption basket and the other excludes oil from inputs of production. We discuss how a fit changes as we move away from our baseline model. We also look into impulse response functions from our DSGE models and compare them with those from "optimal" DSGE-VARs. Finally, we investigate the behavior of deviations from the law of one price in domestic oil prices and the oil price pass-through as the international crude oil prices surges in mid-2000s.

In what follows, we use DYNARE for estimation of both DSGE models and DSGE-VARs. For each specification we generate 125,000 draws from posterior distributions, and the first 25,000 draws are discarded for convergence of Markov-chain.

9.4.1   Prior Distribution

Prior distribution in Bayesian analysis plays an important role in the estimation of DSGE models. By specifying them, we express our own view on plausible parameter values. Actually this process reweights the information contained in the data that are used in actual estimation. That is, we can incorporate extra information that is possibly missing in estimation samples and is developed in the related literature.

To begin with, we calibrate several parameter values that are not identified in our representation. First, the substitution elasticity across differentiated labor v_L that governs wage markup is set to 9 as in Medina and Soto (2005). The price markup parameter v_H is not present in our linearized model. Noting that our model abstracts from government spending, we set the steady-state consumption-output ratio as 0.66, which stems from the average ratio of the sum of consumption and government expenditure to GDP in our sample. The steady-state investment-output ratio is 0.32 and the steady-state export share is 0.38, according to our sample. From these ratios, we can derive other big ratios using steady-state relationships.

Table 9.2 lists the marginal prior distributions for the structural param-

---

4. See http://www.petronet.or.kr.

Table 9.2   **Prior distribution**

Name	Domain	Density	Mean	Standard deviation	Description
α	$[0, 1)$	Beta	0.300	0.100	Capital-oil share in production
η	$[0, 1)$	Beta	0.500	0.200	Oil share in capital-oil
δ	$[0, 1)$	Beta	0.015	0.002	Depreciation rate
τ	$\mathbf{R}^+$	Gamma	1.000	0.750	(inverse) EIS of labor
h	$[0, 1)$	Beta	0.500	0.200	Habit persistence
κ	$\mathbf{R}^+$	Gamma	0.010	0.005	Elasticity: Risk premium
φ_Z	$\mathbf{R}^+$	Gamma	0.300	0.200	Elasticity: H/F goods consumption
φ^*	$\mathbf{R}^+$	Gamma	1.000	0.400	Elasticity: H/F goods in foreign consumption
φ_C	$\mathbf{R}^+$	Gamma	0.330	0.150	Elasticity: Oil and core consumption
φ_H	$\mathbf{R}^+$	Gamma	0.500	0.300	Elasticity: Oil-capital and labor input of production
θ_H	$[0, 1)$	Beta	0.700	0.100	Calvo on price
θ_L	$[0, 1)$	Beta	0.700	0.150	Calvo on wage
ξ_H	$[0, 1)$	Beta	0.500	0.200	Price indexation
ξ_L	$[0, 1)$	Beta	0.500	0.200	Wage indexation
ψ_π	$\mathbf{R}^+$	Gamma	1.500	0.200	Responsiveness on inflation
ψ_y	$\mathbf{R}^+$	Gamma	0.500	0.250	Responsiveness on output
ρ_R	$[0, 1)$	Beta	0.750	0.100	Persistence: Interest rate
$\gamma^{(Q)}$	$\mathbf{R}$	Normal	0.750	0.300	Growth rate
$r^{(A)}$	$\mathbf{R}^+$	Gamma	0.500	0.200	Steady-state real interest rate
$\pi^{(A)}$	$\mathbf{R}^+$	Gamma	3.000	2.000	Target inflation rate
ω_F	$[0, 1)$	Beta	0.350	0.100	Weight on foreign good consumption
ω_o	$[0, 1)$	Beta	0.100	0.050	Weight on oil consumption
ρ_A	$[0, 1)$	Beta	0.700	0.150	Persistence: Technology
ρ_o	$[0, 1)$	Beta	0.700	0.150	Persistence: Oil price pass-through
ρ_{o^*}	$[0, 1)$	Beta	0.700	0.150	Persistence: Foreign oil price
ρ_{R^*}	$[0, 1)$	Beta	0.700	0.150	Persistence: Foreign interest rate
ρ_{π^*}	$[0, 1)$	Beta	0.700	0.150	Persistence: Foreign inflation
ρ_{C^*}	$[0, 1)$	Beta	0.700	0.150	Persistence: Foreign consumption
σ_R	$\mathbf{R}^+$	InvGamma	0.010	2	StDev: Monetary policy
σ_A	$\mathbf{R}^+$	InvGamma	0.150	2	StDev: Technology
σ_o	$\mathbf{R}^+$	InvGamma	0.150	2	StDev: Oil-price pass-through
σ_{o^*}	$\mathbf{R}^+$	InvGamma	0.150	2	StDev: Foreign oil price
σ_{R^*}	$\mathbf{R}^+$	InvGamma	0.050	2	StDev: Foreign interest rate
σ_{π^*}	$\mathbf{R}^+$	InvGamma	0.050	2	StDev: Foreign inflation
σ_{C^*}	$\mathbf{R}^+$	InvGamma	0.050	2	StDev: Foreign consumption

Notes: For the inverse-gamma distribution, values in the standard deviation column denote degrees of freedom.

eters of the DSGE model. In general, the prior distributions used in this study are quite diffuse. As usual, the rule of thumb in choosing the distribution family for each parameter is the shape of the support. Parameters that have limits on both ends, usually confined between 0 and 1, follow the beta distribution. For those with positive unbound support we specify the gamma distribution, with the exception of standard deviations of shock processes for which inverse gamma distributions are assumed. Unbounded parameters are specified as normal distributions. The share of oil-capital aggregator in production α has a mean of 0.3, the usual capital share of an economy. With standard deviation 0.1, 90 percent coverage is [0.15, 0.48]. The oil share in oil-capital aggregator η is centered at 0.5 since no primitive estimate is available. The quarterly depreciation rate δ has a mean of 0.015, implying 6 percent annual depreciation. Inverse of intertemporal substitution elasticity of labor τ has a mean of 1 and standard deviation of 0.75, whose 90 percent coverage is [0.15, 2.46]. Without preference shock as in our model, this parameter is often estimated quite small and even negative with aggregate data. Due to lack of information on the habit persistence parameter h, it is centered at 0.5 and standard deviation 0.2 to have [0.17, 0.83] as 90 percent coverage. The elasticity of risk premium on foreign debt κ has mean 0.01 with standard deviation 0.005. The elasticity of substitution between Home and Foreign goods in core consumption ϕ_Z has a relatively low mean of 0.3 and it is roughly around the calibrated value in the Bank of Korea model (BOKDSGE) by Kang and Park (2007). Its counterpart in foreign consumption ϕ^* is set to 1. The elasticity between oil and core consumption ϕ_C is also low as 0.33, since there is almost no substitute for oil in the Korean economy, especially when it comes to fuel for transportation. The elasticity between oil-capital aggregator and labor input of production ϕ_H is not obvious and hence it is set to 0.5. For more discussion of the estimates of the elasticity of energy or oil with other inputs, see Backus and Crucini (2000). Calvo rigidity parameters for price θ_H and wage θ_L are equally set to have a mean of 0.7. This value implies that prices and wages are reset every three quarters on average. Standard deviations for θ_H and θ_L are 0.1 and 0.15, respectively. Hence, 90 percent coverage implies that prices are reset between 2.1 and 6.8 quarters and wages between 1.7 and 11.9 quarters. Price (ξ_H) and wage (ξ_L) indexation to past inflation are all centered at 0.5 and have a common standard deviation of 0.2. Monetary policy parameters ψ_π and ψ_y are set to have means from Taylor's (1993) values, 1.5 and 0.5, and 90 percent coverage, [1.19, 1.84] and [0.17, 0.97], respectively. We further specify weights on Foreign goods in core consumption ω_F and on oil in consumption ω_o. They are centered at 0.35 and 0.1, respectively. Persistence of shocks, (ρ_A, ρ_o, ρ_{o^*}, ρ_{R^*}, ρ_{π^*}, ρ_{C^*}) have the same specification, mean of 0.75 and standard deviation of 0.15.

9.4.2   Model Selection and DSGE Prior Weight

The main purpose of DSGE-VARs is to evaluate the (mis-)specification of DSGE models under consideration. To begin with, however, we investigate a direct estimation of structural parameters of our baseline model. Bayesian estimations of linearized DSGE models trace back to DeJong, Ingram, and Whiteman (2000); Landon-Lane (1998); and Schorfheide (2000); they use Markov-chain Monte Carlo (MCMC) algorithm for posterior simulator

Table 9.3   The fit of the small open economy DSGE model

Specification	λ	Baseline	No oil consumption $\omega_0 = 0$	No oil in production $\eta = 0$
DSGE		−1329.05	−1499.42	−1389.71
DSGE-VAR	∞	−1278.47	−1412.31	−1387.04
	2	−1220.09	−1219.77	−1293.64
	1.5	−1198.91	−1229.15	−1204.30
	1.25	−1206.11	−1181.97	−1183.42
	1	−1171.12	−1200.08	−1206.92
	0.75	−1185.81	−1199.96	−1211.15
	0.66	−1155.76	−1180.27	−1184.79
	0.5	−1132.41	−1157.48	−1155.61
	0.4	−1155.80	−1146.78	−1136.48

while Kalman filter provides exact likelihood computations. As noted previously, a unified framework for model selection within Bayesian framework, the posterior odds ratio, makes this approach quite popular. Here we consider two restrictions on the baseline model described in section 9.2. In our baseline economy, the entire volume of oil in domestic use is imported from foreign countries and a fraction of oil imports is directly consumed among households. The first restricted model tackles this point and assumes that oil is not included in the consumption basket ("No Oil Consumption"). On the contrary, oil is not used for production in the second restricted model ("No Oil in Production").

The first row of table 9.3 reports the log marginal likelihood of three models under consideration. The baseline model attains the highest marginal likelihood (−1329.05), followed by "No Oil in Production" (−1389.71) and then "No Oil Consumption" (−1499.42) models. That is, the baseline model best describes the data if these models are assigned the same prior probabilities. This result is somewhat expected given that both consumption and production motive of oil use in the Korean economy is sizable and significant, as seen in table 9.1. However, we should note that the marginal data density penalizes larger models like any information criterion and hence this result is not so obvious as it looks.

Now we turn our attention to DSGE prior weight; that is, DSGE-VARs. In practice, DSGE models have VAR representations with the truncation at a particular lag order. Due to short sample periods we restrict the lags in VARs to 2. This approximate VAR representation distinguishes DSGE-VARs from DSGE models even with infinite weight on DSGE priors, DSGE-VAR(∞). This discrepancy is obviously seen from differences between the first and the second rows in table 9.3. For each of three specifications, we try various values for the DSGE prior weight parameter λ and report results in table 9.3. The DSGE-VARs with the baseline model attain the highest log marginal likelihood when $\lambda = 0.5$ at -1132.4, whereas those with other two restricted models do so when $\lambda = 0.4$ (-1146.8 for "No Oil Consumption" and -1136.5 for "No Oil in Production"). That is, the "optimal" prior weight for the baseline economy is higher than those for the other two restricted models. This result again signifies that the degree of the misspecification in the baseline model is less than those in the other two restricted models because the baseline model would put more weight on the DSGE prior. Both from the comparison of log marginal likelihoods of DSGE models and the optimal weight of DSGE priors, we can now draw the same conclusion.

9.4.3   Posterior Estimates

Before proceeding with the posterior estimates of the DSGE model parameters, we should pay attention to the "optimal" weight for the baseline economy. With $\hat{\lambda} = 0.5$, the best fit of the data is achieved by putting 1/3 of the weight on the DSGE model and 2/3 on the VAR model; hence, there is still some room for improvement in the model specification. Del Negro et al. (2007) show that the Smets-Wouters model has around 1/2 weight in their DSGE-VAR analysis. As previously discussed, another interpretation of a DSGE-VAR is to extract prior information from a DSGE model for VAR coefficients; therefore, the posterior distribution of VAR coefficients can be expressed as the posterior distribution of DSGE model parameters, given the tightness of the prior from a DSGE model $\hat{\lambda}$. This refers to the posterior distribution of DSGE-VAR($\hat{\lambda}$).

Table 9.4 reports posterior estimates from the DSGE model and DSGE-VAR($\hat{\lambda}$) of the baseline model. In DSGE estimation, most of the parameters show information gain through likelihood; that is, the prior distribution is updated through the likelihood and results in the posterior distribution. A couple of parameters, δ and θ_H, have roughly the same prior and posterior means. However, 90 percent coverage shrinks as they move to posterior distributions, which implies that likelihoods bring on some extra information. The capital share can be obtained from $\alpha(1 - \eta)$ and its posterior mean is 0.201 for DSGE and 0.4142 for DSGE-VAR($\hat{\lambda}$). The elasticity between oil-capital aggregator and labor input of production ϕ_H attains a very low posterior mean of 0.021. This implies that the oil-capital aggregator and labor are not substitutable in production and hints a big difference in log marginal likelihoods between the baseline and "No Oil in Production" models. In DSGE-VAR($\hat{\lambda}$) the posterior mean of this parameter is much bigger, 0.1750, which implies more flexible substitution among inputs of production and results in smaller change in log marginal likelihoods when we abstract the production motive of the oil use. The model displays relatively high degrees of price θ_H and wage θ_L rigidities, 0.711 and 0.855, with 3.5 and 6.9 quarters of duration, respectively. With DSGE-VAR($\hat{\lambda}$), these durations are 5.4 and 3 quarters, respectively. The estimated slope of Phillips curve, $\beta/(1 + \beta\xi_H)$, is around 0.63 both for DSGE and DSGE-VAR($\hat{\lambda}$), and it is quite close to the

Table 9.4　　　　　　　**Posterior estimates: Baseline model**

		DSGE	DSGE-VAR($\hat{\lambda}$)	
	Mean	90% interval	Mean	90% interval
α	0.2287	[0.2150, 0.2431]	0.4969	[0.4268, 0.5590]
η	0.1229	[0.1122, 0.1353]	0.1665	[0.1239, 0.2101]
δ	0.0152	[0.0150, 0.0155]	0.0118	[0.0112, 0.0124]
τ	0.6227	[0.5195, 0.7242]	1.6634	[1.4049, 1.8997]
h	0.2639	[0.2205, 0.2985]	0.3122	[0.2502, 0.3828]
κ	0.0010	[0.0005, 0.0014]	0.0017	[0.0003, 0.0028]
φ_Z	0.1660	[0.1114, 0.2126]	0.3125	[0.2509, 0.3651]
φ^*	0.9382	[0.8958, 1.0343]	0.8390	[0.7174, 0.9683]
φ_C	0.2852	[0.2657, 0.2996]	0.2064	[0.1607, 0.2463]
φ_H	0.0205	[0.0086, 0.0331]	0.1750	[0.0961, 0.2511]
θ_H	0.7105	[0.6940, 0.7250]	0.8137	[0.7871, 0.8384]
θ_L	0.8545	[0.8392, 0.8763]	0.6626	[0.5779, 0.7433]
ξ_H	0.5881	[0.5029, 0.6503]	0.6000	[0.4947, 0.7151]
ξ_L	0.9790	[0.9625, 0.9959]	0.8811	[0.8243, 0.9346]
ψ_π	1.5720	[1.5413, 1.6193]	2.0209	[1.9161, 2.1411]
ψ_y	0.2711	[0.2323, 0.3247]	0.1828	[0.0831, 0.2845]
ρ_R	0.8569	[0.8477, 0.8704]	0.8179	[0.7889, 0.8569]
$\gamma^{(Q)}$	0.4120	[0.3774, 0.4388]	0.4085	[0.2545, 0.6263]
$r^{(A)}$	0.3368	[0.3131, 0.3646]	0.3328	[0.2717, 0.3966]
$\pi^{(A)}$	4.8804	[4.3918, 5.2561]	2.0724	[1.5934, 2.5767]
ω_F	0.2889	[0.2785, 0.3017]	0.2193	[0.1877, 0.2583]
ω_o	0.1174	[0.1022, 0.1323]	0.1070	[0.0843, 0.1348]
ρ_A	0.8862	[0.8638, 0.9167]	0.7943	[0.7406, 0.8490]
ρ_o	0.9446	[0.9073, 0.9640]	0.9557	[0.9033, 0.9887]
ρ_{o^*}	0.9563	[0.9451, 0.9681]	0.8932	[0.8282, 0.9689]
ρ_{R^*}	0.8229	[0.7971, 0.8500]	0.5262	[0.4542, 0.6228]
ρ_{π^*}	0.1795	[0.1670, 0.1927]	0.0773	[0.0237, 0.1249]
ρ_{C^*}	0.9305	[0.8788, 0.9627]	0.5962	[0.5108, 0.6791]
σ_R	0.0080	[0.0067, 0.0092]	0.0023	[0.0017, 0.0029]
σ_A	0.0189	[0.0157, 0.0217]	0.0188	[0.0148, 0.0228]
σ_o	0.2929	[0.2509, 0.3435]	0.0532	[0.0335, 0.0723]
σ_{o^*}	0.1759	[0.1470, 0.2013]	0.0632	[0.0459, 0.0798]
σ_{R^*}	0.0113	[0.0093, 0.0136]	0.0092	[0.0070, 0.0112]
σ_{π^*}	0.0630	[0.0537, 0.0725]	0.0307	[0.0224, 0.0387]
σ_{C^*}	0.0244	[0.0186, 0.0308]	0.0186	[0.0128, 0.0247]

Bank of Korea's calibration, 0.58. The weight on oil in consumption basket ω_o is estimated as 0.117. Persistence parameters are estimated high except one. The posterior mean of the persistence for foreign inflation shock ρ_{π^*} is 0.180. This estimate is even lower for DSGE-VAR($\hat{\lambda}$).

As pointed out in Del Negro and Schorfheide (2004), information about structural parameters of the DSGE model is gathered more slowly as the DSGE prior weight loosens. When λ is moving away from infinity priors on VAR, parameters become less tight. Therefore, we can expect that the

Table 9.5   Variance decomposition

	Output growth	Interest rate	Core inflation	Wage inflation	Ex. rate dep.	Oil import growth
Money	0.3444	0.0159	0.1953	0.1840	0.0757	0.3268
Technology	0.0580	0.0090	0.0130	0.0040	0.0012	0.0185
Oil*	0.1103	0.1674	0.0691	0.0957	0.0311	0.1226
Dev. LOP	0.2596	0.4039	0.1681	0.2480	0.0709	0.2910
Money*	0.0437	0.3343	0.4347	0.3572	0.2642	0.0502
Inflation*	0.0108	0.0665	0.1174	0.1094	0.5561	0.0147
Consumption*	0.1731	0.0030	0.0024	0.0016	0.0007	0.1762

Note: "Starred" shocks on the first column denote international/foreign ones.

posterior of DSGE-VAR($\hat{\lambda}$) is closer to the prior than the posterior distribution of the DSGE model. For many parameters it is verifiable, especially for the substitution elasticity between oil-capital aggregator and labor input of production ϕ_H, and that between Home and Foreign goods consumption in core consumption bundle ϕ_Z.

Fluctuations of the observables originate from the structural shocks of our economy. Variance decompositions of the observables at the posterior mean are reported in table 9.5. We can easily see that the monetary policy shock has significant contributions to the variability of output growth, oil import growth, and both inflations. However, the contributions of the technology shock are negligible, less than 1 percent, especially for price variables. These findings coincide with the result from a standard New Keynesian economy. The domestic interest rate variability can be explained mostly by the oil price shock (Oil*; 17 percent), the shock on the deviation from the law of one price (LOP; 40 percent), and the international interest rate shock (Money*; 33 percent). We should note that the international oil price and the deviations from the law of one price together decide the domestic oil price, and therefore, we can say that these two shocks have large contributions in explaining the variability of the domestic interest rate, the output growth rate, and the oil import growth rate.

9.4.4   Impulse Response Functions

As seen previously, DSGE-VAR($\hat{\lambda}$) attains higher marginal likelihood than the other two extremes: DSGEs and VARs. Basically, the DSGE-VAR($\hat{\lambda}$) is a Bayesian VAR (BVAR) optimally weighted prior from the DSGE model. Hence, we can use it as the benchmark in evaluating the performance of the DSGE model. As is often the case with indirect inferences (e.g., Christiano, Eichenbaum, and Evans 2005), the performance of a DSGE model is checked by comparing impulse response functions, one from a VAR and another from the DSGE model.

Figure 9.1, panel A, depicts impulse responses with respect to a mone-

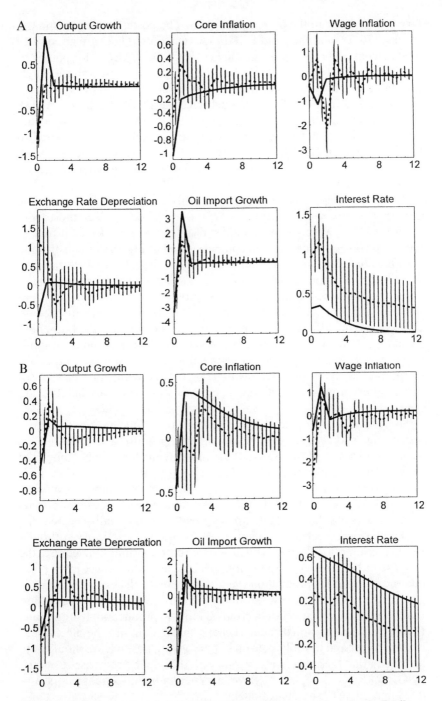

Fig. 9.1   Impulse response functions: Baseline model. *A*, monetary shock; *B*, oil price shock

tary policy shock in the baseline economy. The posterior mean responses of the DSGE (solid line) and DSGE-VAR($\hat{\lambda}$) (dotted line) are given, with a 90 percent coverage band (gray area) for DSGE-VAR($\hat{\lambda}$). Responses of real international price of oil are omitted because this observable is purely exogenous and it responds only to its own shock in the model. We can see that responses from the DSGE model trace out those of DSGE-VAR($\hat{\lambda}$). Most of responses from the baseline DSGE model show hump-shaped and prolonged effects, but these effects are quantitatively small compared to those from the DSGE-VAR($\hat{\lambda}$). These quantitative discrepancies are originated from a relatively low value of $\hat{\lambda}$; that is, 0.5. Some initial responses do not match, such as exchange rate depreciation.

Panel B of figure 9.1 shows responses to an oil price shock in the baseline economy. Again, response from the DSGE model mimics well those from DSGE-VAR($\hat{\lambda}$). When a household is hit by the oil price shock it tries to reduce the oil consumption and compensate its utility loss by substituting with the core consumption bundle. Given that the estimated elasticity of substitution ϕ_Z is low (0.166), however, this desired substitution is not fully accommodated and the aggregate consumption will decrease initially. From the firm's side, the oil input can be substituted by the capital with the unit elasticity of substitution, but this channel also drives out the household consumption for higher investment. Alternatively, the reduced oil input might be compensated by an increased labor demand, but again, the substitution elasticity ϕ_H is quite low (0.021). Therefore, the initial responses of oil import growth, output growth, core inflation, and wage inflation are negative.

The responses of aforementioned variables in subsequent periods are more interesting. As time goes by, more households can adjust to the monopolistic wage in Calvo-Yun setting. Given the higher demand for the labor input, the wage inflation turns into positive. The same story goes with the core inflation, where oil consumption is replaced by the core consumption over time and more firms adjust their Home goods output prices to the monopolistic level. It looks puzzling that oil imports growth that is initially negative due to the oil price shock stays positive in subsequent periods. Even though the oil consumption decreases, the increased core consumption requires the increase in Home goods production; hence, the income effect takes place and the oil input for production eventually increases. The total response is governed by the sum of the substitution effect in direct oil consumption, and the substitution and income effects in oil input in production. If we assume the foreign consumption demands behave similarly, the income effect would be even bigger and it would keep oil import growth positive. We should note here again that these findings coincide with the impulse responses from the DSGE-VAR($\hat{\lambda}$)—a version of Bayesian VAR with not-so-tight priors ($\hat{\lambda} = 0.5$) imposed by the baseline model.

9.4.5 Pass-Through of Oil Price and Deviation from the Law of One Price

The baseline model for our analysis is constructed so that the exchange rate pass-through for all but oil is perfect. However, there is a discrepancy between international oil price and domestic oil price as in (3) and deviations from the LOP are modeled as a stochastic process whose log-deviation $\zeta_{o,t}$ follows an AR(1) process. We can see that $\zeta_{o,t}$ takes value 0 if the pass-through is perfect, and moves away from zero otherwise. From table 9.4 it is obvious that $\zeta_{o,t}$ is highly persistent across specifications, 0.9446 for DSGE and 0.9557 for DSGE-VAR($\hat{\lambda}$). Hence, we can expect that the pass-through of oil prices into domestic price is relatively low. The pass-through rate is calculated by dividing the impulse responses of core CPI index by the responses of oil prices to oil price shock. Figure 9.2 depicts the pass-through rates of the oil price shock into the core CPI evaluated at the posterior means of the baseline model (dashed line) and DSGE-VAR($\hat{\lambda}$) (solid line). Since the initial response of the core inflation is negative, the pass-through for the period turns out to be negative. At the two-year horizon, the pass-through reaches 0.055 for the baseline model and 0.077 for DSGE-VAR($\hat{\lambda}$), which is close to Jongwanich and Park's (2008) estimate on Korea during 1996Q1 to

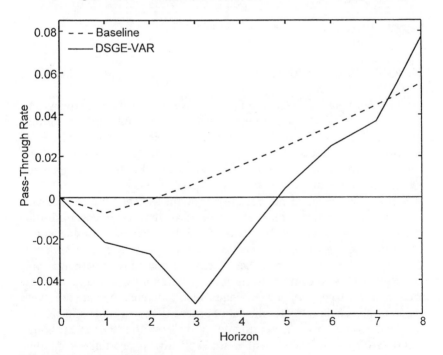

Fig. 9.2   Pass-through of international oil price

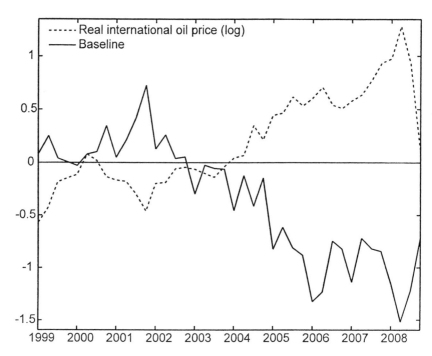

Fig. 9.3   Deviations from the Law of One Price

2008Q1 for Producer Price Index (PPI) (0.07), but much higher than theirs for CPI (0.008).

Since the deviation from the LOP $\hat{\zeta}_{o,t}$ makes one of the underlying state variables of the state space representation, we can obtain the smoothed series via Kalman filter once structural parameter values are fixed. Figure 9.3 shows these smoothed deviations from the LOP. Actual observations of log real international price of oil (dotted line) are also drawn for reference. The international oil price is stable until 2003 and takes off around 2004. We can see that the smoothed deviation from the LOP has also been moving around zero (that means the perfect pass-through of oil prices) until 2004 but decreases significantly afterwards. To explain changes in this deviation, we consider the government's reaction to an oil price shock. First we note that one of the main tax revenues of Korean government is the gasoline tax. Roughly 58 percent of the gasoline price paid by Korean customers is counted as the government revenue. Hence, the government could have lowered the gasoline tax to alleviate burdens of households and this fiscal policy could have affected the deviation from the LOP, even though the behavior of the government is not explicitly modeled in our baseline economy. Figure 9.4 depicts the gasoline price at the pump (solid line), the gasoline tax (dash-dotted line), and the tax ratio on gasoline consumption

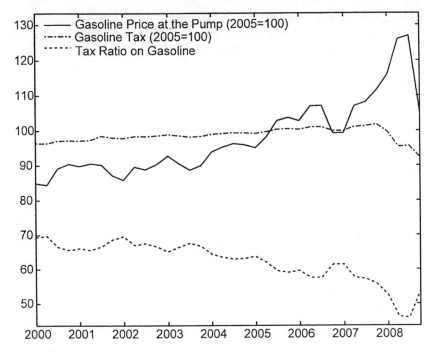

Fig. 9.4   Gasoline tax in Korea

(dotted line) during this period. In Korea, the tax on gasoline consumption consists of a per-unit tax that is time-varying and the value-added tax with fixed rate at 10 percent. As the gasoline price increases due to an oil price shock, the effective tax rate on gasoline consumption decreases because of this composition effect. Actually, the Korean government did not accommodate the oil price surge by changing the per unit tax until the end of 2007. But there was a significant tax cut on gasoline during 2008. Thus, the tax cut that accommodates the oil price shock can explain only a small fraction of the deviation from the LOP.

9.5   Conclusion

In this chapter we present the model economy that uses oil imports either as direct consumption or as an input of production. Within Bayesian estimation framework including DSGE-VARs, the empirical analysis is performed based on the Korean aggregate data. We find that the baseline economy produces reasonable posterior estimates of the structural parameters and works relatively well compared to impulse responses from DSGE-VAR($\hat{\lambda}$), and that the misspecification will be very severe when either consumption or production motive of oil imports is ignored. From the variance decomposition analysis, we conclude that the variability of the domestic interest rate can be explained mainly by the oil price shocks transmitted to domestic oil prices. Finally, the pass-through of oil prices into the core consumption price index is relatively low and the deviation from the LOP has decreased, but the government-accommodating tax policy played a limited role during this period. Therefore, a more elaborate model on government behavior is anticipated to investigate the pass-through of oil price shocks.

References

An, S., and F. Schorfheide. 2007. Bayesian analysis of DSGE models. *Econometric Reviews* 26 (2–4): 113–72.
Backus, D. K., and M. J. Crucini. 2000. Oil prices and the terms of trade. *Journal of International Economics* 50 (1): 185–213.
Blanchard, O. J., and C. M. Kahn. 1980. The solution of linear difference models under rational expectations. *Econometrica* 48 (5): 1305–12.
Bouakez, H. N. Rebei, and D. Vencatachellum. 2008. Optimal pass-through of oil prices in an economy with nominal rigidities. CIRPÉE Working Paper no. 08-31.
Calvo, G. A. 1983. Staggered prices in a utility-maximizing framework. *Journal of Monetary Economics* 12 (3): 383–98.
Christiano, L. J., M. Eichenbaum, and C. L. Evans. 2005. Nominal rigidities and the dynamic effects of a shock to monetary policy. *Journal of Political Economy* 113 (1): 1–45.
DeJong, D. N., B. F. Ingram, and C. H. Whiteman. 2000. A Bayesian approach to dynamic macroeconomics. *Journal of Econometrics* 98 (2): 203–23.
Del Negro, M., and F. Schorfheide. 2004. Priors from general equilibrium models for VARs. *International Economic Review* 45 (2): 643–73.
Del Negro, M., F. Schorfheide, F. Smets, and R. Wouters. 2007. On the fit and forecasting performance of New Keynesian models. *Journal of Business and Economic Statistics* 25 (2): 123–43.
Erceg, C. J., D. H. Henderson, and A. T. Levin. 2000. Optimal monetary policy with staggered wage and price contracts. *Journal of Monetary Economics* 46 (2): 281–313.
Geweke, J. 1999. Computational experiments and reality. University of Iowa. Unpublished Manuscript.
Jongwanich, J., and D. Park. 2008. Inflation in developing Asia: Demand-pull or cost-push? Asian Development Bank. Working Paper.
Kang, H., and Y. Park. 2007. BOKDSGE: A DSGE model for the Korean economy. The Bank of Korea. Working Paper.
Landon-Lane, J. 1998. Bayesian comparison of dynamic macroeconomic models. PhD dissertation. University of Minnesota.
Medina, J. P., and C. Soto. 2005. Oil shocks and monetary policy in an estimated DSGE model for a small open economy. Working Paper no. 353, Central Bank of Chile.
Schorfheide, F. 2000. Loss function-based evaluation of DSGE models. *Journal of Applied Econometrics* 15 (6): 645–70.

Sims, C. A. 2002. Solving linear rational expectations models. *Computational Economics* 20 (1–2): 1–20.
Smets, F., and R. Wouters. 2003. An estimated dynamic stochastic general equilibrium model of the Euro area. *Journal of European Economic Association* 1 (5): 1123–75.
Taylor, J. B. 1993. Discretion versus policy rules in practice. *Carnegie-Rochester Conference Series on Public Policy* 39:195–214.
Uhlig, H. 1999. A toolkit for analyzing nonlinear dynamic stochastic models easily. In *Computational methods for the study of dynamic economies,* ed. R. Marimón and A. Scott, 30–61. Oxford: Oxford University Press.
Yun, T. 1996. Nominal price rigidity, money supply endogeneity, and business cycles. *Journal of Monetary Economics* 37 (2): 345–70.

Comment   Warwick J. McKibbin

This interesting chapter develops a DSGE model for Korea based on the approach of Del Negro and Schorfheide (2004), but it includes oil in production and consumption. In addition to exploring the impact of oil price shocks and monetary shocks on the Korean economy, the chapter also explores whether excluding oil as an intermediate input alone or as final demand alone results in misspecification.

My comments can be divided into questions about the model specification and some comments on the empirical results that require greater elaboration.

The model specification is what becomes a conventional DSGE model, with households, firms, and government making intertemporal decisions. One feature of the model is that money is in the utility function. This is conventional in many DSGE models, but it does create a demand for money that depends on wealth rather than transactions (or income), which tends to be rejected by the data in standard econometric analysis of money demand. A transactions demand for money specification would probably fit the data better. An extension of the standard model is that consumption is allocated between one composite good and oil. In addition, firms choose production based on a CES production function of labor and a Cobb-Douglas nesting of capital and oil. The restriction of a unitary substitutability between oil and capital is a strong assumption. On U.S. data when estimated on a time series of input-output tables this assumption can be rejected (see McKibbin and Wilcoxen 1999). There is no obvious reason for this specification and in future work on the model production could easily be extended to a CES

Warwick J. McKibbin is director of the Research School of Economics and of the Centre for Applied Macroeconomic Analysis (CAMA) at the Australian National University.

KLEM production structure, as in the G-Cubed model of McKibbin and Wilcoxen (1999).

Another assumption that needs further discussion is the assumption of the law of one price for the composite good, but less than perfect substitutability of domestic and foreign oil. The opposite is more likely to be the case given the composite good is an aggregate of many different goods where oil is more uniquely defined.

The fiscal closure is very simple. The authors note that tax revenue from oil is not included (which is a large revenue source in Korea), and I agree with them that this would be a useful future extension of the model.

The model is estimated using a DSGE-VAR framework, which is another strength of the chapter. This technique balances the contribution of the theoretical restrictions of the DSGE with the data in the VAR specification. As far as I am aware this is the first time that this approach has been applied to a model of the Korean economy.

It is not clear why the authors test for the misspecification of only having oil as an input versus only having oil as final demand. From the data in the early part of the chapter it is clear that oil enters in both parts of the model. It is not surprising that the two extreme specifications are rejected by the data in favor of a specification that has oil used for final demand and as an input in production.

The most interesting part of the chapter is the impulse responses to an oil price shock. Unfortunately the discussion of the oil price impulse response consists of a single paragraph, which is surprising given it is the theme of the chapter. A longer discussion of the economics of the results to this shock would be very helpful and would be an important contribution.

The results for pass-through of oil prices and the discussion is puzzling and needs further elaboration. The discussion of the reason for the lack of complete pass-through via government tax changes is compelling, but to imply that it should be included in the model specification in order to avoid the model is misspecification.

There is a lot of potential in this chapter and the estimated model is an important contribution to modeling the Korean economy. Unfortunately, the chapter does not give a convincing answer to the question of how oil prices impact on the Korean economy.

References

Del Negro, M., and F. Schorfheide. 2004. Priors from general equilibrium models for VARs. *International Economic Review* 45 (2): 643–73.

McKibbin, W., and P. Wilcoxen. 1999. The theoretical and empirical structure of the G-Cubed model. *Economic Modelling* 16 (1): 123–48.

Comment   Pengfei Wang

Oil shocks have been assigned a prominent role in contemporary macroeconomic textbooks and models as examples of supply-side disturbances. Most of the studies in the literature focus on the effect of oil shocks on the U.S. economy. This convention, however, has an obvious limitation. The United States is a big economy, so any change in the U.S. macroeconomic condition would have an endogenous impact on the oil price. Due to this endogeneity in the oil prices, it is hence difficult to establish a causal relationship between oil price and the real economy. An and Kang bypass this endogeneity problem by focusing on a small economy, that of Korea. In my view, this is a very innovative way to quantitatively study the true impact of oil shocks on the economy. The model economy developed by An and Kang uses oil either as direct consumption or an input of production. It is rich enough to study different transmission mechanisms on how oil prices affect the economy. The structure model estimation reveals that oil-related shocks explain about 40 percent of output fluctuation and about 60 percent of interest movements. So oil shocks are indeed an important source of economic fluctuation.

I now would like to make a few comments about the model specification for improving this chapter.

First, despite habit formation, sticky price, and sticky wage, the model seems to have a weak internal propagation mechanism, as shown by the impulse responses function in figures 9.1 and 9.2. The impact of monetary shock on output growth is very transitory and volatile. Similar patterns exist under oil price shock also. The reason, I guess, is due to volatile investment. In the presence of habit formation, the household has a stronger incentive to accumulate capital, especially when the shocks are transitory. Although consumption adjustment is constrained by habit formation, if investment is free to adjust, the resulted output change would still be very volatile and transitory. The previous argument suggests investment adjustment costs may be an important additional element to be added to the model economy.

Second, the impulse responses to oil shocks require more detailed discussion. The response of core inflation, interest rate, is not intuitive. It is difficult to understand why the core inflation drops on the impact period of a surprising increase in the oil price. Also, given both output and inflation drop on the impact period, by the Taylor rule, the interest rate should decline rather than increase.

Third, it is not clear why consumption and investment data are not used in the estimation. The estimation is supposed to select a right model among

Pengfei Wang is assistant professor of economics at the Hong Kong University of Science and Technology Business School.

three models: the baseline, model with no oil in consumption, and model with no oil in production. It is natural to include consumption data for estimation purpose.

Fourth, the variance decomposition could be more informative. Table 9.5 only includes information on the contribution of shocks to output growth and oil import growth. Other important real variables like consumption, investment, and net export are missed.

Finally, the chapter assumes that oil shocks and foreign shocks are orthogonal to each other. This assumption may lead to some biased estimation of the importance of different shocks. For example, oil shocks would like to reduce the worldwide output and hence affect Korean export. If so, oil shocks can affect the Korean economy also indirectly through foreign demand channel. Thus, assuming oil shocks and foreign shocks are orthogonal would underestimate the true impact of oil shocks on the economy.

In conclusion, I think this is an interesting chapter. However as I suggested before, there are some issues that require further elaboration.

Contributors

Sungbae An
School of Economics
Singapore Management University
90 Stamford Road
Singapore 178903

Chaiyasit Anuchitworawong
Thailand Development Research
    Institute
565 Soi Ramkhamhaeng 39,
    Ramkhamhaeng Rd.
Wangthonglang, Bangkok 10310
    Thailand

Martin Berka
Department of Commerce
Massey University
P.O. Box 102 904, NSMC
Auckland, New Zealand

Christian Broda
Booth School of Business
The University of Chicago
5807 South Woodlawn Avenue
Chicago, IL 60637

Kalok Chan
HKUST Business School
Hong Kong University of Science and
    Technology
Clear Water Bay
Kowloon, Hong Kong

Mario J. Crucini
Department of Economics
Vanderbilt University
2301 Vanderbilt Place
Nashville, TN 37235-1819

Ichiro Fukunaga
Research and Statistics Department
Bank of Japan
2-1-1 Nihonbashi-Hongokucho
Chuo-ku, Tokyo 103-8660, Japan

Jan J. J. Groen
International Research Function
Federal Reserve Bank of New York
33 Liberty Street
New York, NY 10045

Yuko Hashimoto
Statistics Department
International Monetary Fund
700 19th Street, NW
Washington, DC 20431

Naohisa Hirakata
Research and Statistics Department
Bank of Japan
2-1-1 Nihonbashi-Hongokucho
Chuo-ku, Tokyo 103-0021, Japan

Takatoshi Ito
Graduate School of Economics
The University of Tokyo
7-3-1 Hongo, Bunkyo-ku
Tokyo 113-0033 Japan

Tokuo Iwaisako
Ministry of Finance
3-1-1 Kasumigaseki, Chiyoda-ku
Tokyo 100-8940 Japan

Heedon Kang
Research Department
Bank of Korea
110, 3-Ga, Namdaemunno, Jung-Gu
Seoul 100-794, Korea

Biing-Shen Kuo
Department of International Business
National Chengchi University
Taipei 116, Taiwan

Junhee Lee
School of International Economics and
    Business
Yeungnam University
214-1 Dae-Dong, Kyeongsan-Si
Kyeongsangbuk-Do, 712-749 Korea

Francis T. Lui
HKUST Business School
Hong Kong University of Science and
    Technology
Clear Water Bay
Kowloon, Hong Kong

Roberto S. Mariano
School of Economics
Singapore Management University
90 Stamford Road
Singapore 178903

Warwick J. McKibbin
Research School of Economics
Arndt Building
The Australian National University
Canberra ACT 0200, Australia

Cayetano Paderanga Jr.
School of Economics
University of the Philippines
Diliman, Quezon City, Philippines

Donghyun Park
Economics and Research Department
Asian Development Bank
6 ADB Avenue
Mandaluyong City 1550, Philippines

Arianto A. Patunru
Institute for Economic and Social
    Research
Department of Economics
University of Indonesia
Jalan Salemba Raya No. 4, Jakarta
    10430, Indonesia

Su-Ling Peng
Center for Economic Forecasting
Chung-Hua Institution for Economic
    Research
75 Chang-Hsing Street
Taipei, Taiwan 106, R.O.C.

Paolo A. Pesenti
International Research Function
Federal Reserve Bank of New York
33 Liberty Street
New York, NY 10045

Mohamed Rizwan Habeeb Rahuman
Central Bank of Malaysia
Jalan Dato' Onn
P.O. Box 10922
50929 Kuala Lumpur Malaysia

John Romalis
Booth School of Business
The University of Chicago
5807 South Woodlawn Avenue
Chicago, IL 60637

Andrew K. Rose
Haas School of Business
    Administration
University of California, Berkeley
Berkeley, CA 94720-1900

Etsuro Shioji
Graduate School of Economics
Hitotsubashi University
2-1 Naka, Kunitachi
Tokyo 186-8601, Japan

Joonhyuk Song
Economics Division
Hankuk University of Foreign Studies
270 Imun-dong, Dongdaemun-gu
Seoul 130-791, Korea

Mark M. Spiegel
Economic Research, 1130
Federal Reserve Bank of San Francisco
P.O. Box 7702
San Francisco, CA 94105

Nao Sudo
Institute for Monetary and Economic
    Studies
Bank of Japan
2-1-1 Nihonbashi-Hongokucho
Chuo-ku, Tokyo 103-0021, Japan

Yiuman Tse
Department of Finance, College of
    Business
University of Texas at San Antonio
One UTSA Circle
San Antonio, TX 78249

Taisuke Uchino
Global COE Program Office
Institute of Economic Research, 3F
Hitotsubashi University
2-1 Naka, Kunitachi
Tokyo 186-8603, Japan

Pengfei Wang
HKUST Business School
Hong Kong University of Science and
    Technology
Clear Water Bay
Kowloon, Hong Kong

Michael Williams
Department of Finance, College of
    Business
University of Texas at San Antonio
One UTSA Circle
San Antonio, TX 78249

Doo Yong Yang
Asian Development Bank Institute
Kasumigaseki Building 8F
3-2-5, Kasumigaseki, Chiyoda-ku
Tokyo 100-6008, Japan

Author Index

Subject Index